A bracing trumpet blast against the drear pieties of the contemporary art establishment, and includes witty portraits of encounters with, among many others, the late queen and Sir Roy Strong
Craig Brown in *The Observer*

Julian Spalding, without trying, makes his love of the visual experience infectious ... Certainly a book most art students should read as they embark on their journey as working artists   *New Art Examiner*

Funny, full of interesting ideas, spectacularly rude about people everyone is normally very deferential to, and a reminder of how museum life used to be when museums could be run by someone as robustly outspoken as Spalding   *Sir Charles Saumarez-Smith*

Comprehensively skewers the art world today and takes apart the links between dealers, galleries and public bodies   *Camden New Journal*

Always interesting, lively and well written
Literary Review

Packed with personalities from the art world and anecdotes from the amusing to the hair-raising ... He writes very well and fluently, and movingly about the art he does like—which is generally painting ... Spalding is perhaps too uncompromising and too chippy for today's art world, but his voice is certainly worth listening to   *The Art Newspaper*

Praise for other books by Julian Spalding

THE ART OF WONDER (Winner of the Banister Fletcher Prize)

It does for art what Stephen Hawking's book *A Brief History of Time* did for science ... a thoroughly good read
Washington Daily News

Written with a beautiful lucidity
A. C. Grayling in *The Art Newspaper*

This is not just a book about wonder; it's a wonderful book
James Hamilton in *History Workshop Journal*

THE ECLIPSE OF ART

Elegant, persuasive and timely
Nick Hornby in *The Independent on Sunday*

In every field there are a few individuals—dubbed mavericks or fools, depending on one's perspective—who dare depart from the received wisdom. One such fiercely independent soul in the world of art is Julian Spalding   *Louis Torres* in *Aristos*

THE POETIC MUSEUM: REVIVING HISTORIC COLLECTIONS

Each page is filled with unexpectedly poetic and profoundly alluring insights into past and present   *Choice*

Extraordinarily global, exceptionally non-partisan
Times Higher Education Supplement

One of the most stimulating and approachable books about museums I have ever read   *Colin Ford* on *BBC Radio 4*

Deserves to be read by all in our sector because it is an insider's perspective expressed without fear   *Museums Journal*

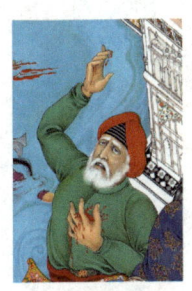

A R T
EXPOSED

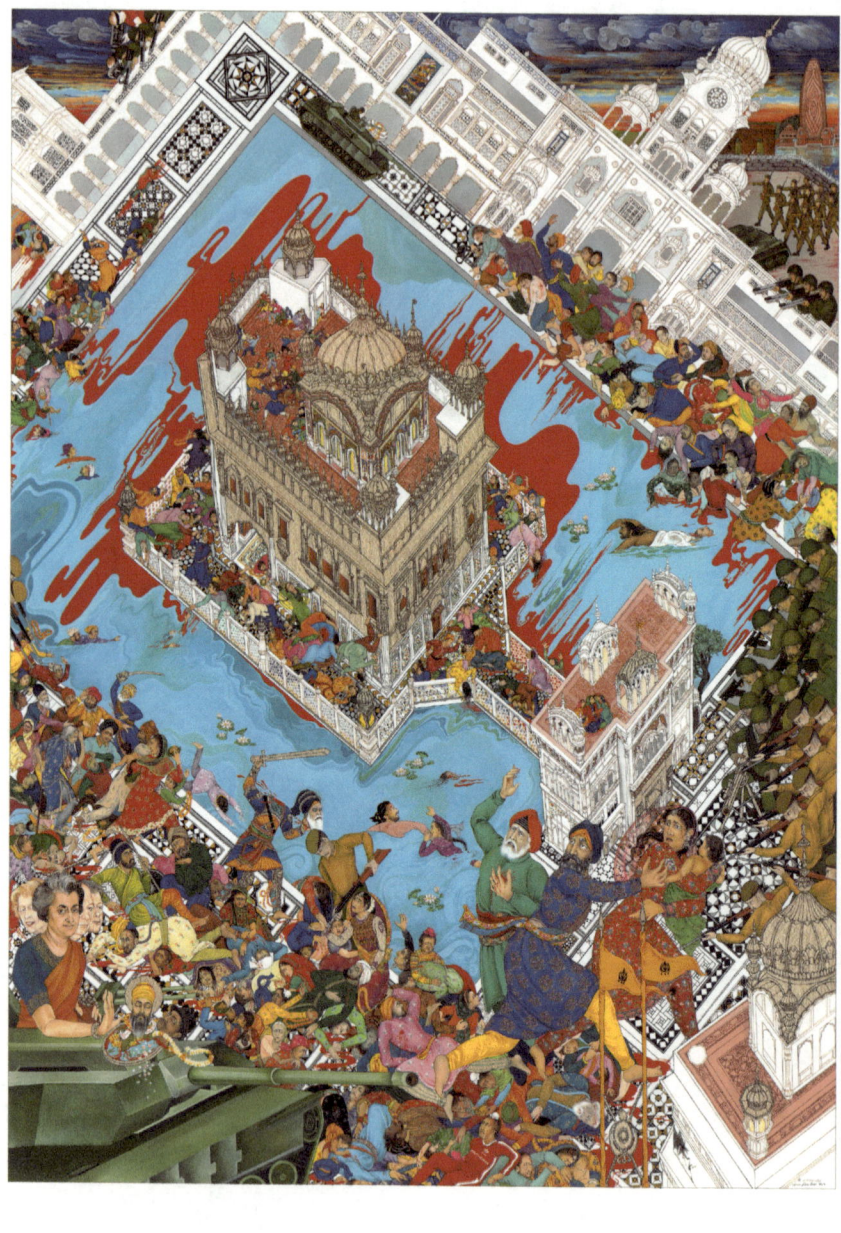

A R T
EXPOSED

JULIAN
SPALDING

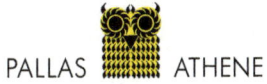

PALLAS ATHENE

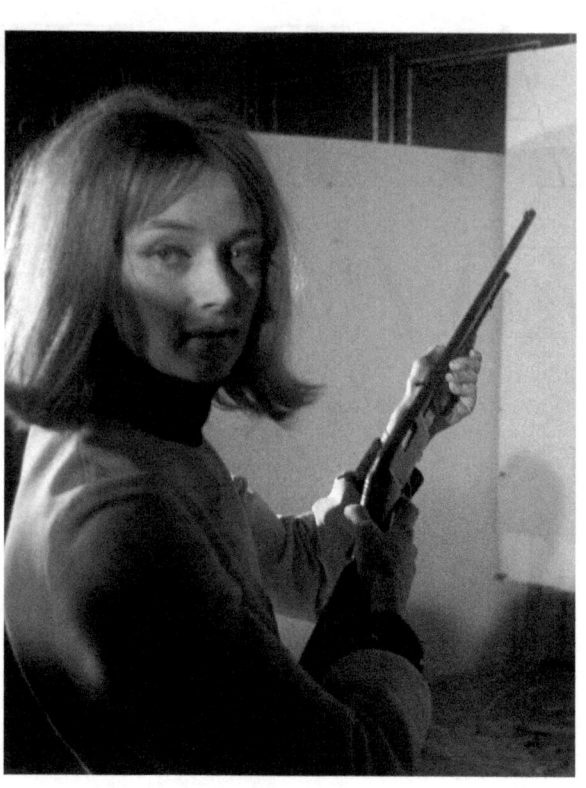

D

F

H

J

Q

R

S

T

W

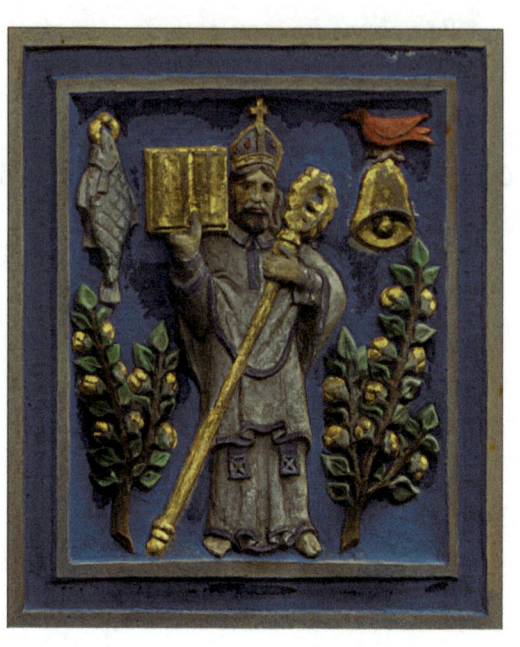

For my son
DANIEL,
& for IRÈNE
for so enhancing
my life

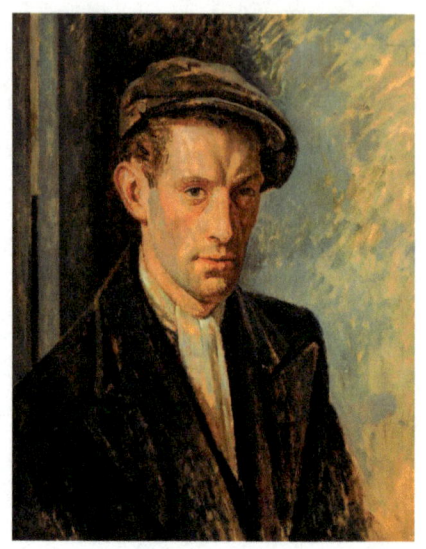

Percy Horton, Unemployed Man, c. 1929

INTRODUCTION

John Nicoll, a man of powerful build with a strangely quiet presence, suggested I write this book. He was the long-term director of Yale University Press, then director of his late wife's company Frances Lincoln Ltd, after which he retired, got bored and started publishing again under the mast of Wilmington Square Books. He came to see me in Edinburgh, though we'd never previously met, found out what I was writing and, to my surprise and delight, published *Realisation—from Seeing to Understanding* and a book I was working on with Raymond Tallis, *Summers of Discontent: the Purpose of the Arts Today*. On a visit to his home, through an odd serendipity, I knew something personal about most of the artists represented on his walls. He suggested I should write a professional memoir—an idea that had never occurred to me. But he added, 'Don't mention your girlfriends— no one is interested in them.' I never got round to writing it while I was working with him, but when I did, I took his advice.

I don't think I would ever have written it at all without the insistent persistence of my old friend and colleague, David Phillips, former keeper of art at Nottingham Castle, whose eyes, the rapiers of his ferocious wit, belie his size. He'd heard many of my stories and was convinced that I should write them down. Conferences of curators often end in discussing labels, because that's their most direct interface with their public. David became briefly famous throughout the profession for pinning ridiculously large labels to his gallery walls, printed in black ink on luminous pink, telling his visitors, in effect, to 'read, you bastards, read!'

David was particularly keen that I keep my text amiable throughout as, rather to my surprise, he said I was, myself, most of the time. 'No one is interested in your old battles any more,' he told me. I would like to hope that this isn't the case, but I am aware that few things are more boring than an old curmudgeon going on and on, and the last thing I want to do is bore. Many things have improved in museums over my time: educational work, hugely, and museum labels, which used to be full of technical data that made visitors feel even more ignorant and excluded, but which now help people understand what they are looking at, and why.

But there are two particular battles that I fought and, regretfully, lost during my career, which I must mention here because they still concern me deeply. The first I promise never to mention again. This is the issue of light levels. Museums, especially art museums, need to be hymns to sight, but instead they've become some of the most dismal places on the planet.

The problem began in 1978 when Garry Thomson, the conservation scientist at the National Gallery, an elegant and amiable man, published his seminal book, *The Museum Environment*. This soon became a gospel for our profession, admirable in every respect but one. The book recommended that no light-sensitive object should be exhibited at levels higher than 50 lux, and no object, however stable, should be lit at more than 150, arguing that it was perfectly possible to see clearly at that level. Overnight light ceased to be a friend in museums, a helpmate to revelation, but became an enemy to be excluded at all costs. I immediately objected and gave a paper at the next Museum Association's conference called 'A Dim View'.

I argued that it's impossible to appreciate art at 150 lux, let alone at 50, even for those with excellent sight. Reading, one of the simplest seeing activities, requires 200 lux, seeing to work requires 500, and no surgeon would operate under less than 1,000. I estimated that you need a minimum of 500 lux, in many cases more, to fully appreciate all the subtleties in a painting. This needs to become the minimum light level in any gallery. But light levels, I argued, can rise higher than that, with proper management. The length of exposure to light is as important at the amount of light—the old method of covers on cases successfully solved that problem. But the overriding truth is that very few objects in museums are actually very light sensitive—apart from some fabrics, a few pigments and badly made paper. The majority of man-made objects are very robust and have survived the rough and tumble of the world until they entered the museum's safe havens. Each object, therefore, needs to be individually assessed so that it can be displayed at its maximum safe light level in order that its full glory can be enjoyed by all, even by those with poor sight themselves. Garry's blanket approach, I thought, would in time kill off galleries for everyone.

Garry was in the audience and came up to me afterwards, saying he hoped I was wrong. I said I feared I was right, for two reasons: one, a blanket approach was simpler to apply and, second, many curators will like it. Gloom in galleries creates a precious atmosphere around a collection, which will appeal to some curators, even though they would never examine the objects themselves under such poor light conditions. They think this is good enough for the public, even though the public are the real owners of 'their' collections. As George Bernard Shaw said, 'All professions are conspiracies against the public,' and museum curators are no exception. I tried to persuade Garry to rewrite his book, but without success. Sadly, wherever I visit museums around the world, I see my gloomy prediction becoming more and more true.

I would love to live long enough to see the day when light, and above all, natural daylight, the most superb light of all, is welcomed back into museums to illumine all the wonders they contain. And—who knows?—we might even be able to welcome sunlight back. One of the greatest experiences of painting in the world is the Mesdag Panorama in The Hague—a rare survival of a once popular art form. The vast encompassing cloud-, sea- and dune-scape is animated daily by direct sunlight falling around it as the earth turns. Staff there told me that the paint hasn't changed in over 140 years due the fact that Hendrik Willem Mesdag mixed starch with his pigment—the colours are still as bright as a daisy —but the sand on the mound in the centre on which you stand to view this remarkable painted scene has darkened over time and therefore has had to be replaced with a lighter mixture. I do not know the chemistry of Mesdag's medium, but it needs analysis, for it could help us create the most magical painting of all, which will remain fresh and brilliant for years to come.

My second battle is ongoing—and, indeed, I am using this book to give it a boost. I have fought and will continue to fight for the future potential of the art of painting until my dying breath. Many of the anecdotes told here, such as those about John Berger and David Bowie, Marcel Duchamp and Nicholas Serota are included here to throw light on that battle. Of even wider significance, public galleries and museums, by preserving and showing people's achievements in the past, can help to inspire us to create cultural expressions that are profound, personal and lasting, as an antidote to the rising tide of brand marketing that offers little of substance, visually, to anyone.

We have a whole planet to save, and one way we'll help to do that is by enriching the world we can see in lasting ways. Considering what is lasting is, in itself, challenging, and seems to be against the ephemeral, ever-accelerating spirit of our times, but this pushes us in the right direction: to create environments that are inspiring and sustainable. Art, in all its manifestations, helps up do this. We need to encourage visual creativity, if only for the fact that living in a city where there is nothing interesting to see is dispiriting or, worse, soul-destroying (if you are fortunate enough to have one).

David suggested the ABC format. Originally it was going to be arranged by themes, like Acquisitions, Buildings, Collections, but I thought arranging it by people's names would be more entertaining and interesting. As my Latin and drama teacher at school, Walter MacElroy—a Californian communist whose perpetually bemused smile belied the sharpness of his mind and who'd quit America when his name was added to Senator McCarthy's red list —used to say, 'The world is divided into people who are interested in people and people who are interested in things.' I'm a people person despite spending my career caring for objects, but I only did so because they interest people and the ones that interested me the most were made by people for other people, or for gods, which many people thought were people, of a sort, too.

The more I thought about it, the more I realised that everything I've done and tried to do was inspired by people I'd met, either personally in my own time or people in the past. Even if you're looking at a work of art from a very different age or culture, what you're doing, in essence, is meeting someone else, and watching as they show you their thoughts and feelings, magically though by no means always seductively. John Ruskin, Charles Rennie Mackintosh and L. S. Lowry are, in many ways, as alive to me as if I'd met them personally and they gave me ideas about what to do today. Meeting living artists was even more stimulating— unforgettable encounters with the likes of David Hockney, Jean Tinguely and Beryl Cook.

To bring the many people I've met to life, I've painted little word portraits of them, as, you might have noticed, I've begun to do already. This is, I'm afraid, not exactly politically correct. We're not supposed to look at superficial appearances, but to judge the person buried underneath. We're taught from an early age not to stare, and never, ever, to point. But this is what artists do all the time, stare and if not exactly point, point out. While I was in Manchester, the idea was seriously considered, in a fit of premonitory wokery, that all interviews for jobs in the council should be held with the candidate behind a screen, because looking itself is packed with prejudices. I argued so are words and voices— prejudices have to be recognised and overcome, not hidden. Thank goodness, this policy was not adopted. Seeing remained a useful tool.

It is therefore only fair that I attempt a word portrait of my-self in the hope that those mentioned in these pages who I have subjected to similar cursory descriptions, and others, might recognise some truth in the face that I have been given and frac-tionally chosen to present to the world. I am thin (or, at least, was) and of average height with a large round head topped by a mess of dark hair and fronted with rather ordinary features that looked as though they'd been flattened, earning me the nickname of 'squash-face' at school. This seemed apt because I often had occasion to be surprised that I have gone through life without being punched in the face, not only because I have invasive, dark eyes but also a tendency to blurt out whatever comes to mind without considering the implications, coupled with my habit of grinning broadly, whatever the circumstances. And, even worse, I habitually erupt into a loud bark that is intended for a laugh— the unfortunate confluence of an irrepressible sense of humour combined with a deep-seated and querulous nervousness. The result of all this was that I sensed many people on meeting me looked at me askance, questioned my stability and, if they were so minded, especially if they disagreed with me, doubted my sanity. So, it is perhaps to be wondered that I got to where I did.

Art only exists to be seen. I would go further and say that art only exists when it is seen. The *Mona Lisa* in a store is merely pigment on a plank. This is why public art galleries are so important today; they are one of the few places where the general public can see the art of their times, and the art people made before. A public gallery's job is to collect and show art that is of lasting quality. But it is a big question, asked repeatedly through these pages, what is the lasting art of today? A gallery curator's job is to begin that sifting. And a lot of fun can be had along the way. I loved the work from the moment I began.

'You're too young to work in a museum.' This quip by a girl I was chatting to (up would be a better word, but I've resolved not to mention girlfriends) in a pub in Leicester, during my first temporary post, stopped me in my tracks. It had never occurred to me that the profession I had just embarked on with such enthusiasm could be a turn-off for anyone. Years later, a colleague of mine at Sheffield City Art Galleries, Mike Diamond, who later become director of the Museums and Galleries of Birmingham, told me that his son Ben's early infatuation with fire engines had stayed with him throughout his youth, to such an extent that he quit school as soon as he could, without going to university, and joined the fire brigade instead. Mike sighed and said, 'Well, I won't tell anyone my son's a fireman.'

'Don't worry, Dad,' Ben replied, 'I never tell anyone you work in a museum.' I was, quite possibly, always too young to work in museums, but whether museums were too old for me, these pages might tell.

My interest in painting began as a child. I was given a box of paints as a birthday present when I was five. My twin brother, Adrian, was too, but didn't take to it. He later earned eternal fame by having a moth he'd discovered named after him: Spalding's Dart. I was hooked on paints, and throughout my childhood that was all I really wanted to do. But two things happened, which overlapped. One thing was that I began to doubt if I really had any talent; my paintings never seemed to take off imaginatively in the way I so admired in a Picasso or Matisse. I felt, perhaps, painting wasn't a creative language for me. I studied art history and art simultaneously, in a combined four-year course at Nottingham University and Art College, a demonstration in itself of my uncertainty.

The second thing that happened was that when I went to art college conceptualism was already, in 1966, beginning to sweep the board. It struck me as fatuous, pretentious quasi-intellectualism from the start. One fellow student Letrasetted the words 'The Raft of the Medusa' across the middle of a huge empty canvas the same size as its namesake. What a waste of the world's resources which, anyone with eyes in their heads knew even in the sixties, were already tragically diminishing. This empty canvas was supposed to be an advance of art. Feebly, instead of resisting, I threw in the towel, abandoned my paints and brushes and disappeared into designing with plastics—a rainbow colour clock for people who didn't need to know the time, which got on to the shelves of trendy sixties shops (I once saw one for sale in Venice!) and a Magnate's Mirror Worry Box that unfortunately remained a prototype when the oil crisis struck and plastic prices went through the roof.

Then I went to work in museums, where wonderful paintings could still be found. I soon came to believe that the great art of painting can't be over, stuck forever in the past, whether I could do it myself or not. I was against the rapidly spreading view that painting was an old-fashioned handcraft that had no place in the age of modern technology. Cartoons, in books and animated films,

which is among the best painting and drawing of our times, dis-
prove that for a start. Painting is the oldest art form that we have,
or at least that survives, from the Chauvet Cave in south-eastern
France to today. It can show us so much about what we think and
feel in our times. So, this book is, in part, a passionate plea for
painting's continuity, and believes in its glorious future. But it's
more than just painting that has to be revived, so does the whole
of visual creativity. All art, whatever it's made of—and art can be
made of anything—has to be a visual creation; it can't just remain
an idea, or be simply 'found'. You have to able to see the art in a
work of art. If you can't see any, the chances are it might not be
a work of art, and if it's only of any value as a work of art, then it
might not be worth anything either.

There is no such thing as Art.
There are only artists.

SIR ERNST GOMBRICH

A is for PETER ANGERMANN

I could hardly believe my eyes. I happened to be in Nuremberg in 1995 and had just walked into a show by an artist I'd never heard of in the local gallery. I found myself surrounded by paintings (brush marks on canvases!), ranging in size from very big to quite small (varying in dimension according to their meaning!), all figurative (not one purely abstract!—as Peter Angermann quipped to me later, 'the thing that's missing in abstract art is the abstraction'), some very freely painted, many summary to the point of being cartoonish in style, others carefully wrought, but all obviously by the same hand (an assured, personal mastery of technique!), and, most amazingly, in a complete colour range, from black and white to the softest greys through to the most brilliant multicoloured radiance (an artist at last who employs the whole spectrum of tone and hue!) and, even more amazingly, dotted here and there among the imaginative creations were, believe it or not, straight landscapes (landscapes!!). I was bowled over. I felt I had walked through a door simultaneously into the past and the future, glowing with light and colour. Painting had never died. And here it was at full power.

I had not that long before been on a trip with other modern art curators attending the opening of the new Irish Museum of Modern Art. We were touring the surrounding countryside in a coach looking at contemporary artists' studios and stores—the country had become something of a rabbit warren tax haven for international big art earners. I remember walking round a display of stone blocks fresh from the quarry, with German sculptor Ulrich Rückriem's semicircular drill marks left down their sides, and thinking how utterly dull and vacuous they were, their popularity with European urban planners and architects presumably explained by the fact they made the buildings they stood amidst and against marginally more interesting in comparison. Public authorities should have the responsibility, as my friend Alexandre Pauvert once remarked, to erect warning notices, 'Beware—Art', informing unwary passers-by in advance so that they can switch paths to avoid such encounters should they so desire.

Outside the factory space where Ulrich was displaying his work, there happened to be a man, of middle age, sitting behind an easel, painting a picture of the view across a canal. The group of curators I was with stopped in bewilderment, and some laughed. One corpsed, 'No one, but NO ONE does that any more!' I was too embarrassed to speak. Fortunately, the artist appeared not to hear us, and carried on, unabashed.

And here I was now in Germany, standing in the midst of a show by an obviously modern artist who painted among everything else he did straight landscapes, and beautifully too. And delight followed delight. Each picture was a new sight, about something different: someone stuck in a traffic jam, painted in reverse perspective piling up around him; a mad insect jazz band playing in a jungle; a crazy scene of grey old geriatrics hobbling and stumbling, one in a wheelchair, into the Fountain of Eternal Youth, and leaping out, thin, lithe, pink and naked, grinning from ear to ear, for it was going to be nooky now for evermore!

Then something else surprised me. There were red spots everywhere. Here was an artist who sold his work to people to hang on their walls! Nor were they in anyway expensive—the price of a good sofa, something to sit down and look at. There was only one big picture left—a painting called *Baggersee*. It showed a flooded gravel pit—there are many in that region of Germany as well as in Alsace—transformed into a popular family bathing site, but instead of people, the bathers were skeletons, charred black, basking in the shimmering waters. No private owner, clearly, wanted to live with such a frightening, if hilarious scene, so I bought it, at once, for Glasgow's new Gallery of Modern Art. It had, I thought, a real place in the public eye.

I had never seen such a powerful or more resonant image of the impact that global warming and pollution were having on the planet, until, much later, I saw his *Aus Grauer Vorzeit* (*From the Dim and Distant Past*) painted earlier in 1979. It shows the origin of all our current trouble, the laying down of fossil fuels, coal and oil, what the British artist David Kemp once dubbed 'dinosaur juice'. A previous, hotter, world is seen in black and white. A volcano erupts in the background, tree ferns shoot up, acid raindrops (beautifully, summarily, painted) pour down, while two dinosaurs copulate: the glints in their eyes revealing their glee at enjoying themselves, her mouth gaping open, his teeth clenching together at the apex of the exquisite crescendo of pleasure, both busy reproducing their species—exactly the same motivating forces that are driving us to burn their leavings to reheat our own environment.

An attendant in the museum where the painting was hanging, noticing my interest in the picture, came over to point out a detail I hadn't yet noticed, his eyes sparkling. He clearly loved the work and wanted to share his enjoyment—exactly what attendants should do—they're not there just to be guards, and their jobs should never be privatised. I peered to where he was pointing. Hidden in a dark corner, beneath a monstrous dragonfly, were an old tyre and a coil of barbed wire, showing that this painting was not just a prehistoric joke but about our current ecological catastrophe—an extraordinary premonition decades before this issue became our main concern. Peter Angermann told me later, when I met him, that he's pessimistic about our future on this planet, but pessimistic, too, about his pessimism, which leaves the door open, just a chink.

Oddly, it never occurred to me to meet the artist at that time. His painting said all that needed to be said. It was only a decade later, long after I'd left Glasgow, and museums altogether, that I got an email from Peter asking if I'd like to write a foreword to a book about his work. So I went to see him in his studio in the countryside north of Nuremberg. He lives bizarrely in an old Nazi barracks, still surrounded by a high barbed-wire fence. He'd painted a sausage and a sickle on the German flags emblazoned on the wire gates. A large plaque of a ferocious German eagle decorates the wall of his house, but he's repainted the block it's carrying in its claws as a packet of Trill bird seed, to feed any little birds that happen to be passing.

Peter is of average build, and normal in every way—you wouldn't think twice about him if you passed him in a crowd. He has a round, bald head and frazzled chin that could belong to anyone, a footballer, accountant or carpenter, and his appearance doesn't say 'artist' in anyway, except when you notice that his eyes, usually slightly closed and down-turned, like a Chinese Taoist monk, as if he were thinking while concentrating, and his mouth, usually set serious but always hesitating about smiling up at the corners, indicate an unusual observational alertness that is, in fact, the mainspring of his imaginative perception, his art.

Then I learnt his story. He'd started angry, but by the time I met him, he'd mellowed hugely, having found, as so few people do, his fullest, perfect means of personal expression—painting. But not without a hard fight at the start. He was a pupil of Joseph Beuys, then the Professor of Monumental Sculpture (believe it or not that was his official title—such was the topsy-turvy world of art at that time) at the Art Academy in Düsseldorf. Beuys believed that everyone is an artist, and everything an artist does is art (his fingernail clippings, for example, are now in the Tate). 'Potato-peelings are art!' he said (as my first literary agent,

Louise Greenberg, commented when she read it, 'tell that to dinner ladies!').

Peter, who is fascinated by and very knowledgeable about philosophy, argued that if everything is art, nothing is art. So, as a student, he sought out the boundaries that have to exist so that art can exist. With a small gang of mates, they did everything they could to get expelled, peeing in corners, attempting to burn down a studio, filling the school with poisonous fumes—as he says, he was not nice to know—but Beuys, God bless him, stuck to his principles—everything was art, and everyone was an artist, so they weren't allowed to quit, nor he to dismiss them.

Angermann abandoned art when he left college, took odd jobs for a year and a half, while, in his spare time, inspired by Robert Crumb, produced his own cartoon featuring a very obedient, armless and legless worm. He knew painting was in his blood—but how could he let it speak? He began by dashing off hundreds of drawings in felt-tip, coloured pens simply of sights around him that he liked—many that prefigure much of his later imagery—and, with two friends, Milan Kunc and Jan Knap, formed Gruppe Normal in 1980 to paint big, imaginative murals together. Painting didn't have to be a precious, introspective journey into an individual soul but could be an ordinary, even normal, collective form of human communication. This was a stand against the whole trajectory of modernistic individualism.

The next breakthrough was perhaps even more crucial. One day in 1986 Angermann was sitting with Peter Hammer, an artist friend, discussing what they could do that day that would be really radical, really avant-garde. Angermann still sensed there were barriers to be broken down. And then it occurred to them: why not go out and paint *en plein air*? So, they kitted themselves out, took a bottle of wine, and much to their surprise had a really enjoyable time.

From that moment on Angermann was hooked. What colour really was the blue of the sky? The green of grass? The brown of earth? Nothing was quite what he expected. From then on, he couldn't stop painting what he saw. Ever since, he has cycled out regularly from his home, with paints and canvas strapped to his bike, found somewhere he'd like to sit for a couple of hours, stops, relaxes, looks around him, and then, and only then, sees something he wants to paint: the brilliance of spring blossom, streetlights illuminating snow, traffic on a motorway. And so, virtually single-handed, Peter has reinvented the art of landscape painting, until he is now, as far as I have discovered, the finest, subtlest master of brush, paint and colour. All this artistry he employs in his imaginative work.

When I went to see him, Peter propped painting after painting on a rostrum he'd pushed against the wall. There were so many, even though so many had been sold. Then suddenly his black cat appeared from nowhere and marched up on to the rostrum where he had just placed a painting, a small mockery of a rich businessmen's banquet I remember, cocked a leg, and peed most purposefully against it, before Peter, shocked, could leap up and stop it. 'You did that on purpose,' he said, as the cat darted away. It certainly looked as though it had—its aim had been so accurate. I am persuaded by Ray Tallis that it's much more productive to ponder the differences between animal and human intelligence than to see consciousness as a continuum through sentient life, but on rare occasions there seem to be overlaps.

Angermann lives on the watershed of both the Rhine and the Danube, at the pivotal heart of Europe. He travelled widely before he settled near where he was born and now rarely goes anywhere. All his art springs from this locality. In this sense, he is an artist of the future who, by concentrating on his vicinity and being passionately local, is helping to make the world richer and fuller again, and therefore bigger for all of us, rather than shallower and emptier and therefore smaller. Going to see him is like walking into one of his paintings—you see things you've seen in his art all around you, rolling fields, shining blue roads, villages huddled under onion-domed churches, bundles of hay stacked in plastic, silver reflections in puddles. Walking into his studio is like entering a brilliant, condensed version of what's just outside.

To the southeast of where Peter lives and works lies a major NATO training ground. He heard the increase in activity in the run up to the Iraq war, and then again, most recently, during the crisis over Ukraine—the booming thuds of trial explosions, which seemed to shake the very ground, and the flypasts of colossal B-52 bombers, blazing trails of dirt across the sky. He then watched, as we all did, the horror of war unfold on his television screen. Local and global; everything we do now affects everyone. When I visited his studio, I was amazed to find a huge painting of this experience, called *Hinten, Fern* (2008), perhaps best translated as 'Far and Near'.

The painting shows a family, Angermann's own, effectively life-size, in the comfort of their home, lounging on a sofa, glasses of wine in hand, the baby crawling on the floor, all of them watching the news, the Iraq war on television. Bombs go off; a man's head explodes in a splat of blood; lined up victims are shot down; and black smoke from shelled buildings billows into the clear desert air. But what's extraordinary about this painting is that this scene is not boxed into the television screen that his family is watching, but fills the whole canvas, just as these events expand in the mind of anyone looking at them.

What Peter has managed to do—and I know of no other artist working today capable of this mastery of light and space—

Overleaf: Hinten, Fern by Peter Angermann, 2008

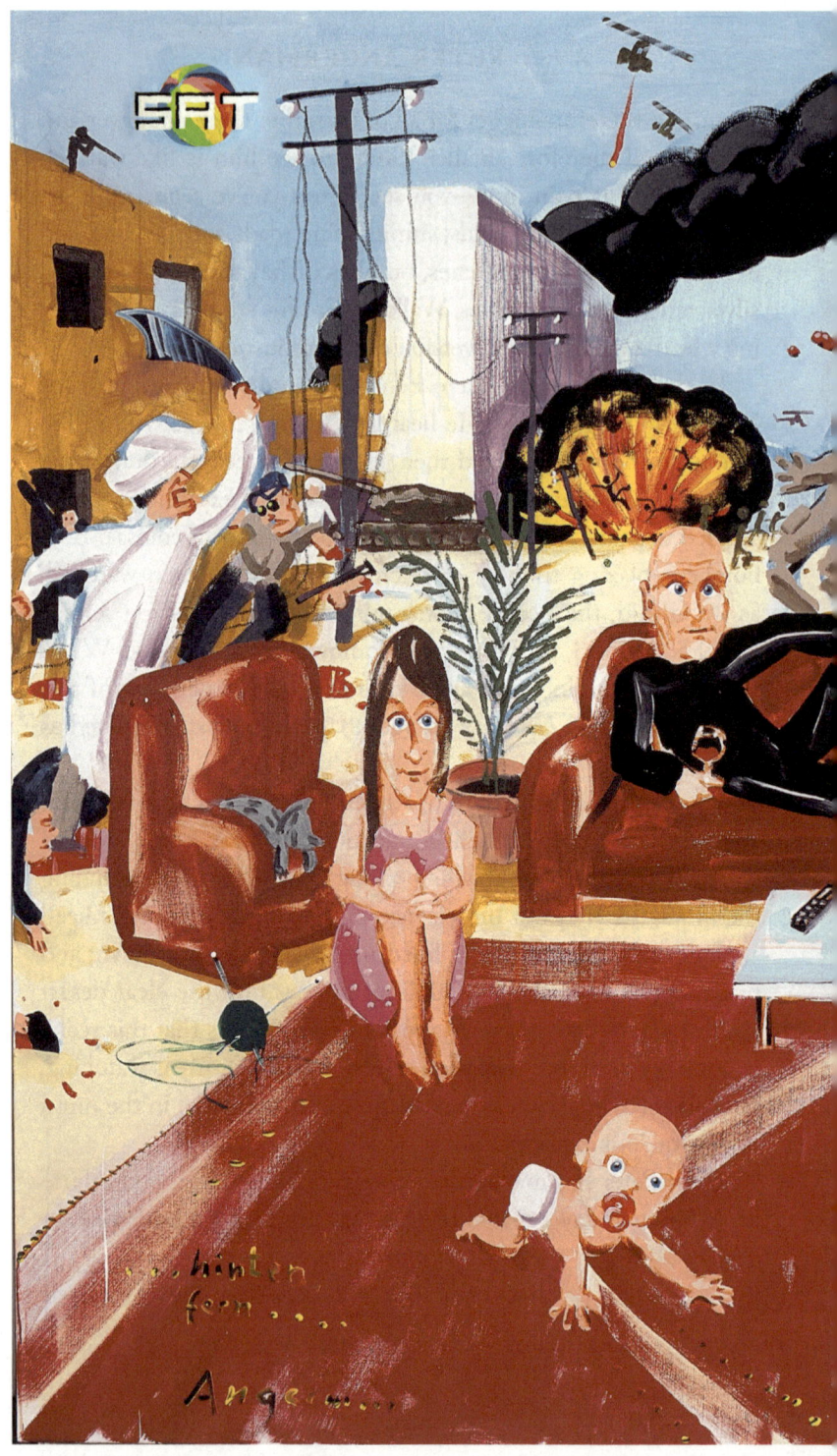

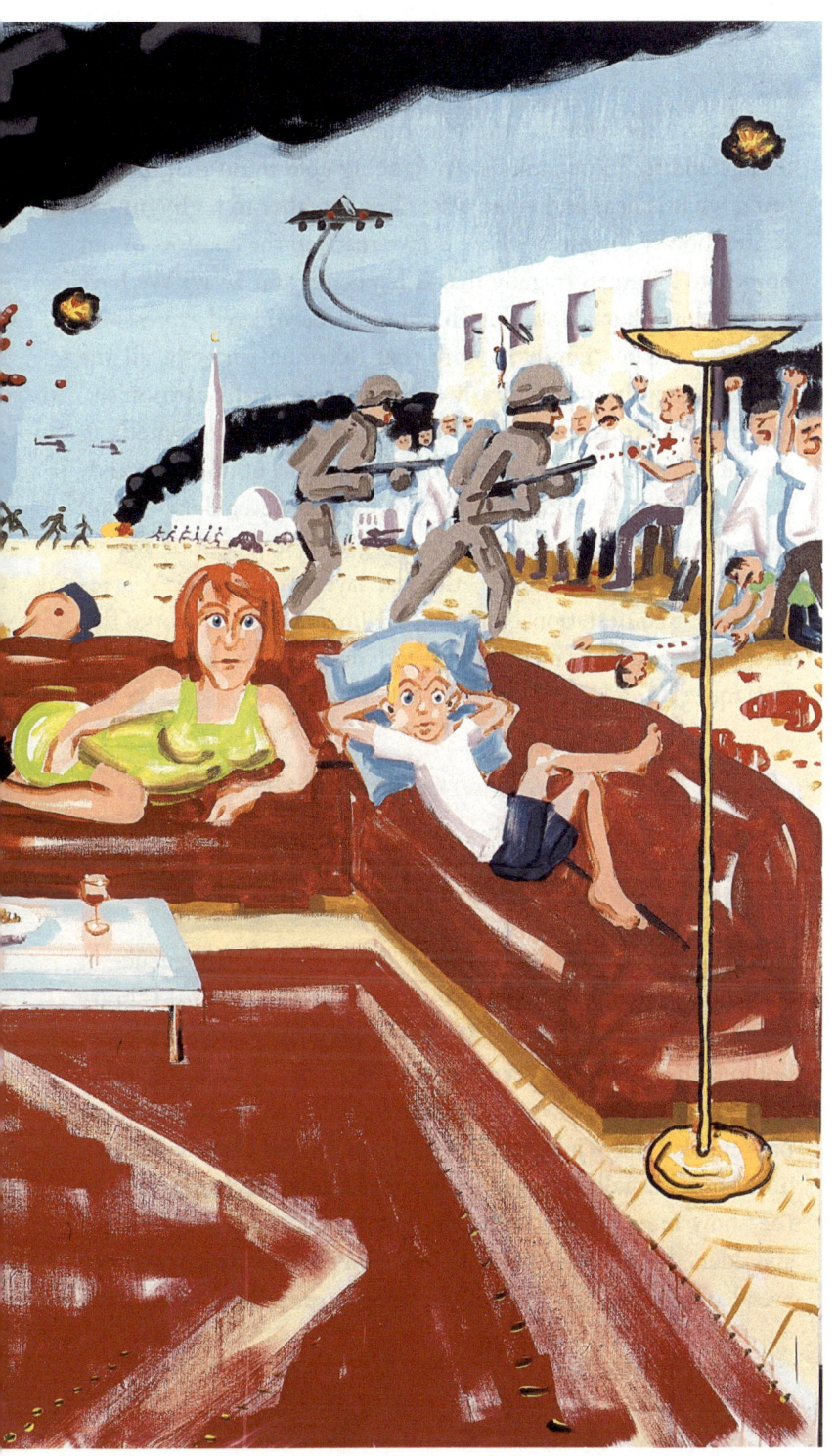

is to marry the glow of the television screen with the glow of understanding in our minds. And, being able to do that, he can bring what is near and what is far close together to highlight our contemporary dilemma—how do we react, in the comfort of our homes, to a human tragedy that is happening far away? We have to react, but what can we do? The stunned, bewildered expressions on Peter and his family capture that dilemma perfectly, all the more poignantly and helplessly for being fractionally cartoonish.

Peter, half-consciously I think, knew he was on to something special, because he took a series of photographs of himself standing beside this large canvas (something he'd never done before) showing the whole painting appearing in a sequence of sixteen overall, sweeping additions—the last layer were the eyes, a remarkable manifestation of the visual imagination at work. This is a great painting, challenging and questioning, in its way a Velázquez's *Las Meninas*, of and for our day.

B *is for* HUBERT BARI

I was surprised by the length of the queue—it stretched all round the block—for a show at the National Library of France in the centre of Paris—about Jean-François Champollion, the nineteenth-century translator of Ancient Egyptian hieroglyphics! What was going on? Luckily my ICOM museum pass enabled me to jump the queue. I was offered a headset, which until then I usually resisted. I was told I had to have one, because the show only worked with one, but I could drop it round my shoulders when I wanted just to look and pick up the story whenever I wanted to start again. One thing surprised me when I did this from time to time was that I discovered that the show was totally silent, even though it was packed; everyone was absorbed, adults as well as children, looking intently and listening, taking everything in. The concentration of the audience was palpable—the exhibits had caught their attention in a remarkable way. No one was wandering around like unmagnetised iron filings, as people often do in museums and galleries, filling the vacuous spaces between the exhibits; here everyone was focused on what they were here to see, and deeply fascinated.

The show was arranged in a series of displays, each introduced by a brief video on a screen, telling you what each section was about—Napoleon's campaign in Egypt, the looting of its treasures, the birth of Champollion, his impossibility and brilliance as a child (the things that influenced him were exhibited in a big playpen), the Rosetta Stone, with its inscriptions in Ancient Greek and both Egyptian hieroglyphic and demotic scripts, and, in the final, extended section, Champollion's slow, meticulous, inspired cracking of the Ancient Egyptian code—a detective story on the walls of a gallery. And then the final, dramatic moment—one of the most moving museum experiences in my life—when I heard, as I looked, as if for the first time, the words of the Book of the Dead, being spoken before me as I read the hieroglyphs.

Horus announces to the recently deceased man who has come before him, as he weighs the man's heart in the scales against the feather of truth, and finds it lighter:

> You have not stolen, been covetous, killed anyone, damaged a grain store, lied, trespassed, practised usury, committed adultery, had sex with a boy, or abused a king—your heart weighs lighter than the feather of truth, you are Maa-Kheru—true of voice—and I present you to the God Osiris—Welcome to Eternal Life.

Here was the communication language museums had to develop, the art of telling stories with objects, about which I had bored my colleagues for so long. And here in France was a master museum narrator, fully formed. I had to meet the exhibition's maker.

Hubert Bari had a round face. His eyes in particular were round, and seemed to stay wide open for a long time, taking everything in. He was at once meditative and emotional and, as I soon found out, very funny, finding playful puns everywhere, in French and in English. I mentioned I'd just been to see Henri Cartier-Bresson when we first met. 'Oh,' he asked, his expression not changing, his eyes not blinking, 'Henri lives in this *quartier*?' It was a delight to work with him.

He told me how he'd got into museums, most unconventionally, not through the very few official schools and channels that are the only way into this profession in France, and this explains, in part, the freedom of his imagination. He lived near Strasbourg, an accountant by training who had developed a passionate interest in the very old, certainly medieval, possibly even Roman, silver mines in the nearby mountains at Sainte-Marie-aux-Mines. A group of top French businessmen were having a conference in this other European capital and one of them had read about the mines and proposed that they all visit. They weren't open to the public, and the only local expert who could be found was Hubert. He told them that he would be happy to show them round but was horrified to see a fleet of long black limousines arrive along the forest track and a group of smart, besuited businessmen get out. He explained that the mines were just narrow tunnels in the ground and they'd ruin their clothes and shoes if they went in like that. They voted, since they were there, to do just that.

Hubert showed me later what the mines were like, so I knew what they'd experienced. The entrance was just a hole in the hill behind some scraggy bushes. This was not a tourist attraction. The tunnel inside was beautifully chiselled, but no wider than your chest, with no room even to turn round. Worse the ceilings were often very low—for much of it you had to walk with your head bent, sometimes crouching almost double. The early miners were small men and wore padded leather hoods to protect their heads. Drawings of them gave Disney's early cartoon artists (some came from Alsace and Germany), the idea for the clothes and hoods of the Seven Dwarfs.

I became increasingly sick with fear and claustrophobia the further we went in—and we walked for what seemed like miles, turning this way and that, and at some junctions, dropping down holes—I couldn't believe we wouldn't get lost—with no chance of turning round! I had, at one point, to jump across a metre-wide fissure in the rock that yawned all-round the passage, below me, to the sides and above my head, a disappearing black emptiness. Hubert explained that this was a seam of silver that had been worked out, and if I fell into it, I'd be lost forever. I've rarely been so terrified in my life, as I jumped over. Then he told me we were coming to the biggest hole in the world. I thought I couldn't take any more. But next we came out on to the mountainside—it was the biggest hole in the world, with fresh air reaching up to the sky. I've rarely ever been so relieved.

The businessmen came out covered in mud, but they'd had the time of their lives. A week later Hubert got a call from one of them. He told him that he was wasting his time being an accountant, and that he'd arranged a post for him in the department of mineralogy and geology at the National Museum of Natural History in Paris. The other curators did not take kindly to their new colleague, and he found himself isolated. But no one was interested in doing exhibitions, so he did that. He first experimented with shows on minerals and mining, one of which the director of the National Library saw. He commissioned him to do a show celebrating the bicentenary of Champollion, remarking that if he asked his colleagues to do it, they'd put a few books in cases, but Hubert, he knew, would do something that would really interest the general public. He did, and this was why we met.

The first exhibition I commissioned Hubert to do, for Glasgow's huge McLellan Galleries, was a celebration of the 500th anniversary of Christopher Columbus's 'discovery' of America in 1492. Anniversaries are very good pegs to hang exhibitions on, but, amazingly, no one else had thought to celebrate the real significance of this one. Perhaps one reason was that celebration was, indeed, not the right word. My idea for the show was to tell the story from the other side, to show what happened to the Native Americans as the Europeans poured in and systematically destroyed their culture and their lives.

And we had a particular reason for doing this in Glasgow. We had a small but unique Native American collection in the museum. Buffalo Bill's Wild West Show was a famous, immensely popular entertainment which performed across Europe in the late 1880s, with real Native Americans and cowboys taking part in its performances, sideshows and set pieces—the forerunner of the many 'Cowboy and Indian' films that used to be shown on TV (before people became aware of their inherent racism). The last port of call for Buffalo Bill's show was Glasgow, one of the most westerly ports of Europe, and they performed in the city in 1892—by chance, another anniversary—before the whole shooting match was packed up and shipped back to the States.

A hanger-on of the show, George E. Crager, sold a bunch of genuine Native American artefacts that were no longer needed to Kelvingrove Art Gallery and Museum. He threw in—since the city wasn't prepared to buy it—what he claimed was a Lakota Sioux ghost shirt, reputedly torn off the freezing corpse of a victim of the notorious Battle of Wounded Knee, when, only two years previously, in 1890, about 300 Sioux, including many women and children, had been massacred by the US army. This was one of the last atrocities in the long struggle between the Indigenous native peoples of America and the invading Europeans.

Some Lakota people, but by no means all, believed that special 'ghost shirts', usually long, pale and embroidered with a few mystic symbols, would protect the wearer from bullets. I asked to see this shirt, which wasn't on display. It was short, brown and looked like any ordinary tunic, nor could I see—I examined it closely—any sign of a single bullet hole, nor any evidence that it had been torn from a frozen corpse, which it would have to have been if it had come from Wounded Knee. But the story that it might have been one of these magic ghost shirts was fascinating in itself. I was very keen for the exhibition to go ahead.

Hubert and his team at Creamuse did a brilliant job. Like his Champollion exhibition, videos introduced each section—and the visitor met each different group of Native Americans before they were outlawed, and many killed. The last display was the most moving. The walls of this square gallery were hung with a replica of a diorama wallpaper, designed in Alsace, which showed North America in the nineteenth century totally populated by Europeans, with their white villas on the hills, looking like miniature Greek temples. Their neat farms were full of European animals and plants, with no trace of Native Americans anywhere, except for one tiny group of 'Indians' in a corner performing a tribal dance for a group of white Americans and a few European tourists. But in the centre of this room, Hubert placed a large wire cage, evocative of the new Indian reservations, inside which were hung the wonderful, sepia photographic portraits of the few survivors of native peoples still wearing traditional dress, taken over two decades in the early twentieth century by Edward Curtis. The only sound in the gallery was an endless loop playing what is effectively the American national anthem, ending with the lines: 'Oh, say does that star-spangled banner yet wave/ O'er the land of the free and the home of the brave?' The irony of 'home of the brave'—my wife suggested it as the show's title— became obvious to everyone. It is the only exhibition I put on in which many visitors left moved to tears.

I involved Hubert with several exhibitions during my career, some of which, like the David Hockney project and the Mackintosh show are mentioned elsewhere in these recollections. Others, like *The Birth of Impressionism*, are wonders gone for ever. But the last one, which ultimately failed to come to fruition, was by far the most ambitious. We were approaching 2000, and, as far as I was concerned, the subject of the anniversary was obvious— though once again it didn't appear to have occurred to anyone else. I wanted to find a way to tell the story of the historical Jesus, informed by all the latest scholarship. There were hundreds of shows that year, including the execrable Millennium Dome exhibition in London, about everything in the world —but not one about why people were celebrating this date at all.

I thought Hubert could organise a brilliant show, which could tour to other venues around the world, asking the simple, but immensely interesting question, who was Jesus of Nazareth? In my dreams I wanted the exhibition to be shown in Bethlehem, but I knew that could be a problem! The ground we were treading was extremely difficult, but I was sure, with the right expert advice and contacts, it could be done. I had got to know Shaike Weinberg, the creator of the Holocaust Museum in Washington, DC, another brilliant storyteller with objects. And I thought he and Hubert could do a wonderful show together.

We met in Israel and visited several museums, some of which Shaike himself had created, archæological sites associated with the historical Jesus and historical collections. There was, without doubt enough material to put on a fabulous exhibition, and with all Shaike's contacts, we were assured wonderful loans. Hubert's idea was simple: to tell the story of Jesus' life as it was told in the Bible. You would just listen to the words of the Gospels on your headset, as you looked at real artefacts from that time, and followed Jesus's life. The Last Supper, for example, was certainly taken on a rug, on the ground. Visitors could listen to the Sermon on the Mount seated on the very same rocks, brought from the hills around Galilee.

We found many extraordinary exhibits: exact versions of the sandals the disciples would have worn when they took them off for Jesus to wash their feet, the storage jars for the wine at the marriage of Cana and, most astonishing of all, the skeletal hand of a man who had been crucified, with the nail still stuck in the bone, which was always driven through the wrist, not the palm, as is conventionally shown in all stigmata. The weight of the body would tear the nail through the hand if it was in the palm, but not if it was lower down, through the wrist. And what came through all these stories about exhibits was the simple but to many people startling fact that the historical Jesus was a Jew.

But the small politics of Scotland, that Graham Stringer had warned me about all those years before, cut the project short—nothing to do with its merits. My job, along with that of the directors of Libraries, Sport and Recreation and Performing Arts in Glasgow were all axed to create a single Leisure Services Department, and there was no one left with the vision, experience or guts to take it on. This was the best show, perhaps, that Hubert and I never did.

B is for JOHN BERGER

I was a child in the 1950s, when everything was brown, lighter than the dark skirting boards, staircase and furniture in my grandfather's terrace house, but brown nonetheless. The bright green and pink jelly ladled out in corrugated paper cups at the kid's street party, held for the Queen's Coronation, surprised me in 1953. I remember being startled, and delighted, by a soft drinks van, with huge bright orange, yellow and red bottles standing on the back, selling fizzy pop to kids on the council estate. Though not to me, because I'd already lost my sweet tooth after a surfeit of rainbow-coloured ice-cream served in tall glasses, called knickerbocker glories, bought for my twin brother and me on holiday with Aunt Dorothy. (My brother has kept his taste for sweetness, and still pours enough sugar into a cup of tea to stand a spoon up in.) At the end of the decade, American culture, colour supplement magazines and, a bit later, colour TV, were beginning to blitz us everywhere. The drab post-war years of rationing, brown paint and consumer restraint soon seemed as foreign and as distant as the Middle Ages. The Swinging Sixties was all up and go and get.

Bruce Lacey, a crazy, brilliant performance artist before such beings existed (except of course for Baroness Elsa von Freytag-Loringhoven) began as a painter. His diploma piece as a student at the Royal College of Art, London, on the set theme 'The Flood' (it was a time when religious subjects were still thought to be essential training for an artist) was, with typically direct aplomb, a huge dark painting, worked up from a photograph, of the bloated body of a cow, one of thousands of victims of the Norfolk inundation of 1953. He told me how he'd been staying in a boarding house at the time and had brought his own breakfast with him—a packet of Kellogg's Corn Flakes, famous for its bright, cock-adoodle packaging. The landlady took one look at it, whisked it away and brought it back neatly wrapped in brown paper. 'We're not having that vulgar thing on the table,' she said.

I was therefore surprised, when I went to Sheffield, as keeper of the Mappin Art Gallery in the early seventies, to find its stores rich with dark brown paintings of the fifties. That's one of the beauties of working in a public gallery: as you pull out its racks, you reveal history. There were several big, impressive pictures by artists I didn't know—Jack Smith and Derrick Greaves, for a start, both Sheffield-born—all of the 1950s. A little research revealed that these were once famous names in the art world. Smith and Greaves together with John Bratby and Ed Middleditch had been chosen to represent Britain at the Venice Biennale in 1956. Now these artists had disappeared under a tidal wave of brightly coloured modernism, largely from America. I was intrigued, discovering something new—a Middle Ages on my doorstep, but only, in fact, one step back in time.

A Jack Smith retrospective exhibition was touring. I booked the show eagerly but was bitterly disappointed. It showed student exercises, drawings of bottles, then abstracted paintings of bottles, then pure abstracts, wriggling, truncated Kandinskys softened in an English light. There wasn't a realistic painting in sight. I looked at the dates. There was a gap of eight years. Jack's social realist paintings, on which his reputation had been built, and which had been the stars at the Venice Biennale, had been deliberately excised. This so-called retrospective was clearly an attempt to rewrite history. My interest was aroused.

I did a little digging. There was a superb, very big, dark painting by Jack in the Walker Art Gallery, Liverpool, of shirts drying on chairs (as they had to in poor apartments) and a dishcloth spilling forks and knives on a tabletop. The room looked as though it had been hit by a poltergeist. Smith had called it *Creation and*

Crucifixion, so I wondered if he was religious. Probably not, I thought; he was just inspired. The Tate had another painting by him, more pedestrian but in its own way just as strong, called *Mother Bathing Child*, showing a cream and brown scrubbed interior with a woman scrubbing a naked, cream kid standing upright in a big, old-fashioned white, square porcelain kitchen sink—a common sight before pink and avocado bathroom suites.

What's more I discovered that this very painting had given rise to the term 'Kitchen Sink', commonly used to describe the plays, novels and films of John Osborne, Arnold Wesker and Shelagh Delaney, Ken Loach and Mike Leigh and, on the Beckett fringes, the works of Harold Pinter, all set in the gritty world of the urban working classes—numbering among them some of the best expressions of British creativity in the second half of the twentieth century. The art critic David Sylvester had mentioned Jack Smith's painting in a piece he'd written in 1954, entitled 'Kitchen Sink' because, as he said, there's everything in these paintings 'but the kitchen sink—the kitchen sink too'.

In this instance the writers and filmmakers had followed the artists, not the other way round. I hadn't known that and was surprised. John Osborne's seminal play *Look Back in Anger* appeared in 1956, the very year that realist painting in Britain simply disappeared. What had happened? I determined to find out. This was a museum's job after all—to preserve and show what is valuable from the past. And it was a movement in which Sheffield artists had played a big role in, so it was absolutely right and proper for Sheffield City Art Galleries to put on a show of the painting of the real Kitchen Sink School. I started out full of enthusiasm but ran almost at once into a brick wall.

I first went to see Jack Smith, the son of Sheffield, in his home on the south coast, near Brighton. He was lean and, I thought, rather sad, with a neatly clipped French beard that fitted his

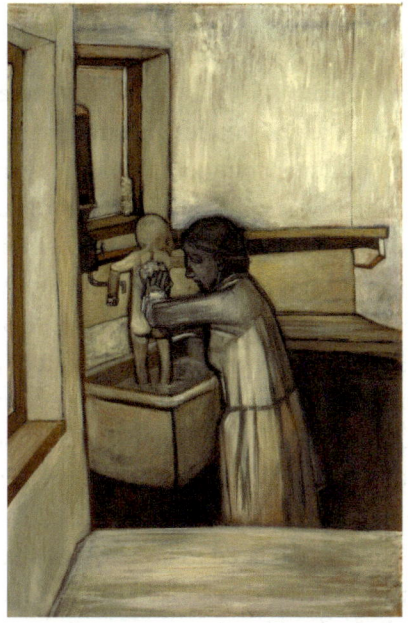

Jack Smith, Mother Bathing Child, 1953

chosen profession, and, behind it, a deadly serious, almost solemn expression. He was, I felt, quietly furious that I should even consider showing his realist paintings. Didn't I know that all modern art worthy of the name is abstract? His realist paintings, he said—they were just student works—steps towards abstraction. 'Yes,' I replied, 'but the best were done long after you left college and can't be just dismissed as you learning something as a student. It was these paintings—some of them very big—that made your reputation and were bought by public institutions.' He could see I was determined to go ahead with the exhibition, with or without his help, and I was politely shown the door. As I left, I noticed some small, sensitive paintings of children's toys, isolated in white, which I rather liked. They were obviously not his; he said they

41

were his wife's. So, she was allowed to be a realist, of sorts, but then, presumably, she was not considered to be serious.

An artist not wanting his paintings to be seen, even those bought by galleries like the Walker and the Tate? It didn't make sense. Something odd was going on. I quickly found out what as I did more research. It was political, and the 1956 date was crucial. The year 1956 was when realist art was celebrated in Britain by the selection of Smith and Greaves, Bratby and Middleditch to represent the country at the Venice Biennale, then the most famous show of contemporary art worldwide. But 1956 also saw the brutal Soviet suppression of the Hungarian Revolution. This gave a boost to the CIA's promotion of American Abstract Expressionism as the art of the free West, against the socialist realism that had been promoted under Hitler and Stalin.

Socialist realism was declared to be a hollow sham, and no artist could produce anything that looked vaguely like it. So, out of the door went all shades of realism, especially any form of social (without the -ist) realism, any observation of or inspiration taken from everyday life. Edward Hopper, the profoundly haunting American realist, had a painting returned to him at this time because the person who'd bought it, when he got it home, thought it looked 'too communist', as if Hopper had ever been one! All the realist artists in Britain in the early fifties either switched to abstraction after 1956 or, if they didn't, were dropped by the art establishment. This explained the gap in the Jack Smith retrospective—he wanted to be seen as an abstract painter all the time.

It now seems strange, with hindsight, that writers and filmmakers were allowed to continue to mine the rich seam of reality, which they did with great success, but that this arena was forbidden to painters. One reason was because books and even films are essentially intimate, personal communications, not public statements, displayed permanently on walls. Painting, being that, had to toe the political line and in the process, the art of painting became brutalised, emaciated and, in its attempt to reach a wider public once again, commercialised—a sorry, complicated tale I've lived through, and which is told in different ways throughout the pages of this book.

The Forgotten Fifties exhibition was the first of my many attempts to reclaim the whole territory of visual art, the full scope of its imaginative potential, its freedom to excavate and express any aspect of human experience. It was also my first taste of many people trying to stop me. I should, of course, have called the show *The Kitchen Sink School*, but shamefully, I admit now, I bowed, at least, to that pressure. The image on the poster and catalogue was obvious, but not allowed. Jack Smith persuaded Sir Alan Bowness, then director of the Tate, not to lend his picture of the kitchen sink to the exhibition. I had to make do with a Bratby instead (a splendid, cluttered kitchen tabletop, I have to add), and the slightly soppy, sloppy, fudging, self-effacing title. How much stronger, more assertive, the proper title would have been. I questioned Alan's decision not to lend. Doesn't a picture, once it has been bought by the public, become public property? Should public galleries be party to the covering up of history? He fell back on what I later discovered was the upper establishment's usual strategy—silence—he simply refused to discuss the matter. But I was determined to go ahead with the exhibition.

David Sylvester, the critic who'd coined the 'Kitchen Sink' term in the beginning, rang me one Sunday morning and spent over three hours—I timed it—trying to persuade me not to do the show. He argued that they—he corrected himself—*we* had got it all wrong: art was solely about expression, and had nothing to do with real appearances, and certainly had no social, let alone any political, function. He said that you couldn't tell an artist's intention from their work. I still find this an odd choice of word. Surely the intention is what is made manifest, even if it surprises the artists themselves, which the truest intentions must surely do. David's favourite artists then (before he got into Jeff Koons) were Francis Bacon and Alberto Giacometti. But John Berger later told me that he dealt in art as well as writing about it, which, if true, makes his criticism, and his own intentions, potentially questionable themselves.

I would not be persuaded by his diatribe and stuck to my own intention. I wasn't trying to rewrite history, still less propose a theory of what art should be. I was just trying to show what a lot of artists had done at a particular time. There are close affinities between Smith's, Bratby's, Greaves's and Middleditch's work as there was with all the other Kitchen Sink artists I unearthed. This didn't mean they were the same, or shared the same intention, but they did share the same interests, concerns and language. They all made art out of the everyday world, like the New Deal artists in the thirties and forties in America, who were funded by the state, before it switched to promoting Abstract Expressionism during the Cold War.

This wasn't just a shift in fashion. Something more fundamental was going on, and there was a class dimension to it to which, of course, coming from my background, I was doubly alert. My first wife, Frances Spalding, was studying the paintings of the Bloomsbury Group, starting with those of Roger Fry before going on to the work of Vanessa Bell and Duncan Grant. This necessitated us spending the odd weekend in the group's country hidey-hole, their modest farmhouse, called Charleston, nestled in the South Downs near Lewes in Sussex, long before it was preserved and opened to the public. I loved its carefree, homespun if then very dusty and musty atmosphere, the bold painted patterning on the walls and furniture, the lights in it and the darks, which is where I learnt the value of warm grey. I did some gardening when I could, because that was in a mess.

The paintings, however, began to pall a bit. I began to appreciate the Bloomsbury nickname for Duncan—Drunk and Can't—and why a researcher for Sotheby's told me they liked to catalogue any unnamed Dutch flower painting, Van Esser Bell. I was once looking at a couple of paintings by them both in Sheffield with my boss, Frank Constantine, when he commented, 'Don't you think any one of us could have got to that level if we'd never had to earn a living?' I had to concur. The Bloomsbury Group's painting is not nothing, but it's not much. Without their friends and family, few would have heard of them. And, of course, they had class.

One Sunday morning there was a knock on Charleston's door. A couple of women were standing there. One asked if she could show her friend inside; she was a neighbour, she explained and lived in the odd little tower I'd seen across the fields. She told me, as I showed them round, that her father was a painter, but I wouldn't have heard of him. She was very surprised when I had. One of my all-time favourite paintings in Sheffield was *Unemployed Man* by Percy Horton—an unforgettable fusion in a face of dignity and shame—a pre-Kitchen Sink painting if ever there was one (see illustration p. 10). She told me her father's story. He was the son of bus conductor in nearby Brighton. His request to be treated as a conscientious objector on pacifist grounds during the First World War was refused. He was arrested as a shirker, and then sentenced to prison with hard labour. After the war, he taught at the Ruskin School of Drawing and Fine Art in Oxford, eventually retiring into the landscape of his youth by renting the gamekeeper's tower, where his daughter now lived.

Duncan Grant, the grandson of the 12th Laird of Rothiemurchus, also applied, with his lover, David Garnett, for exemption from military service as conscientious objectors. They aimed to set themselves up as fruit farmers. Their request was initially refused because their business proposal wasn't credible, but they were told that the Tribunal would look favourably on their request if they could find more suitable premises for such an enterprise. Charleston was the result, where, in effect, they played—two British class stories, cheek-by-jowl across the field of art.

Jack Smith had argued, to me, that his realist paintings were only exercises; he was just painting what was around him, and that if he'd lived in a palace, he'd have painted chandeliers. This was a fudge. He could easily have gone to a palace—many were open to the public—and painted chandeliers if he'd wanted to, but he didn't. The grit of real life was what inspired him at that time, like so many artists of his generation, when socialism wasn't a dirty word, but a legitimate, widely shared aspiration. Smith wasn't a socially motivated artist, like the communist Peter de Francia, later to become professor of painting at the Royal College of Art. I used the exhibition, at his request, to 'save' a striking, big painting of his, *The Bombing of Saskiat*, from being 'buried', he claimed, in the Tunisian Embassy, a complex manœuvre in itself. His best work, I think though, was as a portraitist. Smith was different; he was interested in the magical not the political, and he made things up. Despite the appearance of realism, the baby in the sink wasn't his, but borrowed for the painting. The couple had no children, which added poignancy to his wife's paintings of isolated toys.

I couldn't give up doing the show; I was discovering such interesting things. It was like being born again before you were born, an extension of my own life back in time. Almost, literally as far as the work of Ghisha Koenig was concerned. Her name meant nothing to me, but I really liked her relief sculptures of workers in factories. I didn't realise until I met her that I'd met her before, in a very different context. I must have been about seven or eight. I'd been ill with ... I can't remember what ...

perhaps chickenpox? And the doctor had come round, Manny Tuckman. My mother had removed one of the paintings I'd done of a nude playing the cello which was pinned above my bed with other of my precocious artworks saying, 'We don't want that on the walls, do we? The doctor's coming round.' I was annoyed, but too weak to complain.

The doctor, whose bullet-round head and round eyes swooped down alarmingly close to mine, examined me briefly but was much more interested in my little gallery. 'My wife's an artist,' he told me, 'would you like to come and see her studio?' The two words—artist and studio—almost made me swoon. My dream combination! As soon as I was better, I knocked on the surgery door. He lived in a house on its own at the edge of the estate, at the bottom of the station hill, surrounded by a garden. At the back was a studio, a tall, single building in front of a tree. I went in. It was huge inside—or seemed so to me then—with a crane and hook hanging from the roof for lifting sculptures, and plaster casts of sculptures, models and drawings all around.

On a stool before me was perched a tiny woman—a grown-up whose feet, to my surprise, didn't touch the ground. I remembered that loose lock of hair falling over her forehead, and those intense eyes peering at me through large-rimmed glasses, nearly thirty years later, when I met Ghisha Koenig for the second time. She was a huge help to me with the exhibition. She was the daughter of the brilliant Jewish art critic, Leo Koenig, who I, until then, knew nothing about, but who had such an influence on all the writers at that time, particularly on John Berger. She knew everyone in the London art scene, even though she'd moved with her doctor husband-to-be to a South London council estate, true to the socialist spirit of the age that bore so much art on its wave.

Another discovery of the exhibition for me was closer to my

new home, in Sheffield. George Fullard, the sculptor, was born there but died before I knew him. He was of the Kitchen Sink generation and took his inspiration from what he saw around him, but then took a leap of the imagination. He wrote beautifully about art, being like the follow-through of a dart, when it leaves your hand and lands, due to its own momentum and the accuracy of the throw, in the centre of the bull's eye. I got to know his widow, Corky, and she, like Ghisha, gave me many personal insights into the lives and works of the other Kitchen Sink artists they knew so well. Later I cast a group of his early, realist sculptures for public places in Sheffield, believing that art should be in the streets, not just in galleries and museums. The most famous of these was his *Walking Man*, striding in front of the new (now gone) Town Hall. I particularly admired Fullard's assemblages, memories of his terrible war experience, when he was shot to pieces in a tank, and sculptures that showed children playing war games with domestic tables and chairs. These I think rank among the profoundest war art of modern times, realism with poetic intention.

The research into the exhibition was going well if slowly, but the show wasn't out of the woods yet. During this period, I was promoted in Sheffield, eventually becoming director of arts for the city, with additional responsibility for music and film, as well as running the galleries. Governing bodies, at whatever level, love to play with reorganisations—it makes them feel they're doing something—and I've suffered many. This one was not the worst, by any means, but it did leave my hands full. I handed the Kitchen Sink project over to James Hamilton, who'd taken over from me as keeper of the Mappin. He was a tall, thin young man with a scrub of hair and an intermittent, but when it came on, excruciatingly painful, for him even more than for others, stutter. Much later he became a distinguished writer and biographer of Turner. He picked up the reins of the show, went to see Jack Smith, hoping he could bring him round, but came back to tell me he agreed with Jack and thought we shouldn't do the show.

This was very different from the response of Julian Treuherz, the keeper of art in Manchester, when I proposed, as director, that we do a show about Victorian social realist art, part of my ongoing bid to reclaim the full scope and language of painting. Julian—the first other Julian I had met—was another tall, thin young man, with a tousled knot of curly black hair and penetrating eyes behind thin-rimmed, round specs, with a very finely tuned artistic judgement, immaculate attention to historical detail and a moral integrity as straight as his back. He leapt at the idea of the realist show, though it's true he didn't have to deal with the pressures of contemporary art politics.

We had in our collections in Manchester a superb, moving painting by Sir Hubert von Herkomer called *Hard Times* (1885), evoking the title of Dickens's earlier novel about life in the northern city of 'Coketown'. It shows an unemployed, homeless labourer and his young family, exhausted, by the roadside, staring ahead at the seemingly endless, possibly hopeless road to find work. Julian's exhibition was an extraordinarily moving experience, to find oneself surrounded, in an exceptionally plush public gallery, with paintings, many of them huge and most of them dark, showing the desperate and poor, the sick and untended, the underside of Victorian pomp and splendour, the paintings and drawings that, at the time, so inspired Van Gogh and lit the fuse of his amazing artistic trajectory.

This was later. Earlier, I was only feeling my way towards celebrating the full potential of painting. What could I do about James Hamilton's decision? Technically I could tell him to carry on, but that would have put him in a very difficult position. He'd either have to resign, which would be bad for him and us, or do the show, which wouldn't be any good because his heart wouldn't be in it. I urgently wanted to see this exhibition, and I didn't want to let the artists down I'd already contacted and who were eager to see it as well. So I decided to continue to curate the show myself, on top of my other work.

I went to see John Bratby in his home in Hastings. He was still painting in the same manner, as lively as ever, but with, I felt, an increasingly desperate edge. He was a bullish character, with a big belly and big head fringed with wild hair and a beard that made him look, perpetually, a bit bewildered. He still, I thought, couldn't really believe, let alone understand, what had happened to him. He was in the limelight one moment, the star of art, in 1956, and then totally dropped the next. No one wanted to have anything to do with him. He had a breakdown and wrote a vivid book about it, with that title. Then he picked up his brushes again and carried on, a victim of political exclusion and the narrow, blinkered pursuit of modernism by the art establishment.

There was one voice that was particularly crucial in this movement—that of the art critic John Berger, who'd begun as a realist painter—I included a couple of his own works, not bad if a bit lean, in the show. A socialist vision lapped round all his thinking, to such an extent that he called one collection of his essays *Permanent Red*. He criticised Pablo Picasso, who was a communist, for not being socialist enough. Though never a member of the Party, his influence was such that he got an official invitation to the USSR, much to Peter de Francia's chagrin, who was and didn't. Along with many of the painters, he gave up writing regular art criticism in the late 1950s, concentrated on novels, and soon went to live in the Haute-Savoie in France. He argued that the majority of working-class people round the world were peasants, and he wanted to help give them a voice.

I went to see him in his fine house on the slopes of the mountains, just south of Geneva. I expected to meet a man ingrained in rural life, but I found an intellectual with a garden in a mess. I remember advising him and his partner what to do with their attempt to grow a strawberry patch. The lunch, he assured me was a local speciality: *raclette*. But his was made on a metal contraption at the table, not as I'd had it before, cooked on an open fire in the forest, the smoke from the burning pine logs making the melting cheese taste delicious. He looked like a peasant though, with his weather-beaten complexion, his heavy, sensual features and his aged passion. Disappointingly he had very little to say about the period, no leads to great art I'd missed. It was too long ago, and not his interest now.

I took the chance to talk about his immensely popular BBC TV series *Ways of Seeing*, which in my opinion was having a pernicious influence. It argued, in essence, that oil painting as an art form was over. It had not only been replaced by photography, but, as a language, was itself inherently and inevitably sexist. Oil paint brushed on canvas was an expression of male status and male domination over women—the secretion of the 'male gaze'. Put crudely, paint is semen, a brush a phallus. I argued that this was a terrible over-simplification and reduction of what painting could be. How do Leonardo and Rembrandt, Goya and Van Gogh fit into that? He had to agree. 'We were wrong about that,' he admitted. 'We were not talking about great painting, of course.'

'Isn't that all that matters?' I asked. He shrugged. I wanted him to say that publicly. He shrugged a bit less. In my opinion those shrugs weren't good enough, but I could see there was nothing he was going to do about that. Perhaps meanly, I thought the royalties from *Ways of Seeing* were too good. *Ways of Seeing Differently* could have been even more lucrative as a follow-up. The subsequent closure of the National Gallery's collection at 1900 (see M for Neil MacGregor) can, I think, be dated back to Berger's writing, and that political clipping of the wings of painting in 1956.

Eventually I got a note from Berger, which a bit sadly reflected our conversation. I used it as the introduction to the catalogue. 'I refuse,' he wrote,

> to be wisely critical now of youthful fervour, as sometimes happens with age. I stand by what we did ... During a few years we were not dupes. By intention, with imagination, and with the clumsy anger and dreams of those who see what the privileged ignore, we were close to those without power. None more powerfully and poignantly than George Fullard, whose exceptional work still awaits recognition [we had talked about him especially—as far as I know John hadn't taken much interest in him before]. None of us as a group would claim we produced great art, but in that very closeness we were on the site where great art, when it does occur, is usually born.

He didn't go on to admit that his TV programme *Ways of Seeing* had subsequently helped to ensure that great art, at least great painting, had even less chance of happening again.

Finally the show was on the walls. To me it was a revelation, like lifting a curtain on the possibilities of painting, to embrace, once again, earthy, realistic, humane expressionism, not to flatten feeling into Colour Field Abstraction, or thinned to commercial Pop branding or the self-denial of expression in photorealism, the other trends in art at that time. The Kitchen Sink movement was much wider and richer than even I had thought. But it had disappeared, almost without trace, swept under the carpet of post-war modern art movements.

This exhibition needs to be done again, with artists from Europe like André Fougeron and Renato Guttuso, and from America, Edward Hopper, of course, and the remarkable socialist and communist sympathiser, Alice Neel, whose luminous paintings I only discovered in 2017, fittingly at the Van Gogh Foundation in Arles, thanks to the excellent, perceptive independent curatorship of Jeremy Lewison. Her portrait of Andy Warhol (1970), a minor talent whose name will only survive in the history of marketing not of art, is a brilliant instance of realistic vision. She painted him with his eyes, his main weapons of seduction and defence, shut. The pallor of his feeble body is exposed beneath, with the scar where he was shot, his flab supported by a corset. His fingers fumble before his crotch. Only his highly polished shoes are sharply shown, a tribute to his first, least-exploitative, career as a commercial artist specialising in footwear. There will, I think, be many great works of art in such a show, despite Berger's subsequent determined resignation that there wouldn't be and couldn't, and the work of British artists, including Bratby, Smith and Fullard, would shine among them.

B *is for* EDUARD BERSUDSKY

There are moments you never forget. I opened the long, black, ordinary-looking photograph album, and my eyes, and perhaps too my mouth, fell open. There were photos, stuck on the black pages, page after page of them, of what looked like machines with carved wooden figures, towers with cages containing human beings, animals, goblins. It looked as though some medieval carver of gargoyles had, by some trick of history, been born again in our times. Or, perhaps, some pre-Revolutionary unclean character, like Prisypkin in Mayakovsky's *The Bed Bug*, one of my favourite Russian plays, who is frozen by some fluke and brought back to life in the glorious post-revolutionary era when everything has become, at last, pristine, perfect and pure, but who carries with him, on his resurrected body, a bedbug that escapes and eventually upsets everything in the modern universe. For I knew I was looking at something Russian, and I had been bitten. I knew I had to do something about this. I had no choice.

The album had been brought to me by Barbara Grigor, wife of Murray, the Scottish filmmaker specialising in architecture (later, by an odd chain of circumstances, the official biographer of Sean Connery, whose rich, rolling vowels he could conjure to perfection). The album, in turn, had been given to him by a friend, the furniture-maker Tim Stead—whom I hadn't yet met—who had been excited by something his wife, Maggy, had seen in Leningrad (now St Petersburg). This is how art works, through human connections, hand to hand, eye to eye. Tim had shown the photo album to Barbara, who thought I might be interested, and, what's more, might be able to do something about it. This is how she came to be standing by my desk, watching my eyes grow increasingly excited. So the world turns. And I could see the connections working, the cogs on wheels going round and clicking, triggering actions, in the photos of the sculptures before me, for they were obviously kinetic; everything in them was moving. I was caught and had to see them for real—it was as simple as that.

When I did, I was amazed. Silenced, in fact, just looking, exploring and, quite often, laughing. One sculpture had a little figure of Karl Marx perched on a stand, carved out of wood with a big beard, looking like a predatory garden gnome. He began turning a handle with great effort, slowly and, as he did so, the towering mechanism above him began to click into action— bicycle wheels, weighing and sewing machines, music stands and a horn that went round and round—all things made in early Soviet factories. Soon everything was spinning; it was all working. Then a cracked record began to play a rousing chorus of young voices, the Young Pioneers, youthful members of the Party, singing.

Opposite: Eduard Bersudsky, The Tower of Babel, 1986-89

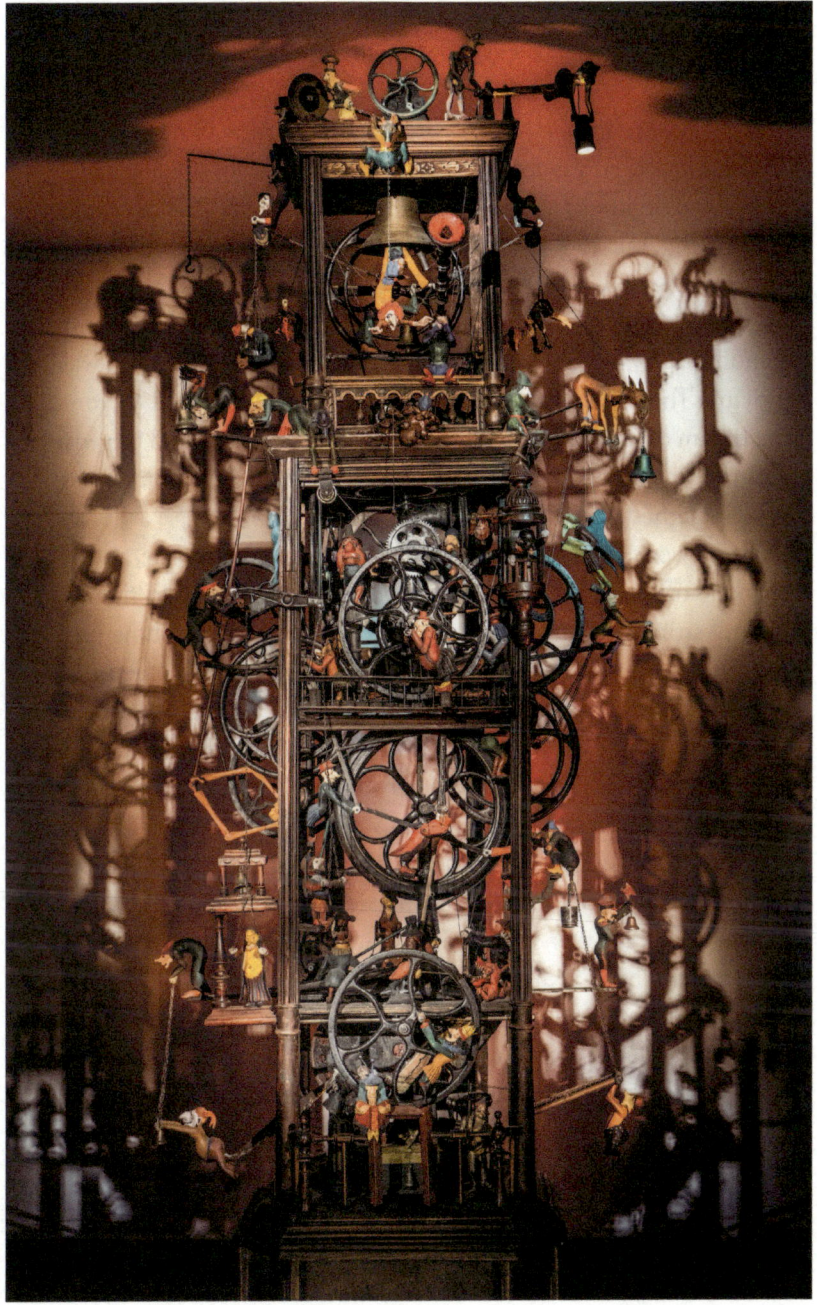

I asked Tatyana Jakovskaya, Eduard's partner, who was with me, what the words meant—'Our train will fly!' (she had been a Soviet pioneer in her youth). 'The next station is Communism! There is no other way forward for us! We have rifles in our hands!' The dwarf figure of Marx went on turning, the machines went on working, but, as I looked, slowly but surely the assembled bits each, one by one, juddered to a halt, until the whole confabulation was still, seized up and silent. Only Marx himself was left grimly grinding away, refusing to give up his belief, but nothing else was moving. The sculpture was called *The Big Idea.* It was all there—the dream of Communism, its hope, its ludicrousness and tragedy, and the impossibility, the futility of trying to change human nature. I laughed, while sensing utter sadness.

There were other machines standing around—a tall one, a tower made of wood, with dozens of small, painted wooden figures, pulling strings, turning wheels. It, too, began slowly, grinding into action, until quite soon everyone was working, doing something, busy with their appointed tasks—I'd never seen such a vivid exposure, amusing, sympathetic but also sad, of the human anthill. It was called *The Tower of Babel*—us building forever upwards in the vainglory of our ambition. There were ominous aspects: a little portrait of Lenin waving his finger, preaching from a pulpit, and in the basement, Stalin, in uniform, wielding an axe.

There was another tower nearby, a dark, medieval one, called *The Castle.* It was a killing machine with a slicing blade, a portcullis clanking up and down, and truncated heads going round and round. One, Tatyana told me, was a portrait of the poet Osip Mandelstam, one of twenty million people killed in Stalin's purges of his real and imagined enemies. These wooden machines were made from discarded bits of furniture Eduard found lying about in the streets of St Petersburg, when it was still Leningrad—for no one wanted wriggly, dark chair legs then—everything had to be straight and modern—and from parts of engines he'd stolen when he'd worked as a ship mechanic. They filled his flat, where he lived with his ex-wife (neither had any other accommodation to go to so they had to continue sharing) and a lame raven he'd saved, which shat modern art on the walls (they'd seen smuggled images of Abstract Expressionism) that became multicoloured when he fed the bird on beetroot and carrot. Eduard was an occasional exhibitor with a group of nonconformist artists. The authorities knew about him, but thought he was just a toy maker—he was by then earning a living as a sculptor carving big animals for a children's park—and didn't take him seriously.

Tatyana Jakovskaya, then a well-known theatre director and critic, was taken by a mutual friend to see Eduard's work in his flat—both of them were Jewish—and, like me later, realised that she had no choice but to do something about it all. Recognition is the essential first step for art's survival. It was her idea to make it work as theatre. It was 1989, before the Berlin Wall fell, and Russia was beginning to open up. She had had the brainwave to rent a space and employ a group of actors and mimes (whom people would come to see—no one had heard of Bersudsky) to perform between the sculptures, which they lit with torches as they sprang to life, one by one. It was poetically trenchant, because Eduard, when Tatyana met him, stuttered so badly he was virtually mute, so depressed was he by the disappearance of his friends, many of them Jewish, one after another, into Siberia. The stutter vanished with the success of the show.

So the Sharmanka Theatre was born. It wouldn't have existed, nor, I think, would Eduard's art have survived, without Tatyana. She's a large, impressive woman, almost a Mother Russia, with a look that is at the same time accepting but misses nothing, and a determination that, once set in motion, there's no stopping, like an armed tank set on the path to victory, whatever's in the way.

Eduard beside her, quiet, at ease in her shadow, is, in fact, an equally strong, looming presence, heavy-browed with a beard more like a lion's mane, with eyes that nowadays have mostly lost their gloom, and thick lips that can break into a quite devilish grin.

Sharmanka is Russian for barrel organ. Eduard's very first animated carving was a compact figure of an antiquated barrel organ player, at the very end of his life; the organ box having now become an extension of his stomach, his huge beard spilling over both, his eyes still staring hopefully ahead, but now looking more hollow than alive. Eduard then had the idea to make his arm move as if, with his last breath, he was still trying to make music, entertain others and earn a crust of bread. He rigged an engine up inside the carving (one he stole from his job in a military factory) and switched it on. The old man's hand ground round. Eduard later told me—through Tatyana, he's never learnt English—that he was so surprised by what he'd done, he jumped back, or rather was thrown back a yard. He half repeated the action for me, as if he'd been kicked in the stomach. Beryl Cook had a similar experience when she started painting. Art often begins as a surprise and is never without it. Eduard had found his language—how he could say what he wanted to say about living in Russia at that time. Everything flowed from that simple cranking fist, non-stop—an extraordinary outpouring of creativity.

These early wooden machines weren't for sale—they were too fragile, and Tatyana needed them to earn income from visitors coming to see their theatre. But since 1990 Eduard had become more and more active. He could now say freely what he'd always wanted to. *The Big Idea*, just mentioned, was a product of that new freedom. So too was *The Dreamer in the Kremlin*—a monstrous, armoured bear's skull, with a rising phallus, under a pulsing red star—its title taken from H. G. Wells's name for Lenin, who had charmed the author on a visit in 1921. There are a lot of rising, and falling, phalluses in Eduard's work, as there are in life, though not usually in sight. In a show Eduard once had in Tel Aviv, one of the organisers suggested it would be better if they were cut out, because such things, phalluses, weren't 'Jewish'. Eduard was furious.

And then there was the extraordinary *Autumn Stroll in Perestroika*, partly inspired by an exhibition Eduard had recently seen of Jean Tinguely's work in Moscow, expressing Eduard's deep misgivings at the real direction this apparent, jolly, opening-up of the Soviet Union was taking. A pair of boots march ominously on a chair. An army is awaking in what appears to be a dreamtime. Eduard was fully aware of the continuing presence of the KGB. His premonition has recently come true in Ukraine. These three sculptures seemed to me the most brilliant summation in art of the whole history of Communism, which had such a profound influence in the twentieth-century world, so I bought them for the new Gallery of Modern Art in Glasgow. And I offered Eduard a show at the McLellan Galleries, for I was keen for people to see his early work. This gave Tatyana the idea to move the whole of Sharmanka to Scotland, lock stock and barrel.

I was against this idea and Tatyana would argue naïvely, but in retrospect, seeing what has happened in Russia, sadly I think she was right. I thought that Eduard was one of the great artists of that country, and his works needed to be seen by the people there, especially since so many of the references in his sculptures are to Russian history and literature—such as the one that plays on the *Aurora*, the navy ship whose gun, legend has it, triggered the start of the October Revolution in 1917, and the superb kinetic evocations of Nikolai Gogol's *Dead Souls* and Mikhail Bulgakov's *Master and Margarita*. Many of these references are lost on British audiences but would resonate profoundly in Russia. I dreamt of seeing a core exhibition of his work in a room in the Peter and

Paul Fortress, the original citadel in the heart of St Petersburg, on an island on the Neva River, used, for some time, as a prison for political criminals—the perfect place for Bersudsky's nightmarish absurdities.

I was going to Russia quite regularly at that time, advising museums about how to adapt to a mixed economy, and Tatyana happened to be there during one of my visits. She showed me something of Eduard's life in St Petersburg: the naval dockyard where he'd worked, the impressive gateway through which he smuggled out bits of machines, oil dripping down his legs, the ancient wooden churches he'd help to restore in the countryside around St Petersburg, the single bookshop everyone went to—the famous House of Books on Nevsky Prospekt, the only place you could buy foreign literature. I was amazed by its staircase, the worn steps (since replaced) which were then so eroded by the traipse of feet that the middle of each was worn down to make a central rivulet—you could only climb the sides—a most vivid expression of the hunger for knowledge and wider horizons, in an era of grim repression.

I wanted to see where Eduard was brought up. Tatyana took me to the suburbs. From the airport to the centre of St Petersburg there is a made-up road, and the buildings along it look quite decent, but the city is in fact ringed by the most desolate public housing schemes I've ever seen: tower block after tower block after tower block stretching to the horizon in a pitted, road-less wasteland, where no foreigner goes. We found the block Eduard lived in and climbed the stairs. Tatyana had warned the new owners of our coming.

The couple had laid a few slices of bright orange sausage on a plate next to a saucer on which stood two slices of burnt toast, leaning together. I declined to eat (knowing that they couldn't have guests in their home without offering them something), saying I'd just had a meal and thinking they'd probably like to have the sausage for themselves. When we left, I said I understood the sausage, but why the burnt toast? 'Oh, that was in your honour,' said Tatyana, 'to hide the smells from the drains.'

When they moved to Scotland, Eduard and Tatyana settled first in a rented house in Blainslie, the tiny hamlet in the Scottish Borders where Tim and Maggy Stead had their home, and he, his workshop. It was really through Eduard that I got to know Tim. We already had a table and set of chairs by him in the Glasgow collection, bought by Brian Blench, the keeper of decorative arts. I was guarded about it. I could see its sculptural qualities, but it was extremely heavy. I liked expressive functionalism in modern design, from Charles Rennie Mackintosh to Charles and Ray Eames to the crazier Ettore Sottsass. Tim Stead seemed, if not a step back, a step sideward, into a rural life. I couldn't place him in the history of modern design as I knew it. I was blind to it, I'm not afraid to admit. Knowledge, like bullshit, can baffle the mind. But my eyes were opened when I first visited his home. I doubt if I'd have ventured there had it not been for Tim's initial liking for Eduard, and the latter's move next door to him.

I realised at once that I was walking into the home of a sculptor, not a furniture designer. He'd carved the whole interior, as if he were living in a cave made of wood. Maggy told me later that when she took the kids on holiday, usually back to France, where her mother and sister lived, Tim rarely went with them. He didn't like holidays. He stayed at home and when they came back a new interior section had been built, a staircase, a fireplace, a suite of cupboards, a loo, doorways, an elaborate bed, all made of wood, undulating surfaces of multicoloured grains, inviting you to touch and caress, live with and in—an extraordinary, containing chamber of love.

I understood then why I hadn't 'got' the table and chair in

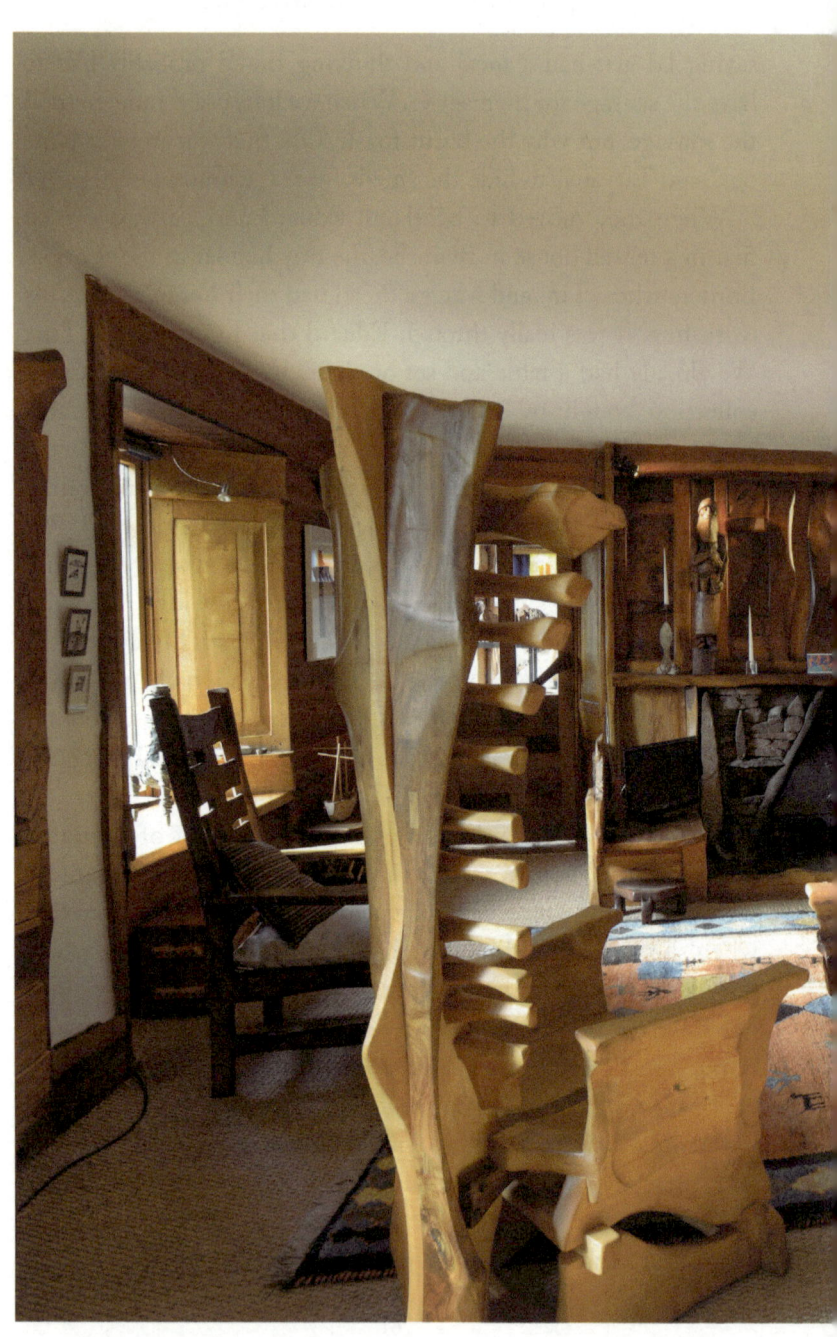

Room in Tim Stead's house, the Steading, with his skeletal chair in foreground

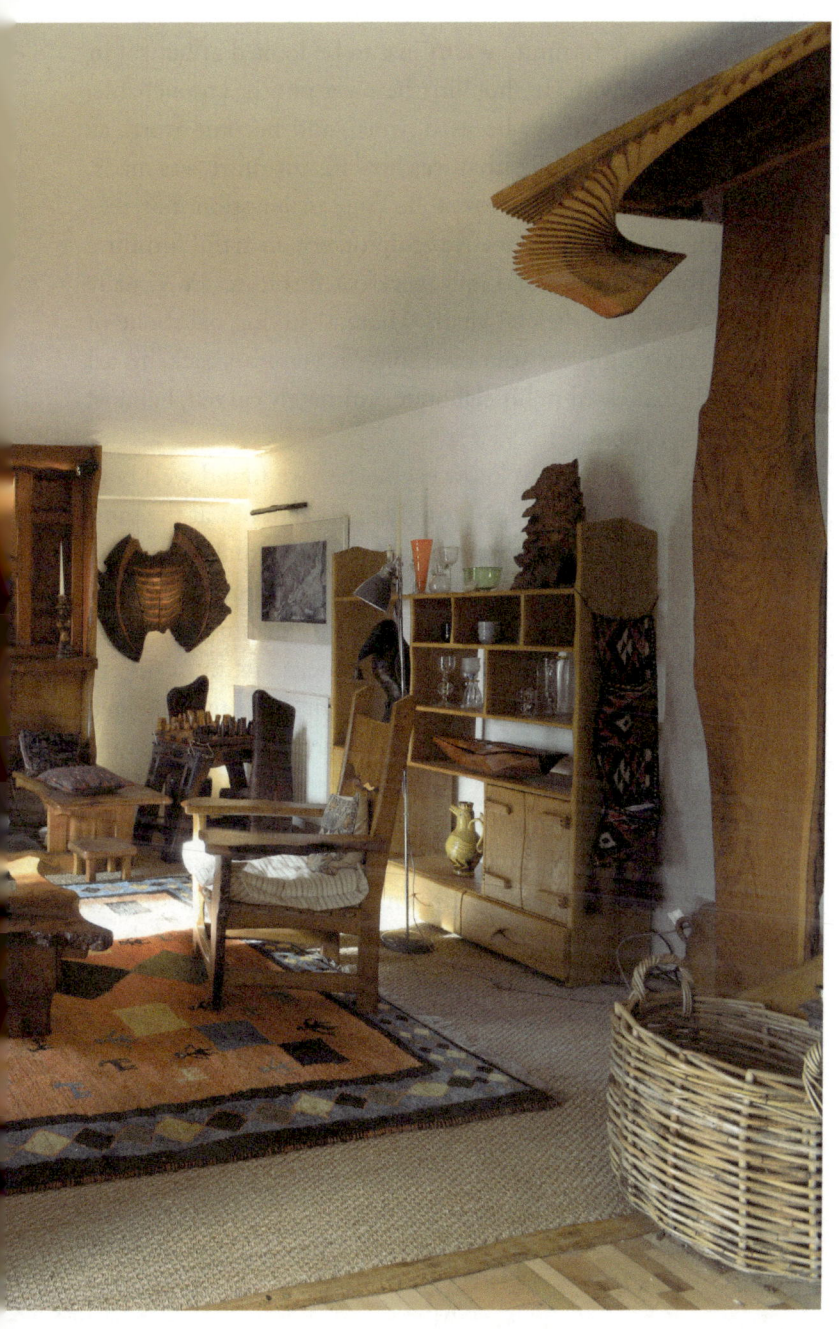

Kelvingrove. Tim's furniture wasn't just to be looked at but sat in and lived in and with. It shouldn't be on a plinth, untouchable, in a museum. It needs to be used, worn, and become worn, as wood can do so beautifully. That was how his furniture was made, by feel, letting the wood speak, following an emotion, not seeing beforehand. He was a creative sculptor, not an artful furniture designer. Though many of Tim's pieces of furniture are visually rich, particularly his skeletal chairs where a curving backbone of sycamore bones supports your own spine as you lean back, his art is most fully expressed in his elaborate, intimately carved, I almost wrote quarried, home.

When Tim and I got to know each other, we found we'd both been to the same art school, Nottingham, though not at the same time. The school had become even more conceptual when Tim got there, and he decided he'd like to make sculptures for people to sit on, not think about. He was driven into furniture design by the barren, cerebral visual culture of his time, a victim of his era. Otherwise, I think, he'd have been a sculptor all along. One gets a glimpse of what he might have done by the haunting sculptures he produced at the end of his short life, his 'excavations', which, though only table-size, acquire immense proportions in one's mind: imaginary dwelling places of early man. I actually think a latter-day Henry Moore was driven off the peak ridge of pure, imaginative creativity by the limited, dictatorial art of our times, by his need to make a living creatively (Tim said to me once, if you spend eight hours a day working, and eight hours sleeping it doesn't leave much time for living) and that vitally necessary ingredient in any full life and all good art, the necessity of not taking oneself too seriously—the need to play and invent. He'd barely begun to get into his true stride, when he died of cancer in 2000, when he was only forty-eight.

His rediscovery of sculpture took off, I think, partly from the inspired commission he received from Murray Grigor to recreate in wood one of the Neolithic houses at Skara Brae on Orkney for the exhibition I invited Murray to do called *Scotland Creates*, about the history of Scottish design. But I was then still thinking of him as a furniture-maker. I got Tim to make massive, truncated tree-trunk seats between the massive pillars of the Royal Exchange's central hall—I'm very fond of seats in galleries—there are rarely enough of them, and, even more rarely in the right position. We discovered during the renovations a tiny room with an inner window on an upper storey where someone could sit and watch what was happening, originally, in the main transactions of the exchange's hall below. We had to make something of it—but what? I handed it over to Tim. He turned this tiny space into a peephole, an organic, wooden vagina, with a curved seat all round, in the very centre of this neoclassical building, something feminine, as Athena stood in the dark heart of the Parthenon. Lovers love to nestle there and watch what's going on downstairs. But when the Queen came to open it, her minders absolutely refused to have her and the Duke of Edinburgh photographed sitting together in this space, knees almost touching, for some reason ...

Having been wary at first, I grew to respect Tim immensely. He was what any artist has to be, a maker first, not a thinker. The theory has to follow the creation—never the other way round. He was a big man, with a ruffled hair and beard, a gentle smile and deep-set, watchful eyes. You had the feeling he never stopped creating. His output never ceased—he was always doing something with his hands, even when he was diagnosed with a terminal cancer in the early 1990s. Things happen, and they have to be responded to; artists go with the flow of life and express what they feel about it. That's their job. It was after all, the Great Storm that swept across southern Britain 1987 that triggered a change of direction in Tim's career. He became fascinated with using native wood, particularly burr elm; there was so much of it lying around. When the central section of his house burnt down, I was amazed how he took it in his stride. Now he became interested in using burnt timber.

The year 2000 was approaching. I had the idea to commission Eduard and Tim to make a great clock to celebrate and, I insisted, mourn—I was feeling this more and more—the passing of the millennium. I had seen many of the great astronomical clocks of Europe, in Prague, Munich and Strasbourg, and Eduard, I thought, was a medieval clock maker reborn in our times and he had to be given his say, at this, his moment in time. After all, he'd lived through some of the worst of it, after escaping, as a boy, the terrible Siege of Leningrad. He was lucky enough to be alive, and he knew it. Tim at the same time knew he was dying. I wanted the clock to be really monumental, ten metres high, at least—after all it was a long century. And they both cursed me, Eduard especially, for the scale of it. They brought other craft workers into project, the real clockmaker Jürgen Tübbecke—to make the actual mechanism—and the glassblower Annica Sandström, half of Linden Mill Glass team. A medieval tower of this size needed stained-glass windows and an all-seeing rainbow eye.

I commissioned the clock to go in the magnificent main hall of Kelvingrove Art Gallery and Museum, which was a sort of Gothic folly in itself, opened in 1901 as a permanent reminder of the first century it had seen. But I needed a grant from the Arts Council Millennium Fund to make it. That meant making an application, and that meant making drawings. The project almost failed, for the first time, at that stage. It was absolutely impossible for Eduard to draw something he hadn't yet made. Any genuine artist is like that. Art is a process of discovery, a building-on, a

Opposite: Eduard Bersudsky and Tim Stead, Annica Sandström and Jürgen Tübbecke, Millennium Clock Tower, 1997–99

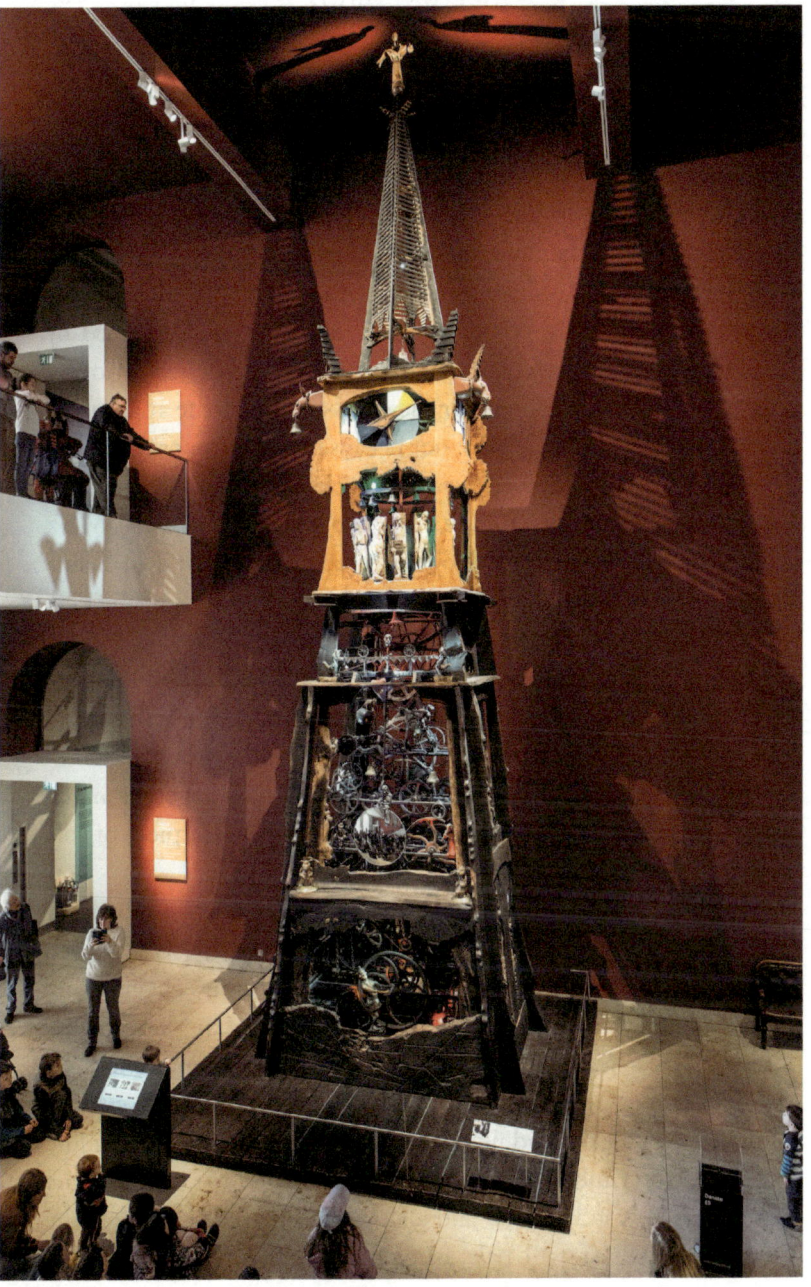

following-through, not an illustration of a preconceived idea (and the best illustrations are that, too). That's why Jim Whiting has never had a grant, nor ever applied for one. So much publicly funded art, however well intentioned, is back to front, arse before mouth. That's why it's so constipated. The creepers and calculators get through, not the firebrands, the creators.

The question was: how could I get this project off the ground, with an artist as 'un-committee-able' as this? Maggy helped by cooking up some drawings of things Eduard had done previously, with some sketches of ideas by her husband Tim. The application was made, but then rejected, not because of the proposal, but because, the panel said, there was too much Sharmanka in Glasgow. This left the door open for the project to go somewhere else. Mark Jones, the director of the Royal Museum of Scotland in Edinburgh, was interested and they had a big hall too, so, in the end, the project went ahead.

The *Millennium Clock Tower* was when realised even more powerful than I'd hoped and even darker in mood, which I think will make it last. I anticipated that Tim would provide the framework for Eduard's animation, but they worked together much more intimately and creatively than that. It's a masterpiece of collaborative public art of our times.

Inspired by the fire in his home, Tim used burnt timbers for the lower stories of the clock, within the dark shadows of which Eduard's figures ply their trade, grind their way, engendering world-wide wars, alleviated only by a diminutive Charlie Chaplin, with a Hitler moustache (after all, as he said, he wore one first) with a slender cane, and a skeletal monkey swinging on a circular mirror (the clock's pendulum), showing us ourselves in the middle of it all. The timbers lighten up above, the tree has survived the fire and the wood is fresh and alive with growth. But here is the darkest insight of it all, pale, ashen figures cycle round and round, chained and tortured, vivid images of how cruel we have been, over the century, to our fellow humankind. Then, above, the timbers blacken again, and rise up to form a burnt, fragile, skeleton of a tower, on top of which stands a woman cradling a dead man in her arms, a *pietà*, which, as Tatyana, observed, sums it all up: 'Caring, carrying and carrying on. Time passing in 2000.' Tim Stead died that year.

Tim's home, the Steading in Blainslie, Galashiels, is now, thank goodness, being preserved, with huge public support, by a trust led by the drive and vision of the jeweller and food writer, Nichola Fletcher. Sharmanka is firmly established in Glasgow, run by Sergey Jakovsky, Tatyana's son, who has used his expertise in theatre lighting to enhance the whole experience. Glasgow, once a socialist stronghold, has taken to its heart the art of Eduard Bersudsky, the latter-day Hieronymus Bosch of Communism and after, until Russia wakes up to realise what she has lost.

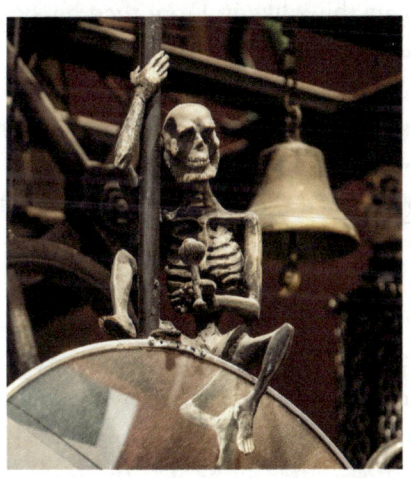

B *is for* DAVID BOWIE

I grew up in the great formative era of pop—first Elvis and Billy Fury, the Beatles and Bob Dylan, the Stones and the Kinks. There was so much, and the songs came so thick and fast that I thought this was the normal background of youth. But after the Velvet Underground, above all their song 'Heroin', I didn't hear much that really grabbed me, apart from some rap, and I lost interest in the whole shooting match. I once went to a concert given by Ravi Shankar, the Indian sitar improviser, in London. Just before he began to play, a mutter went through the audience. The Fab Four were loping in to take their seats in the front row below me. But I forgot about them when the music took over. I closed my eyes. The notes, like jewels exploding in the dark, travelling faster and faster, ceased to be a river passing before me but swivelled round and came full at me. For once, I was in time. I'd never heard anything like it. From then on, pop music for me became the sound of my youth.

Mick Hucknall, who I'd barely heard of, was once invited by my chair, Mike Harrison, to open an exhibition we had on in Manchester. The pop star and I met on the front steps of the City Art Gallery, both going in at the same time. As we walked up together, flames shot out from the roof above us. Men were working up there and, as I found out later, some clumsy workman had dropped a blowtorch. The alarms went. We had to wait. Everyone inside streamed out. The fire engine arrived, plus the press. Cameras flashed. Mick looked at me with amused detachment and asked, 'Did you arrange this on purpose?' If I'd been quicker, I'd have got in first—after all he was the lead singer of Simply Red. Then there was the odd serendipity that Imogen Sheeran, my bright, forever-beaming PR officer in Manchester, when she'd left, gave birth to Ed, who looks quite like her, but that was about as close as I'd ever got to the world of pop, until ...

One day my secretary, Hilary, rung through to say that someone had popped in to see me. 'Who is it?' I asked, since I wasn't expecting anyone. 'He says his name is David Bowie.' She said it in a hesitant way that could mean either she wasn't sure she believed him or, which I found out later to be the case, she thought she'd heard the name before, but wasn't sure. 'Show him in!' I said, leaving my desk to walk towards the door. It opened, and a noticeably thin man walked in, with a very light, cat-like tread. He was smaller than I'd expected, below average height and build, and, rather eerily, looked as though suspended somewhere between adolescence and adulthood. He had an aura of energy around him, a vitality zone that was still his to grow into; he zinged with what can only be called a charismatic presence. I don't think I was backprojecting any awareness of who he was on the person before me as the impression was too unusual and too strong. He was ordinary, and at the same time not at all, as if he'd landed from another planet, Ziggy Stardust for real. I got the feeling in that room, walking across the carpet to shake my hand, he would have emitted this peculiar radiance, whether he'd been famous or not.

And then, as he came close, what was even odder were his eyes, which were of two different colours, one clear blue and one brown. I had the impression he was watching mine as they switched from one to other, not quite believing what they saw—a familiar experience for him I presumed—while his own eyes remained open and fixed. He had not only the agility and tread but also the fixed attention of a cat—a rare breed, perhaps a Burmese. We sat down.

He'd come to the gallery to see the John Bellany fiftieth-birthday exhibition I'd put on. It contained a portrait of Bowie, but I doubt if anyone who happened to notice him looking at it would have recognised him from it. In fact, rather the reverse, for

John's portraits were not his best productions. They're all a bit the same, looking like John himself, in fact. Though John had caught, up to a point, Bowie's needle-sharp features and the two tints of his irises; his eyes, the most telling feature in all John's paintings of faces, were, as was usual in his portraits, those of the artist, not that of his sitter. They were the eyes of a watcher, not a seer. John's eyes always peer out from under their upper lids; Bowie's stare was full and strong, challenging and brazen.

He'd come to see me because he knew about my stand against conceptual art. He agreed with me. We chatted about art in general, John's paintings, and then he let on that he'd started painting himself. That's when I blew perhaps the biggest opportunity of my life. Looking back, I couldn't have been more stupid. I had the chance to do something really interesting, but I was too blind to see it. When, much later, it dawned on me what a chance I'd missed, I was out of art galleries altogether and had no power, no place to effect it. What I should have done, obviously, while he was sitting there, chatting, was to ask him if he'd like to put on a show of his work. And, I have the feeling looking back, that's what he thought, hoped I might ask, but he was certainly not going to mention such an idea to me first. How stupid I was not to realise it. And, worse, if I'd really been on the ball I would have added, did he think he could help persuade Bob Dylan to put on show of his paintings too, and we'd have had a fantastic double bill. But I was too closed-minded to even think of it.

I couldn't think beyond conventional ideas of quality, as if that was all that mattered. The state of the art of painting was much more desperate. I'd seen illustrations of Dylan's paintings and thought they were OK, but nothing special, and I presumed Bowie's would be much the same. What was much more important at that time was that both of them were painting—simply the act of doing it was significant enough. That was the message I needed to get across—and was too blind to notice. If visitors didn't rate their work, so much the better—they'd be inspired to do better themselves. That was the chance I blew, as we sat chatting together. What a waste. And then he left.

C *is for* HENRI CARTIER-BRESSON

I met Henri Cartier-Bresson through his old friend, the painter Georg Eisler. He thought we would get on because we shared similar suspicions of the direction modern art was taking; it was becoming increasing superficial and, at the same time, increasingly commercial. Henri was tall and lean with a round head thrust slightly forward, set with large eyes that looked as though they were shooting rays of light. You sensed you were with an animal about to spring and pounce. He once told me that he thought photography was like pick-pocketing—when he took a photograph, he always felt that he was stealing something. He could, one felt, have been a brilliant thief, even a cat burglar; he was so agile, secretive and light on his feet.

By the time I met him, however, he had become much more interested in drawing than in photography. His experience of photographing people all over the world, for much of the century, had taught him one thing—the world, he thought, was now spinning out of control. We need to slow down, everything, he kept saying. Drawing was, for him, slowing down. It was a totally different activity from photography, he said; it was drawn out, contemplative. He saw himself now not as a pickpocket, but as someone meditating—a somewhat agitated Buddhist, he admitted.

'But you're not entirely giving up photography?' I teased him.

David Hockney had told me how he'd recently noticed a man in Paris walking slowly and purposefully along a crowded pavement with a camera held down at his arm's length, obviously aimed at something. He realised that this man knew exactly what he was doing, and he followed him for some distance out of curiosity. The man was indeed taking photographs, and he seemed to know what the camera was seeing, even though the lens was down by his knees. David had no idea who he was, but then Henri hardly ever let himself be photographed; he liked to be the hidden observer. It was only a little later, at a reception, when David was introduced to Henri that he realised this was the man he'd been following! Henri laughed. Yes, he told me, he'd been very surprised that he'd been followed by someone without him noticing—but then Hockney was an artist himself and knew how to watch. But the problem was, he said, that when we met, all I wanted to talk about was drawing, and all he wanted to talk about was photography. We had nothing to say to each other. Saul Leiter, whose beautiful photographs I only found out about only long after I'd left museums, was also a fine painter. He defined the difference very simply: 'Photography is about finding things; painting about making things.'

I had always in my career collected and shown photographs. It never occurred to me not to. It was obviously one of the great art forms of the twentieth century, and I couldn't understand why Tate—I want to be old fashioned in this book and call it the Tate—why the Tate didn't begin to collect it until 2009. Immediately you start to think you know what 'art' is, and you begin to fall into the trap of predicting it and therefore limiting it. You become blind to the next appearance of the very thing you're looking for. Art curators, who build their careers making visual judgements, on developing what's called 'an eye' are, perhaps, more prone to this sort of blindness than anyone; they can so easily become like doctrinaire priests in a religion. The Tate collected drawings and prints, many of the latter made with photographs, but never photographs themselves all through the great creative years of this art form—a remarkably blinkered approach, if one thinks about it, to contemporary visual expression.

Frank Constantine, the director who appointed me in Sheffield, taught me, among many things, always to keep one's eyes open, which is much the same as keeping one's mind open—including the possibility that what one is looking at might not be art at all! It was Frank who alerted me to the brilliance of Peter Mitchell's small, square colour photos, taken by balancing precariously up stepladders, of his industrial neighbourhood in Leeds and the people who lived in the soon-to-disappear buildings whose last moments he made eternal in his classics of visual construction. This included his remarkable record of the demolition of the Quarry Hill flats, then the largest social housing scheme in Britain.

Frank also bought a beautiful group of Hockney's own photographs. I was once with Hockney talking about photography when he remarked, 'It's simple; you can see visual order anywhere.' He looked down at the table we were standing next to, which was littered with pens and pencils, and making a square with the extended fingers and thumbs of both hands, framed one section. It became a little, explosive Hockney, and still remains as a picture in my mind. His own photos all have that happy, overall completeness, in full colour, of course. Being able to frame a photo is a talent some people have, and some people, strangely, haven't, but it's only a start. Being able to take a photo in which everything looks as though it's 'meant' requires a highly developed level of alertness.

Henri spent a lifetime developing this ability and agility. He told me that he often had a sixth sense that something was about to happen before it happened—a moment waiting to be made complete, a composition to be held in time—a man jumping, a cyclist turning, pigeons flying. The beauty of his photos is that they are life held; they are never dead. His work expresses the essence of William Blake's poem 'Eternity': 'He who kisses the joy as it flies/ Lives in eternity's sunrise.' He captured the moment as he saw it; there was no enhancement after, no cookery in the darkroom. His was a disciplined practice, puritanical looking, with an open heart, in black and white.

Sebastião Salgado is arguably one of the greatest and now probably the most famous current exponent of Henri's approach to documentary photography. In his most powerful pictures, which now number hundreds, he manages to combine passion with profundity, merely by natural observation, without any artifice, in the same way that Henri captured, tenderly, lightly and lovingly. Salgado joined Magnum, the documentary photography collective that Henri co-founded in 1947. Henri told me that when Salgado first wanted to leave Magnum—it must have been in the early 1980s; he didn't give me a date—he stood in front of the door and told Salgado:

> You're not yet ready—you need to be with us longer—if you go now, you'll be swayed by success and commercialism— you can push me out of the way, if you want. But that's what you'll have to do. I'm not moving.

Salgado stayed, leaving eventually in 1994. His extraordinary series *Genesis*—images of nature before the advent of man—also, being in black and white, reads as a requiem for a world we seem set on losing.

Salgado came to see me once in Glasgow, when we'd put on an exhibition of the hundred photos I'd bought by him for the collection. He was self-effacing, like Henri, but in a very different way. Henri's attention was thin, directed and alert, on stilts, like a praying mantis; Salgado's was thicker, still, sedentary, but equally alert, like a chameleon—both of them expert flycatchers. He wanted me to commission him to take photos of refugees around the world. One of the urgent questions that faced us today, he argued, was 'Do people have the right to live where they can live?' I couldn't see how I could spend public money on art that had not yet been done, so I said no. But I wasn't thinking imaginatively or clearly enough. I should have thought of his proposal in terms of a travelling exhibition and a publication, not an acquisition, in much the same way that I was trying to work with David Hockney. I therefore missed an opportunity for Glasgow to be closely associated with one of the greatest artists of our time and one of the most pressing issues. When I realised it, much later, I had no power to make it happen. Another missed opportunity—like my meeting with David Bowie—that I mention in the hope that it will inspire others, in the public sphere, not to make similar mistakes again.

Henri was mostly drawing when I met him. I bought a couple of these small, sensitive sheets for Glasgow (together with a large selection of his photographs) not because I considered them to be great drawings, but because I thought it was historically significant that this major artistic figure of the twentieth century should have taken this step at the end of his career, and anyway one was a self-portrait, which would always be telling. Many thought that Henri, by drawing, was taking a step back—he'd begun by studying painting but had then taken the new art form of photography to its greatest heights, and inspired and helped many others along the way. But anyone who took a stance against the latest development in art, even one who'd done so much to advance and promote a new technique, was, at that time, pigeon-holed as being a reactionary. We talked a lot about this.

He had, for example, been against the building of I. M. Pei's Pyramid in the courtyard of the Louvre (his flat on the Rue de

Rivoli overlooked the Jardin des Tuileries), not because he was anti-modern architecture but because he thought this building was an intervention that belittled, trivialised and obscured the very handsome space it was intended to enhance. He told me he'd once been at a reception where President Mitterrand was present. Though they'd never met, he was surprised to see the crowd part before him and the president, having heard he was there, marching directly towards him. He came right up to Henri and said, without any introduction, 'I hear you're against the Pyramid!' It was one of Mitterand's *Grand Projets*, which each, strangely, had to have a particular, different geometric shape (as if he were planting a sequence of secret—masonic?—symbols across the city). Henri argued that the pyramid was pointless and diminishing—the lobby it covered could easily have been capped with horizontal pools and fountains like those around it, or a low glass ceiling that would not have interrupted the vista in this historic courtyard.

I added that the pyramid was only really useful for marketing purposes—after all it didn't cover the museum, but the museum's shopping mall. We agreed about that too, for Henri was against mixing commercialism with art. He loved the story I told him of Brother Adam, the Benedictine monk from Buckfast Abbey in Devon, famous for breeding gentle bees, who, when asked on television how he marketed his bees, replied, 'Market my bees? Sell my bees?' He shook his head. 'Oh, if the bee is good, it will sell itself.' Henri disagreed strongly with Claude Picasso for selling Picasso's signature to Citroën to name a car. He was distressed, as I was, with the National Galleries of Scotland's marketing campaign to increase visitors by encouraging them to come and see 'the most expensive names in the world', sprawled across posters decorated solely with artist's signatures. Works of art in public collections only have value for their artistic meaning; their financial value, at any particular time, is totally beside the point.

Henri's friend Georg put it even more strongly. 'Modern art museums,' he once quipped to me, 'are tied to the apron strings of the art market.' He was expanding on George Grosz's observation, made in 1920, in his short essay, *Instead of a Biography:*

> The painter, even if unaware of it, is a cash factory, a machine for producing profit, who is used by wealthy exploiters and æsthetic jackasses so they may invest their money more or less profitably and be called, therefore, patrons of the arts.

I understood this influence at work in the art market, but I thought at the time it was a bit exaggerated to extend it to museums. The art galleries I ran certainly weren't tied to any market, for a start. But his words increasingly came to haunt me as these apron strings got pulled tighter and tighter over time (see S for Sir Nicholas Serota). I'm not against anyone making money out of art—people have to live, and deserve to be paid for what they do—but the absurd prices paid for works by a handful of living artists, which bear no relation to the cost of their manufacture, itself in many cases carried out by assistants, suggests that something has gone awry with the way money relates to this activity. Modern art needs to thrive in a different type of non-commercial public space, and it's the job of curators to put it there and argue the merits of each case.

Another incident from my relationship with Henri haunts me. I was once interviewing him in the 1980s for a programme on BBC Radio 3 and we were discussing the increasing prevalence in art schools not to teach drawing any more. He turned to my producer and asked, 'Can you turn off the recorder?' He did so.

'It's off?' he nodded. 'It's all Duchamp's fault,' he said. 'You can turn it on again now.' I was amused, and thought he was just expressing what all like-minded people, like Georg and me, thought at the time—that the rise of conceptual art, which sprang from

Duchamp's exhibition of a urinal, had undermined the necessity for artists to create visually, even, basically, to learn to draw. I never asked him why he wanted the recorder turned off—why he couldn't say what he thought on air. I assumed it was because he didn't want to personalise the debate, but now I'm not so sure. When I discovered that the whole thing literally was Duchamp's fault (see D for Marcel Duchamp), it made me wonder if he knew what had happened, or more probably guessed, because he was precisely right. He was born in 1908 and knew everyone on the art scene in Paris and New York when Duchamp chose to lie and steal. But by then it was too late to ask him. Henri died in 2004.

Though Henri was always serious, he was never anything but charming. On a visit to Edinburgh, we were going to a restaurant on a light Scottish summer evening, when he noticed an American couple taking pictures with a flash. He shook his head, 'They won't get anywhere with that.' My wife, Gillian Tait, suggested he go and tell them. 'I will,' he said, and immediately went over to politely explain what they were doing wrong and kindly adjust the setting on their camera. They thanked him profusely as he came back to us, never realising they'd just had a private lesson on photography from Henri Cartier-Bresson.

C *is for* JACQUES CHIRAC

President Jacques Chirac of France came to Glasgow to look at the regeneration of its huge peripheral housing schemes, the success of which was attracting international attention. There's an exquisite couple of minutes of newsreel footage in the 1950s showing a city planner standing in front of a map of Glasgow, pointing at the densely packed inner city and saying,

'Look, all the people live in slums here. We're going to move them all out here,' indicating, with cupped fists (as if he was lifting clumps of people personally), the hills around Glasgow, 'into the countryside, in tower blocks.' When I first came to the city, I asked to be driven round the whole place by a planner to get a real idea of where I was. We drove through Easterhouse, one of the biggest of the schemes. We turned a corner and saw in a barren, open stretch of land between the tower blocks, a gang of youths idly standing around a gaping hole out of which shot a fountain of water twenty metres into the air. 'Oh God,' my companion complained, 'they've got through to the main drain again.'

I, in a small way, played my own part in this redevelopment programme. When I was in Sheffield, I'd created a local touring exhibition scheme to send small exhibitions to community centres around the city. Having been brought up in a council estate on the fringes of South London, I was well aware that there is a shadow of cultural deprivation around Britain's largest conurbations, London most of all. We had thousands of things in our museum stores—why couldn't we use them to interest people? Our Sheffield service had been a great success, but it was, essentially, a reach-me-down, spoon-feeding service. In Glasgow I wanted to do something different. I wanted to open our stores and invite people in from the community to make exhibitions for themselves.

So I founded the Open Museum. It was got off the ground, brilliantly, by Nat Edwards, who, after a cæsura in his education, had become an attendant at the British Museum, and from there developing an interest in the profession as a whole had applied for the job and come highly recommended by a curator there. One of the most memorable community shows, among many, that we put on was organised by a women's group from Easterhouse, who selected exhibits from our stores showing how men had treated women in the past—tiny Chinese shoes, Myanmar neck rings and medieval chastity belts. The group curated and designed the display and talked, enthusiastically, to everyone who came to see it—our work was being done for us, just by opening our doors. Unfortunately, it wasn't still on when President Chirac came to visit.

His wife wasn't interested in the housing schemes and wanted to see the Burrell Collection instead. She and Prince Charles, who attended in honour of the President's visit, were shown round by Stefan van Raay, the head of art. Three young Cambridge architects, Barry Gasson, Brit Andresen and John Meunier, designed the Burrell in the 1970s, to look like a streamlined greenhouse, or, perhaps more, the classiest modern yacht, in the middle of Pollok Park, with a sweeping lawn in front and trees behind. At the back it had a wall of glass. You walked among the exhibits as if you were in a forest. The royal party had reached that point, and were standing admiring the wood outside, when a lad, having run away from his gang, hid behind a tree, opened his fly and began to pee. He sensed something was wrong, and turned, still peeing, to see a rank of dignitaries gazing at him behind a wall of glass, which he'd just assumed to be a building, a few feet away. He blushed bright red and ran from their silent hilarity. The president's wife could talk of little else when she arrived at the lunch—the best exhibit of her visit.

I hadn't really wanted to attend. I told my wife we'd be at a side table in the vast banqueting hall of the City Chambers, and one can have enough of civic dinners. But to my surprise, when we arrived, we were on the top table. Pat Lally, the leader of the council, told me after that he knew Chirac was interested in art and thought we might want to talk about that. The president's wife was sitting at another table, with Prince Charles. Mine was seated next to the president himself. Gillian Tait was, by profession, a painting conservator, so the chances of a conversation about art was likely, but it took a different turn from the start.

No sooner had the president sat down, than a waiter came up to him and asked, 'Are you the vegetarian option?' His eyebrows shot up his brow even higher than their characteristic upward cock. We were in the middle of the outbreak of mad cow disease, and the beef war between Britain and Europe. 'Is this normal?' he asked, in his deep, friendly French accent. Little did he know that that was like waving a red flag to a bull. 'Normal?' my wife, Gillian Tait, replied, 'What do you mean normal? You don't think it's normal to be a vegetarian?' She was the vegetarian option. She had a bee in her bonnet about this subject and didn't miss her chance not to try to convert the president of France to her opinion. After a bit, Pat Lally diverted the conversation by saying, 'Can't we talk about something less controversial, like football?' When he rose to leave the table, the president raised Gillian's hand to his lips and said, looking into her eyes, 'For a woman as attractive as you, I'm almost persuaded to become a vegetarian, but I have to tell you,' he paused, '... I lurve junk food.' The word 'lurve' rolled off his tongue and was long.

C *is for* HUGH COLLINS

One acquisition I didn't make might have cost me my life. Ricky Demarco, a private gallery owner, was a famous ebullient figure on the Edinburgh arts scene, especially around the Festival Fringe. He was a confusingly small and simultaneously large man who seemed to bounce more than walk or run. One day he phoned me to see if I would be interested in acquiring for Glasgow Museums a life-size stone carving of Christ by an infamous local murderer, Hugh Collins. The victim they got him for, rumour had it, died of thirty-two stab wounds. Collins had carved the statue while he was in prison, as part of an arts reform programme. He'd just got out and was living at a safe distance from his home city, across the central belt, forty miles away in Edinburgh. The carving was here, Demarco said, in his gallery. Would I like to see it? I was sufficiently intrigued to say yes.

The grey lump was impressive but horrible at the same time— a remarkable feat for a man who'd never, so I was told, carved anything in his life, apart, perhaps, from human flesh. And the anatomy was, if a bit skew-whiff, passably correct. But what came over most was the fury. The chisel-marks were plain to see: every one a stab wound. But what was also evident at once was the deadness in its creator's eye—it hadn't anything in it that could be described in any way as love. The whole sculpture was frigid, cold; it could have been hatched in Nazi Germany, vicious heroics over a hollow heart. The piece reminded me a bit of Hitler's own drawings which are, for all their technical competence, exceptionally heartless, as if there was something profound missing in his make-up. It is not totally trivial to remark that Hitler, having failed to become an artist, tried to become an artist in life. You can wipe out a figure in a painting with impunity, but not real people. The reverse was supposed to be happening here, but then I suppose it was asking for a miracle for a murderer to be able to bring anything he touched to life.

Collins wanted £15,000 for it, I was told, a grand for every year he'd spent inside. I always have an immediate response to art, but then I like to think about it for a while, at least over a night, preferably over several. The brain receives visual information almost instantaneously and overall first impressions always tell. This is what art is about: stilling the moment in the heart. If a work of art doesn't go 'boom boom'—as the late, redoubtable, curator at the Tate, and ex-vet, David Brown, was fond of saying—it doesn't even begin. But first impressions can on occasion be wrong, usually by being over-enthusiastic, rarely the reverse, which was why I always liked to ponder, later.

I had never forgotten being impressed by the first exhibition I had seen of Francis Bacon's work at the Marlborough Gallery in London in the early sixties. But then I'd gone back a week later and felt nothing but emptiness. Worse, the sudden spurts of white paint looked like spunk on a blooded wound, a self-inflicted, utterly indulgent show of pain. Collins wasn't in that league of expression at all, but I came to the conclusion on the following day, that he had shown his anger, nothing else, not even, given his choice of subject, one glimmer of remorse. I said no. I didn't want to be entirely negative, because it was, in one sense, a remarkable achievement, and much better for everyone that he was hammering stone not people, so I sent him an encouraging letter giving him my reasons for this rejection. This was a mistake.

A few nights later—he'd presumably just received my epistle— I got a phone call, just after midnight, from the night watchman at Kelvingrove saying that Hugh Collins had just called to say he was going to kill 'that bastard', i.e. me. The night watchman, who knew who Collins was—everyone did in Glasgow—said I should take this threat very seriously, and asked if he should call the police. I thought about it, and the hour. Collin was almost certainly drunk, high or both, and I realised it was my mistake sending him any explanation at all, because there was no way that it couldn't look like anything but condescending crap to him. And, at least, he'd given me a warning, before he'd sent the thugs in, or done the deed himself. So, I said, no, don't ring the police.

Some months later, I was walking with my son, Daniel, down Edinburgh's Royal Mile, when I saw a man striding towards me, very determinedly, bony, lithe and very rugged. It was Hugh Collins. We hadn't met before. His fist was stretched out towards me. I thought my hour had come. But he grabbed me by the arm and shook it rigorously. 'You're a silver-back, you!' he growled. 'A silver-back. It's not the big men that rule the gaol, it's the little ones like you, with brains. I'd be inside again, for life, if you'd rung the police after I'd phoned. I know you could've done. But you didn't, did you?'

His eyes were very close, cold and fierce, but—I don't think I was imagining this—they almost cried. Then he marched on.

Dan was taken aback, especially when I explained soon after who the man was and what a silver-back was. The idea that anyone, particularly a murderer, could have likened his boring, not at all sporty dad to a gorilla was beyond his comprehension. In time Hugh became quite a good column writer for *The Scotsman*. We met several times, afterwards, in the pubs of Edinburgh. Once when I was grumbling about someone, I muttered, 'I could murder that man.' I heard a gruff whisper in my ear, 'That can be arranged.' His matter-of-fact tone chilled me to the bone and made me realise that my non-acquisition had been a dangerously close shave.

C *is for* BERYL COOK

Blackpool was the annual let-your-hair-down seaside haven for the locals in the north-west, before they all flew off to the Costa del Sol (or Costa Packet, as it came to be called), or to the Canary Islands or to Phuket—that is, of course, long before the virus struck. I did a winter exhibition in Manchester City Art Galleries called *The End of the Pier Show*, featuring the saucy seaside postcards of Donald McGill, which George Orwell had written so brilliantly about, and all the other art that celebrates the underbelly of British Life. I'd always had a fondness for genuine popular expression, though not its more recent degeneration into brand commercialism. When people, in the 1980s, began wearing maker's labels on the outside of their clothes, rather than discreetly hidden inside, as they did before, I couldn't believe that this idea would catch on. I couldn't have been more wrong—but I hadn't then understood the motivation and momentum of what David Kemp, apt as ever, dubbed New Tribalism. In the exhibition, we put a sandpit in the middle of the gallery, under bright spotlights, for children to play in while their parents walked round and laughed, and a few deckchairs for those with weary 'gallery feet'.

I'd loved a painting I'd seen by Beryl Cook, her response to a trip round the Museum of Modern Art in New York, depicting two weary middle-aged lady visitors she'd spotted in the café easing their sore ankles out of their pinching shoes, with blissful relief spreading across their faces. No troubling art to look at any more, just a cup of tea and a seat. What an earthy response to a gallery visit. Beryl, I realised, had to be in the show; she was the modern McGill, and a much keener, broader and funnier observer of contemporary life, and her cards, as his had done, sold in millions around the world. She was, I thought, a genuine artist of our time. I borrowed a few things from her dealer, the independent, lively-eyed Jess Wilder of the Portal Gallery, but promised myself I'd go and see her when I could.

I got a chance, a few years later, when I was travelling through Plymouth, where she lived in a modest terrace house on the Hoe. I was by then in Glasgow, and wanted her to paint something of the city, which I'd buy for the Gallery of Modern Art, if I liked it enough. She said, sharply, she never did commissions; she just painted what she wanted. And that was almost the end of the conversation, but tea was served, and we began to chat and the sheet of ice between us, erected by what I took to be an instinctive aggressiveness to hide a deep shyness, and a perfectly understandable suspicion of a museum director visiting her in a suit, began to melt.

She was small, petite even, with a round, bullet head and close-cropped, if a little wayward, white hair, but all her energy seemed focused in her eyes that fixed you, almost, to the floor, while her mouth moved beneath, showing two rows of sharp white teeth. Later, when I knew her better, she showed me a self-portrait she'd done, face on, with a set of dentures protruding from the canvas and a little handle at the side which, when you turned it, made the teeth open and shut, faster and faster, until they chattered, while her painted eyes above remained absolutely still. 'I call it *Giving an Interview*,' she said. I understood then why she had been so nervous about seeing me at first. Your coming, she told me, ruined my day, and the night before. She hated, one: being disturbed and, two: talking about her work, especially, I think, with someone who knew a lot about art.

I had noticed, on that first visit, a small dark painting on the wall, very different from the others. I said I liked it. 'Oh, that's the first painting I ever did.' She then told me the story of how she'd begun to paint. She was in Southern Rhodesia (now Zimbabwe) where her husband was working in a garage as they had wanted to go somewhere different, and thought they'd try Africa. She'd given her son, John, some paints for his twelfth birthday, and he painted a picture of grass at the bottom, with a little house standing on it, and, far to the top, a band of blue for the sky. 'But there's nothing in middle,' Beryl complained. John replied, 'But there isn't anything in the middle, mum.'

'I'll show you what's in the middle,' said Beryl, grabbing hold of his brushes. She painted two big round bare breasts in the centre of a fresh piece of paper, and then added a head on top, with eyes looking sharply to the side, as if to say, 'What do you think you are you looking at?' She had no idea how to paint a waist, so added a fence along the bottom to suggest the woman was standing behind it with her breasts lolling over. Her husband, John, always called the picture 'the Hangover'. She told me that she was so surprised by what she'd done that she felt as if she'd been kicked in the stomach. She had no idea she could paint anything at all. She knew absolutely nothing about and had, then, zilch interest in art. This painting had suddenly popped out of nowhere.

It was only two years later, when the family were back in the United Kingdom and she was running a guest house, that she thought about painting again. She was sitting in her local pub, where they went every Friday, watching people, when she realised that she could paint them larking about. She tried it, taught herself how to paint, began to look at art books, discovered painters like Stanley Spencer, who made a huge impression on her, and began to produce a lot of work, which she hung around the guest house. If anyone showed interest in them, she'd always say, yes, I'm so sorry, aren't they awful, but a friend of mine does them, and I let her show them here out of the kindness of my heart.

The local publican heard about her paintings, which were mostly of his customers, and suggested she hung them in the pub. Reluctantly she agreed. He then said she'd have to put prices on them. She thought this was a joke—no one would buy them—but she put £25 on each, and they all sold. One thing led to another, a show at the local, very enterprising Plymouth Art Centre, national coverage in *The Sunday Times* and the South Bank TV Show, hosted by Melvyn Bragg, and an offer to join the enterprising London dealer, the Portal Gallery. And, as they say, the rest is history, but not as far as modern art museums are concerned, who wouldn't go near Beryl with a barge pole, even though part of their job is preserving art history. They were too busy making up an art history of their own—but that's another story, told elsewhere in these pages.

Beryl soon developed her own instantly distinct style: bright colours, clear compositions, designs focused on expressions, pointing fingers, fat without the fuss of fingernails (Fernand Léger employed the same simplification)—nothing must distract from the direction of glances. Every image was based on something she'd seen. She told me she'd wondered one summer where all her subjects had gone. They took a holiday to Lanzarote, and there they all were! She painted every morning in the front room upstairs. I once saw her at work. She was just scrubbing out a face. 'If you don't get the eyes right,' she said, 'nothing works.' I asked what drove her on. Her own eyes twinkled. 'I always think the next one is going to be really good...' Her eyes added the rest—'but, of course, I'm always wrong...'

I asked her, too, if she ever painted anything 'serious' (I said it with the inverted commas), something she didn't like. Her eyes, once again, dug into mine with that forensic twist of hers, like a surgeon searching for a foreign body. I often felt I was on an operating table when I was with Beryl. 'I did once,' she said, 'or tried to. These two Jehovah's Witnesses came to the door, and I hated them so much I decided to paint them. But they turned out funny in the end. I can't stop it. If I thought it would change anything if I painted things I don't like, all that's wrong with the world, I might do it, I suppose. But I don't, so I don't.'

She did come to Glasgow, to look around, just in case. She and John stayed in the Midland Hotel at the station. We went to a karaoke bar. I watched her watching. She occasionally and very discreetly took quick snaps with a tiny camera, and also made little notes and tiny sketches on scraps of paper she tucked into her handbag. She rang me later and told me she'd done three paintings. I went to see them. The karaoke bar sang in my memory, and there was a busker on Buchanan Street, and ... 'Beryl you can't,' I said ... there was a striking girl in a leopard skin coat taking her dog for a walk along the Clyde, under the arch of a bridge on which an orange double decker bus was passing—everything was OK so far but behind the little dog sniffing at a bollard was a boulder that had 'WOGS OUT' graffiti scrawled across it. 'I can't buy that,' I said.

'But I saw it,' she said.

'Yes ... but.' Her eyes lit up: 'I know what to do ... I'll scrub it out, but leave a trace, as if the Council had done their best to clean it, but not quite succeeded.' The result was perfect. I bought all three to hang in Glasgow's new Gallery of Modern Art.

'The Queen is going to come and open it,' I said, 'you must come along.' But she shook her head. She told me she'd never been to an opening in her life, and never one of her own. It was true; she was chronically shy. 'But you've just got an OBE,' I said. You should be there. She was adamant, but then asked. 'Are you really going to meet the Queen?' I nodded. 'And will you speak to her?'

'Of course.'

'Will you ask her something from me? Will you ask her to stop pestering me with medals?' I did (see Q for the Queen).

There is a coda to this story. Before the opening of the Gallery of Modern Art I was invited to give a presentation at a big international art curator's conference about modern art museums in the Louvre. Nick Serota spoke before me; he'd just had the go-ahead to build Tate Modern, after National Lottery money became available, with a budget of £135 million, as against my modest £6 million, a sum typical of pre-Lottery funding for the arts. I spoke in the conference about the role a gallery of modern art has to play in contemporary society, providing opportunities to see living art that has the qualities to last. I showed what sort of works were going in it, from Scotland and around the world, including the art of Beryl Cook. Her pictures, like much of my talk, were greeted with laughter, which I felt to be warm and genuine, if surprised, but not at all derisory. This could, of course, have been wishful thinking on my part. But when I had sat down, after gratifyingly sustained applause, Nick rose from his seat in the front row, uninvited by the chairman high on the platform, having spoken earlier about his own project, and turned, ramrod-backed, to face the several hundred of our colleagues seated in the raked hall behind him, and solemnly announced, 'There will be no Beryl Cooks in Tate Modern.' He sat down to a silence that was more like a shocked intake of breath. I was cheered over a year after my new gallery had opened, with packed attendances, to overhear a taxi driver say to someone he'd just dropped off near the entrance, 'You should go in there. There're Beryl Cook's paintings in there.' That meant more to me than anything Nick could say.

I was understandably rather taken aback at the time and, though I hate to admit it, a bit upset by this directly personal, public snub, but I was also quite honestly appalled by his professional arrogance. Beryl was still very much alive and firing on all cylinders, so how could he, as the director of a publicly funded gallery, however low he rated her art at present, presume to know that she would never, ever paint a picture of brilliance? I have never argued and would still not argue that Beryl Cook's art is profound, but it is genuine, springing from creative inspiration and very brilliantly seen. It's a fresh response to and therefore a real record of our times, and I think it will last and continue to bring joy, much more than many pieces the Tate has bought. Beryl's work merits a place in any public collection, even the Tate's, when they eventually get round to appreciating what she's done.

I invited Beryl to my sixtieth birthday ceilidh in 2007. She couldn't come, as I knew she wouldn't—she's chronically shy—but she painted a card for me instead. By some fluke, or because she'd looked it up, or perhaps because I'd mentioned the fact in some unguarded moment, she dressed her dancer in a Murray kilt—

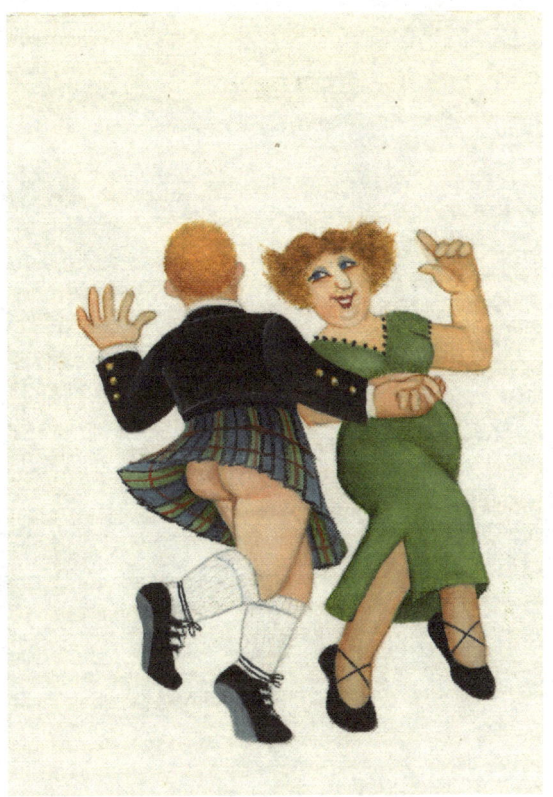

Beryl Cook's birthday card for the author, 2007

which is the Spalding tartan, for people with this name are a sept of the Murray clan, though the fellow can't be me because I never, ever, had red hair. This book was going to be called *Van Gogh's Best Chrysanthemums* (see T for Mrs Thatcher), Nickie Fletcher's suggestion, but Alexander Fyjis-Walker of Pallas Athene, seeing the Cook card, thought it would make a brilliant cover and suggested calling it *Art Uncovered*. My old friend Henry Noltie, a world expert on botanical illustration, polymath and harpsichord player, suggested in his droll tone, the final tweak.

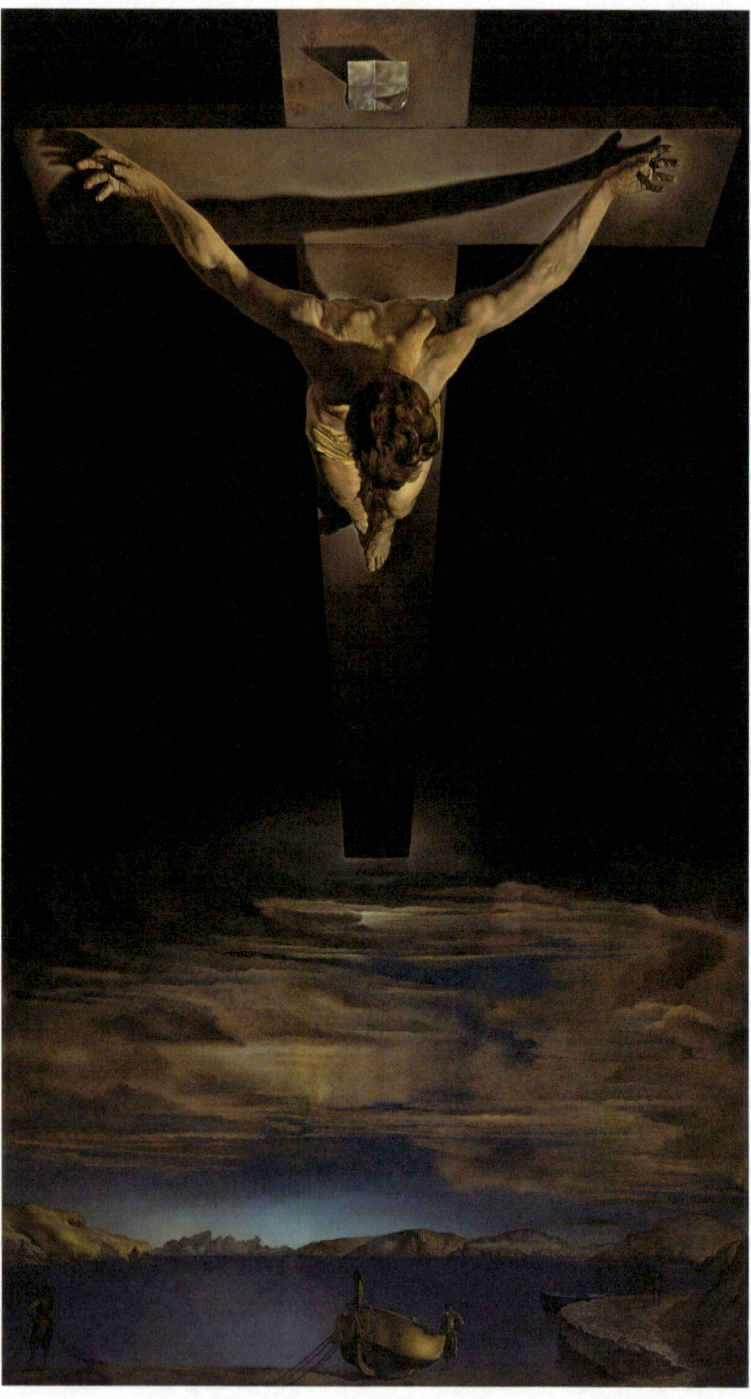

D is for SALVADOR DALÍ

Glasgow has a wonderful battery of paintings on its walls, Rembrandts, Van Goghs, a Titian and a Botticelli, but its most famous painting, by far, is Salvador Dalí's *Christ of St John of the Cross*. The odd title is explained by the fact that it was inspired by a vision of Juan de Yepes y Álvarez, a sixteenth-century Spanish Catholic priest, a key figure in the Counter Reformation who was tortured and imprisoned for his passionate mysticism. He was later canonised as St John of the Cross, because of a vision in which he saw the crucified Christ from above, as if God was looking down on His Son from heaven. The saint made a fairly clumsy little sketch of his vision, but it was enough to inspire Dalí. In his youth, when he was a surrealist, Dalí was a committed communist and anti-cleric, but, as he aged, he turned his coat and became a devout Catholic and fascist. He actively supported Franco's dictatorship in Spain and was granted an audience with the Pope in 1949. Inspired by his new faith, he painted, in 1951, what became perhaps his most famous work, a massive version of St John's vision, executed in his famous photorealist style, showing Christ seen from above, in full Technicolor, hanging on the cross, suspended over what could be the Sea of Galilee, but is, in fact the inlet of Port Lligat, near Dalí's home in Spain.

We held many receptions and banquets in the great hall of Kelvingrove, especially during the year when Glasgow was European Capital of Culture. On one occasion I had never seen so many sleek black limousines slide up to Kelvingrove's main front door. It was as if every mafioso of Glasgow, Rome and Chicago had got together to celebrate the event. The women were given orchids as

Opposite: Salvador Dalí, Christ of St John of the Cross, 1951

parting gifts, the men bottles of grappa. Never had I tasted one as silky smooth. I steamed the label off to get another at Sarti's, Glasgow's famous Italian delicatessen. The staff huddled round. Where had I got it? No one can buy such a rare grappa. Before we got to the gifts, a guest at the feast had seen a poster in the gallery shop. A buzz went round the hall. Was that painting here? I got a request. The visitors rose *en masse*—all three hundred from their tables. I had to open the galleries upstairs. They streamed up to see the Dalí, some bursting into tears at the sight. I'd never seen the like. This was religious art, in action.

Tom Honeyman, the inspired and inspiring director of Glasgow Art Galleries and Museums long before me, who crucially ne- gotiated the gift of the Burrell Collection to the city, had seen the painting in a gallery shop in London and, noting how it was attracting a crowd, suggested to his committee that they bought one of Dalí's drawings for the painting. His chairman asked, 'If everyone's looking at the painting, why are we buying a drawing and not the painting itself?'

'Oh, we couldn't possibly do that,' Tom replied, 'it was much too expensive.' The asking price was £12,000, but the city bought it for £8,200, with the copyright, the income from which has over the years reimbursed the original expenditure many times over. There were objections to this purchase at the time, since that sum could have paid for several houses, and a decade later someone tore at the canvas with a stone, for reasons that remain unclear. He might have been a Protestant. But the picture soon became Glasgow's pride and, to its Catholic residents, its joy.

Personally, I remained ambivalent towards the work. In sev- eral ways, you can't help but be impressed: the drama of the per- spective; the looming, foreboding darkness; the eerie, stormy atmosphere; the flickering halo of light along the edges of the flesh, of the shadows and around the foot of the Cross, and along the ridges of the lifting clouds, as if light, or lightning, was about to stream down from above and illuminate the world. Then there is the empty, expectant tenseness of the scene below, the waiting figures, the beached boat and the unbroken stillness of the water. This, surely, is enough, and it is, in a way. But not being a Christian, not believing in Christ, made me suspicious of the hanging head of hair hiding his face, his expression and his thoughts, and, not perhaps incidentally, his crotch. The painting, for all its impressiveness, had for me a hollow ring. Converts, as Dalí was, are famed for being more faithful than anyone. The painting could only really work fully, I thought, for Christians, and Catholics at that. But for them, it most certainly did.

This set me thinking. Our collections were full of religious art from around the world, from Europe, obviously, but also from Asia, the Americas and Africa. This was hardly surprising because religions have, throughout the history of mankind, been the main commissioner and, it's true, constrainer of art. Hardly any of this art was contemporary, except the Dalí. But then this was also understandable. Many of the major faiths around the world, including Buddhism, Judaism and Islam, had maintained from the beginning that divinity was invisible, a view that had become strengthened after the microscopic and telescopic discoveries of modern science.

I wrote a lot about this later—how the way we see has changed through history—in my books *The Art of Wonder* and *Realisation*, but at this time I was mainly concerned about the role of religious art in museums. Were we right to present these as *objets d'art* arranged in rows, as part of the Western Enlightenment's historicising, scientific, identification project? I'd recently been visiting Russia (see B for Eduard Bersudsky) and seen worshippers flooding back into the churches that had been turned, during the Communist era, into museums, kissing the icons—their previous curators would have been horrified! Was there a way of presenting religious art in a gallery that didn't strip it of its religious meaning?

While I was thinking about all this, a message came round to all departments, asking if anyone was interested in using a building that had been erected by the Friends of Glasgow Cathedral, a unique Gothic survival on mainland Scotland, at first Catholic, but since the Reformation, Protestant. The Friends had begun, as a 1990 project, to build a visitor centre in one corner of the cathedral grounds, to use for receptions and displays, but they'd run out of funds. The building, designed by Ian Begg, in the Scottish Baronial style, was only a shell. Pat Lally didn't want to pull it down but a use for it had to be found. I seized my chance. When you have so many wonderful things in store as we had, as so many museums have, an empty building is a godsend—well, in my case, not literally a godsend, but at least, I thought, an opportunity to find a new way to present religious art. But how?

I held a brainstorming session with senior staff. I argued that we couldn't just present the history of Protestantism in Scotland, but just adding the story of Catholicism was asking for trouble. When I'd arrived as director, I'd discovered whole teams of staff were either Catholic or Protestant. How did they choose their teams, I asked? My colleagues looked at me as if I was naïve, which I admit I was, but then I hadn't thought, when I went to Glasgow, that I was, in some senses, stepping back into the seventeenth century. They told me they find out which school you went to—if it was named after a saint, you didn't have a chance of getting into a Protestant team; if it was, you joined the Catholics. I soon found ways of combining these teams and was delighted how well they all got on. But I couldn't mix the population as a whole. Glasgow was divided into which football team you supported—Rangers for Protestants and Celtic for Catholics. A museum celebrating both, and on Protestant ground, was a bomb waiting to explode.

D *is for* SALVADOR DALÍ

Mark O'Neill, our head of history, a quiet-spoken, thoughtful man, whose high-domed forehead, short stature and unassuming manner kept reminding me of William Shakespeare, asked why didn't we do a museum of all religions? He looked, however, un-usually alarmed when I clapped my hands together and said, 'Yes, of course. That's it! A museum of religious art'—especially as it dawned on him, too late, that he'd have to mastermind such an ambitious project. There was a call from colleagues that we needed to appoint a curator of religion, but I resisted that, arguing that we had collections of and curators for most religious objects in the world, and this new museum could be created by teams work-ing together to bring their collections out and show them in new, inspiring, meaningful ways.

This project would not have been possible at all had I not re-organised the collections as a whole. Soon after I arrived, I had become deeply frustrated by the divisions of collections in Glasgow. Most museums are riven with territorial disputes between cura-tors who think they 'own' their subjects, and therefore the objects that relate to these subjects, even if all objects, of course, can have very different meanings in different contexts. But I wasn't just dealing with sectional divisions in one museum, but with divi-sions in separate buildings. The art curators in Kelvingrove and the Burrell wanted nothing to do with each other, though their collections complemented each other in many crucial ways. The curator of social history at the People's Palace refused to collect the social history of shipbuilding arguing that that was the job of our Transport Museum. They replied that they were a technology museum, and social history was the People's Palace's responsibility. The tragic result of this blinkered approach was that much of the living history of Glasgow's most famous industry from which its wealth and most of its art collections had sprung, not to mention much of its humour and culture (the great Glasgow comedian

Billy Connolly was essentially a product of the yards), had slipped through our preserving net.

I dispensed with these divisions by making the whole of Glasgow's collections one entity, one resource, which all curators could draw on—as well as people outside—hence the Open Museum and shows in all the peripheral estates (see C for President Chirac). I argued that all objects—a painting, a car or a stuffed giraffe—can be looked at from a scientific, historical and, even at a push, an æsthetic perspective. Making these objects safely accessible was the responsibility of the conservation department (and I set them targets to increase safe access—for there's no point in a museum having something if it can't show it). The curators' job was to collect, communicate and research, and they could use any objects they liked from any part of the collection to get their message across. So, we created three large teams of free-roving curators, focusing on art, history and science. And I argued that religion has a relevance to all three—and encouraged them all to get on with it.

We did, however, appoint an external specialist adviser, one of the greatest authorities of comparative religion, Professor Ninian Smart of the University of California, Santa Barbara. He was irrepressible with a roving brain; a Scot who had first studied in Glasgow and was happy to drop in and see us whenever he was passing.

He did make one slip, however, in his own backyard, and in our top floor gallery, which showed collections about the history of religion in Scotland. We'd indicated, somehow, that the Queen was the head of the Church of Scotland, and Ninian hadn't picked this up in his reading of our texts. The Moderator of the General Assembly attacked us in the press. The Queen might be head of the Church of England but Jesus was the head of the Church of Scotland was splashed across the front page of *The Scotsman*. When we told Ninian, he roared with laughter and said what excellent publicity! There would be no *mea culpa* in the media. Mark wasn't happy, but I said we just had to change the label and get on with it. Jesus wasn't going to make a fuss. Nor, I thought, was the Queen.

We would need, I knew, more than flashes of publicity to make the museum work. It had to have a few lasting attractions to keep people wanting to visit, and revisit. I was, from the start, determined to put the Dalí painting there. It looked great from a distance, as a *coup de théâtre*, under an arch at the end of an upper corridor in Kelvingrove. It never looked good hanging in any picture gallery as it was so dramatic; it wiped the floor with everything else and, somehow, because of its meaning, it seemed to be out of place. I felt it needed, even more than many old masters, to be suspended in a church. It simply wasn't doing its full religious work. It could, I thought, in the cathedral context of the new museum, so we moved it there. The chair of our committee was delighted. The painting was going east. Protestants tended to live in the west of Glasgow, Catholics in the east. 'They've had that painting long enough,' the chair commented, coming, as he did, from that part. We had our star attraction that would draw the crowds.

We had beautiful examples of Christian, Buddhist and Islamic art, in particular from the Burrell Collection, but we needed, I knew, a major representation of Hinduism. We had a sporadic collection of this faith, but nothing to match the Dalí in power and presentation. I searched through contacts and was eventually lucky enough to find a superb 183-cm-high bronze statue of Shiva Nataraja, the Lord of the Dance, slowly beginning to move his limbs in a circle of flames, to initiate the whole process of creation. The statue had been long enough in a private collection in Belgium for us to acquire it—it is impossible now to get export licences to bring such sculptures out of India. With hindsight it would probably have been better to commission a new one, from the brilliant Hindu sculptors the botanist and curator Henry Noltie told me about, still working in Swamimalai, near Kumbakonam, Tamil Nadu, if I'd known about them then. Nevertheless, the Shiva became a major religious attraction for Hindus in Glasgow, and the ground at its feet was regularly and spontaneously decorated with flowers, as it would have been if it were in a temple. A god is a god anywhere.

One thing was clear from the start—we had to work with the religious communities themselves. What we couldn't do was to write down on labels what we thought different people of different faiths believed in. This museum needed to be about inspiring and communicating belief, not pigeonholing it or boxing it in. It needed to be about people, not dogmas. I decided to call it the St Mungo Museum of Religious Art and Life, which is what I'd always been interested in—the relationship of art to life. St Mungo was the patron saint of the cathedral, and I'd long had a soft spot for him, being, as he was, the patron saint of adultery (see L for Pat Lally and S for Niki de Saint Phalle).

So, I decided that the key, ground floor display in the museum, flanking the Dalí facing you on the wall you as you came in, would simply take the visitor through the most familiar story of all, the story of life, from birth, puberty, love and work, to marriage, parenthood, old age and death, letting people of different beliefs say how their faiths helped them to understand each stage of life, accompanied by objects and images that made these beliefs clear. Lives simultaneously lived in different religions. Believers, ordinary worshippers, not priests and certainly not curators, wrote the labels in this part of the museum. And we added the touch of putting photographs of the writers next to each short text, to make the whole display as personal, immediate and intimate as possible. This accumulated display, in the end, I found very moving.

The idea was there, but we still had to get the project off the ground and funded. I went to see key figures in all the leading religions in Glasgow for I knew that without their support we would never get members of their communities to give us the essential, personal help we needed. This was especially important because I wanted these outsiders to help choose the exhibits from all the wonderful things sitting along the shelves in our stores. The whole museum could only work if it was a genuine community project. If one leading religious community was against it, I knew the idea was as good as dead.

My most nervous moment was when I went to see Cardinal Winning, a born and bred Glaswegian. He was only the second cardinal in Scotland since the Reformation, and the museum I wanted to create was in the grounds of a cathedral that had originally been Catholic but was now Protestant. He was a big man, and alarmingly intelligent. He'd played a key role behind the scenes in arranging the visit of Pope Paul II (the first ever official visit to the United Kingdom by a pontiff) to Scotland (for which Tim Stead made the papal throne). He listened to my brief summary, adding, unwarily, that it would be the first public museum of religion in the world. He half-laughed, 'Huh, another first for Glasgow. The first to put religion into a museum!' Things weren't going well. I realised then I should have called it a gallery; the alliteration would have been just as good, without the implication that religion was a thing of the past. But when I added that I was going to put the Dalí there, suddenly his mood changed. His eyes expanded with delight. This picture really was magical, and for Catholics most of all. He gave me his full support and from then on everything rolled.

David Page, a local architect—a tall, thin, slightly leaning, deceptively dreamy-looking individual—did a typically beautifully sensitive, self-effacing interior display inside Ian Begg's grandiose, rusticated folly. However, there was a walled courtyard at the back, intended originally for wedding marquees, that looked ugly and needed filling. I suddenly had the idea to put a Japanese dry-stone Zen garden there—Zen Buddhism was barely represented in the museum, hardly surprisingly, because its vision of divinity is almost as invisible as that of Judaism. The garden had to be a genuine religious expression, not, as was so often in the West, a fake approximation. But how could I commission such a thing, even if anyone could make one nowadays? The great days of these gardens were five hundred years ago.

As luck would have it, a major Japanese newspaper wanted to fund a touring exhibition of Impressionist paintings from Glasgow Museum, and they invited me over to approve venues and arrangements. Some of the galleries were on the top floor of department stores—brilliant for accessibility, and made possible by their excellent security. I was impressed by Japanese professionalism everywhere. To my surprise the head of exhibition organisation was a woman. I could judge the importance of the people (all men) she introduced me to by how deeply she bowed —the merest nod on many occasions, but once, suddenly her forehead was touching her knees. She was literally bent double. The owner of a huge newspaper chain was before me. I asked her after how she had managed to rise so high in a man's world. She looked at me wryly and then said, 'by deciding never to marry and learning to swim [her delicate small hand, with the fingers held together performed the waving motion] like a fish'.

I took the opportunity to visit Kyoto and see if I could commission a genuine Zen garden. The British Council arranged a meeting with the current head of the Kyoto Gardener's Association, Mr Tanaka. He sat, with his team, cross legged on the floor on one side of a very low table. I on the other, with the Scottish and Japanese flags crossed on a little stand in the middle, with an interpreter at the side. I spread out the plan of the space and showed some photographs. I explained the project, the budget and the timescale, mentioning that the garden had to be in place for the opening ceremony, which would be performed by Princess Anne (Pat Lally had, as ever, quickly got this event into the Palace diary). There was a long silence while the plans and photos were minutely examined, then some incomprehensible (to me) whispering.

Mr Tanaka looked up, and said, through the interpreter:

Your garden meets all the strict requirements of a Zen garden [to my surprise because I knew of none such]: it is orientated precisely north, south, east and west; it is a regular geometric shape—a triangle is an excellent shape for a Zen garden; it is viewable on the same level from within the building as without; it is bounded by a wall between 6 and 8 feet high, over which can be seen cherry trees [there were indeed, as it happened] and religious buildings [the cathedral].

'And,' he laughed,

Scotland is littered with wonderful rocks—you leave them lying about in fields, whereas in Japan, they have been all owned for centuries and are hard to come by.

Then he asked, 'Did you say Princess Anne was coming to open it?' I nodded. 'Then,' he announced, 'I will do this garden myself.'

He took me to a *geisha* house to celebrate. The *mamasan* (mother of the house), dressed in a discreet grey kimono, met us at the door. He seemed to be a regular from the way they glanced at each other. She led us through, past an exquisite little garden, to a large room surrounded by screens where we sat down on the *tatami* mats. A few other guests I didn't know appeared. There was the sound of giggling. Wall panels slid apart, and the geishas tiptoed in. A *maiko* sat, no, nestled down beside me—a particular honour

I was told later (whether this was true or not, I still don't know), for a maiko is a young, trainee geisha, with a white painted upper lip and red only on her lower (a sign, I was also assured, of her virginity). She had an especially low neckline at the back which revealed a band of yellowish naked flesh on her nape just below her hairline, which, in contrast to the white mask make-up every-where else on her exposed skin, I found, for some reason, absorb-ing. She was a crinkling silk presence beside me, who occasionally sipped but never ate, as the banquet was laid in little bowls before us all. She sat slightly back, just behind my precise peripheral vi-sion, and keeping her eyes on mine all the time, watched where my attention wandered, then reached out to bring me any bowl of food my eyes had lingered on for a moment. It was an eerie feeling, as if I had an additional silk-sleeved arm to serve me what I wanted.

There was dancing and music, and we drank—sake—beer—sake—beer—until we all got quite merry, me not understanding a word, and not wanting to bother the interpreter. My maiko became more familiar, and, laughing, started joking about my eyebrows, which stuck out further and were bushier than most Japanese. She had the idea, whether it was part of her training or not, to start a game to see how many matchsticks (people were smoking) she could balance on my eyebrows, which she pulled out as far as she could—a peculiar sensation in itself. I assumed others were counting too, and possibly betting, but whatever, everyone was enjoying themselves by the exercise. I was forced to stay ex-tremely still ... until, at last, one match from the pile fell down, to everyone's amused delight, and the count was done.

The whole experience was a neatly wrapped parcel (for which the Japanese are famous) of eroticism folded in decorum—rather disquieting for someone like myself reared in puritanical com-munism, but for the others around, it was clearly the name of the game. Sex was central to and celebrated in many religions of the past. Images of aroused phalluses and flowering vaginas abound in what was then ignorantly called 'primitive' socio-religious imagery, as they still do in Hinduism in India—its masterpiece at Khajuraho, Madhya Pradesh—and, now to a lesser extent in Shinto in Japan, where they exploded in the wonderful art of *shunga,* above all those of Utamaro and Hokusai. The subsequent suppression of sex in the major world religions—Judaism, Christianity, Islam and Buddhism—was and still is a mystery to me. It was a theme I certainly wanted to explore in this new museum but wasn't sure how to begin. I came back from Japan, however, determined to start by including displays about circumcision, both male and female.

I also came back with a Zen garden, or at least the promise of one. Mr Tanaka arrived, with a couple of assistants and ancient wooden levers and rakes—everything had to be correctly done, he assured me, with the right tools. I accompanied him, out of interest, to look for boulders, not in fields, I admit, but at suppliers. I was amazed to see him leaping on his toes with excited delight from boulder to boulder as if he'd been reborn in heaven. One has to be like a ship at sea, he told me, another a high mountain. He searched for moss by himself. 'You weed the moss out of the grass in the West. In the East, we weed the grass out of the moss,' he told me. The garden was made; it looked very austere. 'I don't need any trees,' he told me. 'There are trees outside. And one stone has always to be invisible from whatever angle you are looking. That is essential.' He clapped his hands together when it was finished, and said, with some pride, 'You can say all the prayers to the Buddha here.'

The museum was getting ready, and we started staff training. When I'd arrived in Glasgow, I'd abolished the role of attendants—security guards sitting on chairs or standing around, bored out of their minds—and introduced museum assistants, whose main job was to know about the exhibits and help the public, while security remained in the background, which it is also more effective. It was vital that the assistants at St Mungo's should be very well informed about the displays and trained in dealing with the public, for we anticipated trouble in a museum that wasn't about facts but emotional beliefs. In fact, we found our visitors to be exceptionally interested and open minded. The museum was, surprisingly, left in peace.

The only incident that occurred, at least during my time as director, was a man who suddenly, in a fit of passion, seized the wonderful statue of Shiva dancing, rocked it in his arms until it crashed over. The museum assistants were so well trained that they kept the man talking, asking why he'd done it, and he was still talking when then police arrived. The fallen sculpture revealed cracks in it that showed that it had been repaired before and it wasn't as old—or bits of it weren't—as we had thought, which made me regret, once again, that I hadn't had a new one made. The antiques trade is riddled with deceptions, increasingly so as genuinely old things become that rarer.

My new museum assistants were essential to the success of St Mungo's. Years later, long after I'd left Glasgow, one of these staff came up to me in the station at Edinburgh. 'You won't remember my name,' he said. I didn't, but he went on:

> I want to thank you. I was an attendant, and then became a museum assistant at St Mungo's. And because of that scheme you introduced where assistants could learn museum skills and climb up the ladder, I'm now a curator. I'd have been an attendant all my life, but for you. You changed my life.

This was gratifying, to say the least.

I'd had the idea to change the way a museum ran staff development in my second job in Sheffield. The secretary to the keeper of education was Sue Graves. She was so dedicated that she knew more than almost anyone about the collection. She took an Open University degree in art history in her own time, but I knew, such was the system, youngsters with degrees, like me, would swan in and take the plum jobs and she'd remain a secretary all her life. There had to a way, I thought, where a museum could become a career in itself, which you could master from within, by entering at the lowest rung and learning the whole business from there, for, after all, attendants—museum assistants as we now called them— got to know more about the public than anyone else in the museum, and it was the public the whole museum existed to serve.

So as soon as I had enough power, and was running an organisation big enough, in Glasgow, I initiated a museum revolution. My ambition was to turn museums inside out—to put the public's interest first and use the collections as a resource to generate myriad areas of interest, however large or small, across the community as a whole. This could trigger funding from multiple sources, which would augment the allocation from the governing (whether local or national) purse, without resorting to the introduction of entrance charges, which leads to the debilitating downward spiral of falling attendances and falling public interest—the very opposite of a museum's role in society. This revolution depended on making security discreet (and therefore both better and more economic) while putting the museum attendants, now museum assistants, in the front line. As the ever-ebullient Councillor James Mutter commented, when the Museum Assistant scheme was finally approved by the Glasgow Personnel Committee, 'You're creating the best jobs in Glasgow.'

I couldn't have managed this revolution without the brilliant assistance of my deputy director, Stewart Coulter, and my head of corporate service, Seonaid Cowie. I owe almost everything to their unfailing commitment and, most important, to their grasp of realism. They saved me from many pitfalls, I'm sure, of which I am still unaware. Stewart is tall, square shouldered and stylish, who looked as though he could have just stepped out of a Hollywood musical. Seonaid is small, neat and sharp, with a clipped hairstyle and clipped heels to match. Both were quick-witted and very fast thinking. The three of us were called, after the C. S. Lewis fantasy children's story, the Lion, the Witch and the Wardrobe. There was no dispute among us who was the witch, but to both Stewart's and my surprise, we each thought the other was the wardrobe. The creation of St Mungo's wouldn't have been possible without this revolution.

The opening day for the new museum arrived. The staff were all prepared. Mr Tanaka had flown over, not with his wife, whom I'd briefly met, but with the elegant mamasan, dressed, or rather draped, in another exquisite grey silk kimono. A limousine purred to the front door. Princess Anne got out. There was a small group of women protesting. She glanced at them, clearly used to such things, and came in. I liked her immediately. There was only one word to describe her long-faced, attractive, lithe strength—horsey—and I immediately felt she wouldn't at all mind the appellation. The straightness of her body and directness of her mind gave you the impression that you could actually see her thought following her glance, with the precision and speed of a shot.

The garden delighted her. Mr Tanaka bowed. The mamasan bent double. We went inside. 'What were those women outside protesting about?' she asked me. 'Female circumcision. We have a display about it.'

'Show me it.' I did. She was immediately interested.

'They're protesting about that?' I nodded.

'But you're just telling people what's happening, not arguing for it.' I nodded again. The arrow of her look shot out again. 'I'm going to speak to them about it. This is one of the worst things that's happening. Don't they realise?' She marched at once out into the street. I followed at a distance, but unfortunately not quite close enough to hear the exchange (stupidly, I didn't think it would be polite). The protesting women soon looked sheepish. I wish there were more royals like her. Had she been born first (now they've, at last, changed the rules about regal male dominion), she'd have made a brilliant queen.

The museum won several awards, including one given by Loyd Grossman and Lord Lichfield for *Courvoisier's Book of the Best*, presented at a dinner in the Strand where I sat next to the wiry-headed, irrepressible Anita Roddick, another winner, for her Body Shops. A priest from Kansas came to see me, excitedly proposing to make a virtual version of the museum. I suggested he make a real one—exhibits like the ones we used (apart from the Dalí) are not hard to find in museum stores. He said I was living in the past; everyone would soon be looking at computer screens. But they don't go to your church to do that, I said. He looked at me and sat nonplussed. That was the end of that.

The most important and interesting thing that happened was that the museum attracted a new audience. I realised that it served a new community of interest that hadn't existed before—not just multifaith groups, but people who wanted a religious dimension to their lives. People started wanting to be married in it, and we had several requests to have ashes scattered on the white raked gravel sea in the Zen garden. I saw no reason why not. And the small exhibitions we put on were fascinating. We were, for example, the first museum anywhere in the world to do an exhibition about the history and significance of the veil.

And we discovered and showed new artists who were working in traditions outside the usual reach of modernism, such as the devout Ahmed Moustafa, whose *The Attributes of Divine Perfection* is an extraordinarily compelling, contemplative image based on an Islamic hadith that states, 'God has ninety-nine names, one hundred minus one. Whoever enumerates them all enters paradise.' And the multi-generation Linares family, makers of painted papier-mâché sculptors for the Mexican Day of the Dead. Two of the stars of the exhibition programme (planned before I left) were the Singh Twins (Amrit Singh and Rabindra Kaur Singh) who, working together, have revived the traditional art of Indian miniature painting in twenty-first-century terms. They talk of past-modernism, not post-modernism. Their tiny painting *Nineteen Eighty-Four*, showing terrified worshippers fleeing as Indian troops stormed the Golden Temple in 1984, its sacred waters stained red, is one of the little masterpieces of our age (see the frontispiece of this book). We had created an art museum that was living in a new way. Museums, which are a Western, post-Enlightenment, phenomenon, have taken almost all art out of religion. There is a good reason, now, to put some of it back.

For some reason, long after I had gone, Mark O'Neill decided to move the Dalí back to Kelvingrove. This was an odd, retrogressive decision because this outstanding painting has its fullest place in the history of faith, not of art. It's an oddity of a creation, not really featuring in the history of art, and certainly not in that of modernism nor even of the Surrealism for which its creator was famous, on account of the seriousness of its religious subject matter, on oddity itself in the twentieth century. However, as its popularity proved, it was certainly a painting that continued to have a vital place in modern life. I had the feeling, all along, that Mark didn't actually like the brilliant idea he'd had. And as I write I hear grim news that Glasgow City Council are thinking of closing this delightful small museum to make a measly, unimaginative paring in their budget. The staff should put the Dalí back in this museum at once. They wouldn't close the doors on that.

D is for FRANCIS DAVISON

I first saw a collage by Francis Davison when I went to see the painter Mary Potter in Aldeburgh. The composer Benjamin Britten had lived next door in the Red House, which she'd swapped with him after her divorce in 1955. Kenneth Clark, the director of the National Gallery, was an admirer of Mary and her work, and a frequent visitor. The house was full of her glowing, gritty, almost abstract evocations of East Anglican light. Nowhere, I felt, could be closer to the core spirit of English creativity.

I'd recently been given £15,000 by the Arts Council to add to its collection. The condition was that everything I selected was to be shown first in an exhibition that was to travel around Britain. This affected my selection. I wanted a show of a decent size that celebrated contemporary visual creativity. I couldn't blow it all on a handful of works by big names in London, with their dealers taking half the cash. So, I set myself the task of extending the collection's scope by finding works of art of real quality by artists who didn't have a London dealer and who were too absorbed in what they were doing (conversationally, I summed it up as being too mad) to be able to do anything else with their lives. London dealers can't be the only ones to decide what we see. I wasn't looking for geniuses—just artists who had something genuine to say and couldn't stop doing it. Colleagues were disparaging. Alan Bowness, then director of the Tate, told me that the notion that there were unknown geniuses working away in attics was a myth. We know everyone worth knowing, he said.

Undeterred, I started looking. But how was I going to find them? One of the best ways was to ask around, among artists themselves whose work I respected and who understood what I might be searching for. So, I asked Mary if she knew of any. She immediately showed me a small, almost monochrome, rectangular collage hanging in her hall, by someone I'd never heard of called Francis Davison. She'd met him occasionally at local shows and told me that she thought he was 'the real thing' but warned me that he was chronically shy. I was impressed enough to want to see more work. Even this modest piece had a quiet, memorable authority.

Sometime later, after a brief exchange of letters, and an even briefer phone call, I knocked on his door. He lived in a tall, narrow terrace house in Southwold, just north of Aldeburgh. His wife, Margaret Mellis, answered, a sprightly, slim sixty-year-old, with striking blue eyes, widening in surprise, and smiling, bright red-painted lips which looked as though they were about to break into a grin. The house was full of abstract paintings in strong, primary colours, not just on the walls, but stacked everywhere, in the corridor, up the stairs and on furniture, so cluttered you could hardly move. There wasn't a muted collage to be seen.

The only room to sit in was the small kitchen at the back. She led me in. A lean man, of her age, was sitting silently beside the bare scrubbed wooden table, looking at me warily, his eyes set back and shaded under straight brows, his cheeks chiselled and his mouth unsmiling, if not exactly grim. At first, I thought he was angry, and then that he was haunted. His intensity and unease filled the room. My presence was the problem because I could see he was utterly at ease with Margaret. I had the strange impression, even then, that they were totally in love, utterly at peace with each other. She had enough outgoing sunshine for the two of them; he was withdrawn and deeply suspicious. I hadn't liked the paintings I'd seen very much. They were strong, but I thought formulaic, sixties abstracts. I was disappointed. I presumed they were by Margaret. I didn't know she was an artist as well. I had come to see Francis, not her. I made that clear. This, in retrospect, was the best thing I could have said. The handful of people who had come to see Francis's work before, over his long life, had done so because of his wife's connections. I had no idea who Margaret Mellis was.

I remember being totally surprised to discover, on a subsequent visit, that she was the ex-wife of the elegant, wealthy, art writer and painter Adrian Stokes and, as a result, was an inner member of the Hampstead/St Ives set, when the likes of Piet Mondrian and Naum Gabo were passing through London, escaping Nazi Europe. The Stokes were close friends of Ben Nicholson and Barbara Hepworth and had put them and their triplets up in their house in Cornwall during the war. And Margaret was familiar with the younger generation of painters there, such as Patrick Heron, Roger Hilton and Peter Lanyon. I discovered, too, later, to my surprise that Francis was Patrick Heron's best friend at school, and it was through this friendship that he'd met Margaret after she'd parted from her husband, having found out that he was gay.

Francis and Patrick's backgrounds were both privileged but in very different ways. Francis was a Dr Barnardo's orphan, one of two adopted by a Kodak millionaire to be companions for his only daughter, whereas Patrick was the son of the founder of Cresta Silks, a highly successful fabric printing company employing leading contemporary artists as designers. At school Patrick's ambition was to be a painter, Francis a poet. Later, when I tried to interest Patrick in Francis's work, he dismissed it saying Francis was a writer, not an artist, and he should stick to that.

Francis was to some extent to blame for his almost total efface-ment during his life. He wasn't interested in other artists, or any-one, come to that, seeing his work. Margaret told me that Roger Hilton had once come to stay. I was a great admirer of Hilton's work, and put on a show of his late, glaring gouaches, painted with his left hand while his right propped him up in bed, as he died, painfully slowly, of alcoholic poisoning. When he visited

Margaret much earlier, Francis had some of his own works on the walls—he was beginning to paint near-abstracts in black and white. It was before he'd started making collages. Roger, peering at them closely, said how much he liked them—rare praise, indeed, from him. Francis then whispered in Margaret's ear to get him out of the house—take him for a walk, whatever. When they got back, all of Francis's paintings had been taken down and hidden.

When it became clear, on that first visit, that I had come there because I'd seen his work at Mary Potter's, and had no idea who Margaret was, Francis, eventually, agreed to show me some of his work. Margaret's studio was the light-filled, large attic. I went up there much later. Francis worked in the small front bedroom below. A white screen softened the light from the window. Large grey soft-boards were propped up against one wall (this warm mid-grey was vital for him as a neutral background against which the whole range of tones and colours could sing). The bed, and under the bed, were stacked high with papers. There were a few scraps of torn papers on the floor—there had clearly been an attempt to tidy up—and a big tin of wallpaper paste, with a brush sticking out of it. But not a work of art to be seen.

Then, with a reluctant sigh, he began to take collages from the heap on the bed, and pinned them, with drawing pins, onto the boards, one by one. This was when, for me, a life's love affair began. I watched, quite simply spellbound, as one after another collage appeared before me, each distinct, though of a family; some simple and bold, many elaborate and complex, some small, others very large, filling the whole of the bedroom wall, some muted, greys and browns and whites, others singing with all the colours of the spectrum—and all of them—this is what made this experience so unforgettable—complete in a way I couldn't quite put my finger on, for each was a living being, like a butterfly opening its wings and settling, for a moment, on the wall before me. It was their rightness and fullness that made me gasp—this sounds a bit dramatic but I can't think of a better way of putting it—an intake of breath?—and made my eyes open wider each time—with—what?—recognition at seeing something alive, meeting someone looking at me, the complete expression of an artistic personality, a glowing awareness, a beauty that was resonant, breathing and lasting. I realised I was in the presence of something extraordinary.

I'd seen a lot of abstract art, and loved the best, but this was different. These collages looked casual, torn, wrinkled scraps just chucked down, but I saw immediately that they were the very opposite. Every nick, tear, placement was meant but looked as if it were spontaneous. Everything in it had to be alive, not dead, to 'work' and contribute to the impact of the whole. I often had to stay Francis's hand before he removed a collage to pin up another because I wanted to look at one longer, swim in the virile, imaginative pool and relish the play of lights, shades and hues. Each collage had its own presence that glowed in my mind. I was being treated to something exceptional, a life's passionate visual journey was unfolding before me.

What had he been doing all this time, by himself, alone in this room, morning to night, over all these years? He clearly hadn't been communicating with others. I should by rights have dismissed this as self-indulgence—for isn't that what art is about—communicating with others?—but I realised at once that it was the opposite. Here was an artist doing something very different—communicating first with himself—what others thought later was their business. He had to be his own severest critic. That was the rigour of his self-discipline. What he was doing was much bolder and braver, taking contemporary art down to its sparest essence, the fundamentals of its very existence. Before it can have anything genuine to offer anyone else, art today has to be an individual creation, otherwise it's merely illustration. Anyone clever can dress themselves in borrowed robes, but discovering your own form of artistic expression is much harder. Francis took that course. He was the sparest of all creators, working only with given, unpainted papers. A monk of modern art, working in that small room, he built a mountain of new abstraction, which is only just beginning to be seen.

From that moment on, I did everything I could to promote his work, acquiring collages for the galleries I ran in Sheffield, Manchester and then Glasgow and organising exhibitions, one at the Hayward Gallery in 1983. I was chair of the exhibition committee at that time and knew I would be able to get one show solely of my own choosing through the committee process. I was determined it would be Francis. He was furious with me for that because he had to do the framing himself and all he really wanted to do was work. Worse, much worse, he'd just been diagnosed with cancer and time, for him, was running out. He told me he had been driving, but suddenly couldn't use one leg. He managed to get home, went to the doctor who sent him to the hospital where they found he had a malignant brain tumour that was inoperable. He had a year, at most two, to live.

I remember going for a walk with him along the beach, when he could still walk. We talked about everything: art, of course, and literature. He'd read hugely. And religion—he was very interested in religious feelings. He was probably, I think, a mystic Christian, though he never exactly spelled that out. We stopped to look at a large bird that had just flown down and was perched on a fence. It looked like a large sparrowhawk with its barbed chest and long tail, but then I realised it was a much rarer sight, a cuckoo, presumably exhausted after a long flight, because it took no interest in us, even though we moved quite close. Francis looked at it for a while, and then said simply, 'Well, that's it.' We both knew he meant by that the end of his life.

D *is for* FRANCIS DAVISON

He asked me to help him sort through all his work, over thirty years of uninterrupted and undiminished heartfelt creative expression, hidden behind Margaret's public professional persona. These were the most harrowing days of my professional career, driving down from Sheffield to spend weekends with him as he grew thinner and weaker, his eyes never leaving mine to see if I liked the next collage he showed me. He wanted, after all, to communicate with someone else. If my eyes didn't light up, it was often torn up on the spot, and later, Margaret told me, burnt. Goodness knows if I got things right. I was the first 'other eyes' to see much of his work.

It was only then that it dawned on me that there could be an extraordinary, utterly logical development throughout his work. None of the collages was titled, and hardly any were dated or signed, so no chronology was obvious, and he showed me them randomly, whatever was next in the pile. 'Titles, dates and signatures have nothing to do with it,' he told me once. I've never come across a purer dedication to the meaning of a visual image. What I was looking at was a contemporary version of the Lindisfarne Gospels—fragments of them in fistfuls—celebratory prayers to the wonder of existing. A handful were signed when the London dealer, Leslie Waddington, who represented Patrick Heron, told Francis that he would only even consider his work if it was signed and dated. Francis signed and dated a few, with an angry 'FD', but even so Leslie wasn't interested in them. It was only after he died that I worked out the sequence of his creation. I took photos of every piece, mounted them on cards and realised that he'd worked in series: one visual idea leading, absolutely logically, to another—a slow efflorescence, the development of a highly personal lexicon of the language of abstraction.

He'd begun painting small, coloured landscapes; then he shrunk these to purely tonal configurations, patterns of fields, houses and roads in greys, blacks and whites—the paintings Roger Hilton had admired. He began making similar images in paper collage. It might have been, partly, that they couldn't both afford oil paint, as Francis told me. Margaret was the main artist after all, the professional who, from time to time, brought home the bacon. But I think it was really because, as Samuel Beckett replied when someone asked him why he wrote in French, he wanted to impoverish himself further. Reduction, for Francis, was inspiring.

Working only with paper, Francis's art took off. It was a slow elevation. His collages were at first rectangular, small, the same size as his paintings; then they grew larger, but were still contained, landscape-like images on rectangular boards. The boards became the backgrounds, and the patterned papers began to float free with them. These explored series of pictorial themes: bold, balanced contrasts; complex, convoluted vortices; fractured, dynamic spaces—like sequences of visual sonatas, culminating, at the end, when he began to tear apart and recycle earlier collages and meld everything together. The torn streaks of coloured paper left on the dried strokes of glue making them look more and more like paintings. These last works, some very big, would sustain a glowing presence hanging between any Rothko or Pollock. Then, at the very end, bedridden, hardly able to move, he produced a series of small collages, some made out of torn-up envelopes, tiny stars appearing in a setting consciousness. One shines above my desk as I type.

Looking back, I think Francis's work was the major discovery of this early venture of mine into unknown territory—my attempt to lift stones, to unearth hidden contemporary visual creativity. There were many among them who went on to do remarkable things, like Martin Handford, the creator of *Where's Wally?* It's difficult to imagine art more different from Francis Davison's than Martin Handford's, but the argument I was making with this

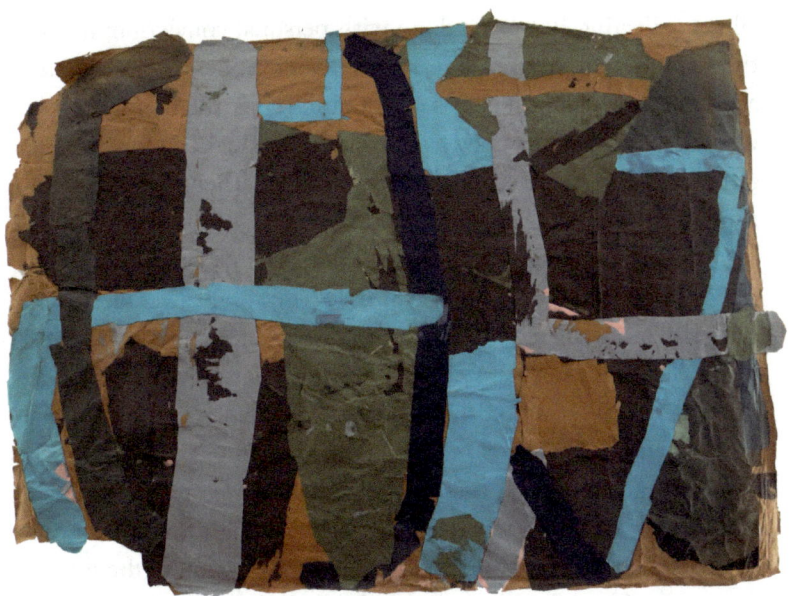

Francis Davison, Collage, c. 1980

selection was that it's not anyone's else's job to determine what art should be. We're the outsider, the watchers; not the creators. We have to leave that to artists, to the people who are responding creatively to the world we live in, as it is, not as we imagine, still less would like it to be. The history of art is made by artists, not predetermined by critics or teachers, still less dealers or curators and even less by theorists like art historians.

Such was the disparity of the art I collected for the Arts Council, that I had difficulty thinking of a title for the touring exhibition in which it would first be shown. I eventually settled on a condensation of a line from T. S. Eliot's poem *The Waste Land*: 'These fragments have I shored against my ruins.' *Fragments against Ruin*, the title of the 1981 show, summed up a lot of my feelings. First of all, it was a personal journey, as in Eliot's poem—

all art collecting has to be done with personal conviction; if not, the aspirational reflections around its emptiness will become apparent over time. Next, the exhibition was fragmentary as a whole—glimpses into many disparate individual creative lives—not, in anyway, an attempt to chart a school. Then it was against ruin. I felt a sense of growing urgency in many of these works, like John Morley's exquisite painting *Noah's Ark* (1977) and Peter Bettany's quintessential sculpture *Sinking* (1974), an awareness, felt rather than calculated, of impending disaster. The casual remark of my teacher at school, Walter MacElroy, that we've come to see ourselves as a disease on the surface of the planet, was beginning to grow and has haunted me ever since.

Over and above all these meanings was my awareness that modern art was born when artists broke through the restrictions of pictorial representation, superficially as a reaction to the invention of mechanical means of reproduction, above all photography, but, much more profoundly, in response to Darwin's discovery, deeply shocking to Christians at the time and still rejected by creationists, that God hadn't made the world as it appears, but that it has changed out of all recognition over time. Fragmentation and reconstruction were essential ingredients of modern image-making. Nothing exemplifies this more essentially than Francis Davison's torn and reassembled scraps of paper. *Fragments against Ruin* perfectly encapsulated his songs in darkness, joy made out of nothingness.

Slowly, long after Francis's death, the art market has begun to become interested in his work. The Redfern Gallery in Cork Street, who showed Margaret's work, put on the occasional show, but the most enterprising has been Mike Goldmark, a beaming, bald-headed bull of a man, who slowly but surely, over five decades, has built up, in the tiny market town of Uppingham, in middle England, a most exceptional, wide-ranging art promotion enterprise, selling, from his premises there—which seem to have spread to take over a whole street—and online, literally thousands of original works of art of all shapes, sizes and media, from oil paintings to prints to pots, within price ranges to suit every purse, every single item worth a look. If most selling galleries are exclusion zones—to increase the value of their chosen few—Mike's is an inclusion zone. He buys what he likes and sells what he likes; the more the better—it's as simple as that. He told me he didn't really like abstract art until he saw a Francis Davison and fell in love with it. Now he shows him whenever he can. Within Mike's expansive, all-encompassing garden can be found one of the rarest artistic flowers of our times. So, slowly, Davison's art is seeping into public consciousness...

This story has a very strange coda. After Francis died, Margaret who interestingly had given up painting and begun to make powerful assemblages out of driftwood, springing from some very early small constructivist collages she'd made before she met Francis, rang me and told me she was being 'pestered' by a young student from Leeds, who had seen my show of Francis's work at the Hayward Gallery, and was obsessed by it. His name was Damien Hirst. I'd never heard of him, nor had anyone else at that time, except his teacher, Glyn Thompson, who, at a later stage was to re-appear in my life with regards to the influence of Duchamp. Serendipity in art is everything.

When Hirst arrived in London from Leeds, he was still raving about Davison's work, but found to his surprise that no one knew about it, even though he'd been given a show in what was then the main modern art exhibition space in town (long before Tate Modern, or even the Barbican). Francis Davison wasn't a name anyone knew, so few went. Hirst then focused on fame.

D *is for* MARCEL DUCHAMP

The god of modern art, the father of conceptu-
alism, spanning my museum career, and still elevated in heaven,
was and is Marcel Duchamp. I was taken in at first, like everyone
else, up to a point, but not totally, because I was, from the start,
confused. I remember looking, for the first time, at his most famous, infamous creation, the urinal (aka *Fountain)* in the Duchamp exhibition in the Tate in 1966 and thinking 'this doesn't
make sense'. Why is it signed on the rim so that it has to be exhibited lying on its back, on a plinth, not placed upright against a
wall as all urinals are? Surely the whole point of it was that it was
to be exhibited, as a familiar urinal, amidst and between a line of
paintings, making the statement that anything can be work of art
if an artist says it is, and inviting, by its very presence, a visitor to
piss into it (if you were a man, and so inclined) and by inference,
take the piss out of art itself?

I did a drawing to illustrate this point for my book *The Eclipse
of Art* (2003). The urinal I was looking at in the Tate didn't, in my
view, say what it was meant to at all, but suggested something
much more complex. And I noted, even then, that the profile of
the thing looked oddly like a seated Buddha, in white porcelain.
I didn't understand it. But then I didn't doubt it either, and lost
interest in it as a bit of puerile nonsense. The show as a whole,
including the urinal, simply didn't interest me. Collected all together, I found Duchamp's work dull.

His paintings were laboured artifices, self-conscious, Cubist-
cum-Futurist concoctions unenlivened by any imagination let
alone by any sparks of inspiration—a young, intelligent man
trying to be an artist, as his brothers were, but failing—producing
pastiches not creations, nothing living. So, to me it was hardly

surprising that he gave painting up and never touched a brush again. His urinal was his revenge on art; his piss-take against the whole shooting match. The 'readymades' he made subsequently I found impenetrable self-indulgences. They looked to me like in-jokes among cronies, without the merit even of being funny. I couldn't get anything visually out of them at all, unlike the playful use of found objects by other artists, like Picasso, Kurt Schwitters and Dalí.

I left the exhibition thinking that Duchamp and his work were boring. He'd gone on and on about how he was against 'retinal art', as if visual art could be anything but retinal! But this was the very sphere of human activity that interested me—how people can communicate by creating things to look at. So, from that moment on I lost interest in Duchamp and in his childish urinal in particular. I hardly spoke about him to anyone, except perhaps to complain about his growing influence in art education and on the young. I was discussing this with David Hockney once, and his only comment was dismissive. 'It's a very un-Duchampian thing to do to re-do Duchamp,' he muttered wryly. And we left it at that. But still Duchampian repetitions went on and on ... *ad nauseam*, and his reputation grew bigger and bigger, until it became, like a dark cloud, hanging over everyone. I wrote about it in *The Eclipse of Art*, still never questioning the primary source. That's when Glyn Thompson stepped in.

I'd first met Glyn at college. We were doing the same degree in Fine Art and Art History—a combined course taught simultaneously at Nottingham University and Art College, which attracted oddballs, like us. We got on immediately, not only, I would like to think, because I was one of the few people he'd ever met who'd actually been to Great Yarmouth, the somewhat forlorn seaside resort and former fishing port on the extreme eastern tip of Norfolk, where he was born and grew up—over thirty years later he muttered under his breath, in disbelief, as we went to the opening of an exhibition we'd put on at Summerfield about the urinal, 'who'd have thought it? A lad from Yarmouth putting on a show at the Edinburgh Festival!'

I like to think we got on because we had a similar wit; his I knew was always keener and quicker than mine, but we were, so to speak, singing from the same scurrilous hymn-sheet. Nothing was sacred, for either of us. Our ways parted after college. He was teaching at Jacob Kramer College, Leeds, where I was told he was known as the Bald Monk—he'd had from early on a fondness for a close-shaven skull—and now, I think, there's nothing left to shave. Meanwhile I was curating at Sheffield Art Galleries. We were not far apart geographically, but worlds apart, in milieu. Unbeknownst to us, however, our activities overlapped.

I was putting on a show of work of the collagist Francis Davison at the Hayward Gallery in London, while he was teaching a student called Damien Hirst, who visited the show and was bowled over by it. Hirst tried to emulate Francis' work, then the assemblages of his wife Margaret Mellis, but failed to get anywhere with either. He then turned, famously, to producing concepts—repeating, in my view, Duchamp's revenge on the retinal art that neither of them could create. Glyn has kept a slide show of the lectures he gave, where some of Hirst's ideas came from, and occasionally re-enacts it, in a lecture called 'Educating Damien'. So, unwittingly, we both sired (if that is the right word) the most famous name in modern art worldwide—me negatively by showing art that Hirst liked but, judging from the couple of illustrations I had seen of his efforts, couldn't emulate, and Glyn positively by giving him ideas of things he could subsequently do. We both helped hatch the monstrous marketing illusion that is Hirst. But neither of us can be blamed for that.

Glyn took early retirement from Jacob Kramer and realised

a long-held dream to open a restaurant, called In Vino Veritas, in Leeds, which housed the first Café Scientifique in Britain, inspired by the Café Philosophique movement in France. He finished working at the restaurant after eight years—a good stint for this gruelling, unsociable profession—and then focused on Duchamp, concentrating on unpacking the working method behind his readymades, explaining why he spent so much time leafing through dictionaries and, above all, analysing the influence of Raymond Roussel on his activities.

Roussel was a very rich, *fin-de-siècle* Parisian playboy, who, after his attempt to write a serious long poem proved a flop, turned to promoting, at great personal expense, performances of deliberately incomprehensible nonsensical plays. There was a method in his madness, which he later revealed, a sequencing of meaningless puns, one leading to another to the obliteration of all sense. This was part of the intellectual climate at the time—Cubism, Dada and Surrealism were, in many ways, all fallouts from Darwin's realisation that God hadn't created the world as it appears. Penises and vaginas could well have been where our noses and mouths now are. The discovery of the cruel and random process of evolution spelled the end of the visible (retinal) world that had sustained representational Western European Christian art and thought for well-nigh a thousand years.

Glyn worked out how Duchamp used Roussel's punning method to create his readymades, which he didn't regard as works of art at all, and never exhibited as such, but which were to be read, not looked at, as verbal puns, essentially rebuses. His wheel mounted on a stool is, for example, a pun on the French words for these two objects: *roue* and *selle*, i.e. it was a representation of Roussel, the godhead of nonsense himself.

Meanwhile, in another part of the country, I was getting absolutely fed up with Duchamp's persisting influence on modern art, which was increasing, not, as I hoped, shrinking. In *The Eclipse of Art*, I had argued that Duchamp's putting a urinal in a gallery effectively said that anything can be a work of art if an artist says it is, and therefore, by implication, anyone can be an artist. This had great appeal to egalitarians, by pulling art down from its pedestal, destroying its exclusivity and making it accessible to everyone, but it also undermined any attempt to make value judgements about quality in art, even to decide what was art and what was not. Outside observers, curators like me, let alone Joe Public, didn't have a say.

Moreover, the idea that anything can be a work of art also had great appeal to educational administrators who'd long wanted to get rid of the all the expensive equipment in art schools needed for painting, printing and sculpture, which they soon did. If an artwork could be a found object, you didn't need to have to learn to make things, not even to draw. So drawing went too. All a student had to do was to develop a concept. It's true that it's perfectly possible to make art out of anything, as African artists have known all along, and as Picasso famously proved again in the last century when he juxtaposed a handlebar and a saddle to create a fierce, fighting bull's head, but I argued that you have to be able to see the transformation. Art has to be created and it has to be visible, and it has to be judged; it can't just be found and a given. This, I discovered, was to be an unpopular position among my colleagues and almost everyone in the art game. I was letting the side down, taking a step back, not forward, as we all were supposed to do to advance something called 'Art'.

Then Glyn came to see me. I will never forget him, quietly and patiently, bending back the pages of my book, and with his finger underlining the facts I'd got wrong. Duchamp never had submitted a urinal to an exhibition, nor did it, in any way, mean what he said. He'd stolen it, much later in life, from Baroness Elsa von

D *is for* MARCEL DUCHAMP

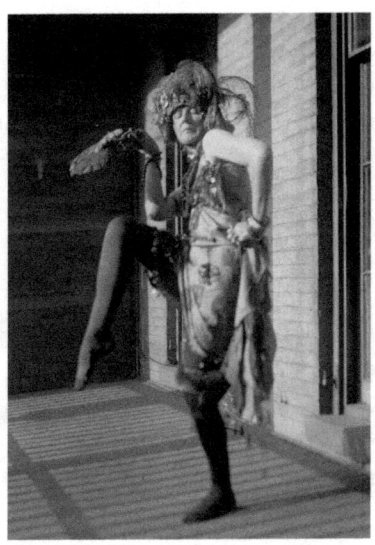

Baroness Elsa von Freytag-Loringhoven, 1922

Freytag-Loringhoven, long after she was dead and, even worse, robbed it of its meaning. I was stunned, but also enthralled. This could explain why the urinal, as Duchamp's work, had never made any visual sense to me.

I immediately read Irene Gammel's recently published biography of the Baroness, which Glyn recommended. The urinal was indeed the fountainhead of modern art, but, as the French film-maker Julie Gavras, who later made a film about Elsa remarked, very disturbingly for the French—it was not only by a woman, not a man, and, even worse, she was German. Pathetically the film was suppressed by the TV channel Arte due to pressure from the Duchamp lobby. The urinal's meaning became clear, which had been hidden by Duchamp's thieving deception. It shone in my mind as the world's first and arguably still greatest feminist, pacifist work of art. Yes, work of art, because the way Elsa had presented it; it was a urinal utterly transformed.

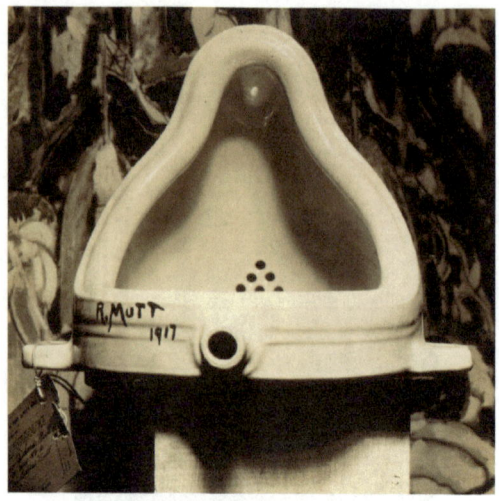

Alfred Stieglitz, photograph of the urinal, 1917

We only know Elsa's urinal from a photograph by the great photographer Alfred Stieglitz, gallery owner and husband of the artist Georgia O'Keefe, taken shortly after it was submitted to, but not shown in, the Independent Artists exhibition in 1917 in New York. It doesn't at first look like a urinal. It's laid on its back with the lower rim standing up. It has, indeed, the profile of a seated, contemplative Buddha. And in addition, as can be seen clearly in the Stieglitz photograph, the shadow of the rim forms within it, in negative, the profile of a pale, veiled Madonna, another image of love to mankind—two great religions enthroned at one. Then you realise it's a urinal—the throne, you might say, in the gentleman's room—and the meaning of the whole thing does a dramatic, almost unbelievable, deeply disturbing summersault in your mind. It's an image of piss as well as peace. Who could have conceived of such a thing?

Elsa was a poet, performance artist and sculptress, a star of *The Little Review* in New York, where she was published alongside

James Joyce. She sent in her urinal to the Independents exhibition on Good Friday (hence the Madonna), the day that America, which she regarded as a gentleman's club (symbolised by a urinal), declared war against her motherland, Germany (hence the signature R. Mutt—*Mutter* in German meaning mother, as well as *Armut*, meaning poverty—as poor as piss). Elsa punned in German, Duchamp in French. But there was another personal meaning behind this gesture. She was saying to America 'don't piss on my country' as her father had done to her mother, inflicting her with syphilis after his frequent philandering, a disease from which she died, leaving Elsa her inheritance, which was, she said, 'to fight'. Like all great works of art, Elsa's urinal has many layers of meaning. These are all hidden under Duchamp's puerile misappropriation.

Glyn kept me in touch with his researches. He was like a dog with a rag who wouldn't let go. In the most remarkable sequence of forensic examinations, sustained over several years, that I have ever witnessed in the field of art history, he unpacked everything that had happened before and during Duchamp's deception. His research led him to become an expert in urinal-making in America, an essential first step. Duchamp claimed he'd bought his urinal from J. L. Mott's, a posh plumbing fixtures store in New York—hence in part, Duchamp claimed, his supposedly punning signature, R. Mutt. But Glyn proved he couldn't have done because Mott's didn't sell the model in the Stieglitz photo and, anyway, Mott's was a showroom, not a shop—you couldn't go in and carry away anything. So, all the cards in Duchamp's hands fell, one by one.

Glyn discovered there was only one model that fitted the Stieglitz photo, and it was sold in Philadelphia where Elsa was at the time, escaping charges of shoplifting in New York (she was that poor herself). What's more, he actually acquired one of these models, which blows Duchamp's later faked attempt to 'replicate' it out of the water. Elsa died, more or less in the gutter, in Paris in 1927, while Duchamp lived on, eventually mass-producing her work as his own in 1964. Glyn has unravelled every tiny bit of the scam, including analysing Elsa's handwriting—it's hers on the urinal. Everything fits: there's no doubt about it.

But there's also a smoking gun, and Duchamp is holding it himself. Two days after the urinal was submitted, he wrote to his sister in war-torn France, as an amusing aside, that 'a woman friend' of his had submitted 'a urinal as a sculpture' to an exhibition. He knew Elsa, as most people in the New York art world did—she was difficult to avoid—but the fact that he referred to her submission 'as a sculpture' is most significant, because his readymades, according to his own definition, weren't in any way to be regarded as works of art. The urinal wasn't his, and it wasn't even a readymade. This letter wasn't discovered until 1983, but it was buried by the Duchamp industry, which by then had become dominant in the contemporary art world, and they've gone on maintaining Duchamp's fiction ever since, despite all of Glyn's superb articles that make nonsense of it all.

I did my bit to help. We wrote to all the museums who owned one of Duchamp's urinal casts, asking them to change the label —the public have the right to the truth. None did, but at least Nick Serota at the Tate had the courtesy to reply. The truth is that Duchamp simply could not have done what he later said he did. That fact didn't fit. The reality is that Elsa submitted the urinal. Duchamp's urinal never existed and any impact it had on anyone is a total fiction. David Lee, the brilliant, independent, art-thinker and editor, published Glyn's discoveries whenever he could, and the whole correspondence between us and Nick Serota as a podcast supplement to his magazine *The Jackdaw*.

We put on a show at Summerhall, the extraordinary, utterly

individualistic, sprawling, artistic brainchild of the artist/financial journalist Robert McDowell, as part of the Edinburgh Festival, called *A Lady's not a Gents*. It was all Glyn's research, but I added my morsel on the implications. These are immense. When people realise that the fountainhead of modern art is a sculpture, not a found object—an imaginative transformation as significant as any by Picasso—then the whole edifice of conceptual art, which began to be erected in the 1960s, after Duchamp's theft, not before, crumbles to nothing, and we can begin to create great, purely visual art again.

This will take some time, because the investment in Duchamp's eminence is immense, in the teaching of art, in its literature, in curation in museums and in all the personal reputations built around these activities, and above all in the vast sums sunk into it. No one will want to admit that all that is worthless, which it is. One of the versions of Elsa's urinal commissioned as his by Duchamp in 1964 sold for $1,762,500 at Sotheby's in New York in 1999. It had come from the gallery of Arturo Schwartz, the art dealer who said, in 1954, 'Duchamp had been completely forgotten. I put him back in the picture.' By faking his past and burying Elsa. Duchamp is a false god and modern art galleries around the world are littered with the relics of his phoney religion. Glyn is a modern-day Luther, pinning his ninety-five articles to the door at Wittenberg, one of the most cluttered with relics he could find. Few have read Glyn's yet. I hope I live to see the revolution that results.

One question remains to be asked—why did Duchamp himself hold such sway? I have written extensively about how the idea of exhibiting a urinal in an art exhibition had such appeal to the new, politically correct egalitarianism of the sixties, but the key point to be made here was how it fitted into world politics. It was the height of the Cold War and the USA was fighting a propaganda battle with Russia for intellectual and cultural world leadership. They abandoned social realist art, as manifest in the New Deal, and turned, with the help of the CIA, to promote Abstract Expressionism, the modern art forms derided by Hitler and Khrushchev.

Duchamp's credentials were impeccable. He was an artist who had been there in the exciting formative years of modern art at the beginning of the century and he was French, and he then moved to America and claimed he'd submitted the urinal to an exhibition—not in Paris but in New York. One of the founding icons of modern art was, in fact, created in the USA, not in Europe, let alone in Russia. Picasso, Matisse, Kandinsky, Mondrian and all the rest became marginal—old world figures, in fact. Duchamp was where it was at, at the right time and in the right country. The latest, most radical modern art sprang from what he claimed was his crucial gesture at that moment. Modern art was, to put it crudely, in its origin American. This whole fake faith was built on that single, cheeky theft.

Glyn is continuing his researches, and I've been lucky enough to include here a recent photograph taken by him on 23 February 2023 of this work in progress (see opposite). It needs to be looked at with the immaculate explanatory text he has provided:

> The image records one of the stages of my analysis of the process followed by Alfred Stieglitz in the production of his iconic photograph of Mutt's (lost) urinal, taken on 13 or 14 April 1917 at his gallery at 291 Fifth Avenue, New York, an enlarged copy of which rests against the base of the plinth on the left on which an actual example in my collection of the same make and model as Mutt's urinal has been posed.
>
> It was my acquisition in 2017 of this, one of the only two known actually surviving examples of Mutt's (lost) urinal, that made my analysis, and the insights it has furnished, possible. That analysis required my painting the full-size of copy

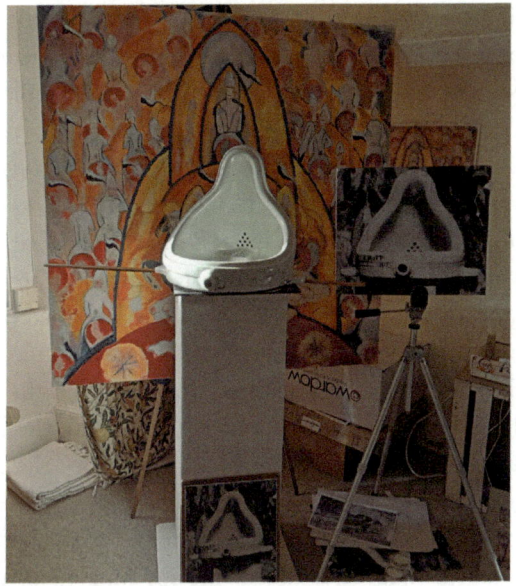

Glyn Thompson's reconstruction of Steiglitz's original photograph, 2023

of the background Stieglitz chose to photograph Mutt's urinal against, Marsden Hartley's painting titled *The Warriors* of 1913, seen here.

That acquisition had only been made possible by my earlier identification—in 2014, for the first time in the history of art—of the identity of the actual make and model of Mutt's urinal, that then lead to my subsequent identification in 2015 of a (unique) location in which an earlier example of that same model had been installed, in 1908—the Magic Chef Mansion in St Louis, MO.

On a tripod, to the right of the urinal posed on the plinth, is an enlargement of the upper section of Stieglitz's photograph, rendering Mutt's urinal life-size for the purposes of direct comparison of the two, showing both their generic similarities and their specific differences in dimensions and proportions: according to industry custom and practice the model of urinal was issued in three sizes; that on the left, a No. 1, was the largest; Mutt's was a No. 2; an example of a No. 3, the smallest, has yet to be located.

Mutt's urinal, erroneously attributed—in 1932, not 1917—to the œuvre of Marcel Duchamp, by Georges Hugnet was, unknown to either, a 'Vitreous China "Bedfordshire" Flat Back Urinal with Lip' manufactured exclusively between 1915 and 1920 by the Trenton Potteries Company, in Trenton, NJ.

Two factors inarguably guarantee this identification, firstly, the dimensions of the three sizes in which the item was uniquely manufactured between those dates, the No. 1 measuring 21" x 18" x 14½" [height/width/depth]: the No 2 [Mutt's] measuring 19" x 16¼" x 12½", and a No. 3, measuring 18" x 14¾ x 11". These sizes are listed in the catalogues of both the manufacturer that made the model and those of the plumbing supply houses that bought examples wholesale from the manufacturer in order to sell them retail to the trade.

The second guarantee is the incorporation of a design feature also unique to the specific make and model, the signature combination of (the triangular) integral strainer perforating the bowl of the urinal and the perforated ventilator attached to the inner back, both unsurprisingly observable in the Magic Chef Mansion example and that in my collection but not in Stieglitz's photograph since, as a result of the æsthetic and physical points of view he adopted, whilst the integral strainer is [only] partially visible, the perforated ventilator has been completely masked by the rim of the urinal; the perforated ventilator had been completely obscured by the flushing rim of the urinal as a result of Stieglitz's desire to conjure the image of a veiled woman from the penumbra of the shadow cast in its bowl.

The significance of Mutt's urinal's exclusive manufacture by the Trenton Potteries Company lies in the fact that the manner in which the sanitary fixtures manufacturing industry had been organised by 1917 made Duchamp's claim [of 1966, to Otto Hahn] to have obtained Mutt's urinal from the J. L. Mott Iron Works in Manhattan completely false, since it wasn't a Mott. Duchamp's disqualification is confirmed by, *inter alia*, Duchamp's confession in a letter written to his sister Suzanne on 11 April 1917, two days after the urinal had been rejected—because Mutt was not a member of the exhibiting society to which the urinal had been sent, not submitted—that not he but a female friend had been solely responsible for the conception and execution of Mutt's gesture.

Thus, since the urinal could not have come from the J. L. Mott Iron Works, then the pseudonym Mutt could not, as Duchamp suggested to Hahn, have come from the name Mott. Rather, as we now know from evidence that Duchamp had no interest in discussing with Hahn, the pseudonym 'R. Mutt'—not printed on Mutt's urinal by Duchamp but by that female friend, Elsa von Freytag-Loringhoven—came from the German for impoverishment and incompetence, *Armut*.

Thus the pre-eminence of Stieglitz's iconic photograph in the institutionally authorised history of the Mutt affair takes on a somewhat different complexion now burnished by its anatomical dissection, a snap-shot of which is illustrated here, recommending that the copyright of its contents should now be de-attributed from the œuvre of Duchamp, along with its subject—Mutt's urinal—which belongs to Elsa.

This statement and this photo dispel any lingering doubt that Duchamp 'did' the urinal. Pictures speak louder than words, for all Duchamp's assertion of the value of the 'non-retinal'—that the idea 'behind' a work is more important that the work itself. His idea of 'non-retinal art' is, of course, nonsense, a contradiction in terms. All art is full of thoughts and feelings, but they are ideas and emotions you can see; that's why they're works of art. If you're looking at a what you're told is a work of art—say an object—but you can't see any art in it, there's a strong possibility that there is no art there. You have to trust your eyes, and I've been trusting my eyes all my life. And if there's no art there, but it's been sold as a work of art, then someone has been totally conned. These emperors have no clothes. The whole multi-million-pound conceptual art investment market is a bubble that is about to burst, and the sooner it does the better, so we can get back to appreciating, discovering and creating real art again. And for that, we have to thank Glyn Thompson, and his brilliant, pioneering, undauntedly stubborn investigation into the actual events of the case.

F is for IAN HAMILTON FINLAY

There was a fleet of cars in Glasgow to drive chief officers around the city, or wherever, but on the day I went to see Ian Hamilton Finlay for the first time all the smaller cars were in use, and they only had the Rolls—hardly appropriate—and one of the two Daimlers left. So a Daimler it was. Ian lived in the hills far to the southeast of the city, down winding lanes, and the driver was amused. He usually drove officers to meetings in town halls and business headquarters, not to a distant, isolated farm, perched at the end of a long, rough, stony track hidden in a copse of weather-beaten trees on an otherwise barren brow of hill. He was even more amused when we dipped down, at the last stretch, to navigate the sleek, black limousine across a pebbly brook past a low wall with the profile of a gun emblazoned on its side, warning, by inference, that anyone who entered there was in danger of being shot.

I'd told him the story. Ian, the artist we were going to meet, had recently declared war on Strathclyde Regional Council (fortunately not Glasgow City itself), because this authority was demanding that he pay rates on a building on his farm where he displayed and, occasionally, sold his work, which he had declared was a Temple of Art. As a religious building, Ian argued, it should be exempt from any form of taxation, but the unfortunate, unwary junior officer who'd inspected the premises had assumed it to be a shop. Hence the battle line. I explained to the driver that Ian loved declaring war on all and sundry. It compensated, I supposed, for his lonely existence. He was famous for suffering from agoraphobia—fear of open spaces—which is why he never left the patch of trees around his farm, for the moors stretched open for miles around. He told me later that this was a myth (not one, it has to be said, disavowed at the time by himself) and that he loved open spaces and walked for miles across the hills every day—but at that late stage in his life he'd begun to find it necessary to go to see people because people had begun not to go to see him. But, when I first went to see him, everyone had to cross a pebbly brook, through a war zone, in a Daimler, or whatever.

I had been an admirer of Ian's work for a long time. Indeed, I was the first curator to buy his work for a public collection, in Sheffield—an engraved plaque of the Battle of Midway—but then I was a fan of Dante too, and felt already midway in my life and a bit lost in a wood, though not so much interested in the battles of the Second World War. I wondered what sort of man I'd meet. He appeared, at first, to be mild, lean and tallish, unkempt, grey-haired, basically wiry and scraggy. He was, it's true, a bit suspicious. His eyes, I remember, were set far back under ragged brows, but, on the other hand, he didn't look at all like a bomb about to explode. There was no sign, even, of a fizzling fuse, just the proffer of a welcoming hand and the offer, in a honeyed, almost silky Scottish brogue, of a cup of tea, for my driver and me. There was no mention, even, of a whisky. Nothing fiery, at all. I was, in a way, slightly disappointed. Had I got this man wrong, all along?

He showed me round. The driver stayed behind in the little kitchen. Gardens weren't his cup of tea. I was delighted by what I saw. Albrecht Dürer's monogram, that elegant overlapping AD, inscribed on a slab of stone under a clump of grass in a pond, as if the great artist had drawn the whole scene. And he could have done. Here, in the middle of a wilderness, was an intimate, enclosed, haven of peace and growth, no sign of war at all. But at the edge of the garden, where it opened on to the moorland, beside another reedy pond, the black conning tower of nuclear submarine ploughed along a path, as if war was lurking underneath. It was a beautiful and disturbing place. I was glad I'd come.

We chatted about all sorts of things: the Ceolfrith Arts Centre in Sunderland, where I'd first seen his work and his printed books. He was a concrete poet then, before he'd got together with Sue and could live on a farm on the estate of her father, a local Scottish laird. She was his emissary, his extended, travelling eyes and negotiated all the commissions and installations for his work, which were, by then, spreading across Britain and Europe. I was impressed by his ability to imagine what his work would be like in far-flung locations, though he, at that time, never left the farm. It was almost always words spelt out, usually in stone. I bought a piece, a huge, monstrously heavy cloud-shaped slab of white marble carved with the lines:

CLAY THE LIFE

PLASTER THE DEATH

MARBLE THE REVOLUTION

This phrase, chiselled in light, intrigued me. It seemed right to hang it in an art gallery/museum, for it spoke a lot about art of the past and today. If you believe the Bible (which I don't for a moment, but it's a good place to start), we were created out of clay, and this is the basic material we've used for making art, from the earliest times until now. Rodin's *The Age of Bronze* was originally modelled in clay, then cast in metal. He was furious when he was accused of casting a real man in plaster first; a few contemporary critics of his thought this must be the case because the figure was so extraordinarily life-like. But this was because it was fired from within, inspired, not shadowed from without, a lifeless cast.

Plaster is slippery and directionless before it sets in *rigor mortis*. Marble is made from clay, and other substances, then transformed by fire, in the heart of the earth, and then carved by artists such as Michelangelo. Ian's summation of art history in stone was so heavy and unmanageable, it had to be permanently installed. I decided that it should hang on the staircase in Kelvingrove between the ground floor, where the natural history and geological collections are displayed, and the first floor, where most of the art is shown. It seemed an apt transition. I think Ian was pleased, though he never let on. But after that, things started to go wrong.

I had two things I wanted him to do. One was to help us put on a big retrospective of his work in the McLellan Galleries—there had never been one anywhere, and it would be interesting to see his development since I'd first seen his work in Sunderland a quarter of a century before. And we certainly couldn't have done the show without his interest and commitment—he'd kept many pieces himself but the rest were so far-flung, it would be a challenge to work out how to represent his installations. I had in mind some brilliant, very large-scale photography and projected films. Secondly, I was beginning to work on the new Gallery of Modern Art in Glasgow, and I wanted to commission him to create something that would be integrated into the building. He was such a big, international figure in Scottish art at that time that I wanted him to be part of the project at its inception, but I wasn't at all sure where or how. He had a new helpmate then—Sue and he had long since parted company—Pia Simig, who worked for the gallery that represented him in Germany, and stayed when she was over in the Temple. She came to see me in Glasgow to discuss the projects and everything seemed fine. Ian, then, was still not venturing forth from his den.

The young Andrew Patrizio took on the task, later professor of Scottish Visual Culture at Edinburgh University, a remarkably untroubled personality who acted as methodically as his mind worked. This was lucky, for he slowly but surely worked out what Ian was up to. He was leading me up the garden path, which was allowable, after all he liked gardens, but it wasn't where I wanted to be. He was playing me along, pretending to get earlier works, but when the project was set and scheduled, all the money raised and the other venues were booked, these earlier works would disappear like morning mist, and he would create a huge installation of new work, his dream creation in a gallery.

That might have been beautiful, of course, but it could equally have been awfully thin; he wasn't necessarily inventing as well as he had, and I had the feeling that his work was getting overextended and repetitive. I'd always promised him an installation of new work in the last gallery, which was only right, but not the whole show. I had to confront him about this and lay my cards on the table. He argued that all creations are reworkings, which is true, up to a point, so a retrospective didn't make sense and a show of new work would be that anyway. I wanted to watch the transformation of a concrete poet into an international installation artist, and to see how his fascination with the French Revolution and his correspondence with the imprisoned Nazi architect Albert Speer had developed, and why. I wanted visitors to be able to follow the emergence of his ideas and his art over time, and that meant seeing works made in time. He wouldn't play ball, so I cancelled the show.

We were still talking—having agreed politely to disagree—for he had the installations in the Gallery of Modern Art to complete. He'd had the idea to put some heads of people he didn't like in baskets, as if they'd just been guillotined, in an odd, little passageway we'd discovered between two floors, which couldn't really be used for anything else. It was as though they'd been found hidden in the building itself. One was a decapitated head of the art critic Waldemar Januszczak whom he didn't rate—and I half wondered if one of mine wouldn't end up in a basket when the gallery opened. But he'd had another more exciting idea, which I was very enthusiastic about.

There were three large, tall windows on the first floor of the gallery behind the pillars under the portico at the front. I'd explained to Ian that one of the principles of this new gallery was that people would be able to see into it from without. There were high, clear windows all-round the ground floor, as well as these three at the front. I wanted the building to be inviting and intriguing, to tempt people in to see the art inside. Most modern art is made to be seen in modern life, as most art always was. We put ultraviolet filters on the windows, to exclude any damaging rays of light, but the glass was still transparent and passers-by could see the works of art lit within. Ian had the idea to inscribe each of these three windows, along the bottom, with the words LIBERTY, EQUALITY and ETERNITY, a delicious play on the motto of the French Revolution, which is still inscribed on the front of most public buildings in France and all schools.

Ian's substitution chimed perfectly with my interest in the lasting qualities of art today. The inscribed words would be readable from outside, by people looking in, but, because they would be in reverse and low down, the letters wouldn't interfere with people's view outside. This flow of inside-outside was vital to the gallery's concept. The commission was set, the panes of glass sent to the engravers, but when they arrived back, I was furious. Ian without telling me had reversed the design, made the engravers frost the whole surface, only leaving the letters clear. No one could see out or in. He said he thought they looked better that way. He refused to revert to his original design, so I drew the line and cancelled the whole scheme.

At the same time—everything was happening then, before the opening for the Queen—Pia was in the gallery setting up the heads in baskets. Unfortunately the staff didn't realise she was still there and locked that section of the gallery up, while other work was being done elsewhere. She was locked in for a couple of hours, growing extremely frantic, until some staff heard her banging on a door. When she got home, Ian immediately rang the press—he had media contacts everywhere—and told everyone that we had 'kidnapped' his assistant, without mentioning the debacle over the glass engraving. But this was all in a day's business, and as they say in Glasgow, 'Today's news is tomorrow's fish supper.' (For those who don't know, it used to be traditional to wrap fish and chips in old newspapers, before the days of health and safety.) Despite all this, Ian was always polite to me whenever we met—he started to go out more, towards the end of his life, perhaps with a growing foreboding that he might be forgotten—seduction and venom seemed for the most part to be confined to the pen.

After my very first meeting with Ian, on the drive back to Glasgow, in the Daimler, I asked the driver what he thought of Ian and his house—he'd stayed in the kitchen drinking tea. His comment was brief: 'Too much oose for me.' (Oose is a wonderfully evocative Glasgow word for the soft, grey rolls of dust that gather under furniture in a house where cleaning isn't frequent.) Perhaps a retrospective would have shown that before Sue left, Ian's work was to the point, but after that it got out of hand, became overblown and began to repeat itself. We'll probably never know, for Ian, aside from being a chimera on the hillside fighting imaginary battles with the world, was, when down to earth, a master of disguise.

H *is for* MARTIN HANDFORD

Where's Wally? has become famous throughout the world. His name morphs a little as you edge round—becoming Charlie in France, Walter in Germany, شلبي in Egypt (pronounced Shalabee in Arabic), हेट्टी in India (pronounced Hetti in Hindi), 威利 in China (pronounced Wēilì in Mandarin), and Waldo in America—but the sound is similarly familiar and friendly, if intentionally a bit simple, while the images remain exactly the same. But few people know the name Martin Handford, though it's on every cover. He's usually dismissed as being the book's illustrator, but he is much more than that.

As part of my commission to acquire works of art for the Arts Council (see D for Francis Davison), I visited as many open submission art exhibitions as I could. Most public galleries then held them annually up and down the country. One of the worst things that's happened in recent decades is that galleries have ceased to hold them as they've become increasingly tied to the apron strings of the international art market (see the story of Mandy McCartin in Sheffield, p. 308). One of the few organisations still to hold an open exhibition is the Royal Academy in London, but then it's run by artists trying to promote their and other artists' current work. The show's packed with the Royal Academician's own works, of course, but it's also an opportunity for new talent. I went there early in my hunt for new art for the Arts Council.

I was stopped in my tracks by two large, very intricate drawings of battle scenes by an artist I'd not heard of: Martin Handford. I've never been interested in war games, real or imaginary, but I found these drawings extraordinarily absorbing visually. He'd drawn each soldier distinctly in such a way as to give each figure a life of its own. Handford had also managed to create with these massed, tiny details, complex patterns of movement that ebbed and flowed across the page. His drawings were immensely enjoyable both when examined minutely and when viewed broadly as a whole—a remarkable achievement, by any standards.

These two drawings were sold, so I got his address from the catalogue and wrote to him, hoping to visit and see more work. We spoke on the phone. He wouldn't have me come to see him but promised to bring some drawings into central London to show me. But where to meet? I suggested the Hayward Gallery, where I had a lot of Arts Council meetings at that time. He asked 'Where?' He'd evidently never heard of the place. I was even more intrigued. This was exactly what I was looking for—artists who weren't part of the modern art scene. I explained where it was and what it was—then the main international showcase for contemporary art, long before Tate Modern. There was a pause on the other end of the line. Then a voice said quietly, 'Oh … that's not the sort of place I usually go to.'

We met. He was a thin young man, barely twenty, intense and intensely shy, holding a big portfolio. It contained two large drawings of amazingly intricate battle scenes. I wanted to acquire both—because seeing the differences between them was doubly surprising, for nothing in them was repeated—there were no short cuts, no devices, in his creations. Every centimetre was genuinely felt. But Martin wouldn't let me buy both. I had to choose. With difficulty I selected his recreation of the Battle of Chacabuco, a crucial encounter in the Chilean War of Independence, fought in 1817, when the Liberation Army of the Andes, led by Captain-General José de San Martín, routed the Royalist Army of ruling Spain. Martin knew a great deal about the battle and told me he'd chosen to draw it because he wanted to depict a conflict between trained and untrained soldiers. He'd succeeded brilliantly in every detail, and in the ordered chaos of the overall effect. The scene reminded me of the wonderful painting on the side of Tutankhamun's sandal-case, showing the pharoah defeating the chaotic forces of the 'vile land of Kush'.

Martin told me each drawing took several weeks to do, and he showed me where he'd drawn himself drawing the whole scene, in the heart of the conflict. He said he always put himself in the battle—it was, I think, a way he had of making the whole event absolutely real for him. But try as I might when I looked at the work on subsequent occasions—I still find this bewildering—I couldn't find him again. Eventually I did, after another day of looking. It was only much later, when I saw his *Where's Wally?* books, which he started producing a decade later, that I realised he'd repeated this ability to hide himself in multiple reality. Most people think he's just an illustrator of an idea; but he's not—he was the inventor of it, Where's Wally's creator. He is, in his own way, a visionary. He told me that when he'd started submitting his work to the Royal Academy Summer Exhibition, Carel Weight, the academician, had encouraged him. Weight himself was a visionary, a painter of strange, ghostly presences in wispy, low-roofed, tree-clustered London suburbs. Artists often need other like-minded artists, if only one or two, to help them get on to their track.

Overleaf: Martin Handford, The Battle of Chacabuco (1817), 1978

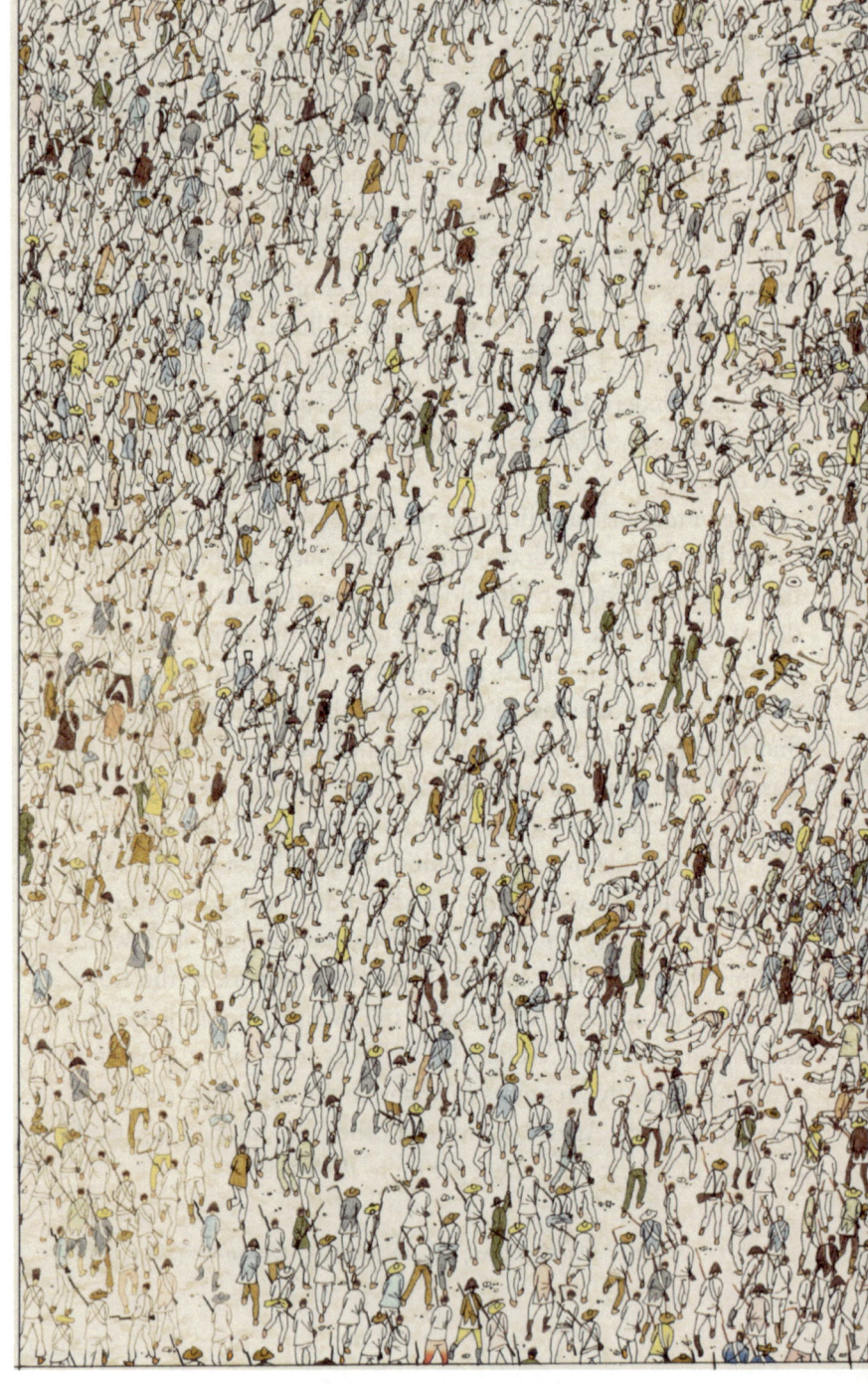

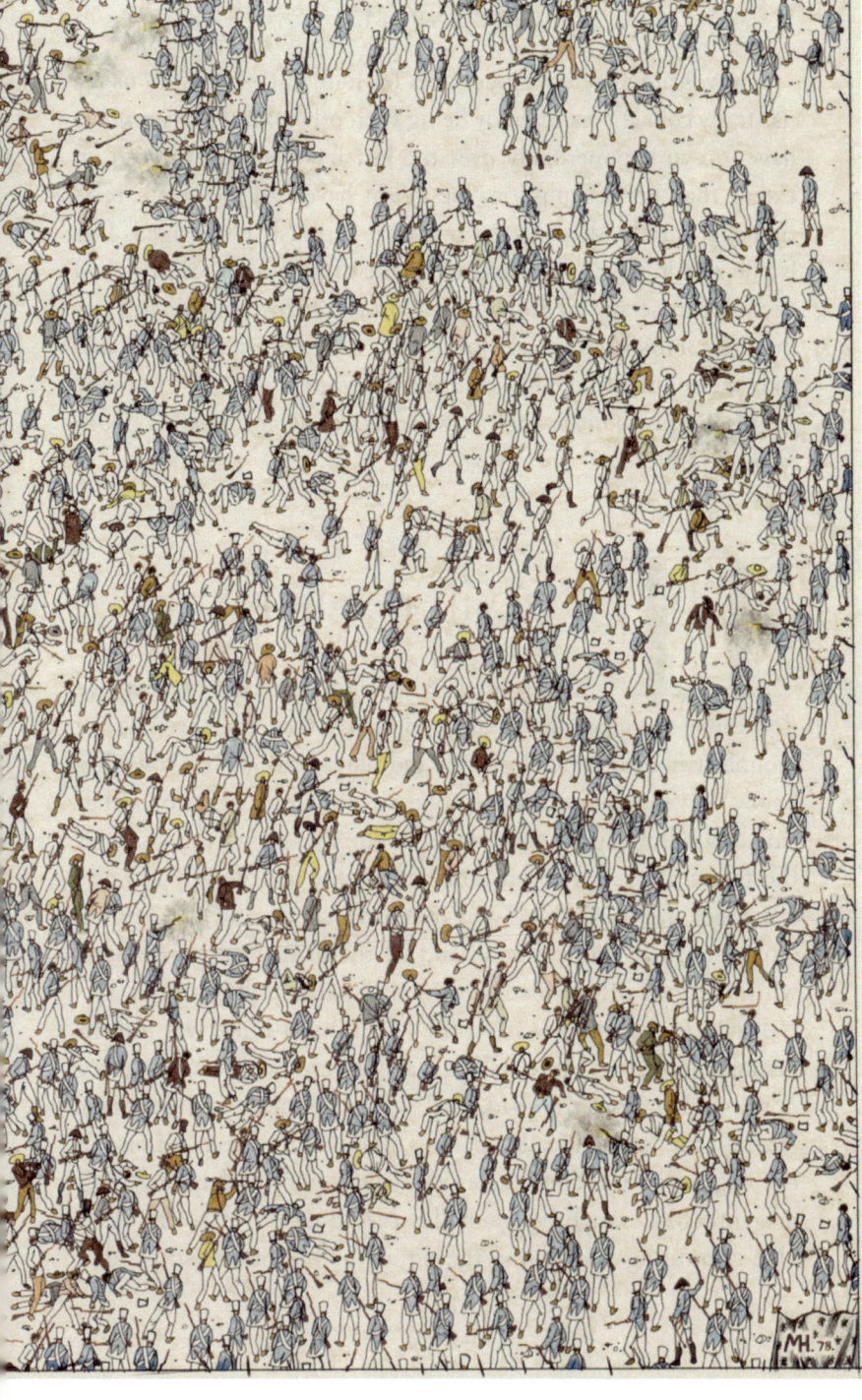

Crowds are not new experiences for humanity—most of us are naturally collective and enjoy being with others. But our numbers have grown exponentially over the last few decades, to such an extent that any assumptions we might have had about our relationship as individuals to the many are seriously challenged. This is one reason why Martin's visual game of hide-and-seek has had such immense appeal around the world. It helps us deal with our numbers. He's become fabulously rich not because anyone wants to make an investment by acquiring his work but because so many people simply want to look at what he's done and buy his books in their millions.

H *is for* DAVID HOCKNEY

It was an amazing sight from the plane as we flew down the coast from San Francisco to Los Angeles. The sky around was absolutely clear, still and blue, as usual, but towering below us was a cliff of black smoke, stretching for miles on either side and billowing up towards us, as the fire ate its way through the forest. I was surprised how narrow the angry red band was at its feet and understood why cats often survive fires by finding a place to hide below ground and let the flames pass over them, while dogs are often killed because they panic and try to run.

David Hockney's house, in the Mulholland Hills, was hidden behind a long, low white wall, just above head height. You can see nothing of it from the road. The surprise comes when you walk through the automatically opening door and find yourself on the top edge of a tree-filled crater, the sides opposite dripping with magenta and orange bougainvillea cascading down to the deep blue swimming pool filling the pit at the bottom. A suspended path led down through the tree's branches to the balconied house half-hidden beneath. It was like walking down into one of Hockney's own paintings, the shadows of the dark brown branches emphasising the dazzling brightness.

Hockney met me on the slope. He was clearly very excited about something. But then he always appeared to be like that, about to explode with his enthusiasm. He is larger in life than he looks in photographs, as if his body had outgrown his boyishness in all directions. He is really quite a big man, but his burning energy makes his movements appear light and suspended, at times even delicate. His blue eyes sparkle within his round-rimmed specks and his mouth, set slightly askew in his round face, always looks as if it is about to or already has broken into a lopsided grin.

'You've seen the fire? You flew over the fire?' he asked in his Bradford drawl, waving aside hallos. I nodded. I've got it on film! I've got it on film! Look!' he said as he rushed me inside, flicking on his big screen:

> I was watching the news, when I saw this. Look! Look! There's my house! Up the coast. Look! Look! See the flames, coming down the mountainside. I couldn't believe it. I flicked on the recorder. I was going to watch my own house burn down!! But look—see that little road. There are the fire engines. See they're stopping! They stopped the flames. Can you believe it? I watched my house being saved!!

His ever-ready appetite for experience was what was so endearing, so catching about him. Peter Goulds, the founder of LA Louver Gallery who was often hanging around, was more down to earth. He told me later Hockney had wanted his house in the hills to burn down so he could build a bigger swimming pool with the insurance and was most disappointed that the fire brigade saved it.

I was over to see Hockney about a dream project I had in

mind for the McLellan Galleries in Glasgow. I had suddenly been handed these galleries to run by the 1990 Year of Culture committee when I arrived to take up my job—they'd never been mentioned to me before. This superb suite of Victorian exhibition galleries, almost as big as those of the Royal Academy in London, was being refurbished for the Year's celebrations. I had to complete the refurbishment—a crazy nightmare in itself—but, worse, programme this colossal space for the foreseeable future without a budget. To my horror, I discovered the whole project had been sold to the council as an income-generating venture—or, at the very least, one that would cover its costs. They'd been told, and fondly believed, that great exhibitions were floating around the world, and the city only had to provide a suitable venue, and the shows would fly in, the public would flock and money would be made. I wanted to refuse to take the McLellan on—I had more than enough to do with the rest of my empire of ten museums and galleries, but Pat Lally put my options bluntly: 'I sacked your predecessor, and I can sack you,' he said, and I got my answer to my refusal before I'd asked it. And part of me, anyway, was sorely tempted to see what I could do, to make big exhibitions really work. But for that I knew I'd need famous names—hence my visit to Hockney in LA. I also wanted to acquire something major by him for the city's collection, and the best way to do that I thought was to involve him in creating an exhibition.

I'd been tremendously impressed by a show of his held at the Hayward Gallery in London called *Hockney Paints the Stage*, an exhibition about all his theatre designs, which then toured the world and was seen by millions—the most popular show he'd ever put on. The exhibits, though, weren't just images of what he'd done, designs in frames, which would have been a bit tame, but reconstructed mini-sets, which visitors could stand in and walk through. Hockney had told me he'd had to repaint most of the sets himself—they couldn't just be made from cut-down theatre flats and props. This gave me the idea.

I suggested he create a walk-through exhibition himself—an installation—which played with spaces, colours, shapes and images. I'd just seen his sets for *Turandot*, which was running at the Los Angeles Opera, and had greatly enjoyed the way he used coloured lights to transform, magically, the mood of the colours before your eyes, and make playful shifts in reverse perspectives, Chinese style. I'd seen several of his productions, from *Ubu Roi* on, and argued that he didn't really need the plays and operas as a starting base but could create a sequence of painted environments to entrance and intrigue visitors himself. 'You're the artist, you can do it,' I argued, and I knew he loved the very act of painting, couldn't stop doing it, and had the energy and persistence of a mountain lion. 'Yes, well,' he said, warming to the idea, 'but the music of *Turandot* is syrup.'

'I like syrup,' I replied.

He laughed, and his look meant we could be in business.

He started working on several individual projects and trial goes at the final visual travelling circus, and he kept me posted with ideas. One was in the Haus der Kunst in Munich, a configuration of lines receding, advancing and climbing—a rope trick on which a number of harlequins, of various sizes, danced and played in space. He dropped me a letter with some photographs. 'Dear Julian, I painted it in one and half days, with a little thought first, but people were very excited by the spaces made ... Perhaps we are thinking too heavily, not enough simple illusion ... keep thinking, Love David.' But the next trial he did was more elaborate and heavier than ever, an immensely complex, abstract, multicoloured painting that curled across the floor and rose halfway up the wall, which he called *Snail's Pace with Vari-Lites*. These top-quality theatre spotlights, with tremendously precise colour rendition, played across his painting in a darkened room in a twenty-minute sequence that was one of the most mesmerising visual experiences I have ever had. I was amazed by the way the space was simply moulded before your eyes—the mysteries of quantum mechanics in action. I realised I could be on the threshold of something really astonishing. I would at last do something artistically creative with the unexpected bonus/nightmare of being handed the McLellan Galleries.

I knew the project would be hugely expensive, but I wasn't worried about that for a minute. If the project got off the ground, the income from the world tour would be immense, not to mention all the marketing spin-offs—the exhibition shop selling signed Hockney prints. The project could go on earning for years if my estimate of its popularity was realised. And, anyway, it was the basic principle I always worked on: money follows ideas. And this I was sure was a very good idea—a Hockney walk-through, visual work of art—like visiting his house, plus, plus, plus ... I was aware, however, that it would need its own independent company to manage the tour. Glasgow Museums couldn't do that. We would benefit from the first showing of the exhibition; income from the subsequent tour, and our collection would be enhanced by the preparatory designs Hockney produced as the whole scheme came to fruition. I commissioned Hubert Bari (see B for Bari) and his team Creamuse to manage the project.

Hubert realised immediately that the problem would be the scale, precision cutting and assembly of the canvases. Hot air balloon technology was his solution—they could cut huge areas of sailcloth to any shape—to build castles in the air, which was what this exhibition was about. Hubert suggested that Hockney, he and I meet in Spain and visit one of the best hot air balloon factories in the world. Hockney was excited by the possibilities, as we watched teams of people cutting and sewing vast areas of canvas. Then the owner asked if we wanted to go up in a balloon—he was test flying a new one that morning. Hubert, of course, had set this up. Hockney was delighted. I declined—I'm not good with heights—and I was even more determined not to go up when I saw the flimsy little woven basket they were climbing into under the vast balloon above, swollen with hot air yet still tethered to the ground. But at the last minute Hockney and Hubert persuaded me to climb in too, and not miss the opportunity of a lifetime. I did, but closed my eyes, not at all sure when or whether I would open them again, if ever.

The sounds of gasps around me tore my lids apart. I was terrified, but astonished. As soon as the ties had been released, without my realising, we had risen silently, without any rush of air, without my feeling anything at all, about a mile into the air. Out of the corner of my eye, I could see the ground far below through the foot holes in the wickerwork basket made so you could climb in with your feet. I didn't dare look down but peered around. There were a few distant threads of clouds. Everything was still and eerily quiet, except for the occasional whoosh of fiery air released by the pilot into the huge balloon floating above. Well, I thought, there's nothing I can do about not dying now, so I may as well enjoy myself, though I still gripped the flimsy basket sides, which rose just above my waist, as if they could be of any help.

Hockney was already enjoying himself immensely, leaning over and almost dancing with delight. I thought something good for the show would come of this, a new perspective in the sequence of galleries—a flying-sensation room, perhaps. The pilot pointed ahead. We were sailing towards a row of low but steep hills, a modest mountain ridge. 'I'll take you right down there,' he said, pointing to the foot of a tree covered slope, 'there should be some good rising thermals there.' We sailed so gracefully and quietly closer and closer, lower and lower until we were almost at ground level.

Hockney suddenly asked, 'How do you steer this thing?'

'You can't,' the pilot replied. I have never seen colour drain so fast from anyone's face. Hockney's eyes, usually wide, suddenly now really stared. 'Don't worry,' the pilot replied, 'I am an Olympic flyer for Spain. Watch.' Suddenly, as we thought we were about to crash into the ground, a current lifted the balloon as if it was a feather and we began to rise up the mountainside, slowly and gently, the basket just scraping the tops of the trees. Hockney, totally recovered from his slight, plummeting scare, flushed again with delight, stretched right out, quick as a flash, to pluck a pine cone from the very top twig of a tree. That was how close we were.

I was totally at ease by this time and watched with delight the shadow of the balloon rise up beneath us, frightening a family of wild boar. Then, suddenly, we rose above the ridge, and were high in the air once more. We sailed for another half an hour or so, watching, from time to time, the team in the Land Rover trying to follow us along the dusty tracks of the flat farmland of Spain. The pilot said he was going to take us down there, pointing to a playing field in front of little village, but just before we touched down, we suddenly rose again, over the roofs—'Missed', he said. Eventually we landed on a field in the u-bend in a river far from anywhere. One thing to go up, a very different thing to come down ... He told us we had to bend our knees as we hit the ground as the basket bounced, and not get out—if we did, the basket could go up again! We bent our knees and stayed put, all glad to be back on solid earth.

Hockney sketched a fine drawing of the flight in the book of his work the pilot had brought for him to sign—in an almost single, elegant line, his mind still in the sky. I spotted, to my delight, the fully grown caterpillar of a Swallowtail butterfly on a branch of fennel as we idled about in the sunshine, waiting for lunch back at the balloon base, and I showed it to Hockney with its brilliant yellow, black-and-white banded body. I remember Hockney looking at it and then at me with surprise. How could I be interested in such things, he seemed to be asking?

I suddenly got an insight into something I should have thought about before. Of course, Hockney's art was about love, as is everyone's. His love of animals extended to his dachshunds but not to insects. But it made me wonder, what would be the line of love in this immense painting project I was encouraging him to undertake? It wouldn't work at all unless it had one. But he wasn't worried; he didn't seem to doubt that one would emerge in time. He was playing with space, colour and illusions—and that was the chief love of his life at that time.

The project looked like plain sailing from then on. Hockney came to Glasgow to look at the McLellan Galleries where the tour would begin. We had on a big retrospective, to date, of Peter Howson's paintings, which Hockney had never seen. He was riveted by them, kept on drawing in his breath with delight at their handling of space. 'I'd come to see the galleries,' he said laughing, 'but I can't stop looking at the art.' Outside we looked at the Mackintosh school, and Greek Thompson's superb buildings. He was impressed by the wide, box-like streets of Glasgow. 'There's a real appreciation of space, here,' he said. He wanted a model of the galleries to work on the project in LA. We sent him one. Then, after a bit, everything went quiet.

We had a mutual acquaintance in Jonathan Silver, a dapper fellow with swept-back hair and a lively stare. He was a Bradford-born entrepreneur of German Jewish descent, who had a chain of menswear shops, with one in Sheffield, where I bought my suits. They were elegantly cut, of good cloth and remarkably reasonable in price—quality for everyone. With typical imaginative flair and foresight, he bought Salts Mill, a huge, handsome Victorian industrial complex at Saltaire in Bradford and turned it into a commercial and arts complex, which has now been recognised, largely due to his efforts, by UNESCO as a World Heritage Site.

Hockney told me how he was being pestered by this fellow from Bradford to open a gallery of his work in this industrial complex. I was an enthusiast for the scheme. I loved the idea of modern art being 'in the streets', and admired Jonathan's enterprise. I remembered opening my jacket and showing Hockney the Jonathan Silver label (in the days when labels were worn inside). Anyway, whether I had any influence or not I can't say, but Hockney eventually agreed to Jonathan's proposal and the two became very close friends. Saltaire is still a major showcase for Hockney's work.

Jonathan fell ill in 1995, and David painted him a get-well card of sunflowers. He propped the painting up beside the vase and painted the bottom of the vase on a piece of paper lying flat in front. He was so startled by the effect that he made a photographic print of the whole assembly (opposite). I was equally impressed when I saw it. The painted flowers look more real than the real ones. They radiate their own life and light and, amazingly, appear to be standing in their own, imaginative space in front of the real flowers, though they are in fact behind. I remember, rather childishly, clapping my hands with delight, and suggesting to David that he call the print *Photography is Dead, Long Live Painting*. We'd just been discussing the impact of digital photography on this art form and on Cartier-Bresson. Photography isn't dead, of course, but it certainly hasn't killed off painting as some, like John Berger, had thought. David hesitated for a second—he's nothing if not political, mentally racing through the implications—and then said OK. He also told me that he'd been in such a hurry to

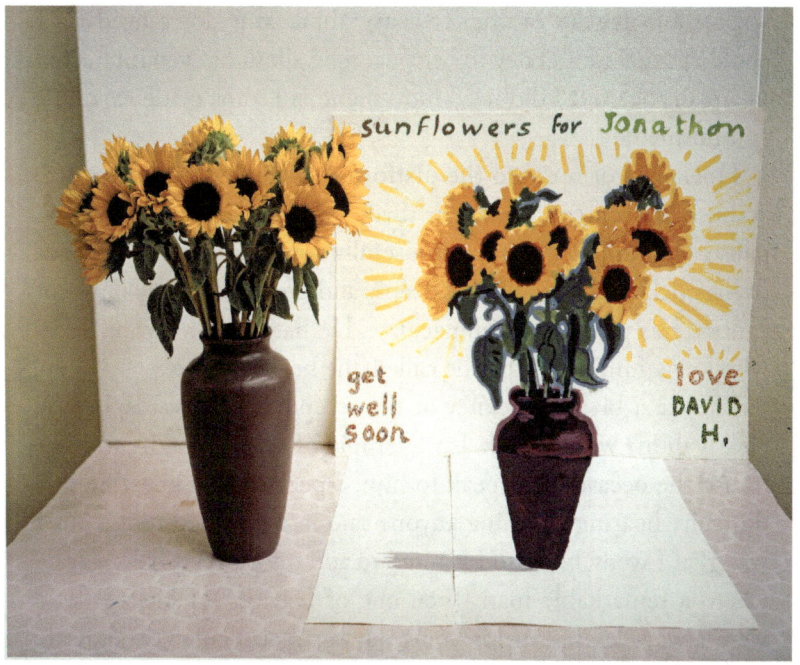

David Hockney, Photography Is Dead. Long Live Painting, 1995

get the card off to Jonathan, that he hadn't looked at the assembly long enough. He realised later that he should have laid a brush across the sheet of paper and the table to make the composition and the significance of the illusion complete.

Tragically, Jonathan died when he was only forty-eight. I went to the funeral, in part, I had to admit, because Hockney had told me he'd been there, and I'd get a chance to talk to him about our project, which had gone quiet. I was getting a bit anxious because I'd earmarked nearly a quarter of a million pounds to get it off the ground, and it's very difficult to carry that sort of money over in a budget from year to year in the public sector. If you don't spend your budget up to the hilt in the financial year, the socially responsible hawks in the Treasury think you don't need it. I couldn't expect Hockney to be concerned about or even interested in any of that, but I did need movement and some evidence of his commitment.

Hockney got up onto the platform—there was quite a crowd. A hush descended. 'Jonathan died,' he said—there was a long pause while he slowly and purposefully fished a packet of fags out of his pocket, lit one, inhaled deeply and breathed slowly out—'of cancer.' His timing was immaculate. He hated, as everyone knew who knew him well, what he called 'the health police'.

I spoke a bit to Hockney at the reception afterwards, but he clearly didn't want to talk. It was stupid of me, I thought, to want to use the occasion to speak to him, especially as I knew he had difficulty hearing anything anyone said in a crowded room, but I was glad I went, because I wanted to add my pennyworth of tribute to a remarkable man. Then one of David's sidekicks—there were always 'extras' in his court—I wasn't a regular enough attender to know them all by name—came up to me purposefully and, quite simply and directly, said, 'Forget it. David won't do that project.' He'd clearly been sent. I was not entirely taken aback, because I'd suspected a cooling, but I couldn't hide my disappointment and my frustration. 'Why couldn't he have told me so himself?' I asked, perhaps a bit peevishly, but understandably. 'Oh,' he replied, 'David doesn't like saying no.' That was it.

I thought a lot later about why it hadn't taken off. Had I overestimated Hockney's imagination? I'd greatly admired his drawings—that show we'd put on years ago in Sheffield was stunning. I remember afterwards hanging one of the drawings we bought from it next to an etching we had by Van Dyck. They sang together across the centuries, with their lucid linear visual intelligence.

Then I also greatly admired his early paintings, when he was (difficult though it is to imagine now) a closet gay, at the time when homosexuality was still illegal in the UK. He painted images of the boys he loved, like Peter C (which I bought for Manchester City Art Galleries), in a lavatory-wall graphic style, his bare finger pointing to the bit of him Hockney was most interested in, framed in two sections showing Hockney's early interest in different perspectives, while painting his own profile as a shadowy image behind, the hidden love that cannot speak its name. One of these early, painful paintings, such as *We 2 Boys Together Clinging*, deserves to hang in the National Gallery (if they would only reverse their decision to close their collections at 1900), as a tribute not just to Hockney, but to the crucial struggle for gay rights at that time.

After that Hockney went to LA, where he could be himself, fly free so to speak, and then oddly, but understandably, his art became much easier, conventional and representational. This was when he painted his most famous summations of his new rich gay life—naked men swimming, climbing out of and splashing into rippling pools in crisp Californian sunshine. His lines lost their nervous edge but still had tension, playing between the flat surface of the picture and the depth within, between the observer standing at the edge of the pool, watching, and the swimmer embroiled within its sensual flow. It was this continual exploration of the nature of consciousness, detachment and involvement, manifest in the play between two-dimensional and three-dimensional space, which is the major recurring theme in all his later work, that I hoped that Hockney could develop on a public stage, in the huge project I had in mind, combined with his love of theatre and eagerness to entertain, his sheer fun and exuberance, and his endless ability to cover acres of canvas with brushed pigment. But the idea, in the end, didn't get a taproot, and only sporadically flowered.

We were talking one day about Disney's *The Lion King*, which

I'd just seen. So had Hockney, and he suddenly reached for a sheet of paper and he said, 'I'll show you what's wrong with the Lion King. The lion has no balls.' And he sketched with typical beautiful ease the back view of a lion. 'This is what a lion looks like from the back, and what you notice most ...', and he drew, perfectly, two large, smooth balls squeezed out between its thighs. We both laughed. It (they) said it all. He added, holding the drawing in his hand, 'What do I do with this?' Of course, I should have seized my opportunity, and suggest he gave it to me—it could have been the back cover of this book—but I didn't and he let it fall into a drawer, where presumably it remains, somewhere in his massive archive.

In a way, perhaps, both of us lacked balls, like Disney's Lion King. On the one hand, I should have persisted and insisted on the challenge I was offering—to interest and entertain a wide public in a new way, artistically, making painting that was both popular and profound—a form of modern, visual, all-encompassing Baroque. I shouldn't have allowed myself to be brushed aside by a member of his court. Hockney, on the other hand, could have had more confidence in his ability to think creatively and critically. But all this is pointless, for there is no 'should' in art. Yet I still regret that this project didn't take off. At least, Hockney has carried on painting. As he wryly commented after he got a critical review of one of his shows, 'At least I paint my pictures myself.' That's something to be thankful for in an era of bland, brand factory production—an artist committed to the personal touch.

His performance reminded me of his brother. We'd put on a show a long time before, in Sheffield, of Hockney's drawings. His brother came to open it. Paul was a smaller version of David, with undyed, still black hair and was the Lord Mayor of Bradford. Bradford at that time was proud of being one of the first clean-air cities in Britain, along with Sheffield, when all its old black-grimed industrial buildings were cleaned, and the stone gleamed. But, unlike the steel mills of Sheffield, its textiles industry had attracted an influx of Ugandan Asians fleeing the murdering regime of President Idi Amin. I asked Paul if he needed a mike at the opening. 'Oh no,' he said, as he stepped forward, bellowing at the top of his voice in his rich Yorkshire drawl, 'I come from Bradford where the buildings used to be black and the people white.' The word white is particularly drawn out in a Bradford accent, sounding more like 'whyat'. By the time that word had ended, the laughter and the gasps of horror had erupted.

J *is for* JACK JONES

One of the most moving artistic experiences of my life was when I first watched the Durham Miner's Gala. You hear the miners' bands playing before you see them approaching from pits in all directions. Then they come into sight over the hills, marching down into the city under their huge banners— music and visual art combined. The paintings waving in the wind, as they draw close, are as colourfully triumphant as the sounds: oil paintings on vast sheets of silk, suspended between poles, with borders as decorative as any fairground or canal barge, framing realistic scenes of workers painted by the miners themselves. We'd recently put on a show at the Durham Light Infantry Museum and Arts Centre (one of my first jobs), selected by the curator, artist and critic Bill Feaver, of the Ashington Colliery painters—an amateur group of artists formed in the 1920s who painted simple, vivid, small-scale scenes of their everyday lives. But here, swaying before my eyes, was the much older, wider cultural tradition from which their art had come.

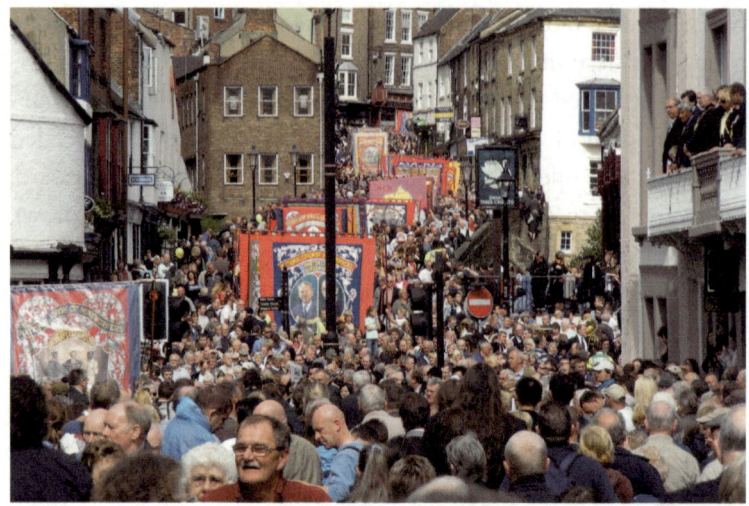

The Durham Miners' Gala, 2008

I was then immediately intrigued when, a decade later, the town clerk of Manchester forwarded me a letter he'd received from the director of the National Museum of Labour History in London. He wondered if Manchester would be interested in helping them find a new home for their museum. Tower Hamlets, the borough in which they were located, was no longer in Labour control, and their future in Limehouse Town Hall, they claimed, was insecure. I knew the collection well—it housed the oldest and some of the finest trade union banners. If this museum wasn't to be in London, its natural home, the next best place for it was in Manchester. What's more there was a vacant listed building waiting for it just down the road from the City Art Gallery—the Manchester Mechanic's Institute where the first Trades Union Congress (TUC) was held in 1868. Everything seemed to fit. I thought if I got the city to say 'yes', the rest would be plain sailing. Little did I realise that it would take me some years to sort out and lead me into the dirty underworld of left-wing double-dealing.

Graham Stringer, the leader of Manchester City Council, gave me the nod to begin to negotiate, in his usual undemonstrative way. I have rarely known such a quiet-spoken or so thoughtful a politician. He always looked as if he'd prefer to be playing some powerful, silent sport, like squash on a court, rather than talking in the City Chamber. So I went to see Terry McCarthy, the curator/director of the museum who'd written the letter, to begin discussions. His actual role was unclear, which proved a blessing in the long run. He was a dapper fellow, of medium height and build, like me, but wore a snappy, dark three-piece suit with a fob-chain drooping from his upper waistcoat pocket. He looked as if he'd just stepped out of a novel by Dickens and spoke with a strong London accent to boot.

To my surprise, he didn't seem at all pleased to see me. He kept on muttering about the difficulties of the move, so much so that I said, if you're not interested in coming to Manchester, I'm not interested in spending my time talking to you. 'No, no, of course we want to come,' he replied, hurriedly, 'it's just that it's complicated.' He told me he'd never managed a move like this, and there would be his board to convince. We'll invite them all up, I said, if you'll give me a list of who they are. We left it like that, and I went to look round the museum, my interest distinctly cooled by his oddly unwelcoming manner.

But my enthusiasm revived as I looked at the collection. The banners were superb, so were the hundreds of posters and photographs. This was the greatest, most genuine and spontaneous socialist art at the heart of the movement's nascence. And the museum had the oldest trade union banner in the world—the Liverpool Tin-plate Workers' banner of 1821. But I was worried about their condition—banners are a conservation nightmare, being painted on silk and waved about, for years, in all weathers. I could see why Terry was worried about the move, but why, then, had he set this ball rolling?

I'd put on a show when I was in Sheffield of John Gorman's collection of trade union banners to celebrate the launch of his very fine book *Banner Bright*. It was wonderful to see them all hanging from the ceiling in the Mappin Art Gallery, in Gallery 5, the large modern space at the back, built to replace the rooms lost in the Blitz. The ceiling there is low, so you could see the banners up close. Many were huge, superb, decorative creations, inset with sensitively painted scenes of labourers at work, the whole waving ensembles ringing with pride and hope, bringing back to life for me that bright summer day of the Miner's Gala in Durham.

All I wanted to do was to turn the museum into a museum, but that exposed me to accusations of being a middle-class intellectual. I was portrayed as killing off the authentic working-class spirit of the museum. McCarthy sold himself as a brother labourer at the mill. No one believed I came from a South London council estate, because I didn't sound like I did. I'd once been caught in the wrong part of the estate—it was divided into gang territories. The leader of the territory I was in, as his gang circled me, asked me why I didn't talk like them. I replied, 'Because I listen to the Third Programme' (as Radio Three used to be called in those days). They were bewildered for a moment, and I took the opportunity to run—I was very good at that, then.

I realised I had to get the board on to Manchester's side. The great and the good of the Labour Party were on it, including the then leader, Michael Foot, and barons of the trades union movement, such as Jack Jones and Clive Jenkins, but there were also stalwart supporters of McCarthy, like the MP Gwyneth Dunwoody, who believed implicitly everything he told them. She came up to Manchester, I found out later, purposefully to rubbish the move. I got a note from Graham Stringer before she arrived, saying, with typical brevity, 'Gwyneth likes to eat.' But she didn't want to stay even for lunch, which was the clearest signal I could have of the motive for her visit. 'One of the troubles is,' Graham said, 'you're trying to preserve a history that the top echelon in the Labour Party is now trying to distance itself from.'

Jack Jones clocked the games that were being played. He was a tall upright man with—I know it sounds a bit sycophantic, but it's true—an almost noble bearing, and an ease of manner that belied the quickness of his mind. He became a great ally, almost a friend. Nothing he ever said suggested he was interested in art, but he could see the value of the banners, and the relevance of their history. He encouraged me to ring him whenever I was uncertain about something and, my goodness, were there wriggles! I'd never seen a performance like it. Jack told me to phone him even when he was on holiday. He always went to the same caravan site. I had to let him know when I would ring—it was the days before mobile phones—so he could stand by the phone box when I called. He was always to the point and knew exactly what to do. Together we secured the future of this remarkable museum.

After a crucial meeting of the board, when they appointed me as acting secretary of the museum, there was a poignant moment. We were all getting in a lift. I was the last, outside, hesitating to see if there was room. Michael Foot turned to make space for me. He already looked like a skeleton warmed up, with that floppy lock of hair that today would make Boris Johnson proud. We looked at each other for a second. Then he said, 'Do we trust you to run a lift?' It was gracious admission of his own previous misjudgement of my capabilities.

With McCarthy gone, the project began to run. Clive Jenkins was the new chair. He was head of the new Manufacturing, Science and Finance Union (MSF), an ebullient small Welshman, with a precision accent and astonishing energy, who, at that time, went on and on about how wonderful Tasmania was to anyone who would listen. Clive got into his stride. He'd met Lord Charteris, former private secretary to the Queen, now provost of Eton, at a posh banquet, and they'd chatted about Labour history. Charteris told him that the boys of Eton had been given a project during the General Strike of 1926 (the one my grandfather played a role in) to collect all the announcements, all the ephemera issued by the strike leaders from their headquarters, and these were still in the school, stored in two tuck boxes. It was a perfect instance of how the establishment runs Britain, by keeping a close eye on things. Clive asked him if they'd give the boxes to the National Museum. Charteris thought, why not, so the gift was arranged.

Clive organised a press conference with photographers for the handover in his luxurious apartment on the top floor of the MSF offices. He offered to send a car for Jack, but he preferred to take the tube. I was present as the official. The boxes were there, cameras and press at the ready. Lord Charteris was expected, when a telephone call came through, saying unfortunately he'd been delayed, and couldn't make it. The photographers started packing up. There wasn't a story without the people. Clive's face crumpled. Jack leaned over and whispered in his ear, 'You must remember, Clive, the upper classes always let you down.'

My last engagement at the National Museum, before they appointed a director, was at a meeting when the National Union of Railwaymen (NUR) handed over a lot of material. They were all there, standing in a circle—Clive and Jack, not Michael, but Neil Kinnock, the new leader of the Labour Party, and new supporters, including John Monks (who'd proved a great help in the last stages), Jimmy Knapp of the NUR and Norman Willis, head of the TUC, a big roly-poly fellow with the persistent energy of a falling boulder. There was a slight pause in the chat, when Neil suddenly pointed at me and said, 'That man removed Terry McCarthy.' It wasn't an achievement I particularly wanted to be savoured. I remembered something. 'Oh, I saw him recently on the tube,' I said. 'He was coming up on one escalator as I was going down.' He said as we crossed, "No hard feelings."' Norman Willis, unable to resist a joke with an innuendo, quipped, 'I hope you replied, "speak for yourself."'

The museum opened in Manchester in 1990 and is now called the People's History Museum.

L *is for* PAT LALLY

Councillor Pat Lally, twice Labour leader, then Lord Provost of Glasgow, wasn't personally interested in art, yet he enabled more artists to reach their public than anyone I have ever known. He is difficult to describe because he was a complex character, and this was manifest in every aspect of his nature, including his appearance. He was taller and larger near to than you would think from a distance, had a high domed, bald head with usually wayward hairs sprouting over his ears, a rounded face, a large nose, a slightly receding chin and, more often than not, a wide grin. His lower eyelids had, rather disconcertingly, sunk to reveal the blood-veined sockets of his eyes which you couldn't help noticing while he, all the time, was peering at you, out of the small, restless, black pupils above. His wit made him dominant. He'd been ousted twice from the Labour leadership, but got back in again twice, which is why they nicknamed him Lazarus but, as he quipped, 'Lazarus only done it once.'

He didn't vote for me on the interview panel, I was told. I never discussed this with him after. Unfortunately, the proper occasion never arose. Perhaps he thought I was too left-wing; he was instinctively wary of officers meddling with politics, and, if they did have opinions, preferred those who were more to the right, whom he could argue with and tell what to do. As a public servant, I'd never joined any political party; I thought it was important to keep these things separate. But it was pretty clear where my sympathies lay.

I'm basically in agreement with Ruskin that 'government and cooperation are in all things the laws of life; anarchy and competition the laws of death.' I wouldn't have been in public service if I weren't. But the actual delivery of those goals is complex and riven with ironies, and have become increasingly so, as 'right wing' and 'left wing' have lost their clarities as opposite poles as we face the increasingly complex problems of saving our round world as a whole. Or perhaps it was more likely that Lally knew I'd got the majority vote, so pretended to go against it, to keep his options open if I put a foot wrong. But in the end, after some close shaves, we had the best working relationship I've enjoyed with any politician in my life.

Graham Stringer, leader of Manchester City Council, had warned me when I took the Glasgow job, that I was entering 'the small world of Scottish politics'. It's true, this got me in the end, but fortunately my time with Pat was in between. I'd applied for Glasgow because the city had just been awarded the status as European Capital of Culture, and they urgently needed someone to run the arts programme in their art galleries and museums—all eleven of them, including the recently opened, world famous Burrell Collection. It was a tremendous opportunity to make a splash, and boost this great service, bigger than any in Britain, including all the national galleries and museums, for the long term.

The only reason why Glasgow had been made European Capital of Culture was because Mrs Thatcher had abolished London.

It was in the early days of the idea—the accolade has now drib-
bled away, as Europe has run out of capitals, and other host cities
had to be found. Thatcher wasn't very fond of government, and
local government in particular. She saw the impressive County
Hall, headquarters of the Greater London Council, emblazoned
with London's rising unemployment figures (a typically provocative gesture of its leader, Ken Livingstone) across the Thames
from the Houses of Parliament, and said, 'We'll close that.' And
she did. An unforeseen consequence was that London couldn't
make a proposal to be a European Capital of Culture when it
became Britain's turn in 1990, simply because London no longer
existed. Glasgow leapt in, with typical cheek, and Richard Luce,
the minister of arts at the time, told me that the government had
no choice but to accept its proposal.

Melina Mercouri, Greek's minister of culture, whose idea it
was to hold this event, was furious. These capitals were supposed
to be capitals, not just cities of culture, beginning with Athens,
Florence (an exception, but Rome might be considered a poor sister to Florence as far as culture is concerned), Amsterdam, West
Berlin (before the Wall fell), Paris then ... err ... Glasgow. Melina
Mercouri was looking forward to being photographed in front of
the Parthenon Marbles in the British Museum, and arguing, now
that we were in the single community of Europe, they should be
returned to Greece. But instead she had to come to Glasgow.

She walked, late, into a banquet in the great hall at Kelvingrove
wearing a long white, body-hugging gown. She looked glorious,
as if she had just stepped down from the Erechtheion, a slow
moving Ancient Greek marble herself. She came and sat down
at the smallish round table where I was sitting; as director of the
galleries, I had a prime place. I was busy talking to junior member
of the French Cultural Ministry, an attractive young woman, and
we were getting on so well I asked her if there was any hidden

meaning in the huge geometric symbols President Mitterand was planting across Paris—the arch at la Défense, the sphere at La Villette, the pyramid at the Louvre and the up-turned table in the new National Library. Rumours I'd heard were that they were masonic. 'Bof!', she threw her hands in the air, and turned away.

I turned to my other neighbour, Mary Robinson, soon to be president of Ireland, explaining how I seemed to have, unintentionally, offended my other neighbour. She smiled. She is one of Mitterrand's mistresses, she explained. I can have an alarmingly loud and sudden laugh, which I emitted at that moment. Melina turned to me. 'Oh, I love a man with laugh,' she said in her gloriously husky voice. We got on very well immediately. There was a slight hiatus when she told me she was thinking of returning to the stage, the English stage, and asked me what part I thought she could play. I suggested, on the spur of the moment, Lady Macbeth—how I could have done so, I still don't know—but it's true, the way she was looking at me now she would indeed have made a wonderful Lady Macbeth. There was a silence. Richard Luce, the minister of arts, who was sitting between Mary and Melina, slid further under the table—he was already a little under—in dreaded anticipation. But Melina smiled. 'Lady Macbeth?' she asked. 'Oh, I was thinking of Cleopatra—she was a mature woman when she met Anthony.' Peace was restored.

She spoke to me seriously after the dinner, about the Elgin Marbles, of course. I told her I had spoken out publicly in favour of their return—they were part of one work of art, and needed to be re-united, as far as possible in a neighbouring museum. I explained some of the difficulties, and discussed strategies. She said, at the end, stroking one cheek, 'You may kiss me here.' I did. I didn't know at the time that she was dying of cancer and had a nurse standing by wherever she went. Richard Luce told me she was famous for never staying until the end of dinner, but on this occasion ... he looked at me a little wearily. I still dream that one day that offer of a kiss to a Brit will be paid back by the return of these wonderful treasures (see M for Neil MacGregor).

It was Lally's drive that got Glasgow the 1990 crown, in his determination to refocus the identity of the post-industrial city. In 1900 half the ships afloat around the world had been built along the banks of the Clyde—it was this wealth that had been turned into the art treasures in its museums, especially the Burrell—but ninety years later, almost none. I thought the city might want me to work on an idea for an Industrial Museum when I got there. But Lally turned away when I mentioned it; he wouldn't even begin to talk about it. Bill English, the city treasurer standing at his side, discreetly pulled the lining out of his trouser pocket. It was the clearest signal I have ever been given to drop an idea. And with relief, I did.

I had, however, said at my interview that we needed more money for modern art. Glasgow had some of the best living painters in Britain, but the service only had £50,000 a year to spend on acquisitions for all of its eleven museums. Interviews are vital occasions for making future bids. A few of the interview panel glanced at Pat Lally when I made my bid, but all he did was to stare straight ahead. At least he hadn't shaken his head. However, the fact that he hadn't voted for me didn't bode well.

I didn't meet him again until I'd been in the job a couple of weeks. I'd been invited to an official banquet held on the stage of the opera after the performance—a typical Glasgow late-nighter. It was a double invitation, so, mid-divorce, I'd taken along Norma Johnson, an eminent painting restorer, an old colleague of mine who'd I'd worked with in Sheffield and found again on my staff in Glasgow. To my surprise we were seated at Pat's small, round table in the centre. The labels on our plates read Mr and Mrs Spalding. I thought I'd better explain. 'She's not my wife,' I said to Pat.

'I didn't ask whose wife she was,' came his instant reply. I liked him from then on.

There had been a march through the streets on the day I arrived, not big but enough to be photographed, carrying a banner 'Spalding Go Home'. They were presumably thinking of the immensely popular jingoistic, anti-English song, 'Flower of Scotland', composed in the 1960s by Roy Williamson of the Corries, which is sung at most football and rugby matches and celebrated the Scots' last victory over the English at the Battle of Bannockburn, in 1314, when Robert the Bruce sent Edward II's army 'homeward, tae think again'. A reporter rang me to ask what I thought of this march against me. I replied, 'I guess it's Glasgow's way of saying hullo.' It's true I was the first non-Scottish director of Glasgow Museums since their foundation in 1854, but I hadn't anticipated what an uphill struggle I'd have to prove myself just because I was English.

Lally didn't know much about art, but he knew what he didn't like. The Strathclyde Regional Council had commissioned the Scottish artist Ian McCulloch to paint a mural as a gift to the new Glasgow Concert Hall, which was being built for the 1990 celebrations. It arrived and was installed, a huge conflagration of slabs of bright colour interlaced with lines, a sort of agro-Dufy. Lally took one look and said, 'We don't have to accept a gift,' and demanded it be removed, and told me to find a replacement that would suit. I was very careful not to make any comment on the McCulloch, and won't now, except to say that it certainly didn't go with the carpet, but that wasn't necessarily its fault.

I pondered the thought of taking the opportunity to organise a community arts project. Until I came to Glasgow, I'd been rather guarded about community arts, which were the burgeoning rage among the left at that time. I was all for community involvement and participation (see C is for President Jacques Chirac) but creation requires single-minded dedication and concentration, imagination and invention, a journey into the unknown which is a territory difficult to walk into hand-in-hand. I was fond of a saying what my old friend in Sheffield, Dave Godin, the music impresario who coined the term 'Northern Soul', used to say, as a profoundly egalitarian, gay vegetarian, 'Democracy in everything; dictatorship in the arts.' Most profound art today is a lonely journey into individual experience; the artist can't take anyone with them quite simply because they don't know where they're going, nor what they will discover. The arts of Francis Davison and Eduard Bersudsky, examined in this book, are just two vivid contemporary demonstrations of such solitary journeys, both proving how various and unpredictable genuine artistic creativity is.

Obviously some arts can be collectively creative to a greater or lesser extent: improvised jazz most famously, but also much modern drama, dance and film. Going to Glasgow made me wonder whether visual art couldn't be collective too; the whole place had such a vibrant, communal atmosphere. Mackintosh had worked collectively with his wife, as I was keen to show. And I remembered walking gingerly along the rooftop of Southwell Minster in Nottinghamshire with the stonemason who was continually repairing it. I admired a carving of a bird on nest between two buttresses. He rather shyly admitted, 'Oh, I did that.' I realised then, of course, that all great religious buildings around the world have always been collective visual expressions. And the sight of the Bayeux Tapestry had amazed me: hundreds of individual hands sewing joy and agony, defeat and victory, inch by inch, for over two hundred feet, collectively.

So I was delighted and excited to discover, when I came to Glasgow, an extremely lively and active community arts group, called Needleworks, celebrating local history, identity and experiences. It had been established by Clare Higney, a small, motherly woman with penetrating eyes and a deep, gravelly voice that always harboured a laugh. She later, under her married name, Clare Hunter, wrote fascinating books, *Threads of Life*—a global view of sewing expression, and *Embroidering her Truth*—how Mary, Queen of Scots, used textiles to show her feelings. Clare, together with the textile artist Malcolm Lochhead, organised/inspired a great sequence of twelve community tapestries, called 'Keeping Glasgow in Stitches' (the laughter always rumbling), which, when they were hung all round the great hall in Kelvingrove Art Gallery, were, I thought, one of the best, most lasting things to come out of the 1990 celebrations as a whole.

But I wasn't at all sure, if four huge community banners would go with the carpet in the Concert Hall, either. So, I took the easier and, I admit, easier to manage option, and used the opportunity to celebrate the work of the four outstanding living painters, the so-called 'New Glasgow Boys', Ken Currie, Steven Campbell, Adrian Wiszniewski and Peter Howson. The paintings they did have lasted very well against the passing of time: Steven's jewelled dream of the opera singer Dame Joan Sutherland, Adrian's lyrical, androgynous quartet, the brute force of Peter's boxer (he'd originally done a drummer, but painted it on the panel the wrong way up, horizontal not vertical, so that's what we got, second try, standing up) and Ken's haunting and haunted quiet choir in a sepulchral wood, the most memorable of the lot.

Unbeknownst to me Sandy Stoddart, a fiercely traditionalist sculptor based in Paisley, a throw-back to the eighteenth century, created a three-metre-high herm (a portrait head on a pillar, in this case without protruding male genitalia at the appropriate height) of Lally, as a celebration of his stand against modern art. I saw it and liked it; it was at the same time funny and a remarkably good likeness, so I bought it for the museum. Lally's political

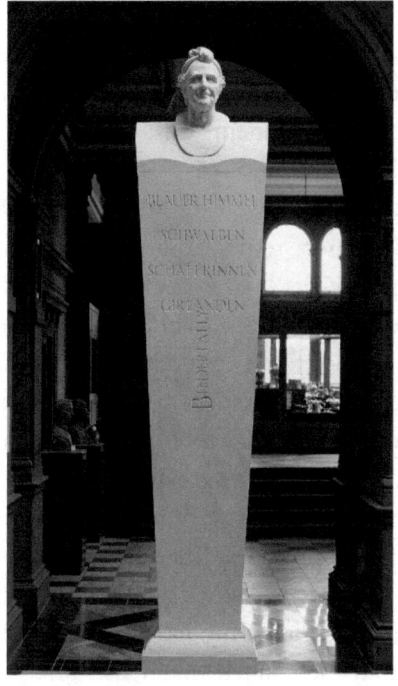

Alexander Stoddart, Biederlally, 1992–93

opponents were furious—they thought I was putting him on a pedestal—but I wasn't. I was just responding to a very interesting artistic debate—and I liked Stoddart's work and this, I thought, was his best sculpture to date. Lally was highly amused. He went round telling everyone, 'I haven't seen it myself, but I hear I've got a bigger bust than Dolly Parton.'

The fact that I could buy this sculpture was due to Lally himself. Just before we all broke up for Christmas at the end of 1990, Pat called me into his office. 'I've got a present for you. You said in your interview you needed more money to buy modern art. Would £3 million do? You can't spend it all at once. But we'll put it into an investment fund, so you can spend the income from it every year.' I was, for once, too surprised to speak. It was a very big vote of confidence in me, but it may well have contained other agendas. There could well be, in the next coming months, a major backlash from Lally's political opponents if there were any major shortfalls in anticipated income from 1990.

I'd expected that the huge exhibition *The Words and the Stones*, which wasn't my direct responsibility, though I had (against my wishes) been put on its board, could lose about £4 million. I'd sent Lally a letter about this, which the chief executive, Steve Hamilton, said he'd refused to receive (though he had agreed to change the show's title to *Glasgow's Glasgow*, because of the original's unfortunate acronym). Steve allowed me, however, to keep him informed, privately, of my growing concerns. When the sums were done, I was proved exactly right, and, as the only council officer on the exhibition's board, I had to face the whole council, in full session, to be cross-examined as to how the exhibition could have cost so much. I knew my job was on the line, but so, too, was Lally's. I told the council that I had foreseen this shortfall. John Young, the leader of the Conservatives, asked me the crucial question: 'If you were so concerned, why didn't you tell your political masters?' I thought of that letter, returned. I had no option but to say, I thought it was sufficient to tell the chief executive. The breath of relief on the Lally benches was almost audible. I'd earned my £3 million.

I started spending the anticipated income from the fund at once (you can do that in local government financing) and after a couple of years said to Lally, 'We'll need a Gallery of Modern Art to put all this stuff in.'

'Oh,' he replied, 'I hadn't thought of that.'

A memo came round asking if any department had a use for the superb neoclassical Royal Exchange building bang in the city centre, which housed a library in its basement, while its ground and upper floors were going to rot. A strong faction in the city wanted it to be sold off, but I'd heard Lally was determined to keep it in the public sector. I looked at it, and realised it could make a superb, if totally unconventional Gallery of Modern Art. Location, location, location, as they say about real estate in the USA. I made a proposal, knowing we only had £6 million to spend (this was before the National Lottery was suddenly forced on a reluctant UK government by the laws of the European Union—had the project been conceived only a couple of years later, I'd have built a spanking new building on a brownfield site). Lally jumped at the idea, and we were all set for opening in 1996.

Then Lally lost his leadership once again, and Councillor Jean McFadden, his arch-rival in the Labour Party, took over. She was a genuinely nice person, a lecturer by profession, with a charming, self-effacing smile, and a very precise use of grammar. She once interrupted me when I was presenting my annual budget to the finance committee, which she chaired even during Lally's leadership, 'Mr Spalding,' she said politely, 'you're getting your tenses confused.' I was. She was on the modernising wing of the Labour Party, which was all the rage then with the advent of Tony Blair. Lally was Old Labour, a diehard working-class politician, having left school at thirteen, and earned his living in the men's clothing business before becoming a councillor full time. I once asked him what the 'new' meant in New Labour. He replied, 'I have no idea. All I know it doesn't mean anything I've been fighting for all my life.'

I heard, via the eminent local journalist, Ruth Wishart, that Jean, on getting power, was determined to stop the Gallery of Modern Art. I immediately hung banners between the front pillars of the building, which was being refurbished at the time, announcing its opening date. Lally went a step further. He'd already had the foresight to get the opening of the gallery into the royal engagement diary. He rose in the Council Chamber and said, 'I hear there's some idea to stop the Gallery of Modern Art. The Queen's coming to open it. Are we going to ask her to close it?' The chamber erupted in laughter. The gallery went ahead, and the Queen did indeed come (see Q for the Queen).

The story of the Gallery of Modern Art is a book in itself, which I wrote at that time. Suffice to say here that I was trying to do something very different from the usual run of contemporary art galleries around the world. For a start I rejected the word 'contemporary' with the implication that 'modern' is now confined to history, as if we're past all that! Contemporary simply means contemporaneous with anything and is meaningless in itself. Modern is a much broader concept, and we're still I think in the modern age, certainly as far as art is concerned—we've only really just begun to explore Picasso. It's also a shorter word and could be carved on the front of the gallery (see Lida Cardozo Kindersley, p. 282).

Also, modern is a more lasting concept—contemporary is fleeting, gone before you can begin to contemplate it. I was against this whole trend to turn art galleries into temporary exhibition venues, shifting installations, started by Nick Serota at the Tate, with his yearly programme of New Displays. I was a great advocate of collection centres, away from expensive city centres, where the museum's exhibits could be used as a resource, not just by the museum but by others (as in my concept of the Open Museum), but not to the point of turning galleries into ephemeral temporary exhibition spaces.

I wanted GoMA, as it soon came to be called, to be like a tree in the centre of the city, changing and growing, as trees do gradually, with exotic birds and animals flying into them from time to time. That's why I kept its temporary exhibition space deliberately small. We held some jewel-like shows there, such as Pierre et Gilles, the French gay artists. But I wanted GoMA to be different. Its main point was to show lasting art of today—works of art that you would want to come back and look at again and again and show to your friends. And this debate—what is the lasting art of our times?—had to be open, shared by our visitors. I wanted a living, responsive and lasting gallery—a bit like a garden of visual delights in the heart of the city, where you could sit and feel at home.

To encourage repeated visits, there had to be one hell of a lot to see—as well as the usual coffee bar, in this case exquisitely and imaginatively painted by Adrian Wiszniewski, with a little room off, which could be hired for private parties, hung with the superb wallpapers of the brilliant Glasgow design team, Timorous Beasties. Art, for me, has to be like a person—it has to be centred, have a soul, if you like, and it has to be able to exist wherever it is. The *Mona Lisa* on a railing in the street is the *Mona Lisa* after all. I'm deeply suspicious of most artistic installations. A few can work—Kurt Schwitters's did—but even they need edges. Most are forms of hollow dictatorship that deprive other artists of that, for them, most precious commodity of all—public space. I was determined to use GoMA's space to the full and put in it as many works of art as I could.

Richard Murphy, the Scottish architect, helped me. We shared a passion for Carlo Scarpa's museum designs, particularly in Verona, and he brilliantly adapted Scarpa's easel to make movable, free-standing supports so we could show paintings, and big ones, in the huge, pillared hall of the Royal Exchange, an apparently impossible 'hanging' space. The hall was surrounded by high windows open to the street, and I wanted passers-by to be able to look in and see fascinating works of art inside. We protected the windows against damaging UV rays, but most modern art is made with modern materials that are unaffected by and best seen in ordinary light levels. We were, after all, showing the art of our times, not precious, fragile objects from the distant past.

My aim was to get the best, potentially most lasting, living art I could find. There were suggestions that the collection should be limited to British, even to Scottish art, but I resisted that, arguing that the gallery would naturally be locally focused, because that's where it was, but that it should also encompass the best contemporary art wherever it was made. I thought we all had to be local and global in our thinking: true to our own experiences and aware of the wider picture. Artists are in precisely this position; their art is hollow if it isn't personal, and limited if it has no wider implications. I envisaged a world in which all the public art galleries everywhere are not stamped with the boring brands of international art, but full of inspiring, original things to see, many of them springing from their locality. The world, I believed, would then become a much bigger, more exciting place to explore. I wanted visitors to Glasgow to see something different, fresh and new.

I began by collecting the best art I could by the most outstanding Glasgow artists. The New Glasgow Boys had been somewhat eclipsed by a younger wave of conceptual artists, promoted by the Tate's Turner Prize, which had switched under Serota's directorship from celebrating a lifetime's achievement in art, to focusing on the younger generation, under thirties—tying the public gallery world closer to the fashion-changing needs of the art market. But what interested me was what these New Glasgow Boys were doing now, for painting is an artistic language that can be developed, unlike a concept, which isn't a creative language at all.

I was proved right. After being in the limelight, these artists were now producing their very best work. Steven Campbell, a bullet-headed and -faced bruiser of a character with red hair swept back over his furrowed brow, who looked as if he was about to hit you (or, at least, me), perpetually hurt and raw, as if he'd been born with his skin the wrong way round, nerves out, at first was a fan of mine. His comment to the press when they announced my

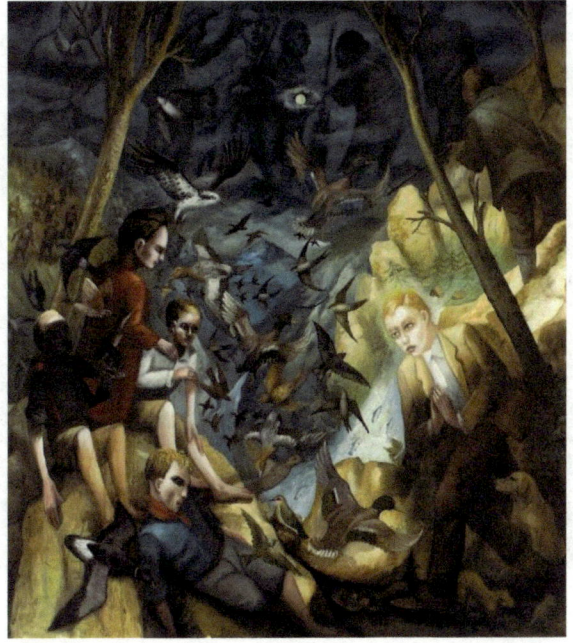

Steven Campbell, Painting in Defence of Migrants, 1993

appointment was 'At last Glasgow's got a man with balls.' But he hadn't met me then. When he did, he didn't want to talk. I knew he'd become interested in Ruskin, but the last thing he wanted to discuss with me, a specialist, was that.

I ignored his touchy intemperance and looked through his work. There was so much of it, and much of it was a miss, but from time to time there was a real hit. I still think his *Painting in Defence of Migrants* is one of the best works of art I ever acquired. The flow of movement in it, of light and shade, of life and death, the painting of the birds flying as they follow the voiceless call to migrate, is totally enrapturing, and, with its implications for humankind, a masterpiece of our times.

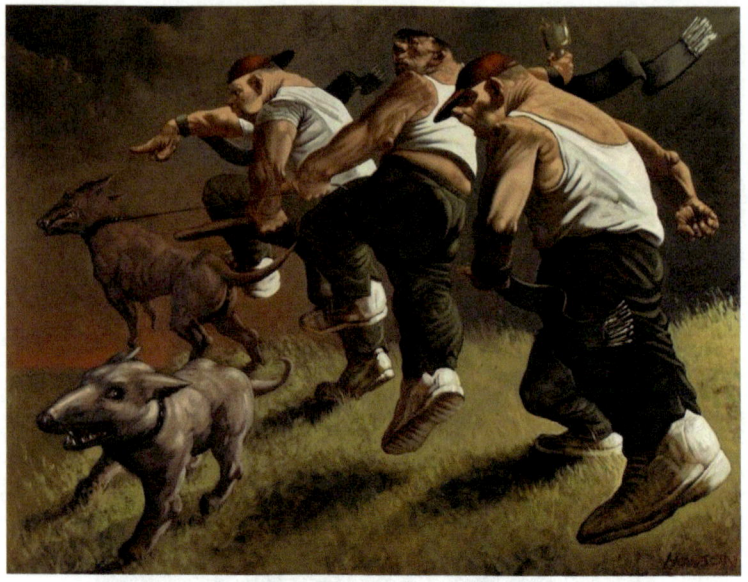

Peter Howson, Patriots, 1991

Peter Howson's *Patriots* is another masterpiece—a perfect, if totally unintended, complement to Campbell's *Migrants*—a superb distillation of the feelings aroused on the other side of immigration, by thugs whose aggression is, in their view, justly liberated by the threat of invasion by outsiders. I'd been used to gangs defending territories in my youth. I'd rarely seen drawing so brilliant—since the painters of the Baroque, few artists have ever been able to capture weight in movement in mid-air as powerfully and utterly convincingly as Howson. He's a most disarming man to meet—big and impressive, like a boxer resting, but with the gentlest, almost sheepish smile, and one of the softest handshakes I've ever known. And yet he can't stop images of aggression pouring out of him. *Patriots* is a high point, one of the most telling images of our times.

I had long admired the art of Ken Currie. I'd greatly enjoyed his murals celebrating the history of the Scottish Labour Movement on the ceiling of the People's Palace—a contemporary artist carrying on the great traditions of working-class art I'd worked to preserve (see J for Jack Jones)—and I'd loved a very big painting I'd bought by him, called *On the Edge of City*, for Manchester City Art Galleries, where his honed skill in spatial composition and *chiaroscuro* had enabled him to chart the dark, ragged hinterland between night and daytime at the edge of people's minds. I was delighted to find him exploring even deeper themes: this time the Holocaust. *The Bathers* is an unforgettable, huge painting of victims, in some modern nightmare scenario, being shepherded into the eternal, cleansing light of the gas chambers, the perfect complement I thought, by utter chance, to Howson's patriotic thugs and Campbell immigrants. Ken Currie is quiet, self-effacing and incredibly thoughtful. I enjoyed, immensely, visiting his studio whenever I could—talking about art and seeing what he was up to. He kept me in touch with real creativity, during the turbulent years of my time in Glasgow.

To my surprise, Glasgow had virtually no paintings by Scotland's most famous artist, John Bellany, but then he was an east coast artist and they were west coast, such were the divisions in Scotland still. I wanted the new gallery to be local and global in its scope—but how could it begin to be that if it couldn't even acquire works by an artist on the other side of its own country? I set about immediately to put that right. I'd known and admired John's work for a long time, having bought his art for public collections before. He was a born painter; he'd begun in childhood and simply never stopped. But then painting survived longer as a perfectly natural, unquestioned form of expression over the border in Scotland than it did in England. It took a while for it to be eaten into by the trivialising notions of conceptualism. John always referred to painting, with a sparkle of pleasure in his eyes, in the most matter-

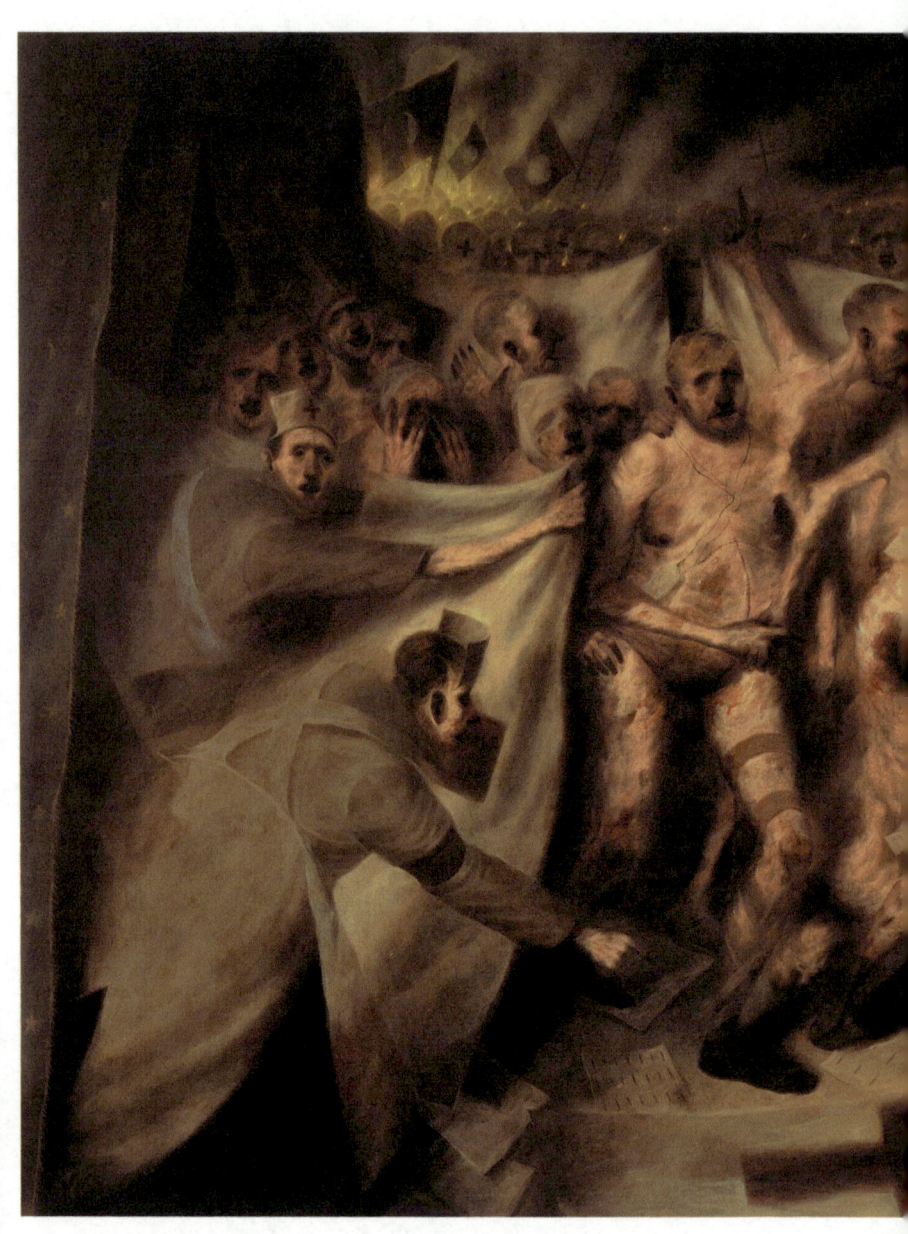

Ken Currie, The Bathers, 1991–92

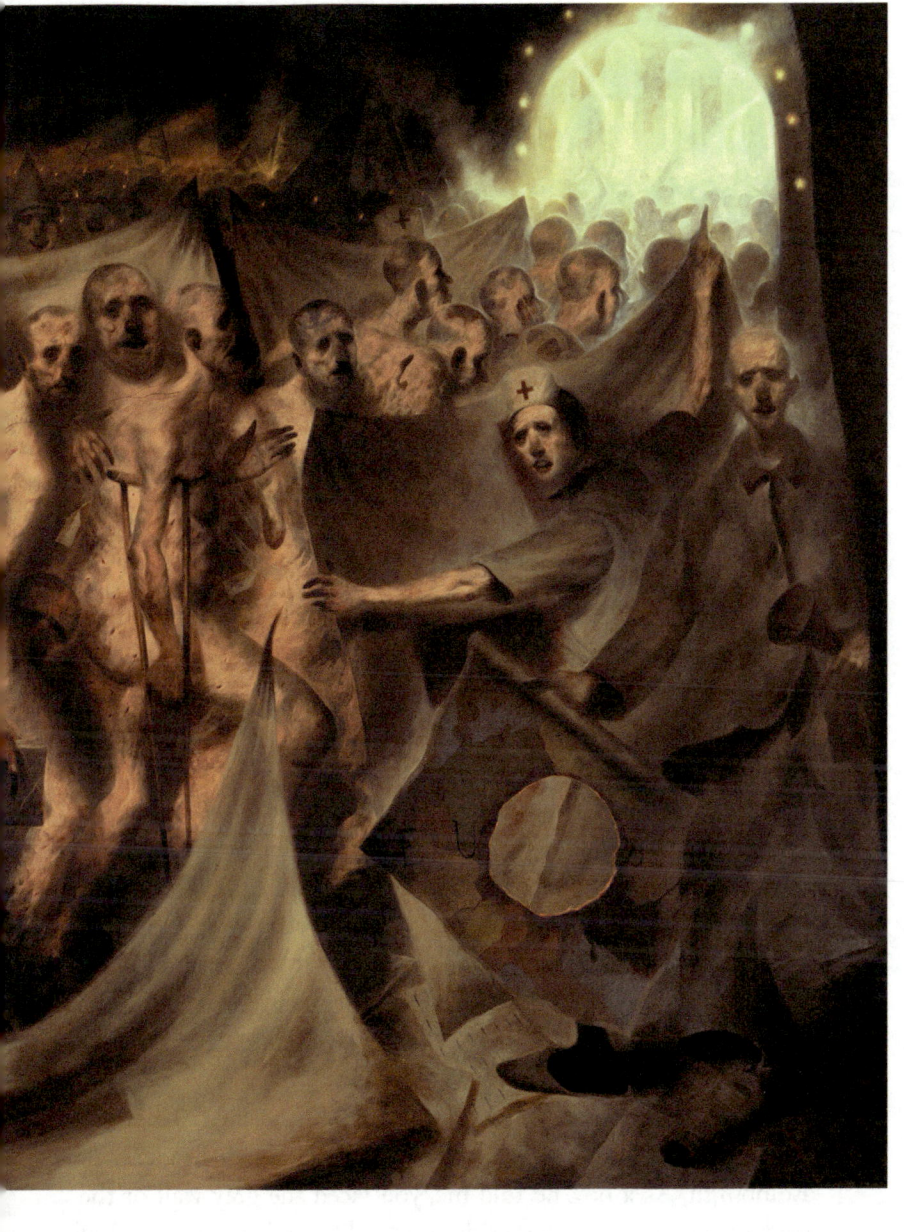

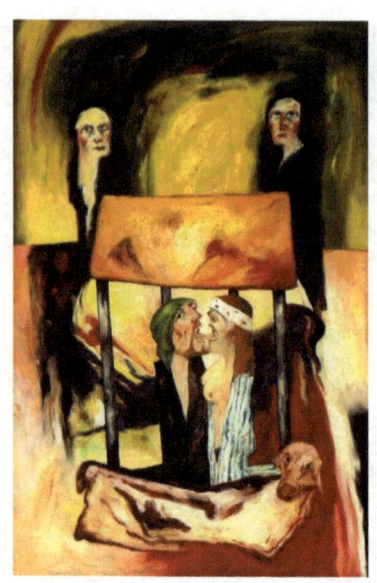

*John Bellany, Triptych: Journey to
the End of the Night, 1972*

of-fact terms, as 'being with his brushes'. It was as simple, and as complex, as that.

John was a big man, in every way, leonine, strong, bearded and beaming, a dominating, charismatic presence. A charming, almost gentle, self-effacing smile, when he met you, invariably played across a small mouth half hidden under his moustache, but his eyes told a different story. They peered at you under half-closed, upper lids—he represented all his sitters with a similar look, unconsciously I thought, even if they tended to stare wide-eyed, like David Bowie. This look of John's, though set back, wasn't in an way wary. I don't think he had a seam of suspicion in him. His look was simply, I think, his visually enquiring intelligence incessantly at work.

Bellany's father and grandfather were fishermen, based in the tiny, rocky harbour of Port Seton on the North Sea, east of Edinburgh. As a boy, he told me, you faced the grey wall of the cold, dangerous sea on one side of your life, and the grey wall of

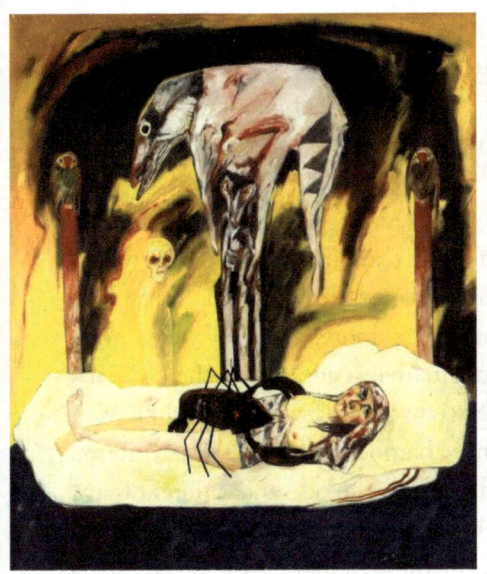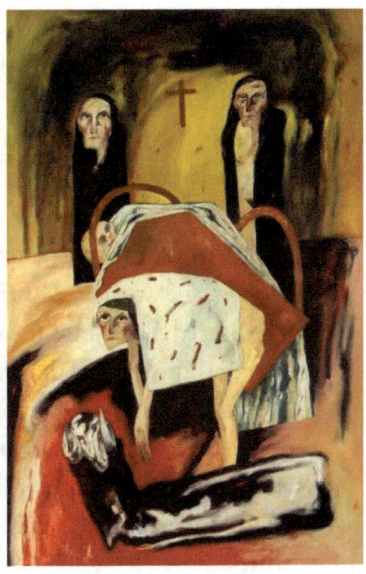

the potentially cold and dangerous community on the other. If you believed in the Bible, you faced a life of rigorous self-denial. If you didn't, you went to hell. But at least that was warm. The choice was stark—either the chilly, spruce church or the crowded, fetid pub. John chose the latter, and never looked back. I bought a fabulous early brutal yellow and black triptych by him called *Journey to the End of the Night*—a black lobster makes love to a naked woman while the fears in her eyes of the sins awaiting her in hell arise in the scenes around.

By the time I'd got to know him well, he'd had a liver transplant and didn't touch a drop. I said to him once, 'John, I think I might have a drink problem—since coming to Glasgow, I'm drinking so much whisky. I never touched the stuff before.' His reply has been a bulwark to me ever since. 'If you're still drinking at your age,' he said, in his ripe Scots brogue, 'you haven't got a drink problem.' Within days after his operation, innovative and risky at that time, he was drawing and painting again, even though still lying convalescent in bed, with tubes coming everywhere out of him. The nurses were amazed—but 'being with his brushes' helped him to live. This series of hospital self-portraits remains some of his best, most haunting work, and I bought a beautiful, small group for the new gallery.

To make GoMA even more interesting—apart from the hundreds of wonderful works of art it contained from Glasgow and all round the world—I wanted visitors to think, or rather feel, immediately they came through the doors, that they were entering something special, an imaginative space, out of the ordinary. That's why I commissioned Niki de Saint Phalle, whom I knew at the time, to design the entrance chamber and the pediment above. The interior spaces, on four floors, were so odd and different that I conceived the notion to heighten this distinction, by linking them with the four elements—fire in the basement (where the pillars were lined with marble—metamorphic rocks formed in our planet's volcanic centre); earth, on the ground floor, where the pillars were massive and made of stone; water on the first floor, where long galleries ran lapping around the building; and air on the top, where the architect, David Page, designed beautiful pyramidal roof lights, oriented north (and glazed, of course, with ultraviolet filters) where the wide open, top-lit gallery could be flooded with natural light. I fixed these zones by naming the floors in the lift—you pressed a button for fire, water, earth or air.

Each space in this gallery had a very different visual quality, and therefore suited different manifestations of modern art. Andy Goldsworthy's evocations of natural ephemera fitted the Water Galleries, as did the narrative, jocular art of Beryl Cook. The massive, serious paintings of Currie, Howson and Campbell looked great among the massive pillars of the Earth Gallery. Interactive and light installations worked beautifully in the darkness of the Fire Gallery.

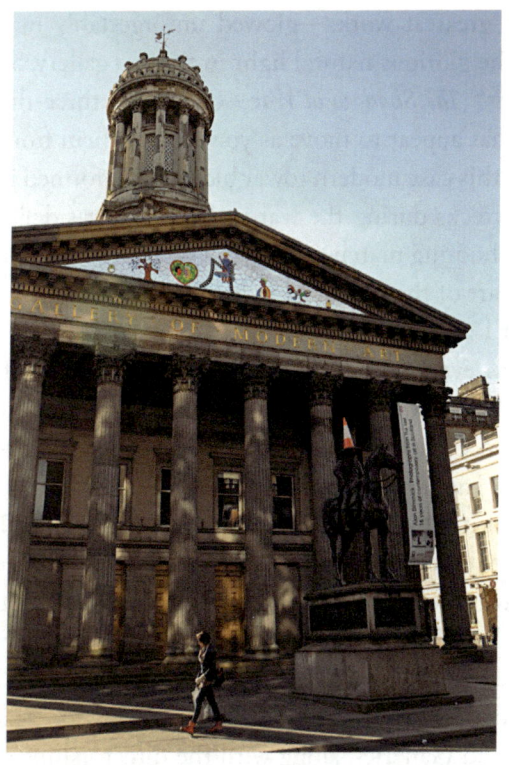

*Exterior of the Gallery of Modern Art, Glasgow, with tympanum
by Niki de Saint Phalle and lettering by Lida Kindersley*

The displays included the head of Bruce Lacey, built big enough
by him so you could climb into it to see a retrospective of his many
inspired responses to life, a robot's 'mate' following her about and
being fired at, collecting rock samples on the moon (the rocks
fell through the bottom of the bags when he brought them back,
because he'd forgotten about their weightlessness above) and his
truly extraordinary *Living Room*, with a slice taken out of the
whole thing, showing what was really going on in the minds and
bodies of its occupants. Bridget Riley's superb painting *Punjab*—

one of her greatest works—glowed unforgettably in your eyes, bathed in the glorious natural light in the top gallery. So did Patrick Hughes's *The Shadow of War*—one of his three-dimensional paintings that appear to move as you look at them from different angles—in this case modern tower blocks transformed into ghastly hollow wrecks during the war in Bosnia. I was delighted with the whole shooting match—art as ongoing fusion, like the sun, in the very heart of the city. And to be able to do all this, I had one person, Pat Lally, to thank.

Lally was eventually toppled by the skulduggery of the little politics of Scotland. He and the whole leading group of Labour politicians in Glasgow were suddenly suspended for 'bringing the Labour Party into disrepute'. The accused took the Labour Party to court, but it took a year and a half for the case to be heard. The week before it did, the Labour Party withdrew all charges because they were utterly groundless. But by then the party had done what it wanted. Faced with devolution, it only wanted one capital city in Scotland and that would be Edinburgh. So it reduced Glasgow to a second-rank city, in part by abolishing my job as director of Museums and Galleries, along with the directorships of libraries, sport and recreation and performing arts, because we were too good at raising money and coming up with brilliant ideas. Lally was sad to see us all go. As he commented, 'Glasgow had the best.'

All our four posts were replaced by a politically run leisure management system. This idea had first been mooted years before in my career years in Sheffield. Councillor the Reverend Alan Billings was the chairman considering a proposed regrouping on departments into Leisure Services. I asked him if he'd like his profession to be regarded as a leisure activity. He laughed, and the idea was dropped. Providing leisure is not a professional skill. Running museums and galleries, libraries, performance arts, sports and parks, and, I'd have to add, a religion, is. Government, at local and national level, only really functions well when dedicated, knowledgeable and imaginative professionals work together with dedicated, knowledgeable and imaginative politicians. That was the lucky confluence I had with Pat Lally. He kept out of art, and I kept out of politics. That was how we worked.

Since the abolition of my professional position, my notion of a Gallery of Modern Art has been slimmed down to provide a changing exhibition venue (as if Glasgow didn't have enough of them)—living art without the lasting. And my vision of recreating the idea of the Encyclopædic Museum at Kelvingrove, in twenty-first century terms, detailed in my book *The Poetic Museum*—an institution capable of responding to and developing myriad foci of interest across the community as whole—initiated and run by front-of-house teams—has been clipped of all its growing points and turned into a deadpan museum, with objects behind glass—lasting art without the living. All very sad. It is ludicrous that Glasgow Galleries and Museums, a service bigger than any national museum, doesn't have its own director. But then the whole debilitating and silly class division between national and non-national collections in Britain needs to be rethought, as part of the potentially inspiring initiative of 'levelling up'. Art galleries and museums need directors, for they have a direction to take.

L *is for* L. S. LOWRY

One of the first letters to land on my desk when I became director of Manchester City Art Galleries was from Carol Ann Lowry, asking if we'd be interested in having on loan some of Lowry's possessions, his Gabriel Rossetti paintings, for example, and his Lucian Freud drawing. She wasn't a relation of the artist, but had inherited his estate, including hundreds of paintings and drawings and the copyright of all his work, and had never from that moment looked back. The story was that her mother had once banged on Lowry's door in Mottram, Cheshire, and when he opened it, said, 'I'm Mrs Lowry. I think we're related.' 'No, we're not,' he replied and shut the door. His fame, by this time, made him used to such unsolicited callers. Undaunted, she tried again next week, this time taking her daughter with her. Lowry liked the look of her, especially since she was called Ann—he had a thing about girls called Ann—and they were both invited in. After that Mrs Lowry became a regular helpmate, and he grew very fond of this lively 'Ann', eventually leaving her everything.

I was immediately interested in her offer. We had one of the great collections of Pre-Raphaelite paintings, and more Rossettis were always welcome, especially ones owned by Lowry, the local hero, and, in my view, one of the most original and profound artists in twentieth-century Britain, and one of the few creative thinkers, aside from Samuel Beckett, to really tackle the ludicrousness of life, and, among the crowds, the inevitability of solitude. The paintings were in her home in Leuchars, Scotland, where her second husband, a helicopter pilot, was in the air force. In another twist in Carol Ann's remarkable, charmed life, he'd saved her from the wreck of her yacht at sea, when her first husband lost his life—their eyes met as he lifted free from the turbulent waves; they fell in love and married.

I went up to see her as soon as I could. I was amazed. There were not only paintings, but her garage was full of Lowry's possessions. Everything was there from his sitting room, where he occasionally gave interviews, very rarely entertained guests and was sometimes photographed, slouching in his armchair, his feet high on the tiled fireplace, surrounded by his grandfather clocks, the piano his mother played, his stacks of records, even the big china bowl in which he used to throw letters sent to him that he never opened. His life came alive before my eyes. It was utterly ordinary—familiar to anyone visiting a grandparent at that time—and yet utterly extraordinary—who else had a huge pouting Pre-Raphaelite Rossetti beauty hanging on the wall above a two-bar electric fire? I suggested we should take the lot and reconstruct his living room as it was.

Then I quickly realised I wanted to go further, and reconstruct not just this 'front' room, Lowry's public face, but the back room down the corridor where he painted—his 'studio' where he worked at night. Everything in it, not just his easel, but also the run-of-the-mill furniture, the table, chairs and walls were spattered with years and years of accumulated paint. The room looked as though it had been used as a pigeon coop, as if there had been an ongoing explosion in Lowry's back room, as, in reality there was in his and there is in any real artist's head. Carol Ann had all this 'studio' stuff, too. The cleaner had never been allowed in there, nor had anyone else. It was the private place of his mind. I had never seen such a vivid juxtaposition of an everyday and imaginative life in these two rooms—creativity happening in Manchester. This wouldn't just be another period reconstruction of an artist's studio, fascinating as these are—such as Constantin Brâncuşi studio in Paris or Francis Bacon's in Dublin—but a telling evocation of something more encompassing: the relationship of art to life, the endless interest of my own.

Sandra Martin, a lively, slender curator who drove a frog-eyed Sprite, and her team did a beautiful job in realising the project, down to researching and reconstructing the original wallpapers, surfaces and paint colours—all the bits that Carol Ann hadn't kept. And she added recordings of Lowry's voice on a headset, so you could feel you were there in the room with him, as you looked around. Then she linked the two rooms with a partial reconstruction of the corridor leading to the front door, where Lowry hung his hats and coats, and kept a couple of empty suitcases at the ready, which he would lift and say, 'I'm sorry, you've caught me as I'm just about to leave,' when an unexpected visitor arrived, when all he wanted to do was to get back to work in the back room of his mind.

I was saddened to hear that Manchester City Art Gallery dismantled this reconstruction after I left and had fond hopes that it would be installed in the new 'Lowry' at Salford Quays. This was a typical major Millennium Project funded by the new Lottery when it came on stream. The Lowry was to be a spanking new, performance venue and gallery aimed not only at providing a new cultural centre but also at triggering commercial development in the huge industrial site at the end of the Manchester Ship Canal, which had been derelict since the dock's closure in 1982. They named the centre after the region's most famous and popular artistic son and transferred the major collection of Lowry's art to it from Salford's Museum and Art Gallery, to complete the marketing package. The other main new attraction on the site was the Imperial War Museum North—which, as David Alston, The Lowry's first art director, commented, managed with its title to combine four words guaranteed to put off the vast majority of its potential public.

I was invited by the National Millennium committee to be the outside expert to judge the validity of The Lowry project, rather to my surprise because I was not, by then, at all popular with the art establishment. I flew down from Glasgow to Manchester, was met by an official car and driven straight to Salford Town Hall, where I was greeted by a rank of leading councillors and officials. We stared at each other for a second, and I thought I'd better clear the air from the start. 'Well, you've got the money. They've managed

to find the only gallery director in Britain who's a Lowry enthusiast to judge your project.' We all laughed. After the bleached
sandwiches and lacerated slices of celery, we looked at the project
drawings and models.

My heart sank. It could work, I thought, as a multi-use
performance venue, but the galleries, wrapped around part of
the outside of the auditorium, looked like an afterthought: art
reduced to foyer space. I couldn't see how you could tell the story
of Lowry there, and what you looked out on was modern toy-
town architecture, not the environment Lowry grew within and
from. He was much better shown in the old Salford gallery, a place
he loved and visited often, and the views outside of Peel Park were
ones he repeatedly painted. You only had to be there to begin to
get to know the extraordinary nature of the man you were dealing with. Lowry in The Lowry was out of place and out of joint.
But did I have the guts to say no to the project? No. They would
have found a way round my objection anyway, another 'expert' to
consult; the momentum for the project was too great. I remained
mum, smiled weakly, and said 'yes'.

Now, years on, I can express my true opinion. The Lowry
should keep one small room dedicated to the artist whose name
it takes—showing the crazier, private sides of his character, his
erotic drawings and late paintings of lonely misfits alongside a
small selection of his most popular industrial landscapes. And the
rest of the 'foyer' gallery space should house changing exhibitions
of national and international contemporary art, in keeping with
The Lowry's main artistic programme. The rest, the whole wonderful kaleidoscope of Lowry's art, should go back to the beautiful
galleries at Peel Park, showing in full his endless artistic inventiveness and psychological intensity, with views out of the window on
the local scenes that inspired him. And here, too, his sitting room
and 'studio' could be re-installed, so visitors can experience what

a remarkable artistic venture began, flowered and ended in this northern corner of Britain.

Lowry's achievement is still underrated and remains hardly known abroad. There are two main reasons for this. One is that he worked in the North, and was totally uninterested in going south, where 'art' is supposed to be 'at'. This was an unforgivable sin. The art world still refers to Joseph Wright, one of the greatest artistic geniuses of the whole European Enlightenment, as 'Wright of Derby' because he came from there, though they wouldn't dream of referring to 'Turner of London' for the same reason. If you are of London, you are of the world; if you come from anywhere else, you're provincial—or so they assume, from down there. I had endless experience of this, as a Londoner working outside London, throughout my career; very few of my townsfolk ever knew what I was up to.

The other reason for the widespread ignorance of Lowry's profound artistic achievement is, ironically, because he was, and still is, so popular. How popular I found out to my cost. I was lucky enough—or unlucky enough, depending on how you look at it— only to have suffered four thefts in my career, but two of them involved Lowry.

We were holding a fund-raising ball for the costume collection in Kelvingrove. Jean Muir, the famous fashion designer, was the guest of honour. My deputy director, Stewart Coulter, persuaded me to take the floor, despite all my protests, with the honoured guest. This was, I knew, a terrible mistake. I had tried, once, to learn to waltz, but not with any notable success. Jean Muir, I realised at once, on the dance floor, could float. I must be one of the few people who have trod on Jean Muir's toes, not once but twice. My goodness was I glad when that was over. Nevertheless, the evening was a great success and even raised some money, which events like this seldom do. I was quite relieved when I got to bed, but hadn't been asleep for long, when the telephone rang. It was one of the night watchmen at Kelvingrove. They'd just completed their regular rounds of the upstairs galleries, when all the guests and caterers had gone, and there was something wrong. Lowry's VE Day had been stolen. They'd just rung the police and they'd be there in minutes. 'I'll be there,' I said, 'in ten.'

My mind raced as I walked to Kelvingrove, through the tall tenement blocks of Glasgow's West End, in the deserted early hours of the morning. Most museum curators are used to being called out because the gallery alarms have gone off in the middle of the night. It's one of the hazards of the job. They're usually false alarms. This theft, however, was real. It was one picture only—and a famous and valuable one at that—so it must have been planned or even, perhaps, ordered. And no alarms had been triggered, so it must have been taken while the alarms weren't on—and that could only have been when the ball was going on and the museum was fully manned. The implications of this were getting more serious at every step. One of Lowry's masterpieces, and one of our most popular works, painted in 1945, to celebrate the ending of the Second World War. For me, this was a battle that was just beginning. The job of a museum director isn't easy; you have to make the most valuable things in the world accessible to everyone. Everything's fine as long as lots of visitors are coming in; but if something goes wrong, there's only one person to blame: in this instance, as I walked those lonely streets, I knew that that was me.

The police hadn't arrived when I appeared. I went up to see what had happened. The glass door to the gallery had been locked when the night watchman went on his rounds, so he wasn't prepared for what he saw. He'd left the scene exactly as he'd found it. There was a gap on the wall where the picture had been, but what was surprising was that, under the large, square black seat in the centre of the gallery, there was the picture's frame, with its stretcher lain at an angle across it. I studied them carefully without touching anything. The thief, or thieves, had carefully unscrewed the painting from the wall—there would certainly need to have been two of them to do that safely, for the painting was quite a size, one of Lowry's biggest. Then they had laid the painting on its front and removed the stretcher from the frame—a precision task in itself.

Then—and this was surprising—they had carefully prised the painting away from its stretcher—most thieves simply cut it out of the centre—by easing the canvas around the many tacks that held it firmly, removing some (which I could see scattered around), and just pulling the canvas over others, which were left protruding from the wooden frame. This must have taken some time, probably about half an hour, which meant that the thieves were confident of not being disturbed. They'd then left through the glass doors locking them behind them, for there were no roof lights removed, no damage to the roof and no other way in, or out, of the gallery. And they'd done all this without setting off any alarms. So, they must have done it, as I had first guessed, when the alarms were off, but when the gallery was locked, after all the day visitors had gone, but while the ball was on.

There was one grain of comfort to be taken from all this. They knew how to look after a painting, for they'd removed it in the best way possible, so it was likely that they knew how to roll it—it must surely have been rolled to hide it in something to get it out of the building. If a painting has to be rolled, it has to rolled with the painted surface outside, not in—which anyone would think to do if they wanted to hide what it was. A paint layer rolled inside invariably gets compressed, cracks and falls off in flakes, unless it is very thin, and Lowry painted thickly, relishing in impasto. So, the painting was likely to be in good condition, wherever it was. That, at least, was heartening.

L *is for* L. S. LOWRY

I looked round the room. There were a lot of easier, smaller, pictures to have stolen, modest-sized Impressionist paintings which were, in fact, much more valuable than the Lowry, and much easier to smuggle out of the country and sell, especially in America or, indeed, in Europe, both places where Lowry's work wasn't known at all. This gave me hope as well. The theft had obviously been carefully planned—the thieves must have brought with them the right tools—but, at the same time, it was ignorant, for they had chosen a work that was only valuable in Britain and very difficult to sell because it was so well known. Anyone wanting to pay half a million for a Lowry, would look up any book on him, and know instantly where this one came from. Fencing the theft would be a real problem.

The fact that they'd chosen a Lowry reminded me of the other theft I'd been misfortunate enough to be involved in during my career. This was of a beautiful little painting by the eighteenth-century painter, Arthur Devis, from one of our branch galleries in Manchester, the Fletcher Moss Parsonage, set in extensive, very attractive gardens in Didsbury. The thieves in that instance just smashed through the front door with a sledgehammer, setting off all the alarms, went straight to the little picture in a back gallery, yanked it off the wall, and left before anyone, including the police, had time to arrive. But they took two Lowry prints for themselves from the shop—having no idea they were valueless but confirming Lowry's popularity and recognisability—proving by doing so that they were ignorant thieves working to order.

The Disdbury theft was clever. Arthur Devis is a little-known artist in Britain—an exquisite painter of 'conversation pieces'—small, intimate pictures of people who have 'made it', owners of modestly grand houses, often only a man and wife, caught together, informally, just chatting in their expensive environment—a delight. These paintings were hugely sought after in America, fetching several hundred thousand, wonderful additions to the country house of a family who had 'made it' over there, small enough to hide in ordinary luggage, and, before the days of the Internet, difficult to trace as a theft.

I thought we'd lost this picture. But I proved wrong. The loss adjuster of the insurance company was brilliantly persistent and had excellent contacts with the police investigators. He rang me several months later to say that the police had found the painting, after a tip-off, in a garage in Wolverhampton. We went to collect it from the local police station. It was in perfect condition, still in its original frame, labelled Manchester City Art Galleries in gold. Whoever had commissioned the theft hadn't been able to shift it at all.

That experience gave me hope, as I looked at the empty frame and stretcher lying beneath the seat. The thieves would have great difficulty finding a buyer for the Lowry, and it had no value abroad. But there was an alarming dimension to this theft. It had to have been done by someone with access to our security keys, and the way it was carried out suggested it was done by someone who either worked in a museum or at a picture framer's, for they clearly knew what they were doing. All that pointed to an inside job, or, at least, an inside accomplice. I had 550 staff in all, and though all were carefully vetted before they were appointed, one never knew what was really going on people's minds.

I cast my mind back to how we had once appointed an attendant in Sheffield who had just retired from the police force, with impeccable references. Soon after, the police discovered he'd been amassing a huge hoard of illegal arms during his long service. He was arrested, but in the famous, if local, case that followed, he was always referred to as an attendant in our galleries, which I thought was a bit steep since he'd only been with us a couple of weeks. Perhaps they knew something already, hence the glowing reference.

My ponderings were interrupted when the police arrived. I shared my analysis with them. They agreed. All the staff on duty would have to be interviewed, and the caterers for the ball and their suppliers. It was an immense and complicated task. Did I want the police to issue a statement to the press? Yes, I decided; it would leak anyway, and the more people who knew about it the better. The police agreed. Was I going to offer a reward for information—it might be worth it since we were agreed that it must have been a local job? 'No,' I said. 'I don't want to encourage copycat thefts carried out to get rewards.' They agreed with this too. I went back to bed. It was too early to ring my chairman, and it was too late for the morning editions, so I had a few hours respite before all hell broke loose.

The press rang me first thing in the morning. I said, 'We'll get it back.' I surprised myself by my confidence, but I felt the only thing to do in the circumstances was to be positive. My chairman's wife told me, when we met a few days later, that 'Glasgow will never forgive you.' So at least I had an idea what the chairman and surely many of my committee really felt. The front-page headline put the boot in: 'STICKMAN PAINTING STOLEN WHILE TOFFS DANCE ON', with a big picture inside of the Lowry and Jean Muir. I knew I was on shoogly (an admirably evocative Scottish word) ground, as I had felt before and would feel again. I had to step with care.

The police interviews with the staff got nowhere. We seemed no nearer to finding out where the Lowry had gone. Then one day the police rang me to tell me they'd got a tip-off—there's always someone on the criminal fringe wanting or rather needing to do the police a favour—that the painting was in a flat in Easter-house—a huge estate on the edge of the city—and that they were going in. A couple of hours later they rang to say they'd missed it. The loot had been moved on before they got there.

Then, a month or so later, I got an anonymous phone call asking me if I'd give him £200,000 for the picture. I said no. There
was a pause. '£20,000?' No. There sounded like a disappointed silence, then a click. The police were amused. 'They don't know what
to do with it,' they said. 'But don't worry, they won't destroy it, as
long as they think they can get something for it.' Then, another
two months later, the police rang again. 'We've really got it this
time. It's in the boot of a car in a hotel forecourt in Edinburgh.'
They told me, a little later, that they went up to the driver of the
car and asked him if he'd got a Lowry painting in his boot? He
denied it. They made him open up, and there it was, folded in half.
'Never seen that before,' he said. 'Don't know how that got there.'
He was arrested, and eventually got two years for handling stolen
property, but the actual culprits were never found, either inside
the museum or out. The damage, fortunately, was not too bad—
almost all caused by the folding. Soon invisibly restored by the
head of painting conservation, Norma Johnson, this glorious
painting was back on our walls, and I had, for once this time, been
proved right, and breathed again.

Lowry's obscure in the art world because he's popular. That's
something modern artists aren't supposed to be. On the con-
trary they are meant to shock the ignorant masses (though not,
of course, those in the know) and in the process prove that art is
advancing. If you're popular, you are, by definition, retrogressive,
not avant-garde. This is one of the most corrosive, divisive and
wrong-headed myths of modernism. It is perfectly legitimate today, indeed admirable for artists to want to reach as many people
as possible, to be both popular and profound, Shakespearian in
their appeal and ambition. Lowry achieved that goal naturally and
imaginatively but has been marginalised as a result, when his true
place is in the mainstream of world art.

Lowry towards the end of his life continually asked, 'Will I

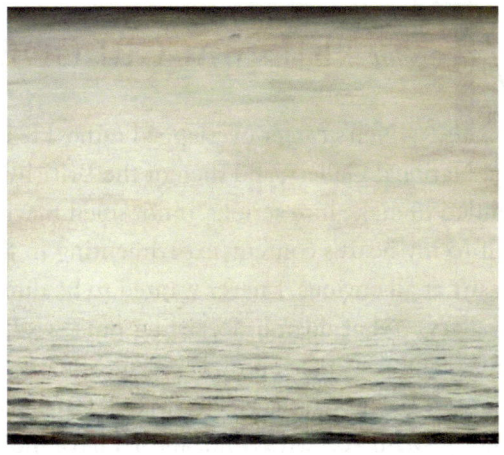

L. S. Lowry, Seascape, 1950

live?' He will if he's loved and understood by those who care for his work, and if people can see it. There are thousands of drawings, for example, all different, the vast majority never seen in public. The fellow hardly ever stopped creating, from his fifteenth year until his death at eighty-eight. There needs to be major exhibitions touring the world. There are so many aspects of his art to be explored. Richard Mayson's new book on Lowry's lamp-posts is an example, lifting a corner on just one aspect of his multifaceted personal iconography. Above all his best paintings need to be seen in the right company where the quality of their brushwork can be appreciated. If the National Gallery reverses Neil MacGregor's decision and continues to tell the story of great painting, then a Lowry or two deserve to hang in Trafalgar Square, alongside Pieter Brueghel, Hieronymus Bosch and Jan Steen—one of his great crowded industrial scenes and his haunting empty seascapes (he had a dream once that one day the tide wouldn't turn back but the sea would go on rising and rising—presages of global warming) and his achievement will, at last, be glorified, not marginalised.

M *is for* NEIL MACGREGOR

Neil's career overlapped mine. He became director of the National Gallery, and then of the British Museum, a role that tended to make him serious, if not solemn, while I could enjoy myself to my heart's content, experimenting in the regions. Oddly, I wasn't at all envious. I never wanted to be director of the National Gallery—what do you do, sitting on a small mountain of wonderful pictures at the top of Trafalgar Square? Mind you, with hindsight, if I'd known that Neil was going to curtail its collection at 1900, I wish I'd made a bid, and I'd have moved heaven and earth, for example, to secure Edward Hopper's *Sunlight in an Empty Room* for its collection—one of the great paintings of our time. But even Neil didn't know he was going to do what he did with the collection at that time. I'd have loved to run the British Museum, of course, but I knew they (the small bunch of really powerful people who run Britain) would never give me it; news of that kiss I'd given Melina Mercouri must have got round. So, my views about Neil MacGregor are not tinted with professional jealousy, not a hint, nor even a glint.

The trouble was that overlapping turned into overshadowing, as time went on. Mind you, I'd always felt a little bit overshadowed whenever I was in his company, rather like having a twin brother (I have a real one who doesn't look like me) who everyone thinks is better than you at everything. We're of the same height, similar build, age and perpetual youthfulness, with slightly too big a head and a face that looks as if it had been squashed by someone at an early stage who had become, finally, exasperated by our assertive boyishness. Worse we have similar, received pronunciation, BBC voices, his tinged with a Glasgow accent, mine with the faint trace of South London. Our similarity was a bit weird, except that I felt, from the start, that he was more refined. He obviously had a very elegant mind, spoke foreign languages fluently, whereas I was bumbling and bouncy in comparison, tripping over myself in my enthusiasm. It was a bit like meeting a version of oneself gone to heaven, with all the vulgarities, not to mention the sins, stripped away, a purer being all round and through.

At first, we got on well. He had just been appointed director of the National Gallery, a surprising choice since he'd never worked in a museum before but had been editor of the *Burlington Magazine*. I was long in museums, and by then director of Manchester City Art Galleries. I had just begun doing a series of interviews about art for the BBC and invited him to be my guest. He'd refused all interviews by the media and the press—he was very nervous of his new role—but eventually agreed to make his first public statement as director with me. The programme was a twenty-minute interval discussion on Radio Three—and proved to be a nightmare for both him and me. He was too terrified to talk, which is odd, since he later made his name as a broadcaster, appearing twice a day on BBC radio in his series, *The History of the World in 100 Objects*. But in his first radio broadcast, which was live, almost all he would answer was 'yes' or 'no', after a thoughtful, painfully long pause. I simply couldn't get any discussion to take off. I saw the end of the programme receding before me, like a black gap yawning ever wider across time, as all my questions, even the feeblest back-up ones I'd prepared, ran out. We only just managed to limp to the end—but I had got him, at least, to say that he was determined to continue the practice, established at its foundation, of bringing the National Gallery's collection gradually if sedately up to date—as the enthusiasm of fashion faded and we were able to distinguish paintings that were truly lasting. And he already had some Cubist works in mind—more, of course, he couldn't say.

We saw eye to eye about art. He was very impressed by Steven Campbell's *Painting in Defence of Migrants* (see p. 183) which I'd just bought for Glasgow's Gallery of Modern Art, which he thought was truly 'lasting'—we'd been discussing the qualities that make art last. On reflection, I think the religious dimension of the work might have appealed to him—one boy is depicted praying, another dying. Religion and sex for that matter were subjects we didn't discuss—we weren't ever that close. But, nevertheless, I felt we were brothers in the same game.

I was very pleased when he agreed to support me in my bid to enable the collection of Sir William Burrell to lend abroad. This was especially good of him, because Colin Donald, the chair of the trustees of Sir William's will, who was vehemently opposed to extending lending, was the head of the firm where Neil first began his training in Glasgow as a lawyer before he switched to art history. Neil, now in the gallery business himself, knew how vital reciprocal, international loans are to keeping these organisations alive and in the public eye. As he said in court, without lending and borrowing, public galleries can quickly die.

This is what had happened to the Burrell. It's opening annual attendances had slumped from 1,000,000 to 250,000, and I knew the only way to keep them up was to put on a brilliant, if small and select, exhibition programme. And the Burrell was ideally placed to have one. We had, for example, some of the best Boudins in the world. The Musée d'Orsay in Paris wanted to do a great Boudin show, and wanted to borrow ours, and we could have the show in exchange. But we couldn't lend because Burrell had given his collection to the city during the Second World War—and he didn't trust ships, being a ship owner himself. Even though he himself had lent widely abroad before, when he wrote the terms of the gift, he allowed lending in Britain, but not overseas.

By all accounts, Burrell was a not an amiable man. He foresaw the advent of the First World War, bought all the ships he could, sacked their crews, and then, after the outbreak, sold them to the government at the highest possible price. He drove around Glasgow in one of his several Rolls-Royces, ignoring everything that was thrown at him. I once drove one of them myself through Pollok Park—an unbelievably smooth, silent experience. But he did a great service for Glasgow, turning all his wealth into works of art, which he gave to the city, seeding its cultural rebirth.

The collection was entirely owned and run by the city, but Burrell had left a little money to be used to add to the collection, and this was run by a small bunch of trustees, who were trustees of his will, not the collection itself, let alone the museum, though they acted as though they were, encouraged by the Burrell staff who dreamt of seeing themselves independent of their paymaster, Glasgow City Council. So, this little rump of trustees proclaimed the moral right of upholding the wishes of their founder against the heathen state. The case came to court, made headline news for a week, ended in us winning, and, as Pat Lally commented, was worth every penny in city publicity. The Burrell could at last join the international community where it belonged, and become a lending and borrowing, lively museum.

But after that, I'm afraid, my relationship with Neil deteriorated rapidly, with good reason, on my part. I was angry. Just after the millennium, I was walking through the National Gallery when I chanced to see a notice announcing that its collection closed at 1900. This came as a cruel blow. The National Gallery in London is and became one of the greatest art galleries in the world because it was from its inception in 1824 a living, growing collection. Its collection is small but absolutely choice. It collected only the highest peaks of painting, lasting masterpieces, and added recent ones as their greatness became apparent.

This process of mist-clearing often took decades, sometimes

centuries, but a few works of genius shone through more quickly. Vincent van Gogh's *Yellow Chair*, for example, was bought by the gallery only thirty-four years after it was painted. That's equivalent to the National Gallery buying a painting painted in 1989, to hang alongside its Leonardos, Rembrandts and Turners, well within the highpoints of the careers of Hockney, Bellany and Freud, and well past the achievements of Bacon, Lowry and Spencer. But now, as I read, the gallery can't do that. It can't even add a Picasso or a Matisse. Nor could any artist of our times, anywhere in the world, dream of a painting by her or him, one day, hanging on its walls. What this little sentence said was that the art of great painting had died in 1900. And with it, I felt, would die the National Gallery. What infuriated me even more was that this decision, so fundamental to painting, the art I loved the most, had been taken in secret, without any professional, let alone public debate.

The National Gallery had a simple, very British and typically pragmatic way of adding to its small, choice collection, without any public expense. The Tate's job is to collect the best art of recent times at home and abroad. It was the first sieve. As outstanding masterpieces became apparent, they were simply moved across to Trafalgar Square—they're all part of one national collection after all, owned by the general public as a whole. So, the National Gallery's collection grew, very slowly, while the Tate went on exploring, searching. This is a very healthy, symbiotic relationship, and I had made sure, in my original BBC interview with Neil, that he would maintain it. I must have had a hunch that it might be under threat—but it was only a hunch; I was just seeking to secure it. It was, and is, obvious to me that a select few twentieth-century paintings should hang in the National Gallery to show the world, at one stroke, that great painting has continued into modern times, challenging artists to pick up their brushes again and show the world who we are, what is happening to us and what we are capable of.

It seemed obvious to me what must have happened: Nick Serota had decided that the new Tate Modern would be the National Gallery of post-1900 art and Neil had bent over backwards and complied. All behind closed doors. There's room, of course, for a National Gallery of great painting, and for Tate Modern. We need both, not the death of one of the great arts of mankind, the first manifestation of our imagination, our ability to make images, from cave art of Chauvet on. Of course, art can be made from anything—I have often demonstrated that in what I've bought—but painting is an especially wonderful form of communicating, with infinite possibilities, that can't be parcelled off as something past. I wrote an article summarising my views in the *New Statesman* which they published on 8 April 2002, under the title 'The Death of the National Gallery'. I was told Neil was not amused. He declined all invitations from me to discuss the issues raised by this in public. Silence is always the safest strategy of the establishment.

What I cannot respect is someone who's been handed power in the public sphere not being publicly accountable for and being prepared to discuss publicly their decisions, which affect everyone. This is exactly what the art of painting has the potential to do. Before the National Gallery was opened in 1824, there was an interesting public debate about whether it should show sculpture as well as painting. The decision was made to concentrate on painting because, it was argued, you looked at sculpture and painting in different ways, one in the round and the other in two dimensions, and they, therefore, required different exhibition spaces to be seen at their best. And the best was what the National Gallery was about. This was a great step forward for the art of painting, in world terms. Neil took that art a step back, without the public being aware, by what was essentially a sleight of hand.

By chance Neil and I found ourselves, later, on the same radio programme. I'd been invited to discuss my book *The Eclipse of Art*. As it happened, we arrived at the BBC entrance desk together to collect our security cards. We both said who we were, but the officer by mistake gave Neil's card to me and mine to him. I was used to us being confused. I said, 'I'm not Neil MacGregor.' He laughed and said, 'I always wanted to be Julian Spalding.' We went up in the lift. He told me how much he'd enjoyed my book—'a passionate plea for painting,' he said. I was surprised. I was going to get a plug from Neil on the BBC, and perhaps, at last, we could discuss his decision to close the National Gallery's collection! During the programme, after I'd said my bit about my book, Andrew Marr, the presenter, turned to Neil and asked him what he thought of it. He replied immediately, 'I don't agree with this book at all. It doesn't deal with video art,' and he went on to talk about Bill Viola, whom he greatly admired, avoiding my eyes ever after.

The South Bank Show, fronted by Melvyn Bragg, got very interested in *The Eclipse of Art*. Melvyn was exceptionally broadminded, coming from the world of literature, where reader's opinions matter, not the exclusive artifice of modern art investment. He had already done a show about Beryl Cook, to my admiration. They rang me to say that they wanted to invite me to do two whole programmes, the first showing what I thought was wrong with modern art, and the second promoting modern art that I thought was really good. I remember thinking, 'My goodness, I'm going to become famous!' I worked out the two shows and presented my list of contents. Then silence. A week later, one of the producers rang with apologies. They had had the biggest row the team had ever had, some for and others against, which in her opinion proved that they were on to something and should certainly do the programmes. But at that point Melvyn came in and argued that it wasn't Hockney or Hirst, but Hockney *and* Hirst, and cancelled the project. This sounds inclusive and egalitarian, but isn't, because found-object art denies all creative judgement (see D for Marcel Duchamp). If everything is art, nothing is art (see A for Peter Angermann). But sadly, the myth goes on.

My relationship with Neil deteriorated after that, to my cost, no one else's. It was a sorry tale of public burial. I'd left museums after thirty years (Neil started much later and was still at the top of the tree) and had begun writing, rather to my surprise. This was due to the encouragement, no, insistence of Louise Greenberg, the head of talks for Radio Three. It was she who got me into broadcasting and set up, among many things, that first interview with Neil. I'd got a call to pop in and see her when I was next in London (I was director of Manchester Art Galleries at the time). I was shown into her office. She was on the phone. 'Find out if the President really said that,' she barked, then swung round on her stool. 'Now I will give you my undivided attention.' She was stocky, powerful, with intensely penetrating eyes. We talked for a few minutes. 'You have the vocabulary to give a Radio Three talk,' she announced. She was always absolutely to the point, to the point of being blunt.

When she left the BBC, she rang me and said she was starting a literary agency. She had Kate Adie and the Chief Rabbi, and she wanted me. But I hadn't written anything, I said, apart from catalogues and the odd art book. 'You will,' she said. So that was it. When I left museums, she rang at once and said, 'Great! Now you can write.' It was she who got me to write about my practical vision for museums, which I'd been developing over the years, in *The Poetic Museum: Reviving Historic Collections*. Then she placed *The Eclipse of Art: Tackling the Crisis in Art Today* and *The Art of Wonder: A History of Seeing*, which won the Sir Banister Fletcher Prize for the best art book of 2006—all with the same publisher,

Prestel. She was a tough negotiator. The giant Jürgen Tesch, the head of Prestel, called her 'my Golda Meir'.

Louise then got Rough Guides interested in me doing a Rough Guide to art, the whole of it—along the lines of their *Rough Guide to Opera*: what it is, where and how to see it, round the world, that sort of thing. They said they'd long dreamt of doing such a book, but didn't know who could write it, until they met me. They were delighted with my outline—everything was full steam ahead, but when they discovered how much institutions and owners, pro-hibitively, charge for illustrations—they'd never done an art book before—they had to jump ship. They then suggested I did a much smaller book—*The Best Art You've Never Seen: 100 Hidden Trea-sures from Around the World* (the perfect lavatory book—with a picture on one page and text on the other).

Rather gloomily, I made a preparatory list. Louise urged, 'No black thoughts! You're not starving and no one's shooting at you. What have you got to worry about?' Then they came back—this was impossible too. I'd chosen such obscure works—like the anonymous Wooden Show Painter of Denmark, a 'Holy Fool' in the early seventeenth century who'd been given free rein to paint whatever he liked on the walls of a few churches (Elmelunde is the best known). He'd 'taken a line for a walk', centuries before Paul Klee, creating wonderful fantasies, almost always including a wooden shoe, hence his name. Such artists were so obscure, Rough Guides said, that no images were available on the web—and they couldn't afford to photograph each entry. If I could find images they could use for the book on the web, they might be able to do it. Could I try?

I wanted to give up, but Louise would hear none of it. 'Don't be stupid,' she said. 'No one else is asking you to do anything. Get on with it.' I spent two months bent over my computer—so continuously and badly that I got a crick in my neck and couldn't hold my head up straight. A friend recommended a good osteopath. The pain was so excruciating, I thought I'd try one for the first time. He began massaging the back of my neck and asked me when it had started. I told him I'd been working on my computer solidly for two months. Then I thought I'd better add that, by the way, I stand on my head every night for five minutes before I go to bed.

The fingers stopped massaging for a fraction. 'On your head, or on your shoulders?'

'On the top of my head,' I replied rather proudly. 'I kick myself up against a wall, then bring my feet vertical, so all the blood runs down to my head.'

The fingers stopped for another second.

'And why do you do that?' he asked, more quietly now.

'Oh, it helps me sleep.' The fingers paused again. His voice was even quieter now. 'And how long have you been doing this ... every day?'

'Yes, every day.' I thought for a bit. 'For about forty years—or a bit more.'

The fingers had stopped altogether now, and silence reigned. I had no option but to turn round. The osteopath was doubled up, almost to the floor, doing his best to suppress his silent, shaking laughter. 'I know it's totally unprofessional,' he said, when he eventually was able to lift himself up and speak, between gasping intakes of breath:

> but I've never heard anything so ... stupid. The bones and muscles in your neck are designed to carry the weight of your head, and at the end of the day they think 'great I'm going to get some relief', when you throw the whole weight of your body on top of them! It's a wonder you have any neck at all. I have only one bit of advice, stop standing on your head.

He ushered me out, and I knew from the laughter in his eye, he couldn't wait to tell everyone what he'd heard. I took his advice, the pain went, and I had no trouble sleeping at all—but then, when I think about it, I never did.

I wrote the book. Louise thought it was one of the best things I'd done—certainly the most accessible and potentially popular. But before it was published, Rough Guide was bought by Penguin. My book was scheduled to come out at the same time at Neil's *The History of the World in 100 Objects*, the book of his BBC radio series. His basic idea came out of all the pioneering work I'd done in galleries and museums (see B for Hubert Bari, and others), summed up in my book, *The Poetic Museum*, about developing the art of telling stories with objects, which is what museum curators have to learn how to do if they are going to make their collections meaningful to a wide public in the digital age.

I was delighted to see this approach catching on, even in the British Museum. But the series, I thought, needed television, not radio, for the whole idea is about gaining meaning through seeing, not through listening. And if I'd been in Neil's shoes, I'd have used the occasion to frontline the curators in the BM, not solely its director, to enable the extraordinary range of world experts on its staff to talk directly to the public about the objects in their care, all their life-time enthusiasms and immense scholarship trickling through. People, not just things. And I had one further criticism, the last objects he chose, such as a credit card, were not ones anyone would want to go to a museum to see—raising the vital question: what do museums collect today? Nevertheless, overall, I was delighted to hear that these two books, mine and Neil's, were coming out at the same time, because some of the objects we had chosen were the same, but our views about them were very different.

Leaving aside the Parthenon Marbles (that kiss I gave Melina

Mercouri again), I'd argued in my book that the Benin Bronzes should be returned to Africa—their theft, during a self-styled 'punitive raid', was one of the most disgusting and discreditable acts of British cultural imperialism. When I was still director in Glasgow, I'd had a run-in about their return with the Black London Labour MP Bernie Grant. He'd asked the Labour Council in Glasgow to return the couple of Benin bronzes we had in our collection. After a lot of thought, I recommended against it for professional reasons, and they took my advice, in the good old days when professional opinions mattered in the political sphere. The return of these few items, I argued, would be a disservice to both the people of Glasgow and Nigeria. It is vital that people round the world have a chance to see examples of the quality of African art—we have to develop, simultaneously, our global as well as our local awareness—and the priority for us all, now, is to put the world first. African art cannot be ghettoised, nor can any of the great world cultures.

The return of these few items would also be a disservice to people in Nigeria. They'd had what were effectively their crown jewels stolen, and they were being offered a couple of brilliants from a bangle and been told to be content with that. I suggested to Bernie that I would support him professionally in a bid to get the Benin treasures in the British Museum back to Nigeria—that would really be significant. The argument that the British Museum Act prevented them from ever doing that is, in my view, nonsensical, because acts can be changed, and Bernie was in the right place to do that, and, anyway, the British Museum has powers to lend its collection anywhere, so they could, if they wanted to, put their Benin treasures on the next flight out, make a long-term loan of them to Nigeria, while the legality of ownership got sorted out.

I was therefore greatly looking forward to the publication of both our books, because together we could get a public debate going. Neil, at last, in open discussion about the hot topic of restitution, not to mention the role of painting in the National Gallery. However, I got the first indication that that wasn't going to be allowed when suddenly, at the very last minute before printing, I had to add one more object and change the title to *101 Hidden Treasures*. They couldn't have two books coming out at the same time with a similar title—that was understandable. But worse was to follow. I was told that there was going to be no publicity for my book at all. I couldn't believe it. If it was a question of money, I said I would pay for it myself. And proceeded apace. Alistair Layzell, the brilliant PR agent for my other books, was delighted to take on the job, but rang to tell me that he couldn't because the publisher refused to send out any copies, in advance, or at any time. This didn't make sense. Any internal PR agent in Penguin would surely have been interested in the marketing potential of a high-profile debate by two of its authors, but not, at all, if one of them wouldn't play ball. Neil, I'm sure, wouldn't. The editor of the book, Joe Staines, one of the brightest among the very bright editors I have had the pleasure of dealing with, told me later, kindly, 'If you'd been on the radio twice a day for the best part of half a year, as Neil was with his *100 Objects*, you'd have sold a lot more copies than he did.' So, my book was systematically buried.

Gabriele Finaldi, one of Neil's successors recently suggested in public that the collection's cut-off date of 1900 should be reconsidered. I went to see him immediately. He was kind enough to offer me coffee in his office. It was now the home to a grand piano (you can judge the room's size), which Gabriele had brought with him because he liked to play to help him consider things, and presumably it helped to drown the din of the buskers in Trafalgar Square outside.

Gabriele is immensely tall with a pronounced chin and eyes set high under beetling brows. He looks more like a Spanish rugby player than a British art historian. He listened to me politely. I ended by saying that he should revive the traditional relationship with the Tate, and move, immediately, Picasso's *Three Dancers,* Chagall's *Poet Reclining* and Ernst's *Elephant Celebes* to hang on his walls. He could never, ever, acquire such paintings now. But he didn't need to because they are owned by the people and need to be seen at their best in the context of the greatest paintings of the past. He lifted his hands slightly, in vague horror, and said, 'I can't possibly do that!'

'Why ever not?' I left him to his piano and the continuing decapitated state of the great art of painting today.

M *is for* EUAN MACKIE

I've only felt the hairs in the nape of my neck stand on end—a most unnerving, involuntary experience—twice in my life. Once when I was cycling to school when I was about twelve. An old man was cycling just in front of me, wearing a long raincoat. We came to a corner, but he went on cycling straight ahead, and disappeared through a brick wall. I must have imagined him, of course, but in that moment, I was sure I'd seen a ghost.

The second time was when I visited Gilmerton Cove. My wife, Gillian Tait, was writing a III guide to places in Edinburgh you shouldn't miss, and she wanted to visit a strange old underground chamber that was supposed to be a pub in the middle of the little, run-down village of Gilmerton on the southern fringes of the city. It had been known about since 1721, when one George Paterson, the cottage owner, had been accused of selling liquor there on the Sabbath, to 'the great many people' who had come to see his very strange caves. He had supposedly excavated these himself, and John Lawson, the current city archæologist, had decided that indeed he had, and that it was, indeed, a pub.

I drove her there and didn't want to go inside. I feel claustrophobic in underground spaces, and had no interest in a cellar, carved for barrels. But I had nothing to read in the car, and for some reason followed her in. The caves were down some steps in the floor of a little old cottage, which had been turned into a local tourist attraction. I edged down, wearing the helmet I'd been given. The low underground passage led to what was simply one of the most extraordinary places I have ever been in. My mouth dropped open in astonishment, and the hairs in the nape of my neck rose virtually vertical. I hadn't seen a ghost, but felt I had, and several.

The room before me, entirely carved out of solid bedrock, was large, oval and bending, like a big kidney on its side. The walls and ceiling, which was easily high enough to stand under, were all curved. But what was even more amazing was that, running the length of the room, in the centre, was a table, also carved out of the bedrock, and curved, like a horn or a truncated, crescent moon, lying on its side, pointed at one end, but blunt at the other, with a beautifully smooth top surface, into which had been carved a single, immaculate large bowl close to the abrupt, wider end. And from the centre of this table rose a beautiful pillar that arched up into the roof—the whole of this elegant configuration cut out of, or rather into solid rock! But—and this was perhaps even more extraordinary—all round the curving walls, edging close to the table, was a continuous, jutting seat which had been carved out of the bedrock too. It was capable, I quickly estimated, of seating at least twenty people, if not more. I had the overpowering feeling that I was in the presence of ghosts, not guests.

This was, obviously, not a pub. There was a dozen of these in Gilmerton at that time, humble licensed premises, at very best a

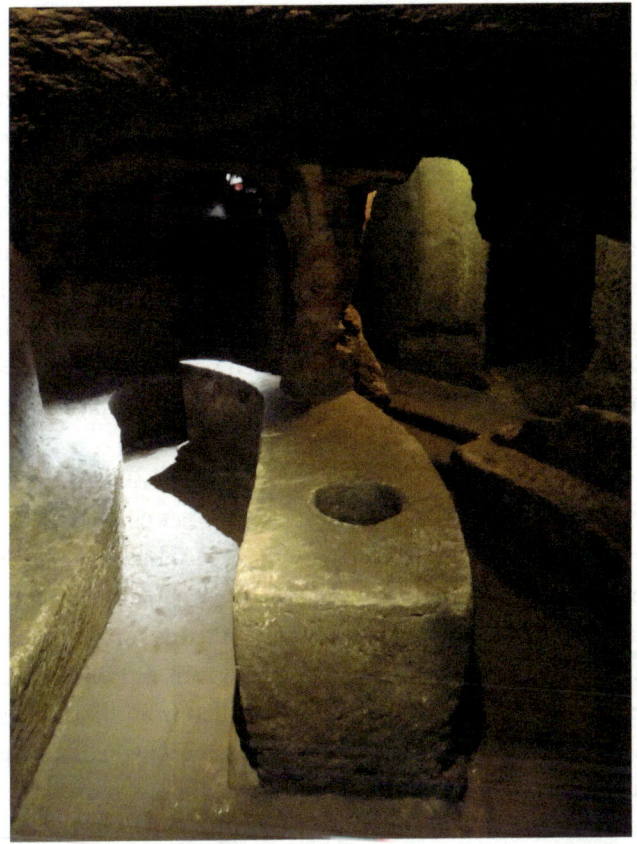

Gilmerton Cove, Edinburgh

couple of benches in the front room of a simple dwelling. Nor had this place anything to do, whatsoever, with eighteenth-century Scotland. That was an age of neoclassical straight lines, the rectitude of state Christianity, with God above, the devil below, and everyone knowing their place in the strict, layered hierarchy of society; this place was all curves, horns and moons—the much more complex, subtler, interconnectedness suggested by Celtic imagery.

If George Patterson had indeed dug it out himself, underground, he would have been accused by the church of devil worship, not just selling beer! What I was looking at was much, much more interesting. I'd visited many ancient underground excavations from Malta to Turkey, India to China, as part of my research for my book *Realisation—From Seeing to Understanding*, and I'd never, anywhere, seen anything remotely as beautiful, sophisticated and strange as this. And the quality of chiselling, in very hard sandstone, was worthy of the finest sculptors in the world. It must have taken a team of men several years to excavate so much open space as this, and to finish every surface so exquisitely and with such care.

And this was only the start of the tour. As I explored the 'Cove' further, I discovered other chambers, with inset tables and seating, long corridors, cavernous rooms with what looked like shelving, and a bewildering low passageway, much too small for anyone but a child to crawl into, receding for several yards into the bedrock, with a channel carved into its base and, even more intriguing, a wide passage, big enough to walk into, filled from floor to ceiling with rubble. The 'Cove' obviously was much bigger than the bit I could see. I was very excited and was sure I had stumbled on something much, much older than 1721, packed with the curved, horned shapes of Celtic symbolism. It was obvious to me that Paterson couldn't have carved this out himself, no single man would have the physical strength, and certainly not in one lifetime. But what he could have done was dug this bit of it out if it had been deliberately filled in with rubble. This made me even more excited, for many ancient sacred sites were filled in and deliberately hidden by their makers. This is exactly what had happened to Gobekli Tepi in Turkey, the most ancient religious temple so far discovered on earth, which I had just visited. And here was possibly another, on my doorstep!

I immediately contacted everyone I could—but to my amazement I couldn't get anyone interested. Edinburgh's archæologist, John Lawson, said it was a pub and he stuck to the opinion. I asked him if he'd ever seen an eighteenth-century pub like that? He just shrugged. Mel Johnson, the archæologist who'd carried out an excavation and wrote the report on the site for the city in 2006, at least came to see it, but she stood at the door of the cottage above and said, 'I don't know why I'm here. I'm not going to change my mind, you know.' I was tempted to say, well go away then, but I was kinder and getting a bit desperate. 'I'm not asking you to change your mind,' I said, 'just to look.' Reluctantly she did and didn't. She still thought it was built as a pub. 'Built?' I asked. I wonder if she realised that it had to have been carved by hand, out of very hard bedrock. What amazed me about all this was that people, perhaps especially experts, couldn't actually see what they were looking at, even though what they were looking was staring them in the face. Mel wasn't the only one who kept on referring to it as having been constructed, when this is the reverse of how it had been made.

Deeply frustrated, I dropped a line to Sir Barry Cunliffe, the top specialist on early British archæology. He'd been kind enough to say publicly that the theory, proposed in my book *Realisation*, might be right: Stonehenge could have been used as a raised, circular ceremonial platform (the stones were stronger supports that replaced the previous wooden ones to cope with the increasing crowds)—in effect like a Mecca on stilts, enabling hundreds of pilgrims to pray to their gods as they followed the circular movement of the stars around the North Pole at night. He replied at once that he couldn't come to Edinburgh right then but suggested I contacted Euan Mackie, who was one of the few archæologists he knew who had the knowledge and the open-mindedness to respond to what I had discovered.

I collected Euan from the station. He was tall and striking and wearing a wide-brimmed Australian hat—he looked as though he'd just stepped out of a film of Indiana Jones. He'd worked in museums too and though we knew many people in common, our paths had never crossed. I drove him to the Cove. He walked around the whole complex, listening to my comments, but not saying a thing. I had, for example, discovered that the narrowing shafts excavated upwards into the ceiling were orientated towards the cardinal directions. Eventually, he sat down on the carved bench beside the carved moon table in the main chamber and said—I will never forget his words: 'I think you've discovered a Druid temple.'

I hadn't thought about the Druids. I didn't know much about them—no one does—but Euan pointed out all that we do know about them—that they were a secret priesthood who effectively ruled northwestern Europe, who memorised all their sacred texts and wrote nothing down (there are no texts or images on any of the walls of Gilmerton Cove—a most unusual attribute for such a complex carving), met in secret places away from city centres, were avid readers of the stars and conducted peace negotiations between warring factions—all of these attributes could have been performed at Gilmerton Cove.

We managed to raise some press interest, which inspired Dr Richard Bates of the School of Earth and Environmental Sciences at St Andrews University to carry out, on his own initiative, in 2017, a survey of the nearby land above ground using a ground-penetrating radar. He discovered evidence of a further large underground chamber directly in line with the blocked-up passageway in the Cove beneath. The exciting possibility is that whole Cove might be almost twice the size of the section currently exposed! And if this infill is original and undisturbed, it should be possible to test the walls for when they were last exposed to light, providing a *terminus ante quem* for the carving of the Cove. If this date is 500 CE or earlier, Gilmerton could indeed be the first Druid temple to be discovered in the world!

Edinburgh City, however, still refused to take any interest, let alone any initiative. I couldn't help thinking what Pat Lally would have done if this discovery had been made in Glasgow. The mere fact that there was a possibility would have been enough for him. The very earth would have moved, and no stone would have been unturned. What other city in the world has a site as potentially as important as Stonehenge within its bounds? And I couldn't help thinking how Gilmerton Cove related to Mackintosh, with his interest in secret Celtic mysticism. How he would have loved the shapes, the forms, the curves! But Edinburgh, perhaps proud of its straight-backed, upright, no-nonsense New Town neoclassicism, has let the whole mystery go hang.

There was nothing left that Euan and I could do but write an article for the *Scottish Archaeological Journal*. Ian was nearing retirement, and, as he said, wanted 'to spend his last years in a beautiful universe'. He just managed to, largely due to his partner, Elizabeth Pitts, before Alzheimers took its toll. He died in 2020. Sir Barry Cunliffe has promised me to come up and have a look—his assessment will settle it—but he was prevented by having to have a hip replacement. So, this story is waiting an ending. I don't believe I'm seeing ghosts again—the evidence is staring everyone in the face. But it's so strong and so unusual that hardly anyone can see it. It is an artefact in itself, created by a team of carvers individually as skilled as Michelangelo working to an equally imaginative vision in their minds. Gilmerton Cove, when it is seen for what it is—a profound and fascinating work of art—if Euan and I are right, will change the history of Europe.

M *is for* CHARLES RENNIE MACKINTOSH

Among the many reasons why I was attracted to the job in Glasgow was the work of Charles Rennie Mackintosh. A city that could not only give birth to but also, much more significantly, commission almost all the major works by such a brilliant artist/architect had to have a lot going for it. We had, in Sheffield Galleries, a high-backed chair by him that had first aroused my interest. I travelled to Glasgow to see his school of art and the flat he'd designed for himself and his wife. I'd rarely ever seen love and wonder so exquisitely expressed, visually, and in a single room. This was an encompassing artistic vision, not simply brilliant design. Art and life, for Mackintosh, were clearly one.

It was the sight of these that gave me the idea to put on an exhibition in Sheffield of a century of British design, from the Arts and Crafts movement to the latest engineering, which we eventually called *Home Spun to High Speed*, for it ended with Kenneth Grange's spanking new High Speed Train (he said he'd only done a nose-job, which was, in a way, true). Another reason for doing the show is that I could harness the abilities of the remarkable Sheffield duo, Fiona MacCarthy, the writer, historian and expert on Arts and Crafts, and her husband, David Mellor, the famous cutler and designer. I've rarely ever met so precise a pair.

Fiona was small, firm and sure, with a lock of hair that fell repeatedly over one eye, which she kept having to brush aside, the waywardness of which betraying a darker, more passionate side to her nature, as did her voice, which was slow, rather deep and thoughtful, but which also always smiled. David was large and impressive, thick-browed and set and appeared totally at ease with himself, which manifested itself in his relaxed smile, and his slow, comfortable Sheffield accent. Both of them were precisely methodical, David with tooling, Fiona with words, seeking always absolute clarity in form and expression. David once told me that if he made one small step forward in something he was doing every day that was enough. It's been a measure for me ever since. They were a formidable combination that resulted in one of the best exhibitions I have ever put on. But even in the array of superb of designs they collected—British visual thinking at its best—Mackintosh shone. His work seemed imaginatively on a level above everyone. I was therefore very surprised to find, when I arrived to work in Glasgow, that this magnificent artist was ignored, even despised, by the city's own galleries and museums.

I make it a point of going everywhere when I take over a new job, looking behind every door, especially those to which a key, mysteriously, can't be found. One such in Glasgow, a store for one of the shops, was actually leaping with fleas when at last it was opened for me and piled high with unsold volumes that were unaccounted for in any audit. Another big store was packed with old tea chests, most of them unopened. What are those, I asked? 'Oh, that's the Japanese Gift, given to the city in exchange for Glasgow sending their experts, a century ago, to teach them shipbuilding.' I got them opened, at last, but it's true they weren't interesting—full of late nineteenth-century examples of Japanese mass-produced ceramics, mostly tedious, over-decorated tea sets, bowls and vases. Japan definitely got the better half of that bargain, judging by its booming dockyards as Glasgow's own declined, though, predictably, not to make teacups instead.

I walked into one even bigger store, at the back of Glasgow's Transport Museum (now called the Riverside Museum). It was piled to the roof with stacks of timber slats. What's all this, I asked Tony Browning, the about-to-retire deputy director who was taking me round. His lips curled in disgust: 'Oh, that's the Ingram

Street Tea Rooms. If I were you, I'd get rid of them as soon as you can.' I'd heard of the Ingram Street Tea Rooms, but had no idea that they still existed, apart from the partial reconstruction of the blue Chinese Room, which was on display in Kelvingrove. Mackintosh built these tea rooms over a period from 1900 to 1912. They were one of his masterpieces. Andrew Stone, the conservation officer in charge of furniture, told me later that the deputy director had instructed him to burn it all, not once but twice. He'd refused both times. They only survived because of his dedication, and his calculation that he wouldn't be fired for refusing to put fire to them. I was determined, from that point on, to get them restored and on display, but had no idea what a trial it would be.

Conservation was one of the strengths of the Glasgow Museums. One star was the brilliant, bright-eyed, gentle, dark-haired Dr Norman Tennant, working at the Burrell Collection, who changed conservation by inventing a glue which set at the same refractive index of the broken glass it was repairing and therefore became invisible. Museums, like any possessive institution, are, at any one point, as much about people as they are about things. On my first visit to the huge Burrell stores (almost as large as the public displays above), I noticed white fuzzy spots that looked like bronze disease on some of the Chinese bronzes. Norman, who was showing me round, raised his eyebrows wearily when I asked about them. 'I've been telling your predecessor about this for years, but he always refused to do anything about it.'

'About what?' Then he explained that the laminated wooden panelling used throughout the stores was emitting corrosive gases that would in time destroy everything in them. The worst place for any object to be was in the Burrell stores! This was not what I wanted to hear. I had enough calls on council funds, facing the advent of the Capital of Culture Year, without getting them to cough up, at once, the hundreds of thousands it would cost to solve this problem. But I had to, and, at least, it was one I could blame on my predecessor. I got the cash and we began the huge replacement work.

Tony Browning had a deep-seated suspicion of conservation. He was based at the Transport Museum (his main passion was commissioning another model of a Clyde-built ship every year) where conservation of an old car meant replacing all the old bits to make it look brand new. When he left, I got the staff, with some difficulty I have to admit, to put on display an unrestored, tattered gypsy caravan we had in store next to the gleaming, fairground version of another one they'd lovingly recreated, to raise questions in the visitor's minds about the truth of what they were looking at in the displays around them.

Those stacks of dark timber slats, saved from Browning's hoped-for holocaust, haunted me. I knew we were sitting on a gold mine, but how to do anything about them, even where to put them? How, even, to get started? Anyone I spoke to wasn't interested, not even Councillor Pat Lally; Glasgow had enough Mackintosh, and it was difficult for them to understand that no one else had any. Worse, to many, Mackintosh was old hat. People in Glasgow wanted to go forward, be more modern, not go back. A prophet always has a hard time being a prophet in his own town, even if, as I repeatedly argued, the town can profit from him.

The 1990 European Capital of Culture would have been the obvious occasion to promote Mackintosh Europe-wide. He had after all a huge influence of European modern design, particularly through his shows in Vienna. But it was too late for me to do anything about that. Graham Roxburgh was building The House for an Art Lover—an unrealised dream based on Mackintosh's designs—an excellent project—while actual interiors by the great man were lying, unloved, in our stores. Moreover, we were committed to a show, organised by Jude Burkhauser, called the *Glasgow Girls*, making the point that there were many of them and equally creative, though so far hidden behind the more famous 'Glasgow Boys'. We were doing the less obvious, but politically correct thing, not promoting big male names, but the women in their shadows. But increasingly, I came to think that this was wrong as far as Mackintosh was concerned. He worked very closely and openly with his wife, Margaret Macdonald, even signing many watercolours with her. I knew of no male artist who had done that, ever. How much more interesting to promote Mackintosh as the first male feminist in art. But the occasion to do that had passed.

Pat Lally eventually got the point. He wasn't particularly interested in Mackintosh but he realised, as he said 'many cities have van Goghs, but you have to come to Glasgow to see Mackintosh'. He backed my idea to do the biggest Mackintosh show ever, in the McLellan Galleries, and I planned it to coincide with the opening of my new Gallery of Modern Art. I decided on this occasion not to tour it to Europe but to America, which was a growing market for Scottish tourism—the Metropolitan Museum in New York, the Art Institute in Chicago and the Los Angeles County Museum of Art all eagerly took the show. One couldn't have had a more prestigious tour. They all, however, as is usual, insisted on having their own designers; they received the loans and then displayed them how they thought best. This proved interesting in itself.

The show got off to a rollicking start with a quarter of a million pound sponsorship from the whisky firm, Whyte and Mackay, secured by our very bright PR officer, Carol Maconachie, who'd come from Edinburgh in the east. She told me once how much she loved her new job—there was only one drawback, she hadn't seen a dry pavement in six months!

We secured fantastic loans, many works of art and paintings that

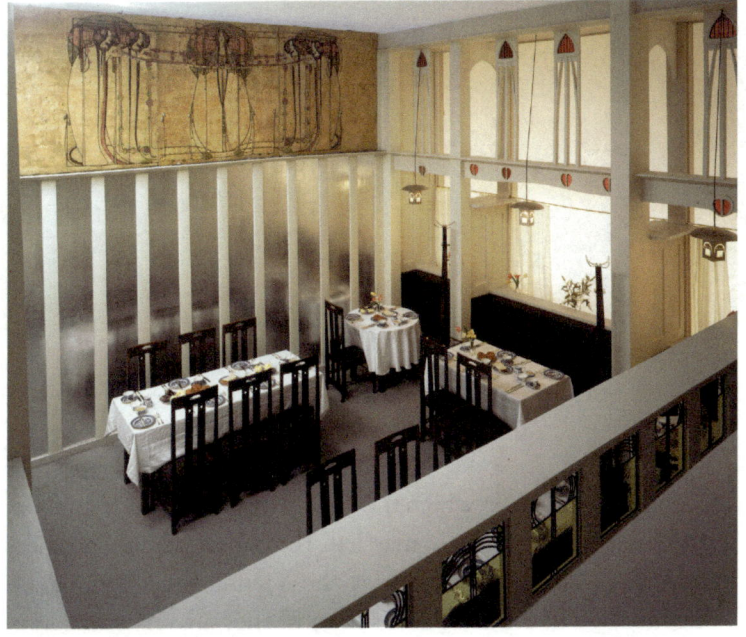

Reconstruction of the White Dining Room, Ingram Tea Rooms

had, over the years, passed into private hands. But the star of the show was the reconstruction of the famous White Dining Room, the first room of the Ingram Street Tea Rooms. We were beginning to make sense of those stacks of timber slats in the store at the back of the Transport Museum. Andrew Stone masterminded the project and discovered that the White Dining Room wasn't actually white, though it had been repainted white over the years, but was originally inlaid with panels of aluminium leaf! The effect, when it was restored, between the beautifully modulated surfaces and detailing of the wooden panels, was stunning.

But what made the room a masterpiece were the two very large, totally original gesso panels, inlaid with string, coloured glass jewels and mother-of-pearl, one by Mackintosh and one by Margaret

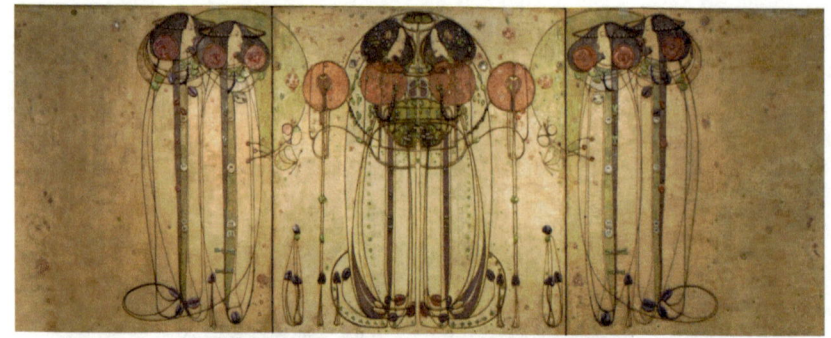

Charles Rennie Mackintosh, The Wassail, 1900
(panel from the Ingram Tea Rooms)

Macdonald, his fiancée, which they worked on side by side, in 1900, in the weeks before they got married. The panels were then exhibited in the Mackintosh Room at the Vienna Secession, before being installed in the Tea Rooms in 1901. They are very similar, yet subtly different, showing willowy and billowy, elegant, elongated women, more plants than people, flowers than faces, swept up in captivating, whirling lines in a dance of loving glances.

These panels, this room, together with Mackintosh's other work convinced me that something more was going on than, simply, design—not that design is a simple process, in any way. His designs weren't function expressed beautifully in form; their beauty wasn't primarily functional at all. Walking into one of Mackintosh's bedrooms and, indeed, this reconstructed aluminium-panelled tea room, was like entering a sacred space: his white-framed beds were like these twin panels, altars for the meeting of bodies, minds and hearts. There were a lot of hints that Mackintosh and his wife were Rosicrucians, and the more I thought about it and looked at his work, the more I thought this could be true.

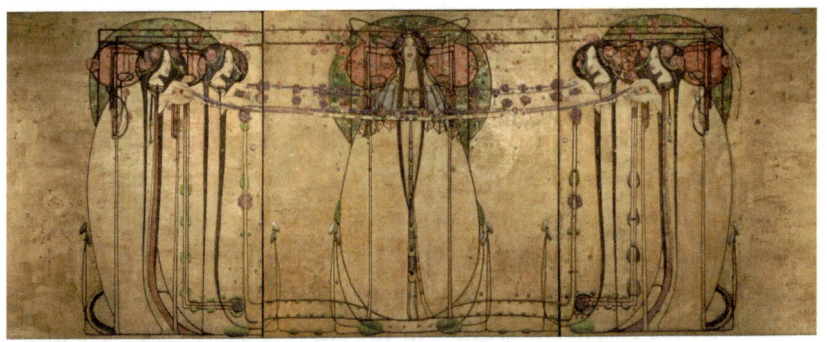

Margaret Macdonald, The May Queen, 1900
(panel from the Ingram Tea Rooms)

The Rosicrucians were a secret religious society, which appeared in the seventeenth century in Europe and believed that a divine order lay hidden within creation and that this had been manifest in Ancient Egyptian, Greek, Judaic, Alchemical and Christian mysticism. Its basic symbols were the rose and the cross. It also held that men and women were not just equal partners but equal powers in creation. But membership of this society was, by order, secret, so there was no direct reference to it in Mackintosh's writings, though, intriguingly, many of his European correspondents had similar secret affiliations. Moreover, all the major founding fathers of modernism, who at the same time at the turn of the twentieth century were breaking through to new forms of abstraction, most famously Mondrian and Kandinsky, were also deeply interested in and inspired by spiritualism. The evidence for Mackintosh being of a similar mind was strong, with a lashing of Celtic symbolism to stir in the brew (see M for Euan MacKie—for another manifestation of secret mysticism in Scotland).

I suggested that the possibility of this interpretation should be explored in the exhibition, but the curators didn't want it. They maintained that it wasn't a proven fact, and thus didn't have a place in a museum exhibit. I argued that the job of a museum nowadays is not only to present truths but to raise questions and stimulate debate. I'd had this argument with the curators of the Israel Museum, Jerusalem. We'd borrowed a selection of their Dead Sea Scrolls. One fragment had a reference to a 'crucified messiah', which might, but only might, be the first historical record of Jesus of Nazareth. I maintained that this tiny section of text should be highlighted as the star exhibit in the show and the case for and against it being a reference to Jesus should be presented in the exhibition. The curators absolutely refused. It wasn't proven, so mustn't be mentioned. So all the visitors passed through unaware of what they might be looking at. I could do nothing about this because it was a loaned exhibition, but the Mackintosh show in Glasgow was our own creation, and I was determined to tackle this issue in an open, non-dogmatic way.

I raised the problem with our designer, Hubert Bari, and his team Creamuse. They'd planned seating areas beside pillars in the corners of the galleries, and Hubert came up with the brilliant idea (yet another) of having Rosicrucian texts reflected in mirrors behind these pillars as an undercurrent of ideas running throughout the exhibition, which you could read or not, much like the hidden belief of Rosicrucianism itself. The curators' labels remained untouched. They were content, and so was I.

I was still intent on restoring the Ingram Street Tea Rooms as a whole, but where could I put them? We didn't have room in any of our galleries. This was a treasure Glasgow was the less without. The National Lottery came on stream to everyone's surprise. They were looking to fund big cultural projects. I had been working for a long time on a major refurbishment of Kelvingrove—a reinvention of the encyclopaedic museum in twenty-first-century terms, no less—with a few handfuls of volunteer staff—what the other curators ironically called my 'dream teams'—and it was obviously the moment to go full steam ahead with that. I wish I had for, with hindsight, it was probably then that I made the biggest mistake, among quite a few I have to admit, of my professional life. The chair of the National Galleries, Angus Grossart, had announced that they wanted to create a new National Gallery of Scottish Art. I thought we, Glasgow, should make a bid for that.

The Mappin Art Gallery in Sheffield, where I'd worked as keeper (as the job was called then, as if anything in it was trying to get out), had an impressive collection of Scottish nineteenth-century painting, and I'd grown to admire the works of artists new to me such as John Pettie, William Quiller Orchardson and Thomas Faed. I began to realise, then, that Scottish art had very different qualities from English art and, almost as interesting, I knew virtually nothing at all about it. I'd been taught the poetry of Wordsworth at school, who was the son of a lawyer who lived a literary life in the Lake District, but not the poems of Burns, a poor peasant farmer, his near contemporary just across the border. I early conceived a mission (among several), long before I went to Scotland, to do something about the English blindness to Scottish culture. And I saw now that this could be the opportunity.

The National Galleries holdings of Scottish art were poorly represented in a desultory, gloomy display in a back basement. What's more, I knew that though their holdings were extensive they were very limited. They had fistfuls of Scottish Colourists, but very few works by the Glasgow Boys and virtually no Mackintosh, whereas we hadn't room to show one of his masterpieces. Edinburgh had, in essence, the national collections of the east coast, whereas we had the national collections of the west. If I could find a way of combining these two collections, we could at last show the world what Scotland had really achieved in terms of both art and design. And we could recreate the Ingram Street

Tea Rooms, since they were only interiors almost entirely without furniture, as the gallery's restaurant and café.

So I put my Kelvingrove 'dream teams' on a side burner and concentrated on realising this long-held dream of mine—to bring Scottish art into the front line. I knew I wouldn't be running the gallery myself when it was operational—it would be run by the National Galleries—nor would I be, in particular, be congratu-lated for its creation—my role would be behind the scenes all the time; the priority was to create a superb showcase for Scottish art as a whole, and get the wonderful Mackintosh Ingram Street Tea Rooms on display, centre stage.

It would have been great if Tim Clifford, the director of the Scottish National Galleries and I had worked together on this new Scottish art and design idea, but he made it clear that, in this project, I was on my own. He wasn't exactly against it, as simply not interested. But to me it was a shoo-in—as obvious a winning project as the money from the newly founded lottery began to pour in.

I gave it my all. This was the best thing I knew I could do for Scotland as a whole. I allocated not just Mackintosh but master-pieces of western Scottish art from Glasgow's collections. We had so much that they wouldn't be missed in Kelvingrove, and anyway they would be seen in a much more telling and exciting context while still being in Glasgow. The National Galleries in Edinburgh had a duty to serve the nation as a whole, so they could show their collections in Glasgow, but Glasgow's art was for Glaswegians, and they would still be seen there. It was a marriage made, well not in heaven, but Glaswegians would argue in the nearest place, for the benefit of everyone.

We held a discreet meeting of some of the most powerful peo-ple in Scotland with strong connections to Glasgow, to clarify our strategy and make sure the project would happen. Angus Grossart was there, a west-coast man himself, and the ever-urbane Lord MacFarlane, head of United Distillers and arguably Scotland's most powerful businessman, who, effortlessly, knew everyone, and so was Donald Dewar, the immensely charming, self-effacing, sloping, loping, bespectacled, highly intellectual Glasgow MP, who looked more like the most honest accountant in the world rather than a politician, a key figure in Tony Blair's Labour government and soon, after devolution, to be Scotland's first First Minister.

The Tories were also represented, by Professor Ross Harper, the head of one of the country's most eminent law firms. I once went to dinner at his house and was surprised, at the end of the meal, to be entertained by African Grey parrots—his wife's favourite pets—flying just above our heads. He was a most charming host.

I was full of flighty optimism when I left this meeting. With backers like these, the project was bound to succeed. Stuart Gulliver, the head of the Enterprise Board, stepped in and bought a building—the superb old, classical Sherriff Court in the heart of Glasgow's Merchant City, just a minute's walk from Queen Street Station, the main link to Edinburgh and much of the rest of Scotland. The building could be totally gutted inside and David Page, the architect, did a demonstration proposal, and the project was submitted to the Lottery Board.

Only then did the Edinburgh establishment begin to get nervous. Sir Malcom Rifkind, the Edinburgh MP, who had served as Secretary of State for Scotland and Foreign Secretary, made the most stupid remark of his career—there might have been others, but of them I am not aware—by asking why should visitors to Edinburgh have to travel another forty miles to see Scotland's art? It was a question that revealed his total ignorance of the fact that the art of Scotland as a whole could not be seen in Edinburgh, and, anyway, the major thrust of the Scottish Tourist Board's new national campaign was to increase the number of 'bed nights' visitors spent in Scotland and encourage them to travel beyond the capital. I became a bit concerned with these rumblings and rang Angus to discuss them. He was bullish: 'I had to climb up Everest in plimsolls to found my bank [Noble Grossart—the Noble is the name of his partner not an adjective, though Angus was to be ennobled later, as a knight]—this is nothing. Scotland always has a habit of having a good idea then dithering for decades until it does finally it.

'This,' he assured me, 'won't happen this time.'

The Lottery Board came on a visit. The key figure on it was Sir David Wilson, former director of the British Museum. He told me, confidentially, how impressed he'd been, particularly with my offer to contribute major works of art. 'At last,' he said, 'two museums working together, not being defensive about their own collections!' He effectively told me that the money for the project was in the bag, but then added 'the only question is does Scotland want it?' I felt a whiff of a chill. Surely, I thought, Donald Dewar —for the decision would be up to him—couldn't renege now, having given the project his support from the beginning?

But that is what must have happened—though I could never get a straight explanation from him or anyone close to him. He gave the impression of never wanting power, which is one reason why everyone liked him, but, sadly, when he got it, he didn't really know what to do it. He was a leader who wanted to be lead. And I think he was influenced by those around him who feared that a National Gallery of Scottish Art could feed into Scottish Nationalism, which was then on the rise and would, indeed, soon take over. This was selling Scotland short, for this gallery would have shown that Scotland is not a suppressed back yard full of also-rans (which is how it is treated by the National Galleries now) but a vital, distinct cultural part of the United Kingdom as a whole.

A National Gallery of Scottish Art and Design has to happen sometime. The recently opened V&A Dundee is no substitute. It's an odd outreach project by the London museum, housed in a rather moving building on the outside by Kengo Kuma, a sort of Fingal's Cave turned on its side. Inside it contains two standard, dark rectangular blocks (they could be containers dropped within), one for travelling exhibitions from the V&A in London and other exhibiting a confusing, ragbag of Scottish artefacts, including the oak-panelled room from the Ingram Street Tea Rooms, the dullest and least telling of Mackintosh's work there, lent by Glasgow. There's a much, much bigger and more beautiful, fascinating story to be told. And Mackintosh and Macdonald's aluminium-panelled love nest needs to be at the heart of it.

M *is for* DAVID MEASURES

My earliest memories are of wildlife, seeing how many snails I could get into my top shirt pocket—not many (they kept stretching out their necks and protruding, magically, out of their smooth brows, their amazing, prolonged eyes while trying to crawl up and out—I'd tap them back in)—and attempting to race frogs—utterly hopeless as they hopped in all directions except the one I wanted. I knew the names of all the common species of butterflies and moths, amphibians and flowers—many rare now, some endangered, like the mottled great-crested newt and the weird herb-paris, which we took for granted—that lived in the ponds and on the scrub wasteland opposite our house, before the council cleared it with bulldozers and grassed it over when I was about eight, eager to improve this eyesore. They left a useless sloping, barren field with one swing, which they called a 'recreation area'—a traumatic experience for me as I watched the bulldozers plough up and kill, in utter ignorance, all the creatures and plants I loved, and my first taste—one that has stayed with me all my life—of the potential meanness of the unimaginative, municipal mind.

So I was a bit surprised when I went to art school, having thought I'd 'put aside childhood things' to discover a teacher who not only shared but also still delighted in this early interest of mine in natural history. David Measures was an oddball in every way. He'd been born with an inability to sweat, which meant his dry skin was more like a lizard's than a man's. I remember him as bald, which might not always have been the case, but he often grew a big beard. He was thin and extremely agile as if about to leap from the tips of his toes, rather than the flats of his feet. He had thick lips, always curling into a smile. But what was most extraordinary about him, almost alarming, were his eyes. They were greenish and large and seemed to take everything in, while he himself shrunk to nothing behind them, and became almost invisible. At moments like this, he was more of a chameleon than a human being.

This happened particularly when he was painting, which he always did outside, in nature. He carried with him a board clipped with sheets of thick watercolour paper, a small black tin of watercolours, a couple of brushes and a biro pen. Water often had to be abandoned, as well as brushes, and he was left making do with his fingertips and nails dipped in pigment and dampened by spit to capture on paper his elusive, darting quarry. His speed of working and seeing was extraordinary. He was, and still is, the only artist I have known who could paint a butterfly on the wing. To do that he had to remain very still, not to scare them away in the first

Opposite: David Measures, Purple Emperor Butterfly, 14 July 2007

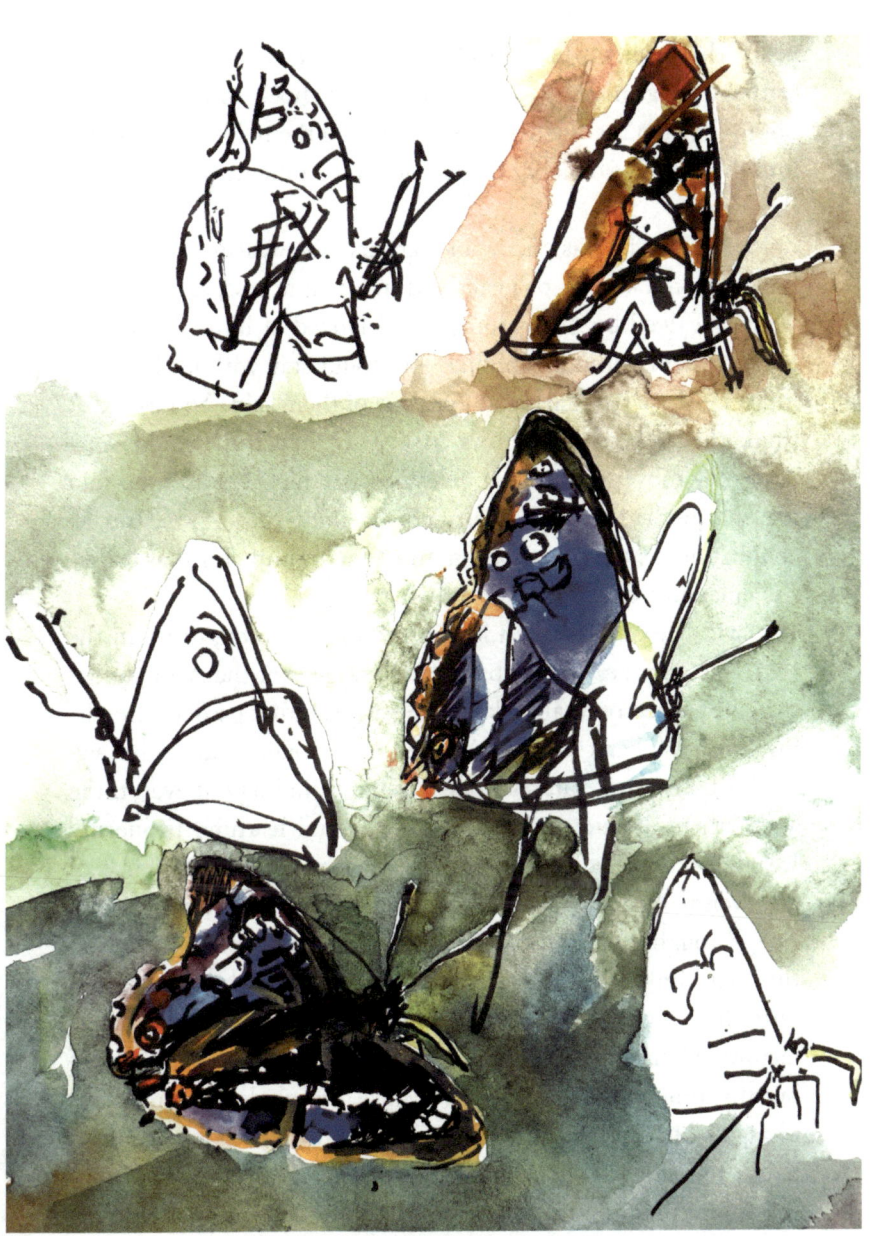

place—butterflies often flew close to find out what or who he was, settling, for a moment, on his clothes or shoes—and, above all, not to frighten them when he was painting them. He fooled them into thinking his dancing fingers were just some leaves playing in the wind.

He told me he was once standing very still, wearing an old long raincoat, on a stretch of heathland in a nature reserve when two women walked by. They stopped and looked at him—he looked back at them without blinking—he could stay without blinking forever—then, still staring at him, one of them said, 'You wouldn't think they'd need scarecrows in a place like this, would you?' And they moved on, totally unawares. He had to admit, he told me, that he had great difficulty not breaking into a grin. But he couldn't move: the hunt was on, this time, I think, for that exquisite emerald treasure, the green hairstreak.

David Measures had an idyllic childhood—brought up in the Old Toll Cottage, by the abandoned bridge over the Avon, under the cliff topped by Warwick Castle—its beautiful garden, stretching down the bank side, is still open to the public, run by his sister, Julia. His main interest then was birds, finding out everything about them, including dissecting them and learning taxidermy. Leaving school, he couldn't decide whether to study science or art, eventually choosing the latter, which led him away from nature, through constructions into analysing pure colour, which in turn led him back to nature again, for he found the colours in a butterfly's wings more wonderful than anything he could manufacture. All his childhood interest in wildlife had flooded back—but this time with art as well as science, his whole awareness was engaged. He described in words on his drawings what he couldn't paint, and painted what he couldn't write, in his intense attempt to capture the totality of experience, the wonder of existence. He wanted, simply, to experience the whole thing.

He wasn't, for a minute, trying to make something called 'art'. He was much bolder and more original than that. He was just doing what fascinated him as best he could. He told me he felt he'd achieved something, lived as fully as he could, if he'd 'caught something' in his paintings and note-taking. It was as elusive and as specific as that—almost as elusive as the butterflies he tried to catch, not by killing them and pinning them on boards, as collectors used to do, but by letting them live. Like Henri Cartier-Bresson's photos, they too capture the essence of William Blake's poem: 'He who kisses the joy as it flies/ Lives in eternity's sunrise.' This is something we all have to learn to do, enjoy nature without destroying it if we are going to save our world. By wanting wholeness, by crossing barriers between science and art, David Measures extended the language of art for our times. He was a truly modern radical.

You wouldn't think so from the derisory comments I engendered for buying a group of his paintings, for virtually nothing, for the Gallery of Modern Art in Glasgow. This gossip reached the ears of Donald Dewar, who confronted me, when we happen to meet, with the question: 'What's all this trouble about your Gallery of Modern Art? I hear you're even buying butterfly paintings!' I fixed him with, I fear, a stony eye, 'I regard them as some of the best watercolour paintings I have seen, brilliant, free and precise, delicate and exuberant all at once. And anyone who says that butterflies aren't in the front line of global warming, and not a legitimate subject for art, hasn't begun to think.'

He looked sheepish, and said, 'Oh dear, I should have thought you'd say something like that,' annoyed with himself that he'd allowed his own judgement to be swayed by an ill-considered opinion he'd overheard.

I refrained from pressing home my advantage, and telling him that anyone who fed him that opinion was clearly in ignorance of Damien Hirst's work, who often uses butterflies in his work as symbols of nature's beauty and fragility, but he does it by killing specially bred ones in their hundreds and pinning them on boards. But I didn't. It's up to artists to extend the language of art and they often surprise themselves and others by doing it. Art is always a step into the unknown and we need to be doubly suspicious of artist who claims they know where they're going before they've got there.

I could have told Donald Dewar, too, that other artists were beginning to follow David's breakthrough, by adding notes of observations to their work, such as Darren Woodhead, in his spontaneous, very large outdoor sketches, James McCallum and a new international movement called Artists for Nature formed by the enterprising Dutchman, Ysbrand Brouwers (see also T for Hock Aun Teh). A leading figure surfing this swelling tide of what I've dubbed 'Live Art'—like 'live film' it records the moment, and is misrepresented as 'wildlife art' or 'nature study'—is Kurt Jackson, an artist who, like Measures, couldn't at first make up his mind whether to become a scientist or a painter, but chose the latter path, after an inspiring year spent crossing Africa, mostly on foot, with his wife. He is the first really big artist of the era of Global Burning, charting the spirited sallies of Greenpeace and changes in the environment in many places around the world, above all in Cornwall, where he is based. And he writes notes on many of his works, in the Measures way, knowing now that we urgently need to grasp the implications of everything we can see, the science in it and the art, if we're going to save the world's wonder, which his paintings often praise so beautifully.

Jackson is the equivalent in art to the films of the natural world, such as those of David Attenborough, Alastair Fothergill and Keith Scholey. I met David Attenborough once at an exhibition in Edinburgh. We had a long chat on the gallery sofa. I tried to persuade him to make a film about what was going wrong with the world as well as what was going right. I asked him to swivel the camera round to show what has happened to so much of nature since he'd begun filming as a young man. He was totally against the notion. 'We have to praise what is wonderful,' he said, 'that's the only way to make people want to save the world.' I told him I'd written a book about wonder—*The Art of Wonder*. He asked to see it, so I sent him a copy.

He disagreed with one of its main theses—that the scientists of the European Enlightenment had stripped nature of its wonder—wonder in the sense of something being eternally mysterious, beyond grasp, and therefore plausibly a divine creation. Newton's unpacking of the rainbow—anyone could make one with a prism and a lens—and Goethe's determination to prove him wrong (he showed that colours could be created by spinning black and white discs—the rainbow as a product of moral conflict) perfectly exemplified the battle over the ownership of mystery. Attenborough argued that the discoveries of science make nature more wonderful, not less. This, to me, is wishful thinking. We've grown arrogant towards nature because we think we understand it; it's in our grasp to use. I think one of the great challenges we face is to recover our sense of wonder and our capacity for praise, while still being totally realistic about what we are doing to our world.

Fortunately, Attenborough and his film crew have now, nearly two decades later, totally changed tack and accept they have to warn as well as praise. Other voices must have persuaded him. They've swivelled their cameras round from the few remaining idyllic spots and shown the disaster that's encroaching. Their filming of a lonely orang-utan clinging to the upper trunk of a blasted, leafless tree, surrounded by the felled branches of what was once the Malaysian rainforest, laid waste for the planting of palm oils, is one of the most telling images of our times.

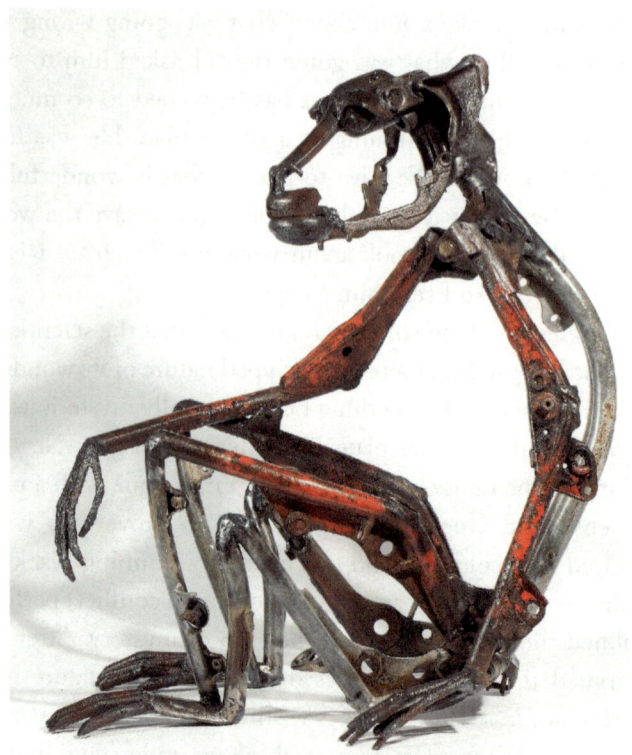

Helen Denerley, Rock Ape 1, 2016

Helen Denerley, the Scottish sculptor, approaches nature from a very different angle. Using scrap metal, discarded fragments from the very fossil-fuel-driven machines that are destroying it, she recreates in her studio, the breathing presences of a wolf, a leopard or a stag. What's extraordinary about her sculptures is that they are mostly made of space, the air they take in that gives them life, their alertness and—this is magical—the light in them that enables them to look out. You sense their presence, forgetting how little there is there. Her sculptures are so vividly real

246

that she once had to take one of her horses away from a bankside where she'd placed it because a farmer complained that his horses, in the nearby field, were crowding close to the fence to look at it all the time and forgetting to feed. Then when what they're made of resurfaces in your mind, you realise that the machines we build are really only extensions of our own muscles, movements and bones.

Measures lived in an earlier age, not that long ago, certainly within my lifetime, when it was still possible to be optimistic about the future of nature—there was still enough of it about, as there was in the little scrappy wood of my childhood, full of wonderful wildlife, before being cleared away for 'improvement'. Children now rarely see frogs, and virtually never the magnificent spotted orange belly and fierce dragon face of the great-crested newt. Measures was able to paint all the species of British butter-flies in their natural habitat, even the large blue, though it became extinct in his lifetime and had to be reintroduced. He was able to help with its successful reintroduction, because he'd noticed that it, like other males in the family of blues, needed immense height to perform a dance before mating. The first reintroduced males were caged and didn't mate. They had to fly free to multiply.

There is a joyous enthusiasm in David's work, which might strike some as being simplistic to such an extent that some would claim it can't be included in the 'art' of our time—and certainly this was an element in the mockery gossiped about me for ac-quiring this artist's work. But art has to be positive, or what is the point of making it? There was, it's true, a vein of naïvety in David's hopefulness, which is partly what made him such a joy to be with. He told me once he was on the Bass Rock with his friend the bird painter, John Busby. They'd been staying at a B&B in North Berwick and had been given packed lunches to take on the boat— they'd be away all day. David put his open on a rock beside him as he painted. Feeling hungry, he turned to look at and, delighted to see a shiny black olive, popped it in his mouth. It was a slug ... that had crawled into his salad pack when he wasn't looking. I can still imagine the grimace on his face. In a way, all David's slugs were olives and one couldn't help loving him for it.

A major representation of his extraordinary life's work is now in the Natural History Museum in London, bridging the crucial gap between science and art.

P *is for* PABLO PICASSO

I was very surprised to see on a map of Picasso's travels—he hardly ever went anywhere outside France after he'd left Spain—two little dots in the UK, one for London and the other for Sheffield. He passed through the capital on his way, as a Communist Party member, to the World Peace Council held in the city in 1950. The Home Secretary at the time let him in, saying he wasn't a serious politician, but excluded Shostakovich who he said was. One of our attendants remembered the occasion—Picasso had his hair cut, he told me. I was chair of the Hayward committee at that time and we were putting on a big Picasso show; I happened to mention this fact to the Arts Council PR department who were delighted and got the *Sheffield Telegraph* to advertise for the barber, offering him a free trip to London to see the show. The fellow responded and came. He remembered Picasso very well but didn't have much to say about cutting his hair other than to remark, 'Well, he didn't have much of it.'

Had I known what I do now, I would have gone to see Picasso and got a painting from him, preferably two, exploring peace and war, to celebrate his visit to the city, and I'm still kicking myself, metaphorically, that I didn't. But it simply never occurred to me to do so. It was just that I hadn't then realised the significance of the role that galleries can play in people's lives, in the minds of the general public and of artist's, of course. I'm sure I would have been successful, and what a tale I'd have to tell! I was only twenty-five when the artist died, but that's no real excuse.

The statures of both Picasso and Matisse have, if anything, grown over the century; they tower above art today, even higher still, and the shadows of their achievements spread even further into our future. I went to an unforgettable retrospective of Matisse in New York which showed how his art wasn't a single mountain slope climbing to abstraction—his late paper cut-outs didn't take off from Fauvism. His trajectory was a series of summits with extended dips between. Each time he peaked, he dived down to start drawing again simply what he saw in front of him, and beginning from there aimed at a new, even higher horizon. He did this several times during his life. Picasso was doing it every day, sometimes every hour. He dated his work meticulously, sometimes even timed it, because he said he didn't know how he got from here to there, but someone would he thought, in time, and these notes and dates might be helpful. I became fascinated by this process of discovery, partly, it has to be said, because I knew I didn't have it. Picasso was my biggest influence when I discovered him when I was about eight, but I knew even then that I could imitate and calculate but I couldn't really create. This was brought home to me during my first full-time job at the Durham Light Infantry (DLI) Museum and Arts Centre Durham.

The keeper-in-charge (such was her title) was Nerys Johnson, a ferocious, diminutive, wide-eyed woman crumpled from birth by rheumatoid arthritis. She told me that she'd never known what it was like to run. She had a three-wheeled, blue-painted fibreglass invalid car to get about. When she first got into it, she was so excited that she drove it as fast as it could go (not very), but then realised that she had no idea how to stop it. It careered along the road and then, at a bend, rolled over into a ditch on its side. She managed, by wriggling round, to poke her head out of the window and signal to a passing car. It stopped. A man got out, pulled her out, lifted the vehicle with two hands back onto the road, set it upright, told her to get in at once and drive, but this time, he suggested 'Use the brake.' She never, really, did use a brake.

We put on a roller-coaster programme of invigorating exhibitions by living artists, all with packed education programmes. Nerys loved visitors painting and drawing in the galleries and when she could, she joined in. I did too at times. In a show about portraits, we had empty frames hung from the ceiling between two chairs, with pencils and papers provided, and visitors could draw their friends. To my surprise the chairs were always full. Later, in a show I did about watercolours, I put vases of flowers on tables, with sheets of paper and watercolours. It was amazing how many visitors tried their hand.

I remember sitting drawing near Nerys once and suddenly noticed her concentration change. I could see she was becoming inspired: her lines flew, as they never did for me. When she retired early—the disease ate into her so much she could hardly lift a brush, get out of a chair, let alone drive a car—she dedicated all her energies to art, even though, towards the end, she always had to have student assistants sitting with her to lift all the materials, even the smallest sheet of paper. She produced a unique small œuvre of hand-sized flower paintings that glow as gloriously as stained-glass windows.

Nerys made me realise that what I had to look for in art was inspiration, that glow of heightened, imaginative awareness that lifts a creation out of the ordinary run so that it shines with a wholeness that enables you to enjoy and contemplate the mystery of existence—not that I was able to articulate this experience in those terms until I met Raymond Tallis. I knew I didn't have this ability myself, but I could spot it in others. Picasso, of course, had this ability in bucketloads. He reinvented art or to put it in another way brought invention to the foreground in art. It has always been there—and it is what we now value most about art from the past—but it had been buried under art's social purpose. Art today has no purpose (see Tallis again), apart perhaps being a bit to do with belief (see D for Dalí); invention is its essence. And invention is always a discovery of something new. As Picasso said, 'If I knew what I was going to do today, why would I do it?' This became the leitmotif not of my art, which I didn't create, but of my professional life.

I'd heard that plans were being made for the opening of a Center for African Art in New York in 1984, and I remember remarking at an Arts Council meeting that there must be black art in Britain. There isn't any was the common observation around the table. 'Well, we won't know whether there is or not unless we look for it,' I said. We can't only do what we know. I resolved there and then to put on a show of whatever black art we could find at the Mappin Art Gallery in Sheffield, where I was working at the time. I loved journeying into unknown territory. But I knew I was unlikely to get very far if I charged in as a white curator and made the selection myself, tempted as I was. Asking around, I found two excellent black selectors, the photographer Pogus Caesar and the painter Lubaina Himid. The show, *Into the Open*, 1984, was a humdinger.

Among the stars, hidden behind the clouds of ignorant white presumption, were Tam Joseph's brilliant, funny gem of a masterpiece *UK School Report*—a row of three almost identikit snapshots of youths but with gradually extending locks, one in red (likes sport), the next in white (likes music), the last in blue (needs

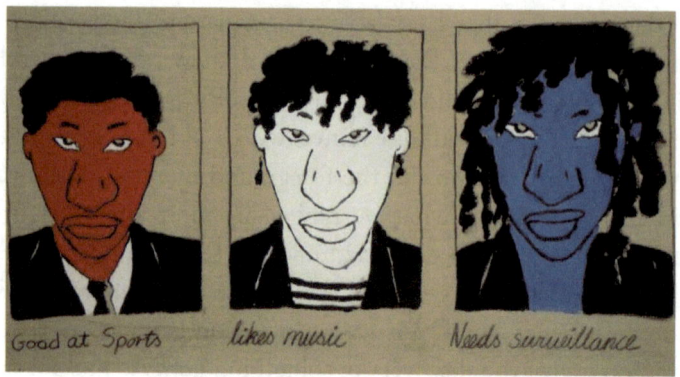

Good at Sports likes music Needs surveillance

Tam Joseph, UK School Report, 1983

surveillance), none black, but then this is Britain. I bought that for Sheffield. Tam told me later that Picasso had been a big influence on his art—it wasn't obvious from looking. Among other discoveries were Keith Piper's sorrowful hangings. I bought one later for Manchester, *Untitled 1986*, a huge close-up of an Ancient Ife head with great sad eyes and a helicopter flying through its red-streaked facial striations, killing life in the jungle. Claudette Johnson's big drawings of nudes took my breath away—they were so direct, naked and honest, with inspired seeing and searing lines that reminded me of Nerys.

All these, then, were unknown discoveries—unknown, that is, by whites such as me. My dealings with black artists, then and subsequently, showed me many incidents of how deeply ingrained racism can be, even by the most well-intentioned. I was interviewing Tam Joseph once for a radio programme in Broadcasting House, London, when, just before we began, the producer popped out from his box, and said to Tam, 'You do know that there's no swearing—this is the BBC.' Then he popped back in again as the live programme was about to start. 'Do you get this often?' I asked

P *is for* PABLO PICASSO

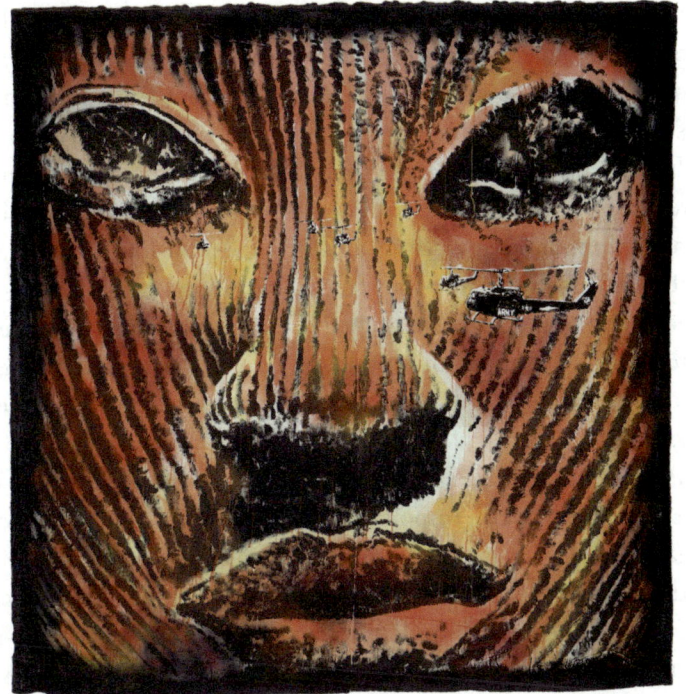

Keith Piper, Untitled 1986, 1986

Tam—I realise now naïvely. Tam looked at me and sighed, 'I've had it all my life.'

Throughout my career, and since, I've been fascinated by Picasso's journey into the unknown, his process of discovery. He famously said (and he said very little about what he was actually doing), 'I do not seek, I find', but later thought he should have said this the other way round. It amounts in fact to the same thing. I dreamt of doing a show of Picasso's creative process—with closely dated and even timed works in series, taken from his whole career. A perfectly realisable project for the backbone of the show would be the prints he made where he kept every stage, and these are in several editions, and therefore easy to borrow. I got the support of John Richardson, Picasso's superb biographer, for the show—'At last,' he said, 'a real exhibition about something that has to be seen in an exhibition!' I went to see Picasso's son, Claude, in his sumptuous Paris flat—I thought the contorted metal furniture was by Diego Giacometti but was told later that they were by Claude himself. He was short and strong—a bit like meeting an embodiment of his father but containing what I imagined was a much gentler nature. He was equally enthusiastic about the idea. But, as with the Jesus exhibition (see B for Hubert Bari), I failed to deliver it due to the political quagmire that Scotland turned into for me.

After I'd left museums, I tried to interest the Royal Academy in the idea. I got a warm response at first, and then a wall of silence. I had become, I was told, by Maurice Davis, a former colleague and most likeable fellow, suave and urbane in mind and physique, but by then keeper of the RA collections, a *persona non grata* in that institution due to my stand against what I dubbed Con Art (con short for conceptual and contemporary, in addition to its usual meaning), even though I had been the first person to buy the then-president Christopher Le Brun's work for a public collection—his early, superb cross-over landscape/abstracts—Claude Lorrain meets Rothko with a dash of Franz Kline. But now apparently I couldn't put a foot right or at least not a foot in the door of the RA, not even on a subject as noncontroversial as this—Picasso's creative process. This is still a wonderful exhibition waiting to be done, for it has so much to teach us. I hope someone does it while I'm still alive to see it.

Q *is for* THE QUEEN

I was once sitting in a pub in Eyam, a village in Derbyshire, with my parents, when a small slip of aged, yellowed, neatly folded newsprint fell out of my mother's handbag. 'What's that?' I asked, picking it up. My father was equally curious. He hadn't seen it before either. 'Oh, I always keep that in my bag,' my mother explained in her matter-of-fact way. 'I've had it for years, move it from bag to bag.' She was about to slip it back, when I unfolded it. She didn't mind. It was an account, now faint and yellowed, of how the Queen Mother made her guests march up and down in front of her after dinner carrying fire pokers, tongues and shovels over their shoulders pretending to be soldiers. 'Why do you keep this?' I asked. 'Oh, to remind me how much I loathe the Royal Family,' as if that was obvious.

I met the Queen twice, and each time I had an hour effectively alone with her, which, now I come to think of it, is rather an unusual occurrence in a life. At the time I thought it was just part of my job and one I was, for the first time but not the second, not particularly looking forward too. I had been brought up on a council estate in South London, and one of my earliest memories was of a children's party—I remember the grown-ups standing around, but not sitting down with us. It was organised by someone with an exceptional public spirit on long tables along the concrete road on the hill near our home, to celebrate the Coronation in 1953. I was five, nearly six. Fortunately, the weather was fine. I remember the bright green and orange jelly in my paper cup and wondering what all the fuss was about. I wasn't very fond of jelly, even then. And when I grew up, I became a staunch republican.

So I wasn't particularly looking forward to meeting the Queen. Was I supposed to bend my head, or even bow? Certainly not, I determined.

The first occasion, when it happened, was a bit bizarre. It was not the usual run of such events when anything that was wrong or could go wrong was swept under the carpet so Her Majesty could sweep through the occasion unaware of any trouble, in a land where the sun always shone, owing partly, as everyone agreed for that moment, to her very existence. On her visit to Glasgow, she knew and I knew I was walking her into quicksand. The exposure of the issue, or rather the fissure, was entirely my fault. Had I anticipated this moment, when I would have, metaphorically speaking, to guide the Queen by the hand through a quagmire partly of my making, I might have shut up earlier and pretended everything was all right. That in retrospect would certainly have been the easier path. But I didn't, and doubt if I would have had anyway. It's never been my nature not to say what I think, and by the time I've opened my mouth, which I tend to do at once whatever the consequences, it's too late not to. It's a bracing way to live, if nothing else.

I need to explain. One of my jobs when I arrived in Glasgow was to refurbish and open the McLellan Galleries, a magnificent suite of Victorian exhibition halls, a little smaller, though not much, than the Royal Academy of Arts galleries in London, and built equally high and ample, on an imposing scale. After the Year of Culture, I knew I was expected to run these galleries as a charging exhibition venue, which would be a very tall order, especially in a place like Glasgow which embraced a great deal of poverty in its hinterland. Given the ambitions for its future—ones I'd inherited with much misgiving and never ones I'd have chosen myself—it was vital that these 'new' galleries opened with a show that would draw large crowds and raise the public's expectation for what they would see there. The Arts Council's *British Art Show* had already been booked in for this opening exhibition by the 1990 Year of Culture team.

I was very happy with this, after all the *British Art Show* had been my idea decades before when I served on an Arts Council committee. I was aware, working outside London, that very few people get to see the art that critics were talking about, the latest Hockney, Freud or Bellany show, for example, and all the new work that was exciting interest because most of these exhibitions were seen in small commercial galleries that few people living in London visit, let alone people from further afield.

My idea was to do a survey show every five years, touring the regions, of the best of recent British Art selected by critics. The year 1990 was time for the next, and it would open in Glasgow in the McLellan Galleries. Nothing could be better. I knew that mature Scottish artists had been doing some wonderful new work and looked forward to seeing this in a national context. But when I asked to have a preview of what was going in the exhibition so I could talk up interest in it, I was shocked. The three young selectors, none of them distinguished critics, had decided to restrict the show to new, mostly unexhibited work produced by young artists who had just graduated from art school, a high proportion of whom came from Goldsmith's College in London where one of the selectors, David Ward, taught. The original concept was out the window, and with it the idea to introduce a wide public to the best modern art that had been created in the last five years. It was an all too typical slip into the easy celebration of youth culture. This wouldn't have been totally awful if the art selected had been any good, but the show contained some of the feeblest expressions of the worst post-Duchampian urinal art I had seen (see D for Marcel Duchamp)—acres of it. And this was the show I had to launch a new gallery with—one that had to earn a substantial income in the future from ticket sales! I couldn't imagine a worse way to put off a future public.

And I suspected something else, which was later confirmed, that the public art world was beginning to be manipulated. The Tate had just announced that the Turner Prize, which they, or rather the patrons (i.e. private funders) of the Tate (the Tate itself being a public body couldn't award prizes) awarded every year to artists who had produced an exceptional body of work, wouldn't be open to any artist as it had been until then, but would be restricted to those under thirty. The decision came as a surprise, without any public discussion. Had there been, I would certainly have argued that creativity isn't a particular attribute of youth, especially not in the visual arts, which require years of development. I knew of many mature artists who were producing remarkable, profound bodies of work, which deserved public recognition and attention, all of which would be eclipsed by this apotheosis of the young. And the Arts Council now, by shifting the focus of the *British Art Show*, had lamely followed suite.

My first instinct was to cancel the show and open the gallery with a real British Art show, with fantastic recent works by the best artists in Britain, of all ages. Pat Lally, the leader of the council, was happy with this. 'If you don't think it's good enough for Glasgow,' he said, 'it isn't.' But he rang me two days later to say that the sponsor for the show 3i, an international and private equity and venture capital company, had told him that if we cancelled it, they would withdraw all their other funding for the Year of Culture, so he told me I had to keep it.

The only way to do that, I thought, was to make the debate public by expressing my reservations about the first show, and putting on another show of my own choosing and letting the public decide if the second was any better. That, at least, would be good publicity for the new venue. Pat Lally agreed with that;

so, this is what I did. But this left me with the task of showing the Queen, who had long been booked to open the refurbished galleries, round an exhibition I had publicly declared I did not rate. Hence the quicksand in this situation. The director of art for the Arts Council, Joanna Drew, a poignant amalgam of a discreet civil servant with artistic passion, told me, with a sparkle in her narrowed eyes, that she was highly amused by the dilemma of my position, but I gathered, as the twinkle turned into a glint of biting coldness—a look she mastered throughout her life—she also thought it served me damn well right for being so outspoken about one of the Arts Council's own exhibitions.

The Queen arrived. Her appearance was too familiar to surprise, but she was much smaller than I'd expected—barely shoulder height. And what struck me at once was her contained energy; she almost bristled with it. I didn't bow, or even bend, but just said hullo, without, of course, shaking hands, which seemed to go down all right. The beginning was OK. She'd come to open the building, after all, not the exhibition. I led her up the grand spiral staircase. The architect had wanted a fancy modern chandelier hanging in the centre to light the space, a zigzag of wires and fluorescent tubes, but I thought it would conflict with the very elegant, Victorian interior. I favoured a conventional chandelier, but a modern version, made with minimally clear glass.

The famous Scottish firm Caithness Glass offered to sponsor it, partly because the chief glass blower on their staff was Franco Toffolo, who had been born and trained in Murano, the island north of Venice where the best chandeliers in the world had been made for centuries. I left it entirely up to him to make it, a tumbling cascade of swirls of molten glass erupting into leaves and flowers. I pointed it out to the Queen as we climbed. Franco stood at the top of the staircase, with his wife. I introduced her to them. Tears suddenly began to trickle down Franco's face. The Queen didn't bat an eyelid; she seemed used to this. I asked him after-wards why he'd been so moved. He told me his father had made the great chandelier for the Met Opera in New York. Now he'd made his great chandelier. Sometime later, I happened to be in Murano and passed a glass firm called Cesare Toffolo. I popped in and asked if they were related. Tears flowed again. They loved their Uncle Franco in Scotland.

We walked into the exhibition space, an extensive sequence of imposing white-painted, top-lit galleries with bits and pieces of artworks littered about, mostly on the floor, some hanging from the ceiling and others occasionally on the walls. I'd decided on the way I'd take her round, avoiding, purely selfishly I have to admit, for my own ease of explanation in the event of being asked, the more explicitly referenced sexual parts. Call me a coward but give me break: I didn't rate the work anyway. I would normally, taking anyone round an exhibition, say a few things to introduce my enthusiasm, but in this instance, I was simply tongue-tied. I knew the Queen wasn't very interested in art anyway and in this art, nor was I. The Queen, I'm sure, had been informed about my opinion. I hadn't exactly kept quiet in the press. But now I de-tected an impish twinkle in her eye at my inability to say a word. (I was already beginning, rather to my surprise, to like her.) So she helped me out.

'Is that an exhibit?' she asked. Her voice took me by surprise. She spoke very fast with a grating, high-pitched edge to her tone. Her voice was clipped and sharp, totally unlike her public, delib-erate, low-tuned drawl. I suddenly sensed I was in the presence of a very different woman and didn't know her at all. Her choice of word was perfect—you get exhibits in exhibitions; they don't have to be works of art. And that's exactly what they were: exhibits, not works of art. I felt more at ease, but still didn't really know what to say. She was indicating some oversize spoons covered in white fur leaning against a wall, a play, I suppose, on Méret Oppenheim's famous fur teacup made in 1936, art echoing art, but for why, I wasn't sure. So, having nothing to add, I just nodded and we moved on. Every so often she asked, 'Is that an exhibit?' But I realised she wasn't really expecting an answer, so I stayed numb, just nodding each time, enjoying the game.

Then she asked, at the end of one gallery, 'Is that an exhibit? What's that?' The additional question caught me off my guard.

'It's bunches of grapes cast in lead—I think it's lead,' I looked more closely, 'yes, lead—hung on wires from the ceiling.'

'Thank you for telling me,' she replied ironically.

Then we turned a corner. 'What's that? Is that an exhibit, too?' she exclaimed, looking at a row of grey filing cabinets with their bottom drawers pulled out, into each of which was stuffed a length of rolled up carpet. I didn't want the Queen to get too close, for the carpets stank and were crawling with bugs, some of which had fascinated our natural history department when they had been called in by conservation to see if the museum should be worried by this possibly invasive species. It seems there were some unusual specimens among them, but none could do us any potential harm. I nodded. A further question followed. 'And who's that by?'

'It's by an artist called Melanie Counsell. She got the idea, I think, when she worked in a mental hospital.'

'Her mind was affected, was it?' Came the quick-fire retort, as usual ambiguous but precisely to the point.

The art of indicating what you mean without saying it, which the Queen has honed over years of practice, was displayed beautifully at the official banquet held in the City Chambers after this visit. Her Majesty read her speech from a little rostrum propped for the moment on her table. 'This morning,' she said in her familiar, slow, mannered drawl so unlike the zappy tones I had just enjoyed, 'I visited the McLellan Galleries.' The room erupted into

laughter, and continued for some time, breaking into little ed-
dies here and there as people imagined her encounter with these
'exhibits'. The Queen looked round the room, her eyes slightly
widening in surprise. She waited for the laughter to die down.
Then, without looking down again at her notes—which made me
think her next remark was unscripted, a rare occurrence for someone who had learnt for years never to depart from a text—she
said in her official slow voice, 'I enjoyed the experience.' The room
burst into laughter again, and so did I. My feelings precisely.

I've only ever done that once since: make a politician—and the
Queen has to be thought of really as a politician—depart from a
set speech. I was once invited to open an exhibition of the work
of Joachim Wtewael, a seventeenth-century painter whose pictures were charged with eroticism, in the gallery of the town of
his birth, Utrecht. I mentioned in my talk that I'd seen in this
exhibition the most beautifully painted nipple in the history of
art. There were several, but one stuck out. The Mayor of Utrecht,
who followed me, ended his read speech by saying, 'now I must go
and find that nipple!' He told me afterwards that in all his long
career in politics, he'd stuck religiously to the golden rule—never,
ever depart from a scripted text. I was the first person who'd ever
made him step out of line.

My next meeting with the Queen was even more fun. Partly, I
have to say, because I was looking forward to it this time. The occasion was the opening of the Gallery of Modern Art I'd created
for Glasgow in Exchange Square, in the middle of the city. There
was a crowd waiting for her behind the railings the police had
erected. Stefan van Raay, the curator of art, was surprised: 'There
would never be such fuss for the Queen of Holland, where I come
from,' he said. She immediately stepped over to them when she
arrived and shook hands with many. I had the distinct impression
that she was happier talking to them than going into the gallery,

fearful, no doubt, of what she might find. But duty eventually called, and I led her in.

There'd been a sweepstake among the artists to guess what colour she'd be wearing. I heard that the painter Stephen Campbell had won, though I never had this confirmed, by guessing that she'd be wearing puce—so bright a puce that it was almost fuchsia—complete with matching hat. I now understood why she could wear these dazzlingly bright colours so naturally; they chimed with the contained energy in her small frame, an energy which, when you are actually beside her, is almost fierce. I had no difficulty in talking to her this time, partly because I'd met her before, liked her and recognised the amused twinkle in her eyes, but most of all because on this occasion I could enthuse freely about what was on display, knowing, at the same time, that I mustn't talk too long nor necessarily expect a response because she wasn't really interested in art at all. I'd therefore arranged for her to meet artists, which I thought she'd much prefer rather than only looking at their art. It was a living art gallery after all.

Usually, galleries are cleared of folk when the Queen opens them and goes round, but I wanted people to be in them, so the arrangements were complex and had to be agreed with her security officer beforehand, step by step, almost minute by minute. And one loo had to be totally secured, the day before, in case it was needed. The tour was to last an hour. Selecting the artists who were to meet her was not an easy task. Scottish, of course, and from the rest of the British Isles, but I also wanted her to meet some artists from afar, because the gallery was deliberately local and global in scope. I, and in particular my secretary, experienced a lot of discreet, and sometimes not so discreet, lobbying by people who wanted to be included and I quite possibly made more lasting enemies among those I didn't select than in the whole of my somewhat tempestuous career. I'd thought of lining them all up so that the Queen could shake hands with each one, as they do with actors after a play, but there were too many of them and there wasn't enough room. Anyway, I wanted the Queen to see the art with the artists themselves. Helen Mirren once told me she was in a line on the stage when the cast was presented to the Queen who'd attended the performance. When she got to Helen, the Queen said, 'I suppose you think you should be doing this.'

Eventually the list was settled, the walking tour arranged and the day came with the artists, with or without companions, standing by their works. The gallery was then totally sealed for security reasons. This distressed the wife of one, who having curtsied lower than I'd ever seen—her skirts spread out across the floor—when the Queen had passed, leapt up and rushed to the exit, exclaiming, 'I've met the Queen! I've met the Queen! I must call my mum! I must!' This was in the days before ubiquitous mobiles. I saw her out of the corner of my eye flailing at the security guard at the door, like a butterfly at a window, distraught with exhilaration and despair, but they couldn't let her out.

We walked past some paintings by Beryl Cook, who'd declined to come—she hated attention and crowds. These were the only works of art in the gallery that the Queen knew who they were by without being told, even though the displays contained typical works by many famous British artists, including David Hockney, Bridget Riley and John Bellany, and even works by artists whom I knew she owned, such as Alan Davie. The Queen was delighted to see the Cooks. I told her what Beryl had asked me to ask her—if she would kindly stop pestering her with medals (she'd just received an OBE). The Queen laughed. I'd not heard the Queen's laugh before. It was short and sharp, but genuine and unforced. I liked her more and more. But her reaction to the artist I introduced her to soon after stirred my republican feelings again.

I'd wanted her to meet international artists, for the gallery was global in its scope. Mathias Kauage, a painter from Papua New Guinea, was one who'd accepted the invitation. I'd seen his work by chance in the basement of the Rebecca Hossack Art Gallery in London and had been bowled over by its inventiveness, exuberance and subject matter. Rebecca Hossack is a lanky, Olympian promoter of genuine Australian Aboriginal art with the real flair for independent judgement. I bought three of Kauage's paintings immediately: a pair showing what happens when a) a girl marries for love, against her parents' wishes—it was called *Leg-over,* and showed her beaming with happiness, her legs wrapped round her lover, encircled by a rainbow—and b) a girl marries the boy her parents choose. This one was called *Suicide,* showing the girl driven to hang herself in the moonlight because of her husband's incurable jealousy. And next to these was Kauage's great, big painting, *Buka War,* showing the battle between local indigenous people and an international mining company—an iconic image of our times.

As an illiterate, unskilled, Highland worker, Kauage had got a job as a cleaner at the university in Port Moresby, where he became fascinated by the paintings of the artist-in-residence there, Georgina Beier, wife of the well-known cultural impresario, Ulli Beier, who'd done much to encourage writing and theatre in Nigeria. Georgina told me later that Kauage kept on pestering her by showing her paintings he'd copied from books, which she repeatedly rejected until one day she saw a crazy spider he'd drawn in one corner. She said she liked that and he suddenly took off. He'd found his style and there was no stopping him: a fabulous, intense fusion of traditional tribal design with modern experiences of life.

Kauage flew over from Papua New Guinea especially for the occasion. That in itself proved a problem. As a Highland tribal

Overleaf: Mathias Kauage, Buka War, 1990

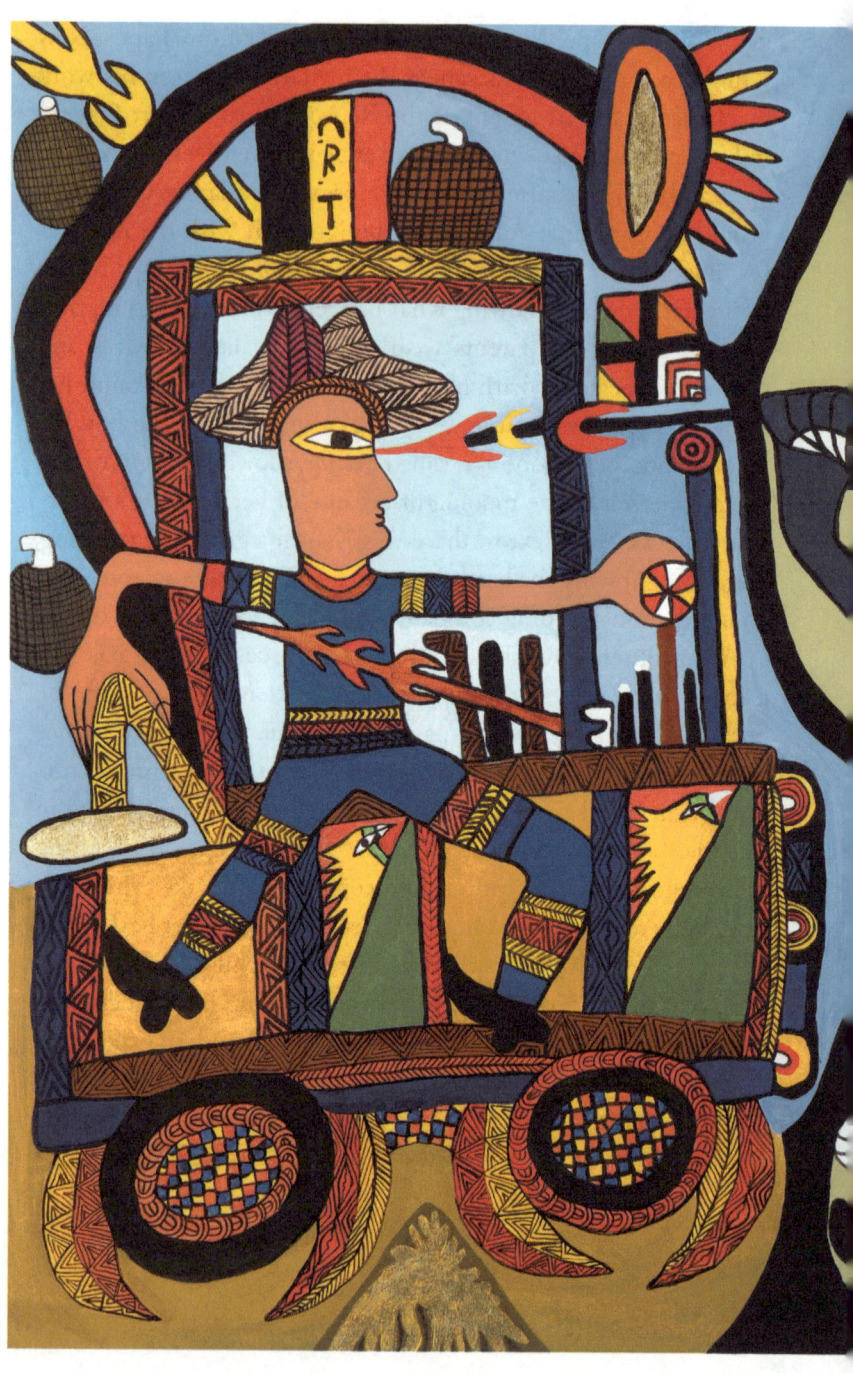

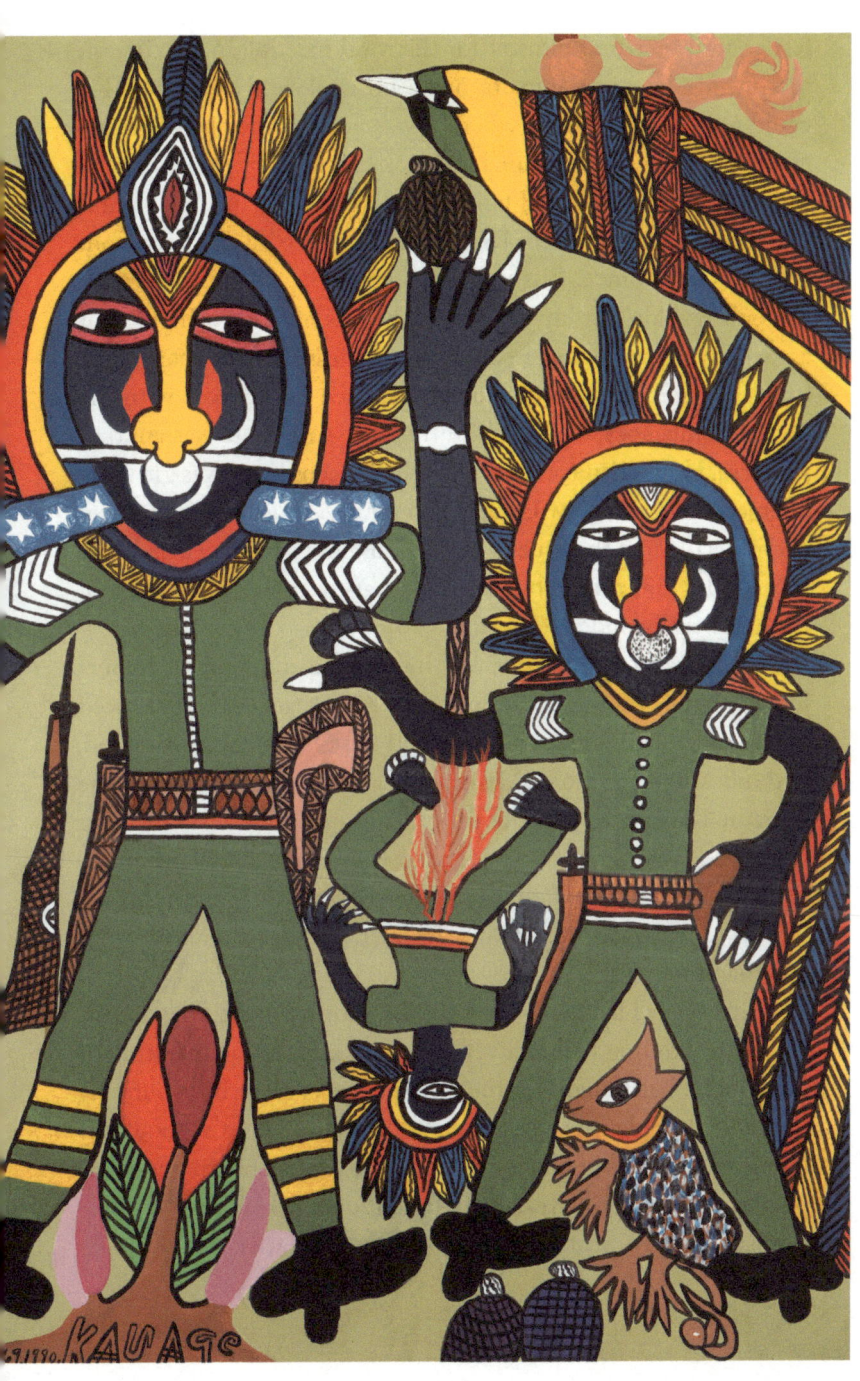

leader, he'd prepared himself for the royal meeting by putting on his full regalia and complete make-up while still at home. This could not have been done when he was here for the procedure included pinning into his bunched black hair birds of paradise, beak first, with their wonderful tail feathers spread out in a ray around his head. Thus accoutred, he sat on the plane all the way from Papua New Guinea. But when he arrived at Glasgow Airport, customs wouldn't let him in because he was not only bringing but actually wearing endangered species of birds. It took nearly nine hours of negotiation, indefatigably pursued by Rebecca with the relevant embassies, to allow him through. And there was another problem. He'd written a speech for the Queen. There was great excitement in Papua New Guinea about his visit; no one from there had officially met the Queen before. I did my best to persuade her office to let him read it, but the diplomats were having nothing of it. I never really understood why.

So Kauage stood massive and mute, a superb spray of colours in front of his brilliant paintings, as we approached. I introduced them, said a little about his work, and the Queen shook his hand, without uttering a word. My republicanism hovered back on the horizon. Kauage did some beautiful paintings later of his meeting with the Queen, him resplendent in his full regalia, her diminutive in bright pink, swinging a handbag. They clearly hadn't talked. He was awarded an OBE two years later, but that was a token, not a human moment.

A little later I led her up to meet the Scottish artist, Alan Davie, who was standing before a very big, striking abstract painting of his, which I had bought for the gallery: a great black horn bursting into a field of plenty, as bright as Kauage's work, but without any narrative. At seventy, Davie could claim to be the premier modern painter in Scotland, a very early practitioner of Abstract Expressionism, not just Scotland's but Britain's own Jackson Pollock. As

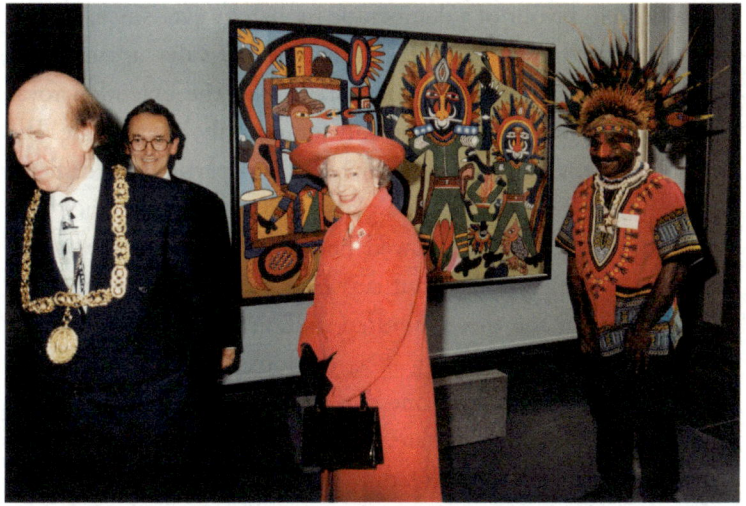

Lft to right: Pat Lally, the author, the Queen and Mathias Kauage, 1990

such he'd become the Queen's official painter north of the border, and for this reason she had one of his works in her collection. He was standing bolt upright in front of his painting, with his imposing white beard looking as though it had never been cut, next to his wife who still wore a towering beehive hairdo of the sixties. She looked a bit like Marge Simpson, except her hair was white.

I was just introducing them, when Alan lunged forward, grabbed the Queen's sleeve and shaking the cloth a bit said, 'That's a lovely colour!' in his rich Scottish brogue. Oh dear, I thought, what's coming next? One thing you don't do is touch the Queen—I thought even he would know that. 'You've got one of my paintings!' he announced. The Queen, shaking herself free and glancing nervously behind him at the huge splashy abstract, suddenly remembered and said, 'Oh yes, we've got a small one.'

'You should get a big one.'

'Oh,' she said, quick as a flash, 'I'd have to move house.'

I've been in favour of a democratic monarchy ever since, a powerless, inherited head of state, a human safety valve against despotism, despite the real-life soap opera that the extended royal family has tragically, and I hope only temporarily, has become. The only job of a royal is to be human, but this is particularly difficult for them, living as they do in a glass bowl when they're not fish. And inheritance can be allowed here too, though it seems old fashioned and hierarchical, but isn't in reality—the happenstance of one sperm in the three hundred million in the average single ejaculation fertilising an egg is as random a way of selecting a king or queen as any. And one day, who knows, a reigning royal might, as people sometimes are, be interested in art, and that could provide a huge boost for this dimension of communication. The last one to do so seriously in England, the first Charles—the Royal Collection still benefits from his enthusiasm—however, didn't end well. A love of art usually helps you hold your head up high, but not his unfortunately which ended up on the floor. Art, as an assertion of individuality, is a powerful antidote to repressive ideology and any dictatorship and it chimes well with the presence of a democratic monarch.

R *is for* JOHN RUSKIN

I had vaguely heard of John Ruskin when I took up my post as keeper of the Mappin Art Gallery in Sheffield, but no more. I had no idea a big chunk of my life was about to be taken up by him. I was surprised to find, mostly in the stores, a clutch of Ruskin's exquisite drawings of a withered oak spray, weeds growing on a stone arch in Venice and, most astonishing of all, a peacock's breast feather, tiny and delicate, with all the iridescence

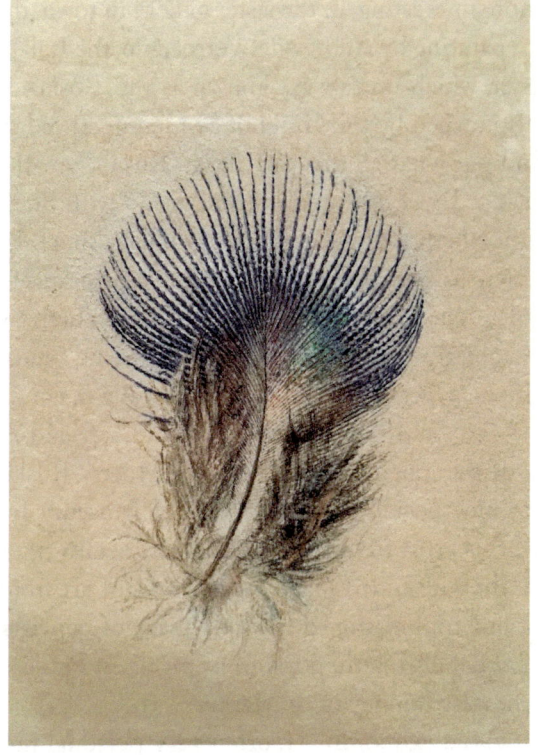

John Ruskin, Peacock Feather (detail), 1873

but none of the showiness of the tail. All the drawings were labelled 'Collection of the Guild of St George'. And there were
other things, nineteenth-century photographs of architectural
details, Dürer engravings and a huge painting of St Mark's Ba-
silica in Venice, by an artist called John Bunney, deadly and
laborious in technique, but nevertheless mesmerising overall.
Bunney spent months painting the picture *in situ*, and I learnt
later that Whistler, Ruskin's sworn enemy, had pinned a note to
Bunney's back while he was working, unbeknownst to the dedicated, concentrating artist. The note read: 'I am blind.'

Even more interesting, in the sister gallery in town, the Graves, there was a painting by Andrea del Verrocchio, the Italian Renaissance master, which was always known as the 'Ruskin Madonna' and was also owned by the Guild of St George. It didn't take me long to find out what all this was about. Ruskin greatly admired craftsmanship. Though he had nothing to do with Sheffield—an industrial northern town wasn't his natural habitat—he considered its cutlers to be at that time the best metalworkers in Europe. He wanted to encourage them to produce even better work and had the imaginative and generous notion to create a museum specially for them, a localised V&A—Ruskin was a major inspiration behind the Arts and Crafts movement and a friend and major influencer of the much younger William Morris. Ruskin bought the Verrocchio specially for his Sheffield Museum because he considered this artist to be one the greatest metalworkers in Italy in his day. Then he added many more works of art from his own collection and commissioned a whole team of copyists to paint architectural details that he'd found inspiring in France and Italy, included the vast Bunney of St Marks.

To this whole extraordinary, often very personal mélange, he added dozens of engravings of wildlife and flowers, including a set of John James Audubon's magnificent *The Birds of America*, and a wonderful collection of mineral samples, because he wanted the craftsmen of Sheffield to be inspired by the works of nature as well as the works of man. With that aim, he opened his museum in Walkley in 1875, high on the hills on the outskirts of the city, with views of the beautiful Peak District, thinking that the walk up to it would, in itself, do its visitors good. He wouldn't have anything to do with local politics, or with the industrial community, and left the whole enterprise to the Guild of St George, the charitable organisation he'd established in 1871 to put into practice some of his ideas for improving the quality of

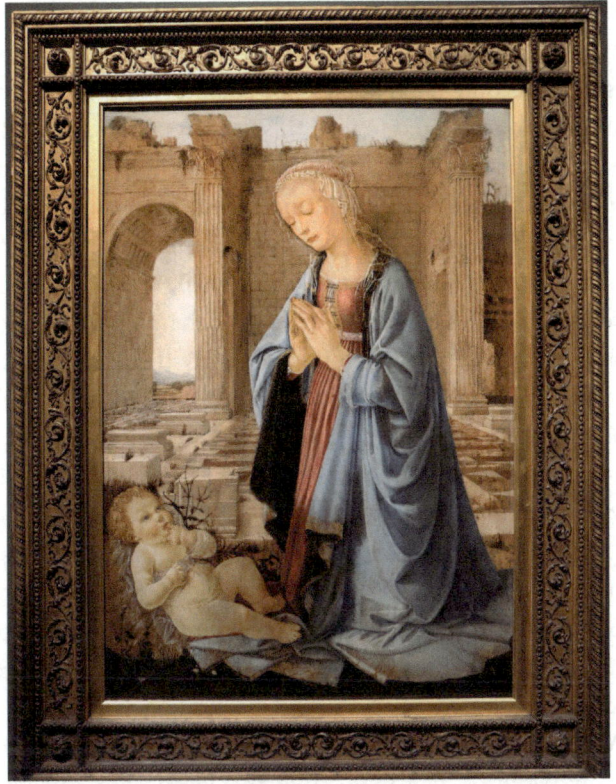

Andrea del Verrocchio, 'Ruskin Madonna', c. 1470

life, particularly in the area of what we would now call ecological agriculture.

The museum was so popular it clearly needed bigger premises, and the city moved it, at their own expense, to Meersbrook Park, in 1890, where it attracted even greater attention, not just in Britain but abroad as by the turn of the century Ruskin's influence was at its peak. The members of the new Labour Party founded in 1900 were asked what books had inspired them—the majority replied, the Bible and the works of John Ruskin. Tolstoy built a new artistic theory on his vision, Ghandi a new politics and Proust was translating his work. But by 1950 his reputation had sunk to its lowest ebb. Second-hand bookshops couldn't sell his numerous fat volumes. No one wanted to read this verbose old Victorian. In this post-Freudian age, his sex life—the annulment of his marriage on grounds of non-consummation, and his affection (surely innocent) for teenage girls—was all people, ignorantly, talked about then. His socialism was thought to be marginal, if not suspect. He'd written, after all, that he was 'a Tory of the old school and redder than the red'. This was confusing to say the least. The Labour Party by then wanted nothing to do with him, and they were solidly in charge in Sheffield.

In 1950 Ruskin's St George's Museum was closed—it was full anyway of funny old Victorian copies that had nothing to do with modern media, let alone TV—and the master cutlers, who it aimed to inspire, were beginning to close their workshops. It was an idea out of time, swept away as the whole city was rebuilt after the war, boldly modernised to face the gleaming future. The collection was moved into storage in Reading University, where the Master of the Guild, after a complex chain of inheritances, was now based. A few items, like the Verrocchio, remained on display in Sheffield as token memories of the museum that had been. This was the state of play when I arrived and uncovered the sad tale of the past.

Then the situation suddenly got worse. The Guild decided to sell the Verrocchio. The price they were asking was £360,000. This was a huge sum then, but a joke now, especially as at least one scholar had argued plausibly that the very beautiful misty view through the arch in the background showed the hand of the young Leonardo when he was training in Verrocchio's workshop. I thought this sale must be challenged. There are virtually no great Italian Renaissance paintings in public collections outside

London, and the idea that one given to the working men of Sheffield by one of the greatest writers in the nineteenth century should simply be lost to the city was, in my view, untenable.

I went to see my boss, Frank Constantine, the director of Sheffield Art Galleries who was based at the Graves Gallery, to argue that we had to fight to stop this. He was a small, immaculately stylish man, with a fine lock of grey hair flopping across his high forehead and an elegantly trimmed beard to match. He had a special glint in his eyes, which was a peculiar mixture of world-weariness (he'd fought in the war) and amused intelligence. He'd started his career in the picture restoration department in the galleries (now called conservation), following his father who'd held the same position, and then risen through the ranks to be director, the only top professional, in my experience, to have done so. He was a fine painter himself and the first acquisition I made when I followed him as director, partly as a tribute to his exceptional, long career, was to buy a beautiful little painting by him of cold winter sunlight shining through a back-garden greenhouse.

Frank's main passion was for adding to the collection, and he was brilliant at doing this. He had an immense, intimate knowledge of British painting, knew everyone in the business and had one of the best 'eyes for art' I've ever had the pleasure to work alongside. And it has to be added, being a Yorkshire man, an eager eye for a bargain. I remember him trying to persuade my colleague Anne Goodchild to have a cake in the coffee bar (which he'd fondly created) in the gallery. She resisted. She was on a diet. 'Oh, come on Anne,' Frank said, 'I'll buy you one.' She was so surprised—Frank had never been known to offer anyone anything— she said yes. But when we got the table, Frank said, 'I know I bought it for you, Anne, but I want half.'

But to my suggestion that we must fight to save the Verrocchio, he merely shrugged. 'I won't stop you doing what you can,' he said, 'but the city can't afford it. What can we do? You won't win.' This was not encouraging. Nor was the chair when I spoke to her. Enid Hattersley was the mother of Roy Hattersley, a rising political star, later deputy leader of the Labour Party. She had an extraordinary capacity to talk non-stop, for over an hour at a time (we timed her), so we called her Lady C, short for Lady Chattersley. I can't remember getting much of a word in but she made it clear that no one in Sheffield wanted anything to do with Ruskin any more. The Verrocchio was the main point, not Ruskin, but the painting seemed to be tarred with his brush in Sheffield eyes. With hindsight, I think that the city's lack of interest in trying to keep it was partly due to the fact that people concerned at the time, which included Enid and Frank, were actually a bit ashamed of having let the Ruskin museum close and didn't want their lack of action brought to light again.

Whatever, I was left to fight alone. I wrote to Lord Clark, former director of the National Gallery and now famous for his TV series *Civilisation*, who had also compiled a brilliant selection of Ruskin's writing called *Ruskin Today*, hoping to see him to get his support to keep the Ruskin Madonna in Sheffield. I didn't get a reply—I was too junior, I guess, in years and profession— but I heard through a mutual contact in the Arts Council that he thought if Sheffield wanted the picture, they should buy it. This I knew was a non-starter, with my director and chair prepared to let it go and certainly not wanting to bid for an extra budget. Perhaps Clark was annoyed by the way Sheffield had let Ruskin's museum close. I never knew. But there was no help there. What could I do?

I wrote to *The Times*, as one did in those days. The great paper, before it went tabloid, was known as 'the Thunderer' and a letter published in it was a lightning flash. Mine was followed by silence. I still hadn't quite given up. I did a bit of digging and realised that anyone could apply to become a Companion of the Guild of St George. I did and got a polite acceptance note from the secretary. I was eligible to attend the Annual General Meeting, held at Reading University. I remember it was a Saturday, and I'd done some shopping in London and went carrying two plastic bags. I had no idea what to expect, when I was shown into a very large room with a row of very distinguished-looking people, almost all men, seated around a very big table. I hurriedly slipped the bags to one side and sat down.

I realised very quickly that I'd walked, unawares, into what was something like a subcommittee of the Senate Board of Reading University. As for the Madonna, they were just selling an asset that had nothing to do with them, the history of which it soon became evident they knew virtually nothing about. The Master of the Guild at the time was Professor Tyler. I asked what they were going to do with the money they got when they sold the Verrocchio. He replied that one of the ideas was to establish fellowships in his own discipline, chemistry. Ruskin, it's true, was interested in everything, but I argued that his Guild had very particular aims, and studying chemistry wasn't one of them. They had, for a start, to make the Guild's collection accessible to working-class people, preferably craft workers in Sheffield. My repeated questioning, which I found fascinating for every stone I lifted revealed the board's ignorance of what they were dealing with, became tedious for the majority and I was shut up by one member proposing a motion of no confidence in the board, which he argued summed up my position, which he and the others then voted against. I was silenced, until next year.

Meanwhile, the Guild sold the Verrocchio. The buyer was Hugh Scrutton, director of the National Galleries of Scotland. I wrote to him, before the deal was sealed, asking him not to go ahead with the purchase. It seemed absolutely crazy to me that the British government (who funded the National Galleries of Scotland) should spend £300,000 (there was an additional small grant from the National Art Collection Fund) moving a painting from Sheffield to Edinburgh, especially one bought specially for that city by a great writer to inspire metalwork. I knew that the painting wouldn't be given an export licence to be sold abroad, so without Scrutton's purchase there would be no sale. Hugh declined to reply to my letter. Silence won again.

At the next Guild board meeting, unencumbered by carrier bags, I launched again into my questioning barrage. What were they going to do with the money? What were they doing with their collection in store? Shouldn't some of it be used to make it available to the public again? I was gradually getting more support. Some members wanted nothing more to do with this, and certainly didn't want to involve the university in opening a Ruskin museum. Tyler stood down as master, graciously admitting privately to me afterwards that if I'd joined them earlier and had been a bit older, they'd never have been able to sell the Madonna.

Jon Thompson, a former Reading student, a fulsome fellow who looked as though he'd never quite outgrown his puppy fat, now teaching at Goldsmith's College in London, where he later guided, if that is the right word, Damien Hirst, was elected Master. He was a pataphysician. Things were looking up, I thought, for I was an admirer of the movement's founder, Alfred Jarry, and had recently seen a production of his fabulous play *Ubu Roi*, designed by David Hockney.

'How do you become a pataphysician?' I asked him.

Jon replied, 'By telling a pataphysical joke.'

I asked him to tell me the one that had got him admitted to this exclusive club. He obliged. It was unbelievably convoluted and tedious: something about going on a journey using different modes of transport. When he'd stopped speaking and I'd realised this was the end, it didn't occur to me to smile, let alone laugh. But the joke obeys every pataphysical rule, Jon assured me—firstly by not being a joke, I presumed. Nevertheless, despite our divergent outlooks, which were to diverge much further as it turned out, together we negotiated the return of the Ruskin Collection to Sheffield.

Of course, it would have been better if Sheffield had done what Lord Clark advised, bought the painting and got the Guild to use the money to return the collection—but, unfortunately, I didn't have that foresight at the time, nor did Lord Clark suggest it to me. As a second best, I commissioned the conservator, Philippa Abrahams, to reconstruct a replica of the painting using the same pigments and techniques—Ruskin always used copies when he didn't have originals. Nicholas Penny at the National Gallery ridiculed the idea, but it worked beautifully. This doesn't mean that if Scotland votes for independence, I won't be among the first to call for the return of cultural property, the Ruskin Madonna to be brought back to its rightful home in Sheffield, England, from which it was wrongfully taken in the era of British Imperialism.

Recreating the Ruskin Gallery in Sheffield was after all this a sheer delight for me, literally a dream come true. I found the right building to convert, the old Hay's Wine Shop on Norfolk Street in the heart of the city centre—a suitable venue since Ruskin's money originally came from the sherry business his father founded. The building had wonderful tall arched, north-facing front windows, which gave a beautiful interior light with the harmful UV rays easily filtered out, but which were also potentially a security risk—a smash and grab raid at night. I commissioned forged bars for them which looked like growing branches—very Ruskinian, crafted by the brilliant blacksmith Giuseppe Lund, who also created a superb, equally organic, staircase and railing inside.

We needed lettering. Only the best would do. I commissioned

the veteran lettercutter David Kindersley, who'd been trained by Eric Gill. 'Oh, we've got a big Gill carving in the collection,' I told him. The panel, two and three-quarter metres high and over a metre wide, had been set into a wall in the Mappin Art Gallery. As fashions changed, it had been covered over with thick, encrusted Anaglypta wallpaper, regularly repainted white. It had, in its way, gone the way of the Ruskin Collection—obliterated by modernisation. This covered panel was a nuisance, however, because we couldn't hang anything on it, so I had the wallpaper removed and the panel exposed. It showed a naked boy leaping through some foliage.

I showed it to David. His face flushed red. His past had come back to haunt him. He told me that his very first job when he'd joined Gill as an apprentice in the mid 1930s was to go to Shanks' bathroom shop on Bond Street and alter a carving Gill had just installed at its entrance. This was the one that had eventually ended up in the Mappin. Gill, being Gill, had cut the boy's penis perkily pointing up. The wife of Shanks' owner wanted it turned down. David had to spend the day in the shop's entrance way, with all the people passing down Bond Street, grinding down the penis and recutting it as the owner wished, pointing down. The worst day of his life, he said.

He came up to Sheffield to carve the entrance panel to the Ruskin Gallery—he had to work on site on the huge slabs of green Westmoreland slate, chosen for its association with Ruskin's home in the Lake District—to a design I'd been delighted with, the letters interwoven with gilded wild rose briars. They were all open but, I said, one needed to be a bud. He didn't know how to draw one, so I did it and he cut it. The bud between the T and the H is my proud contribution to the gallery. David brought his new, young wife, Lida Lopes Cardozo, with him. She was pregnant and their ages together added up to a hundred. He told me later that he'd not been allowed in to see her in the hospital when she was in labour—only immediate relatives were allowed—until he explained that he was the father, not the grandfather—though his magnificent, flowing but well-clipped white beard made him look like an ancient Victorian ancestor. Lida Cardozo, his third wife, blond, prepossessing while being deceptively strong, told me her unusual story.

Born in Leiden, in the Netherlands, she wasn't interested at all in any conventional academic career, not even grasping the basics of spelling, though, oddly, she found, being left-handed, she could write fluently backwards without making the mistakes that usually tripped her up when she wrote forwards. She told me she saw an exhibition of letter cutting and instantly realised that this, of all strange things, was what she wanted to do with her life. This led her, in time, to bang on David Kindersley's workshop door in Cambridge. He was, she thought, the best letter cutter in the world. He opened the door and told her he wasn't taking on any apprentices and shut it again. As she walked away, she thought this is not what I want to be doing. She turned back, banged again and, with great reluctance, he let her stay for a day, thinking she wouldn't last even that long. He was wrong. They forged a great creative partnership until his death, and she continues to run his workshop to this day.

Lida's work at its best is even better than David's. It has a clarity of space around it that makes the letters appear to be full of light and life, yet at the same time strong—an exceptional yet natural combination, a perfect embodiment of Ruskin's phrase 'to see clearly is poetry, prophecy, religion, all in one'. I knew I needed to have Ruskin's words in this museum but wasn't sure how to do it—they couldn't be printed, still less Letrasetted—until I happened to see some of Lida's handwriting. It wasn't formal calligraphy, but beautifully formed. I commissioned her to write several of my favourite Ruskin quotes in gradually changing coloured inks, and to be framed and exhibited as exhibits among the exhibits—words as rainbows, visual poems.

I employed Lida later, after David had died, to carve the big lettering on the façade of the Gallery of Modern Art in Glasgow. Conservationists argued that the building, being Grade One listed, shouldn't be touched, but I replied that buildings need to have a record of their uses through history, and that Lida's carved lettering was entirely in keeping with the classical design. The planning officer agreed with me but wouldn't let me gild the incisions. You won't be able to read them, I argued, but decided to go ahead on the condition he'd look at them again when they were done and make up his own mind. The gilding can always be removed anyway, I said. Lida cut the stone, the inspector came, agreed that the lettering couldn't be read, and said 'gild them,' so Lida finished the job as I'd wished. I'd learnt before that if you can't make a leap, the next best thing is to take a step.

The blank architrave on which these letters had been carved ran round the whole building. I wanted her to continue and carve the whole length with quotations of Ruskin: 'There is no wealth but life' and 'The true veins of wealth are purple—and not in Rock but in Flesh'—I loved the idea of the word 'purple' being cut in stone and glowing gold—and I loved the sentiment because the building was being turned from a bank and stock exchange into a gallery, but I didn't have the guts to fight for this with the conservationist lobby and the planning officer. One battle fought and won was all I dared, though I've regretted my diffidence ever since. I couldn't see how a step could make this work in time.

There was a sliver of wasteland next to the new Ruskin Gallery in the Hays Building, facing the Crucible Theatre in Sheffield. We used it to build a gallery and shop to show contemporary crafts, so Ruskin's intended vision was, eventually, complete. The little duo operated exceptionally well—I am all for small galleries with clear purposes—but the two were unfortunately moved long after I left and incorporated into the Millennium Galleries, a few metres away, and their distinct quality and charm, and much of their incorporated crafts, including Giuseppe Lund's remarkable hand-forged bars, were lost when the Ruskin Collection was absorbed into what is little more, architecturally speaking, than an upmarket shopping mall. But at least it is still there.

My involvement with Ruskin increased rather than diminished when I left museums. I was voted Master of the Guild and I had to take possession of the Master's copies of the Complete Works, all thirty-nine fat volumes of them, and buy a bookcase to hold them. In 2000, the centenary of Ruskin's death, we received the last two bottles of Ruskin's father's personal cask of sherry, sealed in 1871, from the company he had founded with the Spanish grower Domecq. As Master, I decided the only thing to do was for the board of directors to drink it. It was black and thick, and tasted like charcoal ground with honey, an odd but not unpalatable mix.

I then decided that the best way we could celebrate, or rather, mourn, Ruskin's death, was to launch a campaign for drawing. Ruskin, like Leonardo, drew most days of his life. It was, for them both, a way of seeing and a way of living. Ruskin, as usual, put it better than anyone:

> The greatest thing a human soul ever does in this world is to see something and tell what it saw in a plain way. Hundreds of people can talk for one who can think, but thousands can think for one who can see.

Drawing, for him, was the basis of art, and yet in 2000 it was not only not being taught in art schools, it wasn't even being practised. Promoting drawing seemed to be a good way to celebrate and mourn.

We appointed Sue Grayson-Ford as campaign director. She was the founder of the Serpentine Gallery, one among many of her trailblazing achievements. She had a thrusting gait, a lock of dark hair falling over her face and in her eyes a black-eyed fierceness that combined depth and openness with determination and an exceptional catholicity of taste. She conceived, hatched and fire-fed the Big Draw, which, for one day in the year, got everyone drawing. By the time she had ended her directorship, with the help of her brilliant education adviser Eileen Lawrence, the idea had caught on around the globe.

I will never forget seeing the immensely long pedestrian tunnel between the Science Museum and the V&A teeming with people drawing everywhere, and, a year later, the central court and side galleries at the British Museum almost afloat with sheets of paper over which groups were huddled with collective concentration. In the lecture theatre downstairs, Sir Roger Penrose, the Nobel-prize winning physicist, was drawing a self-defining grid with mesmerising simplicity and complexity, only to be followed by Quentin Blake sketching on an overhead projector an angry woman pointing at something. 'What is she pointing at, I wonder?' he asked the gripped audience. Then on the blank white screen sprang, in a few lines, a little boy who had, one could tell from his contorted embarrassed posture, clearly done something he knew was wrong.

The Big Draw was a celebration of line that made everyone want to take part. As Quentin Blake remarked, it showed that drawing, usually thought to be a private, personal process, sheltered behind a covering arm, was actually very public, a communal activity that could involve everyone. In this way it was very unlike writing. If you're writing a letter, no one would dream of looking over your shoulder to read it. But if you're painting a picture, even if your back is against a wall, passers-by will have no qualms about peering round the canvas to see what you're doing. Art is a public expression that naturally exists in the public sphere.

Many big names were only too eager to take part, particularly illustrators and cartoonists, who in many ways will come to be viewed as the most genuine, inventive and perspicacious artists of our times, such as Steve Bell, Posy Simmonds and Gerald Scarfe. Scarfe's sculpture of Chairman Mao as a red chair is a masterpiece of gross, cushioned, scheming, consuming aggression, a profounder work of art than any Claes Oldenburg or Andy Warhol. He told me once that he'd entered as a kid a painting competition and had come second. The winner was an unknown boy called D. Hockney. That's a fairer judgement of his true prowess and even that might in time be overturned. Quentin Blake was always eager to take part. The problem was that, whenever he appeared, there was always a queue of children, and adults, lining up to get their books by him signed. I asked him, 'Doesn't the signing get tiring?'

He replied, 'It's not the signing that's tiring; it's the smiling.'

I had been elected Master of the Guild through the encouragement and canvassing of the companion, Mark Harvey. A Quaker, he was one of those rare individuals who simply exude goodness. He was an artist and art teacher who loved carving spoons out of wood, of all sizes and for all purposes, and made tiny, monumental sculptures of loving couples out of wooden pegs that weren't the slightest bit sentimental. I stayed with the Guild for as long as I did due to the good offices of its secretary, Cedric Quayle. His father, like Mark's, had been a leading figure in the Guild in the past. The Guild was back in the hands of its rightful, purposeful clan. Cedric was one of those rare people who exude quietude. A short man, one wouldn't expect sensing his unassuming presence that his personal, largely achieved ambition was to climb all the highest mountains in the world. He'd climbed one in Antarctica and told me it was so beautiful looking around the vast white stillness that he'd burst into tears. I have never been to Antarctica, and probably now won't get there, but Cedric sharing his vision of it with me remains one of my key motives for doing what I can, however little, to combat global warming or, as I prefer to call it, burning.

I was impatient for results—the Guild was created by Ruskin not to think and contemplate but to act—and Cedric sometimes had to hold me back. I wanted to move on from drawing. Campaigns, like ours, however good, are difficult to sustain and should, I think, have a fixed term. They are battles for awareness, which after they're won, need to be dropped so we can move on. I wanted to start a campaign for painting, with one specific aim: to reverse the set back in the great art form at the National Gallery in London (see M for Neil MacGregor). Cedric warned me that the idea wouldn't get accepted by the board of directors. He was right. It didn't. They wanted to get back to things more Ruskinian. I couldn't think of anything more Ruskinian than encouraging the art of painting. But life's too short to try to dance with someone who doesn't want to dance. I was sad about it but I bid farewell.

Ruskin remains, however, a living presence in my life. I've read so much of his writing, and peered so closely at his drawings, that I feel it's almost as if he were standing at my elbow, a shadowy presence, and a bit at the back, but still young, standing, perfectly straight. I was startled seeing some of his articles of clothing, which survive at his home in Brantwood—he was so thin, elegant and upright. His mother was famous for travelling in a coach across Europe, all the way to Italy, without her back once touching the back of her seat. I imagined her son to have a similar, perpetual rectitude. It was, I thought, a manifestation of his moral vision.

I sometimes imagine what he would think now if he could see what has happened to the world since his time. He was after all the first person to write in effect about the advent of climate change in his two lectures, *The Storm Cloud of the Nineteenth Century*. He would I think in all probability fade away to nothing in horror or, at least, be unable to stand. Nor would he have been able to face the art I loved, of Picasso and everyone after, arguing, as he did, that Darwin couldn't possibly be right that the beauty of a peacock had evolved solely to interest a peahen. And he gave to his museum in Sheffield, his extraordinary drawing of a single peacock's breast feather to demonstrate the wider, encompassing wonder of creation. It's this feeling of wonder that I think we have to recapture, without now denying any scientific discoveries, to motivate us to save our world. Ruskin's vision of nature is still an inspiration to me. But so too is his moral vision, his rectitude and his insistence on fighting for what he thinks to be right. And his presence at my elbow has given me that backbone.

S *is for* NIKI DE SAINT PHALLE

I was taken aback. Tears were streaming down her face. Niki de Saint Phalle, even in her sixties and plagued with ill health, was a strikingly beautiful woman—her perpetually natural mouth-pout, wide eyes, arched brows, small nose, set in a perfect vase-like face—and she was very well aware of the fact and had the poise and self-confidence to carry it off. She was still the fashion model who'd appeared on the front cover of *Life* magazine in 1949, when she was only eighteen. And here she was crying, not that that made her look any less attractive. Not a bit of it.

She'd just been walking round the huge retrospective of her work, taken from Bonn, I'd put on at the McLellan Galleries in Glasgow. She said:

I don't know how you've done it, but you've arranged the show so that every time I've stood in the doorway to the next gallery, left one and moved into the next, it's been a time when I've just had to walk out of my life, leave everything behind, when everything got on top of me—I just walked out, and had no idea what I would do next, if anything, and here …

She looked very moved again:

I stood on the threshold and could see everything I did sub-sequently, things I had no idea I would do, laid out before me, when at the time I had given up everything, was so de-pressed I thought nothing would happen again.

Then she added, very simply, 'I've relived my life here.'

I had to admit it wasn't really anything to do with me. I'd sim-ply arranged the works chronologically. Then if in any doubt, I'd put things together that I felt should go together, and I was just lucky that the galleries fitted the sequence of her development. That was all. There was no magic to it. But I think Niki trusted me after that, so much so that I became part of her intimate laughing circuit. Her lungs had been so blown apart by all the chemicals she'd used in making her early sculptures that her doctor advised her to laugh whenever she felt she needed to. She would ring me up at any time of the day or night—it was often in the early hours of the morning after she moved to San Diego—and all I'd hear was her mellow laugh at the end of the line. It was infectious, and I would laugh too. We'd laugh for a few minutes, sometimes as long as five, without saying anything, until she became obviously exhausted, out of breath, and we'd hung up.

I'd been very keen to get some major pieces by her for the Glasgow collection and showing a retrospective of her work was a good way to begin. I regarded her and Jean Tinguely as two of the most telling artists of our times, and the fact that they'd worked so closely together, been married for a while and even after they split rang each other virtually every day, was all the more interesting since their work couldn't, almost, be more distinct. It's hard to imagine any sculpture more opposite to Tinguely's raw, grinding and twitching mechanics—engines without bonnets—than Niki's massive, fat, inflated, multicoloured, floating balloon women—all bonnet, or perhaps bosom, so to speak, plus a boot perhaps, or backside, with no engine within. They seemed to be going in opposite directions, which suited them both, I think, very well. But they both shared a similar vision that their art should be in the streets, part of modern life, not stuck away in art galleries—what Tinguely came to call 'shit art venues'.

Niki upset art dealers and certainly got up the noses of those curators who thought art should be exclusive by producing and selling popular multiples of her work. She did it for a good reason, not just to widen the audience for her work, but also to fund many of her public enterprises. She told me that the scent she made, sold in a Niki snake-twist bottle, helped to pay for her amazing Tarot Garden in Italy. Jean gave a bottle of it to my wife, when we saw him in Lausanne, but said, 'Don't put that on here—the bulls will charge out of the fields.' Niki's interest in popularity impressed me, as did Jean's. Any artist of any ambition must, surely, want to be both popular and profound, and Niki and Jean were both in bucketsful.

Niki was extremely generous in the works she gave to the gallery. A fantastic addition, for us, was her *Altar of the Dead Cat*. This is one of the most harrowing works of art of the second half of the twentieth century. It was one of series—and in my view the most powerful—of '*Shootings*' (in French, *Tirs*) she made after she had 'walked out' of her first marriage and started to make art seriously. She buried everyday objects and bags of paint in plaster panels

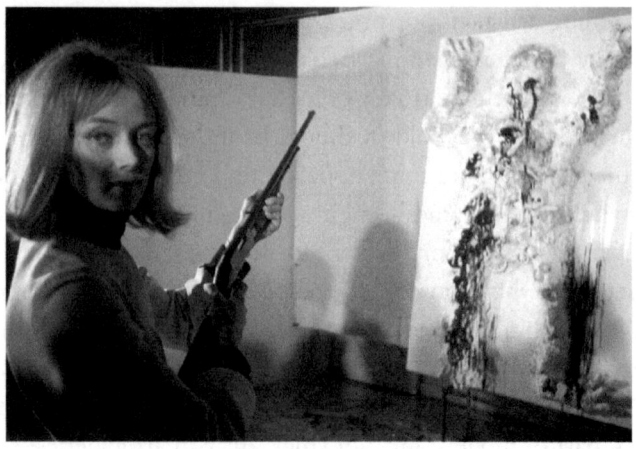

Niki de Saint Phalle executing a Tir, 8 February 1963

and shot at them with a rifle, wearing, it has to be said, a very glamorous body-hugging pure white suit, which attracted huge media interest. Her fabulous style had a serious intent.

As she said later, 'I was shooting at myself, society with its injustices. I was shooting at my own violence and the violence of the times. By shooting at my own violence, I no longer had to carry it inside of me like a burden.' And she had a lot to shoot at: being sexually abused by her father since she was eleven, a bigoted, restrictive Catholic upbringing (she was expelled from convent schools, twice)—a childhood she described as 'hell' (both her younger brother and sister committed suicide later in life). Her profound feminism found its feet in these works which, after she'd 'walked out' again, took wing with works that celebrated joy. She gave us a wonderful version of her sculpture, *The Devil*, winged and horned with a multi-phallus-fingered hand reaching out at its groin. These gifts led to more gifts. The collectors Eric and Jean Cass in time gave their whole collection of Niki's sculptures to Glasgow. That's the way public galleries need to go—not buying

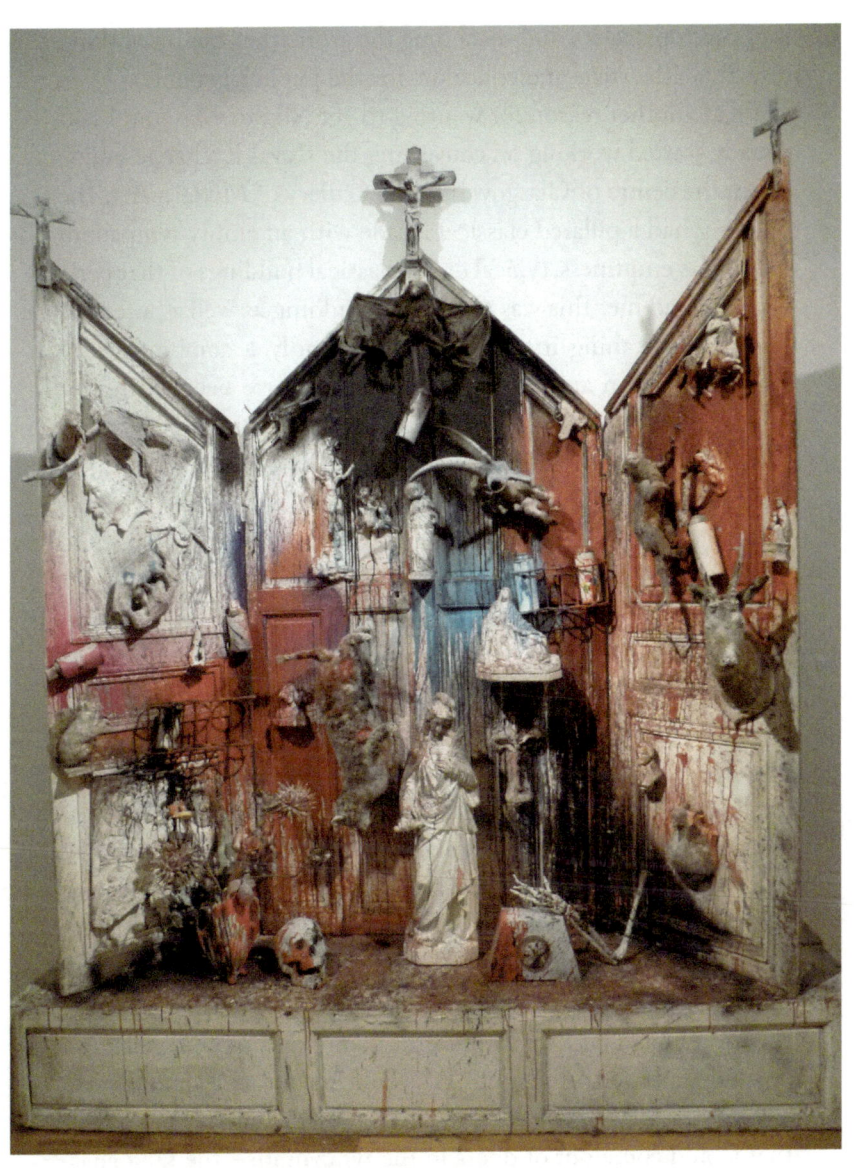

Niki de Saint Phalle, Altar for the Dead Cat, c. 1963

art from top dealers, and sustaining the art market, but by working directly with artists and collectors for the public's benefit.

I had another reason for wanting to get Niki to Glasgow. I had already started working on converting the Royal Exchange building in the centre of Glasgow into the Gallery of Modern Art. The building had a pillared classical façade with an empty tympanum on top. Its emptiness, typical of neoclassical buildings of that period, bothered me. This was to be a fun building as well as a serious one. The one thing it couldn't be was deadly, a combination of all that's solemn and boring, which might have been fitting for a bank but not for a gallery of modern art. Genuine, not neo-, classical façades, those in Ancient Greece and Rome, were enlivened with brightly painted figures, gods and goddesses, warriors and demons going about their business. I wondered if Niki could do something for me.

Tympani in ancient times told stories. The best story this tympanum could tell, I thought, was the tale of St Mungo himself, the patron saint of Glasgow and, intriguingly, of adultery. A Scottish queen in ancient time had given her young lover a ring that her husband, the king, had once given her. He spotted the ring on a sleeping soldier's finger, flung him into gaol and the ring into the river and demanded that his wife brought him the ring or else her lover would be killed. Desperate, she dashed to see St Mungo, who told her not to worry, just to ask her maid to go fishing in the Clyde. She did and the maid caught a salmon with the ring in its mouth. The queen put it on her finger and peace was restored to the royal house, and her lover to the young queen's bed, when opportunity allowed. I thought Niki would like the story, and she did.

Her first idea was to make moving three-dimensional figures that would come out of doors in the tympanum—the king chasing the queen chasing her lover as the maid chased the fish with the ring—that sort of thing. Jean Tinguely had recently died and, as a tribute to him, Niki was trying to make moving art. I loved the concept, but it proved too difficult to construct, and anyway the heritage lobby, led by Gavin Stamp, the author of the famous 'Piloti' architecture column in *Private Eye*, was threatening knickers strangulation for what I was proposing to do to a not-so-ancient monument that had started life as a slave-owner's house. I simplified the project and asked Niki to design a sparkling, jewelled panel telling the St Mungo story, one that could in the future, if necessary, be removed without damage to the fabric of the building beneath. Peace was, just about, restored.

I also asked Niki to design a mirror-panelled entrance lobby, lit by a Tinguely lamp he had made for her, because I wanted visitors immediately they stepped into the gallery to feel they were being transported to a magical, imaginative space, a world of art separate from life, however vividly the art inside reflected it. I had recently been to see her Tarot Garden at Garavicchio in Tuscany, Italy, and had my mind blown apart. I slept in the left breast of the *Sphinx*, which certainly put me in a responsive mood. Nevertheless, it is in my opinion one of the greatest works of art of the late twentieth century, a labour of love for over twenty years, a sprinkling of twenty or so giant figures (if you can sprinkle giants) and countless smaller demons, angels and other beings within an olive grove. A dazzling effect is created by looking up into the bright blue sky through the olive trees' lighter under-leaves. You feel as if you're swimming in a river of imaginative light, a dream world made visible in her mind. This extraordinary realisation, made decades later, springs from a couple of tiny paintings Niki made before she become an artist during her first breakdown—her initial 'walk out' from life—which showed a magical garden where she would like to be. Her life's work was to make this place exist. I wanted Glasgow to have a glimpse of that, and it has—the only public art by this great modern public artist in Britain.

S *is for* SIR NICHOLAS SEROTA

We didn't see eye to eye from the start. We first met in our very early twenties, when I was an assistant keeper at the Durham Light Infantry Museum and Arts Centre and Nick was a regional officer for the Arts Council of Great Britain. It wasn't professional jealousy, not at least at the beginning, though Nick, I think, knew where he was aiming for even then, but he can't have regarded me, a graduate of Nottingham University, not Oxford, as future competition. I was just enjoying the very interesting and highly entertaining job I'd found myself in—it never occurred to me that I might one day become a director of any gallery, let alone the Tate. Our feelings were much more basic; we simply didn't get on.

Nick's an odd man to look at, more bone than flesh, tall, thin and vertical. The only horizontal line in him is the closed aperture in his mouth, which is thin-lipped and straight and, on the rare occasions when he smiles, gives the distinct impression that something in him has cracked. But this was no reason to dislike him. Machiavelli had a similarly lean face, but his writings reveal an amazingly fertile and amused inner mind. Nick has hardly written anything, so it's difficult to know what he thinks. But the division between us was even more fundamental than that.

I separate people into two types—as much for self-protection as anything else: those I can look at works of art with and those I can't. It's a peculiar activity, looking at art—it's at once personal, obviously, but it's also, or can be, communal. I don't know how it works—but then who understands the sharing of human consciousness? I once looked at some paintings with Raymond Tallis—and few people alive today know more about and have written more beautifully about consciousness than him—and was amazed how alert we both became to each other's awareness. Most mysterious!

When looking at art with Nick, however, as I first did in Durham, I felt nothing come out of him. His presence beside me was dead as if he weren't actually seeing what I was looking at. It was a very odd sensation coming from someone who I supposed was interested in art. I've never forgotten the moment. Worse, he seemed to be waiting for me to say something. I didn't oblige, and have never done since, not that he's ever given me any opportunity to do so. Once he became director of the Tate, I was never invited to the institution, for any reason, not even to an opening, even when one of the museums I ran had lent something. My chairman got invited, but not me. It was an extraordinary, planned exclusion, if you think about it, in a small country like Britain, which helped to ensure that I had little chance of establishing contacts with powerful people who could challenge Serota's regime in the coming years. As for the annual Turner Prize shindig, I was always *persona non grata*, despite being a major voice, though I say it myself, in the contemporary art field, but that was more to be expected because I did have different opinions from him. The RA invited me to their shows, and even their banquets, every year, but Nick, never.

There was one exception. I was invited to a Tate opening for the *Ruskin, Turner and the Pre-Raphaelites* exhibition. I think I got through the net because I wasn't wearing the usual hat. I was invited as the Master of the Guild of St George, not as a director of a gallery, and I really had to be invited because the Guild had lent major works to the exhibition. There was I, much to my surprise, at a private 'do' at the Tate after all these years! It wasn't the grandest of openings, a sit-down banquet, but a splendid one nevertheless with endless drinks and nibbles. I was enjoying myself chatting away to friends and acquaintances in the Ruskin world, when suddenly through a gap in the crowd, who should I see walking directly towards me but Nick with Virginia Bottomley, recently appointed Secretary of State for National Heritage, introducing her to guests. Nick saw me, stopped and his mouth dropped open in shocked disgust; then he suddenly swung the former minister round at a right angle and marched off to introduce her to someone else. I could have been imagining things, of course, or it could have been chance, but that's not what I thought at the time. I saw it as a painful little dance, a vivid expression of my place in his estimation of worth.

Mark Fisher MP, a most likeable and amiable, rotund fellow who always looked slightly surprised that he himself was alive, let alone talking to someone else, was for a long time shadow arts minister under Thatcher and briefly junior arts minister under Blair. He told me he was keen on freedom of information when Labour got in and went to every meeting about it. Peter Mandelson also attended, but never said a word. When he left at the end, everyone always discussed what his body movements might have meant. At the next reshuffle, they'd all gone, including Mark. He was surprised when I told him how persistently Nick had excluded me from the Tate. 'You know,' he told me, 'there's only one explanation. I thought Nick wasn't afraid of anyone, but clearly, he is—he's afraid of you.' This was a small solace for my treatment in a way, but Nick had no reason to be—the power was all in his hands. He'd made sure of that. There was something of Mandelson's cold calculation about Nick, which was admirable in its way for it got things done, but I couldn't help feeling it had nothing to do with art.

Not that Nick has ever said much about what he thinks, still less feels, about art. In one short lecture, he argued that Matisse's *Red Studio*—one of the most wonderful baths of imaginative radiance in the history of art—led directly to Joseph Beuys's assemblages of fragments and felts. I don't know which is worse: glowing reds being reduced to lifeless greys or the luminous space of the human imagination being restricted to the given dimensions of a public gallery on which Beuys's installations depend. Nick's admiration for Beuys was shown to be totally misplaced when it was discovered that the rolls of felt, lumps of lard, torches and sledges, which he used to litter public galleries around the world, were fake relics of a rescue that never happened, a myth concocted by Beuys about himself, perhaps to bury a Nazi past, for only party members were usually allowed to join the elite Luftwaffe in which he served.

This was the fundamental difference between Nick and me. I believe art has to stand alone, shine from its own centre, survive, as André Breton said, 'the breath of the street'. Nick thought the gallery space, which he controlled, was paramount. I thought it should self-efface. I once took my committee in Glasgow to see the state of the walls in the galleries in Kelvingrove. I wanted money for an extensive redecoration—it would be expensive I knew to replace all the tatty old damask with a repaintable textile. One councillor muttered, 'I thought people came to see the pictures, not the walls.' I laughed. I got the money, but he had a point.

Alan Bowness resigned as director of the Tate in 1988 and, by then, having been director of Sheffield and then Manchester, I felt bullish and ambitious enough to apply for the post. Eight candidates were interviewed in the first round, and then only four were left—John Elderfield, curator of painting and sculpture at the Museum of Modern Art, New York; Norman Rosenthal, keeper of exhibitions at the Royal Academy London; Nick Serota, director of the Whitechapel Art Gallery in London; and me. I thought John and I were the only real contenders because Norman and Nick had only run exhibition spaces and had no experience of managing a major permanent collection, which was the key job at the Tate.

The last four of us had to write a seven-year plan for the Tate and to do that we were given an office in the Tate for a day, could look at any papers we wanted, including all the budgets, and interview anyone we liked on the staff and board. It must be remembered that at the time no one anticipated the appearance of the Lottery. It had long been the government's intention to split the Tate in two, to turn the Millbank site into the National Gallery of British Art and to establish a National Gallery of Modern International Art on the site that had been specially earmarked and left vacant for it, adjacent to the Festival Hall on the South Bank, on the other side of the railway, in front of the Shell Building where, incidentally, I'd worked before going to university, first on the loading bay, and then promoted to being a Lamson pneumatic tube operator (transporting cash around shops). Alan Bowness, the outgoing director had given up hope of the money for this project ever becoming available and he had plans to build a sculpture gallery on a plot of land next door, celebrating the art of Henry Moore and Barbara Hepworth, his mother-in-law.

I asked to see Alan during my day at the Tate. I wanted to know why he was leaving early, after only eight years—he could have stayed ten, two five-year terms—and, obviously, to hear about his future plans and anything else he wanted to tell me. With his chubby face and buffant hairdo, he'd always been quite approachable, even friendly. I was looking forward to it. He told me he was leaving early because he thought it was important that one person didn't stay in this crucial post for too long (if only his successor had had the same intelligent humility). And, anyway, he was leaving to take up the post as director of the new Henry Moore Foundation, which was so rich that it had more money to spend on art than the Arts Council itself. Moore earned so much at the end of his life that he was one of the few people whose tax return was dealt with personally by the Chancellor of the Exchequer.

Alan then suddenly stopped and looked at me squarely across the desk and said, without blinking an eye, 'You do realise this is Nick's job, don't you?' I have to say my heart stopped and dropped. I was totally taken aback. I thought I was living in a just, egalitarian country, where opportunities were open to all, and all would get a fair hearing. I had, until that moment, believed in Britain. I knew Nick had been brought up in central London, the son of the eminent Labour peer, Baroness Serota, was connected to everyone and that he'd been chairman of the Young Friends of the Tate, when I didn't even know it had any, or even needed any. All I knew about the Tate when I was a kid growing up in a South London council estate was that it was free and was full of things I wanted to look at. I saved up my pocket money to take the train up to London whenever I could to visit it and all the other wonderful free museums and galleries in the centre of town. The idea that I was being interviewed for the Tate's directorship was, until that moment, a wonder in itself.

My utter disappointment and despair must have been all too clear for, still without blinking, a sneer spread across his puffy face that I will never forget. It meant one thing: if you didn't know this was Nick's job obviously you don't move in the right circles and don't deserve to get it. I can't remember what I asked him after that. Looking back, I should of course have challenged him, but I didn't have the heart. I happened to meet his secretary, Edwina, by chance, at an unrelated party some years later. I asked her if she knew about what he'd said to me. 'Oh yes,' she replied cheerily. 'We discussed it. He thought it was kinder to let you know before.' I actually don't think that was his reason. I actually think—perhaps I am flattering myself—that he did it to unsettle me and put me off. They (and I'll explain who I think 'they' were in a bit) were still worried that I might get the job, as the interview itself proved. Had I imagined the sneer? I thought not.

I went through the process of doing a seven-year plan—no easy task, especially when one's heart wasn't in it—and attended the interview. I walked through the door and, to my utter surprise saw that the chair of the Tate, Richard Rogers, who I knew slightly and admired, wasn't in the chair, but to one side. Someone I didn't know, a civil servant, was sitting in his place. I found out later that Richard had been persuaded that since he was dyslexic and had difficulty remembering people's names, he should relinquish this role, which sadly he did, not that the outcome would probably have been different if he hadn't, but it might have been: Richard was extremely imaginative and London might have had a modern building for Tate Modern, not an old conversion.

But what slowed my steps as I walked towards that chair was the face I saw on the panel to the right. Lord Gowrie was sitting there, the former minister of arts in the Thatcher government, who'd recently left the post, complaining that he couldn't live in London on a salary of £33,000 a year (showing his sympathy for the poor), and had become a director of Sotheby's, the major art auction house, instead. The Tate at that time was spending about £2 million a year on art, and there was no way that a representative from the trade should be on that panel. My mind raced. It was the longest, shortest walk in my life. I should refuse to be interviewed by that man, I thought.

My heart sank. I remember thinking clearly, I'm not going to get this job. Why should it always be me that has to spill the beans, pull the plug, say what's right? Nick's only going to be here for fourteen years at the most (they'd changed the rules to make it a seven-year, not a five-year contract, and one could only do two terms). If I rocked the boat now, I certainly won't get the job, but nor will I get it next time round. So I walked on. Gowrie asked my one question, 'What private collectors do you know?' I quipped back, 'apart from you?'; Gowrie had bought a work by David Kemp from a show I'd put on. Gowrie huffed, 'Oh, I'm not a big collector.' The chair disallowed the question—but it had been asked to show the panel what sphere I walked in.

Nick, of course, got the job, but the Civil Service Union immediately complained that the interview process had broken civil service rules and the appointment was invalid. Gowrie, they said, should not have been on that panel. *The Times* ran the story. The government simply ignored the objection. Had I walked out, they couldn't have done. My step to that chair was the most cowardly step of my career, and I've been paying for it for years.

The words of my friend Georg Eisler came back to me, 'The art gallery world is tied to the apron strings of the art market.' Bowness had tied the first knot by establishing the Patrons of New Art at the Tate. They were independent from the board and the staff, formed to help the gallery acquire modern art. Innocent enough, one might think, until one realises that these acquisitions worked both ways. An acquisition by the Tate affects the value of an artist's work in the market place. These patrons were effectively run by a select group of top-of-the-market art dealers and very rich collectors of—a better description of them would be investors in—contemporary art. It was they who awarded the Turner Prize, because public bodies like the Tate can't give money to individuals, and correctly so. But the trade, via the patrons, can.

The prize was at first awarded to artists of any age for the 'contribution' they had made to art, not for a specific work of art, which would have made some sense and encouraged debate about what is really 'lasting' in art. Then in 1991, Serota focused it on young artists exclusively, and it became the main means of promoting the 'next thing' in contemporary art, much to the delight of clever fixers in the art trade, particularly the collector/dealer Charles

Saatchi who'd recently decided to switch his marketing expertise to promoting contemporary art. And this 'next thing,' Nick decided, without any public debate, was going to be conceptualism.

Serota's whole philosophy of modern art, and indeed his whole curatorial practice, is based on his belief in Duchamp, in particular his act of sending a urinal into an exhibition, claiming anything can be a work of art if an artist says it is. We now know that Duchamp didn't do this, nor did the urinal mean what he said (see D for Marcel Duchamp), a fact that scuppers this whole philosophy. But no one knew any better at the time. I think conceptual art appealed to Nick particularly because it elevates the status of the gallery. Duchamp's urinal only becomes a work of art when it's exhibited in a gallery. This ups the role of the gallery and the curator; they become essential players in the art game, and— the inevitable result of Lord Gowrie's presence on that interview panel—tools of the art trade.

Damien Hirst summed up this cosy companionship when reporters asked him what he thought of my claim in my admittedly rather provocative e-pamphlet *Con Art—why you should sell your Damien Hirsts while you can*, that his work wasn't art and therefore wasn't worth investing in. He looked around at his exhibition in the Tate and said, 'Well, it's in an art gallery, isn't it?' The idea that something in a public gallery, especially one as prestigious as the Tate, might *not* be art is very difficult for the public to understand, hence the difficulty I had in making my case. But this is also why I can't respect Serota for not accepting my challenge, as a professional art director of standing, to have an open debate with me about what he actually saw in Hirst's work, taking him back, in fact, to our first meeting, when we looked at art together.

Worse than that, he didn't even allow me into the Tate, despite it being a public space, to say what I thought of Hirst's work myself! London Television, a French and a German radio station and

La Repubblica, the distinguished Italian newspaper, all wanted to interview me in the Hirst exhibition at Tate Modern, but Nick wouldn't allow it. I had to be interviewed standing outside, which made it more difficult for me to make my point. Jeremy Paxman, the famous TV interviewer, happened to walk past. He asked me what I was doing there—I'd contributed to his programmes in the past. I told him I hadn't been allowed in. His jaw dropped. 'You must be joking!' he said. I wish I had been. It's the job of a public gallery to encourage informed debate, not suppress it, but this is exactly what seems to have happened during Serota's term of office.

A few days later, the *Mail on Sunday* smuggled me into the Hirst show when it was open to the public, with a clandestine cameraman, and a reporter to cohere my comments. She was very interested in my observations about how long visitors looked at the exhibits—rarely more than derisory glances. The smell of the formaldehyde, leaking from the cases containing the dead shark and sliced-up cows, pervaded the whole exhibition. The title they splashed across the whole double spread, 'IT STINKS', summed up my feelings and the show's meaning precisely.

It was also, I think, Serota's fondness for conceptual art that led him to choose to convert the grim Bankside building for Tate Modern rather than build anew on the South Bank site long held vacant for it. Conceptual art, being an incomplete art form, like a hermit crab with claws but a soft behind, needs a borrowed shell to crawl into; a 'found object' can't become a work of art on its own. It needs curatorial help. A urinal in a lavatory is not a work of art, nor is one lying about in the street. I couldn't believe Nick could throw away the chance of building a spanking new art gallery in central London, when he had a vacant site to play with and all the money he needed, now the Lottery had come on stream. The opportunity wasn't just golden, but had the potential to be, artistically speaking, a nuclear explosion. Nor was his choice a question of self-righteously saving public money; Bankside Power Station, despite its meanness of appearance, cost twice as much to convert as Frank Gehry's Guggenheim Museum in Bilbao did to build from scratch. And modern architecture is an art form in itself, and one to which architects in Britain were then making outstanding contributions.

I can sympathise with Serota's nervousness up to a point. Architects notoriously take their revenge on art. The most famous example is Frank Lloyd Wright's Guggenheim in New York, built for showing paintings and sculptures (before the era of installations), in which the walls all curve and the floors all slope. Its Bilbao daughter is not much better: a stunning building but pretty hopeless for showing art in. Very early in my career, I arranged a meeting for fellow art curators to see the new Sainsbury Centre, opened in 1978 to house the collection of African and modern art given to the University of East Anglia by Sir Robert and Lady Sainsbury. The Sainsburys met us to show us round. They told us that they'd commissioned the young Norman (now Lord) Foster to design the building, one of his very first jobs. They'd invited him to their London home and told us he'd been impressed by the light coming from either end into the main room where their collection was shown, which had given him the idea for the barn-like glazed shed he built. By an odd fluke, I happened to be at a lecture Foster gave about his work a week later. He said he'd designed a universal building that would suit any client who next came through the door. They happened to be the Sainburys.

The great challenge of the unique opportunity Serota inherited, which he totally ducked, was to commission a modern building that was at once beautiful, a great work of art in itself, and worked superbly well as a museum. Sir Philip Dowson, the chief architect of Ove Arup and, at that time, president of the Royal Academy agreed with me that Nick's wish not to commission a new building for Tate Modern shouldn't be taken without some public debate. We did our best to interest the media and politicians but came up against a blank wall. Nick seemed to hold them all in a snake-like thrall. Difficult to believe, but true. He did it by the simple policy of refusing to speak. The media can do nothing if there's what they call 'an empty chair'. Say nothing and keep power. Talk and you're immediately exposed, which is what I do all the time, in the fond belief that discussion and debate are the natural lifeblood of art.

There was one exception to this muteness, towards the end of his career. He actually answered a letter I'd written to him, with Dr Glyn Thompson, asking the Tate to change the label on Duchamp's urinal and accept the authorship of Baroness Elsa von Freytag-Loringhoven (see D for Marcel Duchamp). I think he began because he thought he was on pretty safe ground. But we challenged all his arguments as he dug himself further and further into a corner. Eventually he ended the correspondence by arguing, effectively, that no one would ever know what really happened, and that he preferred not to believe what Duchamp had said at the time, but what he said much later. What he didn't calculate on was Glyn's extraordinary persistence, by not only unearthing an actual urinal of that time, identifying Elsa's distinctive handwriting and working out, precisely, the sequence of events in the submission, all proving that Duchamp simply could not have done what he later said he did. Elsa submitted the urinal. Duchamp's urinal never existed. It would have required a braver man than Serota to admit that he had been wrong all this time, for he'd totally bought into the Duchamp myth, and even bought one of his fake urinals for the Tate to celebrate the Millennium. The whole of our correspondence was published as a podcast by *Jackdaw* magazine, one of the very few instances where Nick was incautious enough to let slip what he actually thought.

Sealed-lip power has been Nick's operating principle. When he hatched Tate Modern, he devised the extraordinary internal management policy of separating responsibility for collections from responsibility for buildings. The head of collections had art but nowhere to show it and the heads of Tate Modern and Tate Britain (and, incidentally, Tate Liverpool and Tate St Ives) had galleries but nothing to put in them. This policy of divide and rule made sure that the final decision for everything was in Nick's firm grip. Of course, this dictatorship should now be split up. Nick's umbrella job abolished, Tate Liverpool handed over as an exhibition space to the National Museums and Galleries of Merseyside, Tate St Ives to a local organisation or the Hepworth foundation. Most significantly, Tate Britain and Tate Modern should have their own directors, boards and collections so that they can grow in their own way, according to their own priorities, led by imaginative directors.

And while they're at this reshuffle, they should, at last, honour Turner's wishes (as Selby Whittingham, the dedicated Turner authority, has been arguing for years) and hand over all the works he gave to the public, so many of which lie unlooked at in their stores, so that a new, glorious, independent Turner Gallery can be built, with views, preferably, of his beloved Thames, perhaps using the brownfield site Nick ignored on the South Bank, to show the paintings and watercolours of this truly world-class artist, and alongside it changing exhibitions of the many artists who have been and continue to be inspired by him, and by nature, in Britain and around the world. And this new gallery will strike a most timely cause, for Turner was the world's greatest painter of skies, and it is the beauty of the world's atmosphere that we have, most urgently to save.

If I were asked to sum up Nick's career, I would say that he chose the wrong art, chose the wrong building and stayed much,

much too long. One thing he did that was good: he held the line against charging; we saw eye to eye about that, at least. But it still bewilders me how the powers that be enabled him to stay in post for a totally unprecedented twenty-six years—virtually a whole career, and certainly swamping mine. This can only be explained by the fact that they must have been frightened of him, like everyone else, apart, that is, from me. I was once talking to Morley Safer in New York, the famous acerbic American TV broadcaster, who became a fan of mine after reading my book *The Eclipse of Art*, and I was explaining what enemies I had in Britain, Serota and MacGregor topping the list. 'That's the trouble with a small country,' he said. 'Here we judge people by the power of their enemies.'

Not that I would have fared better in America. There was a major problem: I was not American. This was brought home to me at a museum director's conference I was once addressing in America. I felt bewilderment in my audience, little more, until one of the delegates came up to me afterwards and said, 'You must remember that Americans don't understand poetic, elliptical and ironic thought.' I was invited to attend a small meeting of directors that was discussing what sort of museum should be built on the Twin Towers site—it was shortly after September 11. I kept quiet, having learnt my lesson, until Elaine Gurian, the chair of the session, turned to me to ask me what I thought of what I'd heard so far. I had to say that the proposals they were all talking about—above all researching the stories of the victims—sounded to me like a mausoleum, not a museum. A museum, I added, needs to explain why things happened, why a lot of people around the world hated America. It needed, above all, to say something about Osama bin Laden. There was a horrified silence, broken, eventually, by Elaine saying, 'Well, you must understand, Julian is a European.'

I once asked my old friend and former colleague, Graham Beal, an exceptional Brit who was ending his eminent American career as director of the Detroit Institute of Art, if I could ever get a job in the States. 'No,' he replied, totally frankly, 'because some people think that Frank Stella's latest work is crap, but you'll say so. One of your board will have one, and you'll be out.' Museum directors in America spend much of the last months of the financial year working with their trustees' accountants to determine which items in their collections have increased in value enough to be offered to the museum.

The game works like this—a curator at the museum advises a trustee to buy a group of objects that s/he would like to be in the collection. If the curator advises well, these items may well increase in value over time, enough when presented to the museum as a charitable gift to—hey presto!—offset a tax bill. This can work to everyone's (both the public's and the private donor's) advantage, and can be legitimate in many fields of collecting, but in the area of modern art the process becomes extremely dicey. This is because the acquisition of a contemporary work of art by a museum lifts it out of the common flow, declares it to be lasting and therefore worthy of investing in—and raises at a stroke the value of this artist's stock. Museums provide the gold standard for modern art; they're the banks around which the dealers do their business, and create their exclusion zones, for only a few stars can shine in investment heaven, whether they have anything to contribute to anyone else or not.

There is a sad coda to this story. I am an adviser to the Nerys Johnson Fund, which helps public galleries acquire paintings by living artists. I recently arranged for them to offer a superb painting by the Sheffield-born artist Mandy McCartin to Sheffield City Art Galleries, where I was once director. McCartin developed a vivid, personal style, a fusion of figurative art with graffiti—she's a British Basquiat, and in my view more interesting.

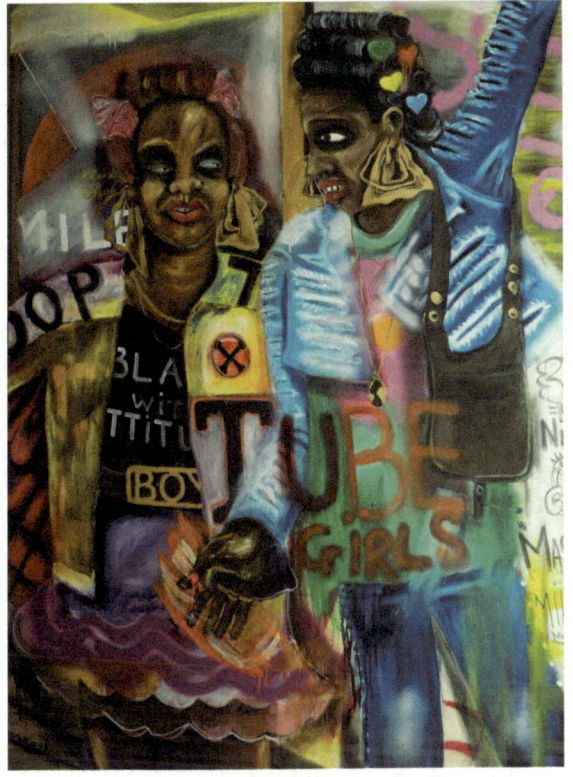

Mandy McCartin, Tube Girls, 1993

Her early lesbian paintings blaze with love, and the one I recommended that the fund buy for Sheffield, called *Tube Girls*, was a superb, ample rendering of two black women, laden down with bling, she'd seen on the London Underground. To my disbelief, this gift was rejected by the gallery, even though the director, Kim Streets, admitted that it was 'an extremely strong work of art'. She told me that they only acquired art from 'well-established artists'. I asked what 'well established' meant. I was told it meant artists in the stables (as they say in the trade) of a small group of London contemporary art dealers, none of whom represented Mandy McCartin, so a work by her could not even be accepted as a gift!

Curators now tend to leave that first process of sifting to dealers. It will require guts and vision to reassert the independent contribution that public art galleries have to make, but it's vital for living art that they do. They need to hold, again, annual open submission exhibitions, as Sheffield and many other public galleries used to do every year, and search, search everywhere, for the art of our times that is truly lasting. There are Kafkas under stones who aren't creating anything for money, or fame, but are really digging into and speaking of our times.

I do not want to inflate my own significance, but that ignored hesitation in my step, as I walked forward and allowed myself to be interviewed for the chief job at the Tate by a director of Sotheby's, was the beginning of a rot I could have helped to stop. This rot has spread. It led directly to that blinkered and most hurtful rejection by Sheffield's own gallery of a zinging painting by an artist of outstanding ability born and brought up in its less wealthy streets, depriving its public of seeing one of their own, when what this gallery needed to do was to accept the gift and celebrate it by putting on a glorious retrospective of Mandy McCartin's exceptional life's work.

S is for BRIAN SEWELL

One day I went down to London from Sheffield to bid for a Paul Nash snow scene, with three standing trees, which we wanted for the gallery. Nash had a tendency to mix all his colours with a dash of white, which was an easy way to create a harmony, but in this painting, partly because it was a snow scene, the trick worked. My train, however, was late and I arrived at Sotheby's just as the hammer was falling on the lot we wanted. It had sold for £900, less that we were prepared to bid. I spotted who'd bought it: a thin, elegant man with a bouffant hairdo whom I didn't know. I wondered if he was a dealer, so went up to speak to him. He was. I told him I'd failed to buy the painting. He was sympathetic. 'I'm not greedy,' he said in the cut-glass voice that was later to become famous, 'Give me a hundred and you can collect it directly from Sotheby's.' We did, and we did.

I didn't see him again until Sir Anthony Blunt was named in the House of Commons as the, until then, unknown fourth man in the Cambridge spy ring, after Donald Maclean, Guy Burgess and Kim Philby. His earlier confession, a closely guarded secret, was publicly revealed by Mrs Thatcher on the day she had to double VAT, burying very bad economic news, after a carefully staged sequence of preparatory leaks, under banner headlines announcing that the Surveyor of the Queen's Pictures, a Knight of the Realm and himself a relative of the Queen had handed secrets over to the Soviets for over a decade, before, all through and after the Second World War. The man who opened Blunt's door and subsequently shielded him from the press was the man I'd seen in Sotheby's, the art dealer and art historian, Brian Sewell.

Without that event, it's quite probably he'd never have become famous, but his handling of the media proved that he had what it takes to deal with them, a fearless, quick wit, and the media, for their part, spotted his talent. He became, quite soon after, the art critic for the *Evening Standard*, London's main popular paper. He relished the role, and quickly proved himself to be brilliant at it, never talking down to his readers, explaining technical terms whenever he used them, an authoritative, obviously knowledgeable voice, moreover, that maintained what the vast majority of his readership believed, that there were things called beautiful paintings and sculptures and that these had nothing, or virtually nothing to do, with the art that was being promoted today.

I was naturally sympathetic and, as chair of Arts Council Exhibition Sub-Committee, which included running the Hayward Gallery, I suggested that Brian should be invited to join us on the advisory panel—his was a genuine, informed voice we needed to hear. This was naïve of me. The officials froze. There was no way I was going to get my way. They argued that he was a dealer, and we couldn't have dealers on the panel. This was a bit ripe, especially with regards to what has happened to the art world since, and that everyone knew at the time that the art critic David Sylvester, chair of the Art Panel itself, was dealing on the side. I'd asked Brian before I submitted his name if he'd agree to stand. He was keen. Then I had to explain the reason they gave for not allowing him. 'But I'm not a dealer anymore, I'm a critic,' he complained. I tried to get the decision reversed, but without success.

Nearly a decade later, in 1994, the contemporary art world was growing increasingly irritated with Brian's relentless and increasingly popular sniping. I happened, by a peculiar fluke, to be visiting David Hockney when he showed me a letter he'd just received from Nick Serota, asking him to sign a letter to the editor of the *Evening Standard* requesting the dismissal of Brian, because he was bringing contemporary art into disrepute, at home and abroad, adding that Nick couldn't possibly sign it himself given his position as director of the Tate, but he hoped David would. Others already had.

'Don't they know how these things work?' David asked me, shaking his head. 'If they send this, they'll make him famous. The editor will splash the attack on the front page, raise his profile, give him more space, and a photo on top to head his column ... I can't possibly sign this.' And this is exactly what happened.

Artists, such as Michael Craig-Martin, himself a trustee of Tate, Eduardo Paolozzi and John Hoyland, and dealers, including Karsten Schubert and Nicholas Logsdail, signed the letter, showing how closely the art establishment was tied to the trade, and the money it generated.

I had my suspicions, however. The supporters of the letter might have been simply pawns in a more sophisticated game, being played by people who knew exactly how these things worked. I penned a satirical novel about what I thought was really going on behind the scenes in the contemporary art market at the time—called *Nothing On*—which no one was interested in publishing, and now drifts about somewhere as a dark, irritant speck in the depths of the web.

In Manchester I was intrigued by all I'd heard about the Haçienda nightclub, and decided, on one strange, floating, late evening, to pay it a visit. I was a bit out of place, being older than anyone, but no one noticed; it was too dark, and there was too much smoke. It felt a bit like walking into one of Piranesi's prison etchings, with levels, pits and ceilings disappearing in front, below and above, as house music pounded in my ears. There were bars seemingly suspended in space serving beer in bottles (without glasses), while people danced and drifted, apparently suspended as well—the whole sensation deeply disturbing to someone like me who basically likes to know where he stands. There wasn't a direction in the place, no guidance, no texts, not even, I recall, any exit signs or arrows, showing the way anywhere, including out. Everyone there knew where they were, even the way to the loos. I was in a different world.

I wandered down some dark steps and to my surprise came face to face with a huge, blown-up photo, in black and white, of Sir Anthony Blunt, the only image in the whole cavernous jungle. I couldn't understand it. Who, I thought, here knows who the hell this man is? There was no explanation, no label, nothing. Then I went down a few more steps, turned a corner and read above a bar its name 'The Gay Traitor'—the only words I'd seen in the whole shooting match. I told Brian about this experience when I next met him in London. His lips curled. 'I knew I loathed the North,' he said in his slow, mannered drawl, 'and now I know why.'

S *is for* PADDY JAPALJARRI SIMS

By far the oldest continuous artistic culture in the world, dating back at least 40,000 years, is that of Australian Aboriginal people. I was determined to put down markers from the start showing how I wanted the new collection of Glasgow's Gallery of Modern Art to grow. The collection mustn't be parochial, but had to reach out naturally, as far as possible. I needed something in the collection to make that clear. You couldn't get further away from damp, cold Glasgow than the arid deserts of Australia, where the indigenous people were now obliged to live, having been driven centuries ago from their fertile homelands on the coastal fringes by invading Brits, many of them transported convicts, a large proportion of these Scots.

I had long thought that traditional Aboriginal art ranked among the greatest contemporary abstract painting in the world, and as for optical effects, at its best, it knocked most of Op Art into a cocked hat. Many museums, like Tate for example, don't regard Aboriginal art as art at all, let alone as contemporary art, even though it is because it's being painted now, and they certainly don't rate it as abstraction, even though it manifestly can be nothing else. They dismiss it, too, because it's religious and spiritual, as if that excluded Rembrandt, Rouault and Kandinsky from the canon of visual creation! Aboriginal art at its best sings as wonderfully as any art today.

An Aboriginal painting then seemed in so many ways an ideal marker to pin the extent of this new collection's global reach. The problem was: how to get a really good one? So many of the paintings I'd seen were cynical, slick productions aimed at the tourist market, without any profundity of feeling at all. How could we get the real stuff? I knew I wouldn't have time to go myself, even though I'd love to have done—one of the few occasions I've regretted being a director. And I knew the business of finding and then collecting the real stuff could turn out to be long and arduous. So I sent out a message to all staff asking for a volunteer to go to Australia and collect. I only got one reply, from a young curator just starting off, Tamara Lucas, a quiet-spoken, deceptively soft-eyed vegetarian. I'd pay for all expenses. We'd deal with the price of the art when we got to that. My condition was that she had to find art that had been created for genuine spiritual purposes, not for tourists or the art trade.

She flew out to Australia and talked to colleagues in museums and representatives of indigenous people in the government. She was dissuaded at every step from going to see the Aboriginal people themselves. Racism was rampant in everything she heard—she was even told that she'd smell these people a hundred miles away, even before the plane landed. If she went, she'd be in and out in a flash. No one stayed for more than a day, quite simply because there was nowhere to stay, and she wouldn't want to sleep in the open, on the ground. The only thing to do was to buy works from one of the dealers specialising in Aboriginal art, as every foreigner did. She made it clear that this was not what she was there to do, and eventually got her way, obtaining permission to fly to Yuendumu, a remote community northwest of Alice Springs.

She did indeed have to sleep on the ground, and, though a vegetarian, eat kangaroo meat. They kept their tails sticking out of an open fridge in one of the houses the government had built for them that they didn't use. She told me, by fax—then the only available method of communication—that the mosquitoes were terrible, and her eyes were so swollen that she could hardly see. But she said she absolutely loved the people, above all the women who endlessly laughed and told stories in a language approximating to English, which she'd begun to understand. She went hunting with the women—the men just hung around—chasing kangaroos in cars and driving into them to kill them, and then cooking them and eating them on the spot. One victim had a baby Joey in its pouch, which she snatched to safety before they could kill it and cook it too. Much to their surprise she kept it with her as a pet for all her stay. They probably reckoned, she thought, that she was a bit touched. But then one day one of the women suddenly looked at her, said she knew who she was, and gave her an Aboriginal name.

All at once, being one of them and having a name, she had a father, Paddy Japaljarri Sims, a tribal leader, who had the major responsibility of keeping alive, literally, the night sky. Paddy expected all his daughters to cook for him and complained about everything Tamara tried to make. On many mornings, she woke to find a man standing patiently waiting for her to wake up, sometimes more than one, occasionally a whole row. They'd walked for many miles, having heard that one of Paddy's daughters was unmarried, and offering their services, which Tamara had, with difficulty, to refuse, explaining that she was already married, elsewhere, though this wasn't true. But, among all the activity, she saw very little painting, and she came back eventually with only a few small canvases, good but nothing special. Altogether a fascinating trip for her, but for me very disappointing.

But we had a surprise in store. A few weeks after her return, a fax arrived in my office. Tamara's father, Paddy Japaljarri Sims, told us it was time to do a Night Sky Dreaming, which he conducted every twenty-five years or so. If his daughter came back, he told us, he would give the painting that resulted to our gallery. They had no use for it after it was done—the doing was all—and they wanted the world to learn more about their culture, which they wanted to keep alive.

Dreaming is at the heart of traditional Aboriginal culture. Put rather simply, Aboriginals believe that the world was dreamed—a good modern word for this would be imagined—into existence. They don't believe in a creator god as such, or at least not one who appears in any form, but in a thinking essence that thought creation into being. The only task that Aboriginals have to do on this earth—eating is just keeping oneself alive—is to keep the world itself alive by redreaming it, reimagining it in their minds. If they don't do this, and go on doing this, they believe the world and they themselves will die. Their whole culture is, therefore, built around repeating the stories, in dances, poems and paintings, of how the kangaroos, the water holes, the rivers and mountains came to be. And they've been doing this probably ever since they first arrived in Australia from Africa many millenia ago, making their imagery the oldest in existence. A redreaming of the whole night sky sounded very special, and I sent Tamara back at once.

When she arrived, nothing happened. She hung about for weeks. Her father kept telling her it was about to begin, but then when it didn't, he told her that it wasn't time. Time simply didn't mean the same thing for them. I faxed her asking her to wait as long as necessary, if she could. She did. Then, suddenly, it started—weeks of it. She was utterly exhausted. Paddy and a group of men slept during the day and stayed up all night and she was expected to do the same—a special privilege. They traipsed miles to different sacred spots across their territory, settled down and when the sun set, sat watching the stars until dawn, telling and chanting stories about them all, and how they had come to be where they are, laughing and enjoying themselves uproariously. Tamara told me she'd never seen so many stars—the night was thick with them, all of so many hues shimmering in the sky. She pointed out shooting stars at first but was greeted with a hush and told to look away, for these were spirits dying and it was unlucky to catch even a glimpse of one.

When they got back to base, the painting, the dreaming began. In the past they used to do this straight onto the ground, with earth and vegetable pigments, and let it sink back into the earth or be blown away after the ceremony was over, just as the Northwest Native Americans used to let their totem poles decay back into the forests, as some still do, returning to the forest growth trunks which they had taken and carved. Now the Aboriginals use huge stretches of canvas, which provide a firmer and easier surface to work on, and they love the brilliant luminosity of modern synthetic paints. Tamara's father, Paddy, first painted the whole four by three metre area in a bright, almost shocking pink. Tamara was horrified and told him so. He angrily told her to shut up and mind her own business. He was in charge of the painting. She had in the end to admit he was right. The whole canvas was eventually covered with tiny dots, and not a sliver of the pink underpaint could be seen.

Tamara took photos, made notes and tape recordings of the proceedings, with commentaries by Paddy and others, all of which are in the Glasgow Museum's collections. It took about thirty men and women, over three weeks, to complete the painting, laughing and telling stories, and often breaking away to dance, then returning to add, under Paddy's strict supervision, minute dots to the canvas, as many as the stars in heaven or the souls of people in the past, every touch delicately felt, nothing mechanical, not a centimetre of automatic filling in, everything intended, no pattern making—an extraordinary community abstract creation.

When it arrived, I was taken aback. I had never seen such delicate, precise, painted feeling sustained over such a broad canvas. Glasgow had, by the greatest good fortune, I was sure, been the recipient of one of the profoundest works of art of our times. I searched everywhere for traces of the shocking pink Tamara had told me about but couldn't find the merest hint. But I was sure that it was this bright underpainting that suffused the whole picture with its extraordinary glow, the restrained rainbow light that Tamara had seen in the totally unpolluted Australian night. This was intended artistry at its finest.

I had seen the stunning telescopic photos of the night sky, taken with natural light, by David Malin at the Australian Astronomical Observatory, and decided to buy some to be displayed alongside this acquisition. These photos were not only beautiful in themselves, but demonstrated how close the actual colours of the starry firmament are to this millennial-old Aboriginal vision. A local journalist, hearing about my acquisition of a few science photos for the Gallery of Modern Art, and wanting to stir up trouble for me—an ongoing game in the Glasgow press—rang the famous art critic Brian Sewell in London to get his opinion. Without bothering to ring me and find out what I'd done and why—even though I knew him well—let alone coming up to look at the photographs and paintings himself (that would have been impossible—it was in the North)—he tossed a remark off the top of his head, much to the delight of the local hack. 'He's finally gone mad,' he said.

Overleaf: Paddy Japaljarri Sims, Night Sky Dreaming, 1992

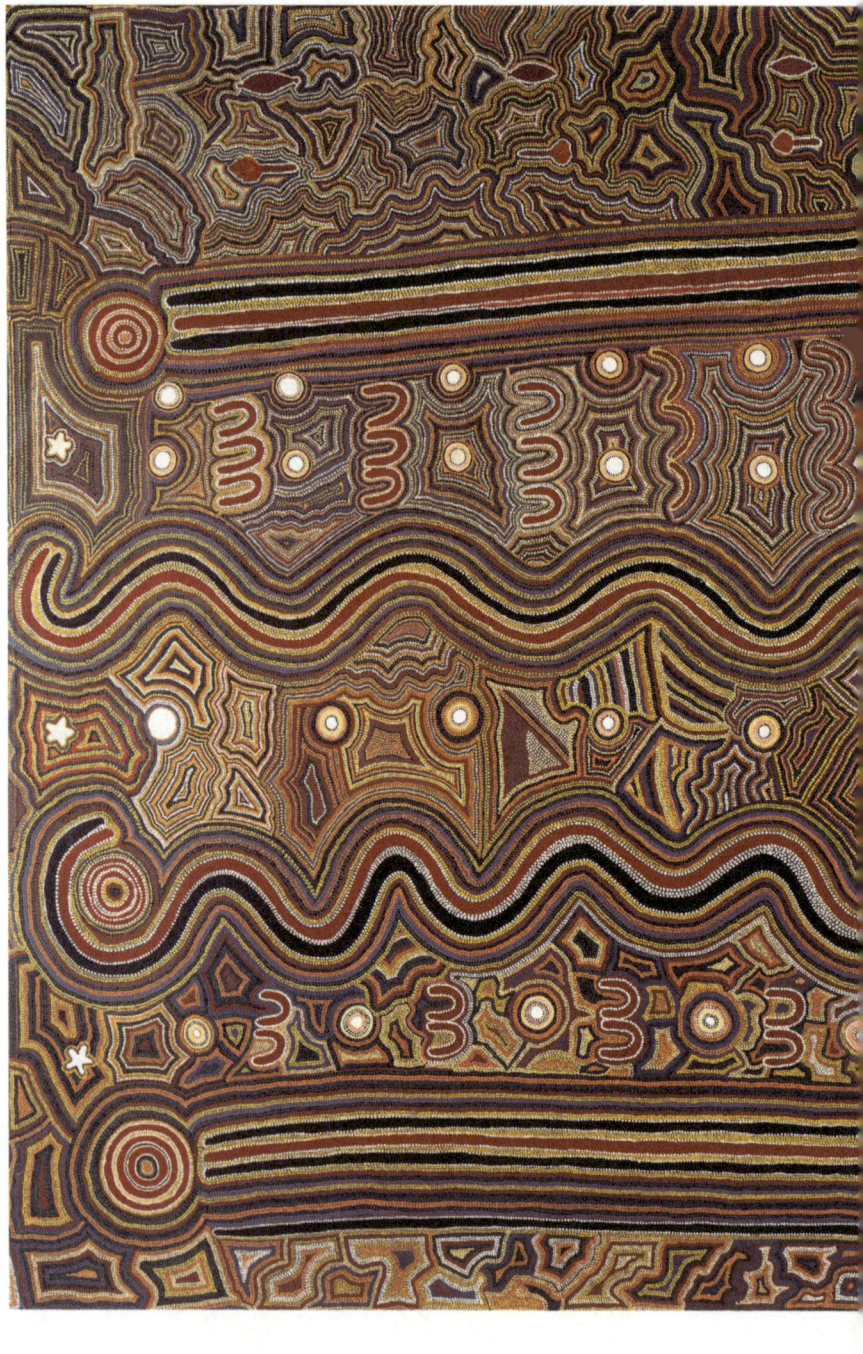

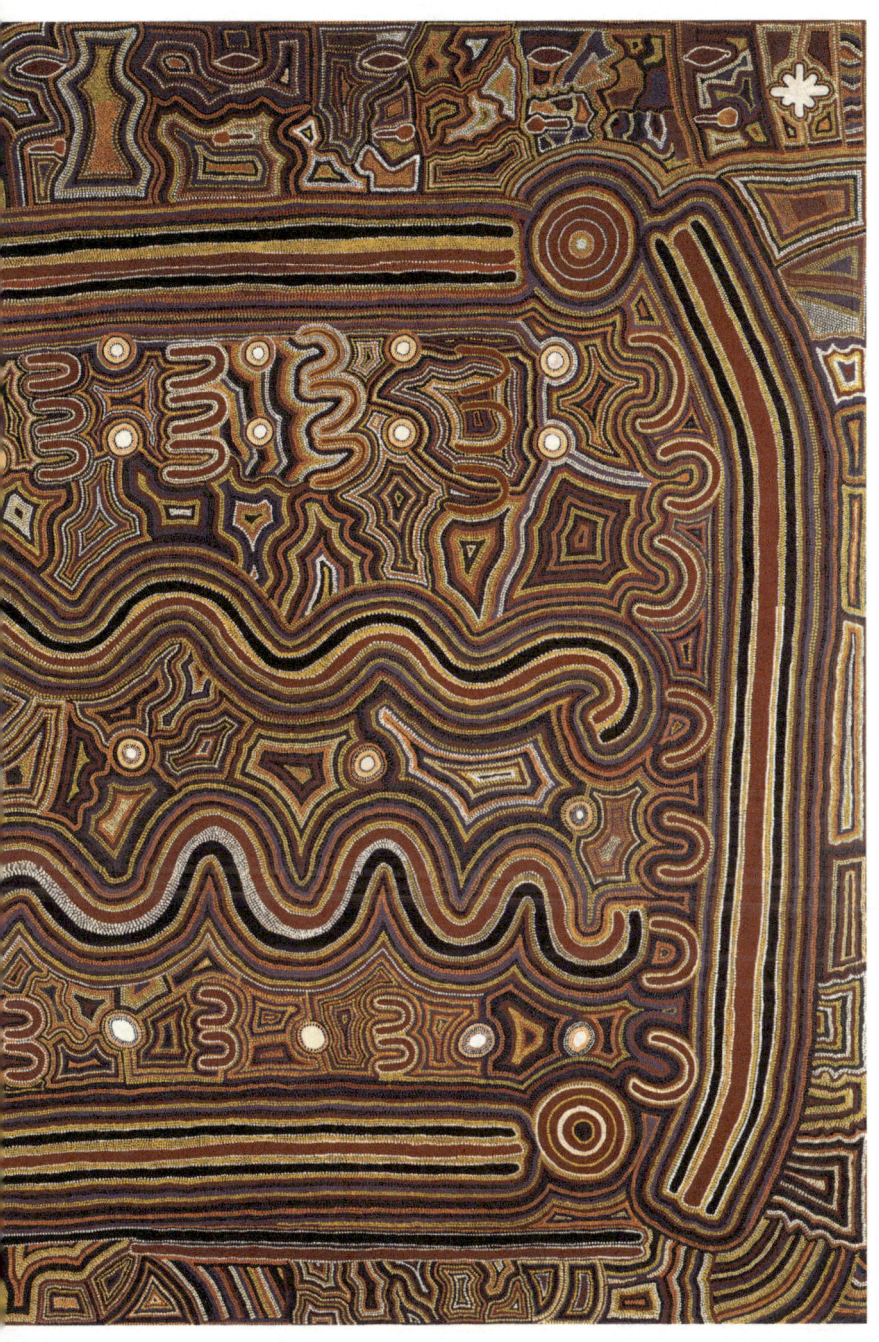

S is for SIR ROY STRONG

Sir Roy Strong, during his time as director of the V&A, complained endlessly, loudly and publicly about the terrible state of the museum's roof, which obliged him, he said, to introduce entrance charges. 'We can't even afford to mend our roofs,' he whined. He was fond of looking sad and crucified, with open hands held wide. I went to see him to try to stop him introducing charging and he, being nothing if not approachable, agreed to see me.

Sir Roy came from a lower-class background like me, and had, like me, what used to be called an 'aspirational accent'. He had already become famous, while he was director of the National Portrait Gallery, for donning a white suit, a sartorial decision, he told me once, that had been his breakthrough. He was following, by doing so, the brilliant American novelist and cultural commentator, Tom Wolfe, much in the same way that David Hockney followed Andy Warhol by dyeing his hair blond. What was it that made white so significant in the sixties? That mad spiral of competitive advertising by washing-powder manufacturers, all claiming on TV that their brand washed whiter than everyone else's, one even claiming to wash whiter than white, if such a thing was possible on earth. What were we all trying to wash away—the war?

Roy was famous in part, too, for his flamboyant news-grabbing directorship of the National Portrait Gallery, which he claimed to have put on the map, wilfully ignoring the considerable achievements of his predecessor, Sir David Piper, whose book *The English Face* is still a gem. Roy was respected, too, for his considerable scholarship, in *English Elizabethan Portraiture*, his knowledge of garden history and his waspish tongue. He had a wicked wit; he once told me that the architects had got the slope of an access ramp in the museum wrong—we were all fitting them at that time—which 'had driven the disabled [as we called them then] hopping mad'. On meeting, he was moderately tall but almost painfully thin, his haggardness of face emphasised by an outsize, then-black moustache. His large round specs made his dark round eyes look larger, rounder and darker than they were. He once described one of his colleagues to me as having 'mad, staring eyes', but it was an attribute I, forever after, associated with him.

I walked into his office and was immediately offered a drink. I can't remember what time of day it was, but certainly not evening. 'A Pernod,' I suggested, feeling the need for something nippy. He opened his drinks cabinet, which was full, and then turned, 'We don't have any French peasant drinks here.' I now know that the best pastis is not Pernod but Pontarlier-Anis.

'Good gracious,' I said, sipping a whisky, and looking round. I couldn't hide my surprise. I was about to say, 'I didn't know anything like this had survived.' I'd only been in colleagues' offices before, not the director's, and they'd all been stripped bare, lavatorial distempered walls and bog-standard government-issue furniture. But this was sumptuous, a unique survival from Victorian times. 'Do you like it?' Roy almost squeaked with delight, 'I've just had it done! I found the marble fireplace in the stores, and the carpet and the desk, and we had the wallpaper specially reprinted.' So there was no shortage of money here, I thought.

I launched into my usual spiel against entrance charges: museums are not one off-visitor attractions, like theme parks, that you go to once, see everything, and perhaps don't visit again. They're more like parks, libraries and shopping centres—especially the big ones, like the V&A or the British Museum and all the large regional museums. They're places that you visit briefly to see one thing or wander around and browse. They're places that you go to again and again, which become part of people's lives. Charging entrance fees doesn't make economic sense. Shopping centres don't charge you to go in but take money off you inside. That's how museums need to make their money in shops and cafés, lectures, concerts, films and specialist services, including difficult identifications and, above all, by putting on stunning exhibitions. Philippe de Montebello at the Met always complained that he couldn't charge entrance fees for his exhibitions, because the public weren't prepared to pay twice. But they'll pay thrice, or more if you put on more shows, I said, which you can easily do in the V&A.

And, I added, charging at the entrance favours the better off. It makes it more difficult to attract new audiences, especially young ones, and widen the museum's reach into the community. I told him how as a young teenager I used to save up my pocket money to buy a train ticket up from the suburbs to London, and then spent the day exploring the museums which were all free. And if you start charging at the V&A, it'll have serious implications for museums in the regions, which need to be much more closely locked into their community. Right-wing councils will immediately follow suit and our regional museums will become as empty as those in France. And where will the income from charging go? Into the coffers of the government; they'll reduce your budget by that amount. Charging is a tax on tourism. Director Michel Laclotte told me he couldn't get Parisians to come to the Louvre. 'Charging at the door,' I said to Roy, 'will halve your attendances [I underestimated this—they fell by two-thirds when charges were introduced], lose you income in the café and shops, and above all from your exhibitions. You'll be a loser, all round.'

I stopped. Roy was looking at me, but not really listening. He just waved his hands and said, conspiratorially, 'Oh you've got to give up all this welfare-state-museum nonsense. You're living on a past ideology.' I thought I was just making economic, not to mention social, sense. I realised sadly, then, that Roy wasn't actually interested in museums, let alone in the museum profession as a whole. He was merely a figurehead on a great ship he in fact cared little about. John Mallet, keeper of ceramics at the V&A, once told me that Roy had never once put a foot in his department. 'He didn't dare,' John told me, 'because he knew absolutely nothing about ceramics, nor was he particularly interested in them.' If you're a director of a museum you have to be prepared to go anywhere, no, you have to *want* to go everywhere, even if it's only to learn what's going on. Ignorance is as good a reason to ask questions as any. Roy took the easy option and remained above it all.

After my disappointing meeting, I went along the corridor to see Michael Kauffmann, the keeper of paintings, whom I greatly admired. We chatted about Roy's new office. He muttered, 'Yes, he's spent all that on himself, and it takes us months to get a light bulb replaced.'

'So there *is* a money problem?' I asked.

Michael replied, 'For some.' But the truth was actually worse. When I came to be interviewed for the directorship of the V&A, I had access to all the books. 'What's this underspending here?' I asked the head of finance. 'Well spotted,' he told me, 'there's always been enough money to repair the roofs, but his staff could never get their act together to clear the stores and galleries and do the work.' The repairs and maintenance budget, year after year, has always been underspent—hence the buckets in the upper galleries, Roy's endless complaints to the press and the totally unnecessary introduction of entrance charges.

Charging was a crucial issue in the times I was interviewed for the post of director of the V&A, a job I would have loved (because its collections are where art—visual imagination—and life come together—the very frontier that so interests me—*Vita* & *Arte*—

the term I wanted to coin, but never got the chance), but not on any condition. The first time, Lord Carrington, former Foreign Secretary and General Secretary of Nato, was in the chair. He opened the interview by saying,

> I must make one thing clear, we don't want anyone with ideas, you know. We've got the ideas and we want someone to carry them out. Now you can tell us what you think about the museum. You've got five minutes.

I opened by saying, 'Well, just in case you haven't thought of everything ...' They laughed. But there was no way I was going to get that job because they were adamant about charging, and I was adamantly against.

The fact that someone like Lord Carrington was interested in chairing something like the V&A (though, it's true, he had a house just round the corner) suggested to me that the top echelons of the civil service were using the V&A, as a little regarded back door, to introduce charges across the board of national museums—with their sights on the big income to made from the British Museum and the National Gallery. This view was confirmed by my second interview—this time chaired by Lord Armstrong, formerly principal private secretary to the Prime Minister, and not known for his interest in the arts or museums. He was very interested in my approach about how to run the place—he asked me all the questions at the interview (he wouldn't let anyone else speak!) but baulked at my insistence that free access at the door was vital for artistic, social and economic reasons. This did not fit in with his plan.

There might have been other reasons, of course, for my failure to land this wonderful job. One was suggested to me by Lady Tollemache, a Lady of the Bedchamber to the Queen, whom I met at a reception in Manchester. She congratulated me on being interviewed for the job—the short list had been aired in the press—and commiserated with me for not getting it, but, as she explained, 'They don't know you in London—and it's very important that they know you.' I couldn't help wondering who these 'they' were. I'm a Londoner after all! But obviously I didn't know the 'right' Londoners—such is the little circumference of the English class system.

T *is for* RAYMOND TALLIS

Hay-on-Wye is the home of Richard Booth, the brilliant bookseller and self-appointed King of Hay, of the Hay Literary Festival and more recently, after the economic crash of 2007–8, of the HowTheLightGetsIn philosophy and arts festival, spun out of the creative, ceaselessly pondering mind of Hilary Lawson, the philosopher and media entrepreneur. This little town, straddling the border between England and Wales, is nearly an hour's taxi drive away from the closest railway station at Hereford. Another man was waiting to be picked up in the tiny, deserted station forecourt. A little over average height, he was dressed in the conventional suit and tie of a not very successful businessman, his face hidden behind what looked like an impatiently home-trimmed moustache and beard. But what marked him out was his large, wide-rimmed, bright-red felt hat decorated with a broad dark band. The taxi arrived, called both our names, and in a minute, we were on our way to Hilary Lawson's jamboree.

We didn't need to introduce ourselves. The taxi driver had done that for us. Neither of us had heard of each other before, me less forgivably. Ray is one the most eminent of doctors, neuroscientists, philosophers and polymaths around, on every panel under the sun, with dozens of books already under his belt, and dozens more under his hat. He took it off when he got in to reveal one of the most perfectly rounded domes I've ever seen. But what caught my attention even more were his eyes, among the most insistently probing I have seen, while his mouth, fringed under febrile growth, was consistently playful, as if about to crack a joke, which it frequently did, often a pun, usually sexual or scatological, typical of doctors faced continually with human realities. We started talking and didn't stop and in a way we haven't still, mostly about art I'm afraid to say because I'm essentially ignorant of all his other topics.

The luxury of not having a full-time job is that you can concentrate on one thing at a time for as long as you want. After that chat in the taxi, and hearing him talk at Hay, I went to the National Library of Scotland and read all the books of his I could—approaching twenty of them at that time. I spent nearly three weeks totally immersed in Tallis. I found them absolutely fascinating. Not only were they extremely enjoyable to read—never laced in jargon: specialist terms beautifully explained—they opened my mind to a subject that I had been interested in, but never really focused on—the nature of human consciousness.

Philosophy had always intrigued me, but almost always left me floundering as if I was up in the clouds, gasping for air, with nowhere to stand to catch my breath. Ray's writing was realistic, down-to-earth in fact. At the same time what he showed was wonderfully mysterious. I felt he'd put his finger on something that was crucial to the future of art, and I suggested that I would select a group of his writings and put them together in a way that could interest a different audience involved with art. He was delighted—a book he didn't need to write! I did the edited selection, and we wrote the last chapter in tandem—he wasn't quite sure how to end the story—and compiled *Summers of Discontent: the Purpose of the Arts Today*.

Ray's theory is that art has no relevance to our ordinary lives when we're hungry, thirsty, in pain or frightened, or when we go about our daily business of ensuring our survival. Art becomes of interest to us when we're free of all these urgencies, however briefly, when we have the time and space to simply be. We should then, you would have thought, be totally happy and content. But we're not. Ray has written beautifully and at length about our nagging feelings of discontentment. One exquisite, extended essay asks when we actually feel we have 'arrived' on the long-anticipated holiday before it's time to pack our bags and go home—never quite, is the answer. When we, to all intents and purposes, have everything, we still have a sense of incompleteness that we are, somehow, not fully living. This is what Ray calls, 'the wound in the present tense of consciousness'.

His argument is that art helps us heal this wound. Our consciousness doesn't enable us to fully experience our experiences and as a consequence we can become haunted by the sense that our lives are somehow eluding us. Art, by lifting us out of ourselves, enables us to experience life more fully, both emotionally and intellectually. Elevated by a Shakespeare play, an opera by Verdi or a painting by Matisse, makes one feel unforgettably as if, at last, one is really fully alive. Art makes us feel, however briefly, that we are no longer victims of time. We are aware when listening to music that the notes that have just gone are tied to the notes that are to come and both illuminate the present. Art makes us consciously aware of the moment. As Ray put it, 'The perfected journeying that is music is continuous arrival.'

More than that, great art can give us the sense of recovering or, rather, repossessing an entire world. He quotes E. M. Forster's description in his essay on *War and Peace*:

> After one has read *War and Peace* for a while, great chords begin to sound, and we cannot say exactly what struck them. They come from the immense area of Russia, over which episodes and characters have been scattered, from the sum total of bridges and frozen rivers, forests, roads, gardens, fields, which accumulate grandeur and sonority after we have passed them.

This feeling of oneness with a larger world that art can bring adds another dimension of meaning to Ray's perception of the sense of disconnectedness that he has identified to be the downside of human awareness. We are the only animal that is aware that it is going to die. We also know that we face death alone and can be painfully aware of our individual isolation while we are alive. Even though we know we can't literally be apart from the world we breathe in and walk on, the wound in the present tense of consciousness that Ray has identified makes us feel we are cut off from everything and our awareness of our ultimate, solitary end isolates us further. Art enables us to face and in a way overcome our terrifying loneliness.

Meeting Ray and reading his books has, for me, been like coming up for air. His writings have enabled me to explain why I have long felt that the arts are vital, not just to my life, but to everybody's lives, even though I have not been able to say exactly why before. They don't feed us physically, it's true, but they feed our minds with something we really need. I've never met anyone who doesn't welcome some form of musical or visual expression or one of the many forms of storytelling. These are all arts, however entertainingly they might start. That is one reason why there is a Beryl Cook on the cover of this book. She was an artist, whatever Nick Serota might say.

Ray has shown that the arts aren't marginal to our lives, a luxurious add-on to material gain, still less the dictate of exclusively cultivated taste, and even less a way of investing cash, but fundamental to the basic business of being fully human. That's why everyone needs access to them, whether as a participant or appreciator, or both, around the campfire. They merit major funding. Ray has identified, quite simply and humbly, factually, without any fuss or fancy theory, a fundamental purpose for the arts in modern society, and by doing so, he's opened a big door in people's minds and hearts that will, in time, change how everything looks and how we lead our lives. The glow of feeling more fully alive is the imaginative light that illumines and connects all the creative art celebrated in this book; the glow that comes with the moment all artists feel when they say, at last, 'it works', everything hangs together so that the whole is more than the parts—none more purely and astringently, perhaps, than in the collages of Francis Davison, but this principle applies to all art, however representational.

The implications of Ray's observations are, I think, immense, now that the arts have no clear religious, political or social function to perform. He has discovered the role of art today—at once personal and encompassing. When, over time—if we have the time—as his ideas seep into public awareness, they will change how we think about the arts and what we expect from them; how governments subsidise the arts; how the arts are taught in schools and colleges; how we validate and analyse the arts; how we make decisions about what art to preserve from the past; and, even more crucially, how works of art are created today, the sources from where they spring. Above all it will make us ambitious for art, particularly great art again. Why should other ages have had Botticelli and Bosch, Velázquez and Goya, Picasso and Matisse, when we're supposed to be content with a shark in a tank, a soiled bed and a can of shit (literally; one was bought by Tate)? Of course, great art is being made now—it has to be, among seven billion of us—it's just that that the curators responsible for showing it have to search really hard and wide to find it.

Ray's theory is that the arts help us address our profound discontentment. This is currently alleviated, in the main, by consumption. This is eating, relentlessly, into the dwindling resources of the planet. The arts are immaterial, and almost without exception their creation and appreciation are, like physical sports, eco-friendly and sustainable. The arts can help us save our world not by telling us what to do—that is the job of scientists, civil servants and politicians—not even by warning us what is about to happen (though that can help)—but by celebrating the wonder, however troubled, of being alive. Life doesn't need to be a tedious repetition, a labour or a ceaseless process of acquisition: it can be a continuous expanding discovery of existing.

This possibility, this journey into freedom, is open to the artistic feeling in every one of us, whether we are creating artworks ourselves, or choosing which art forms we want to enjoy and explore. For the surprising and hopeful implication of Tallis's simple and beautiful observation is that our massive collective discontent, which has the potential to destroy the planet, could be transformed, by our own agency, into a massive collective benefit. All the world eats, drinks and even makes love, basically, in order to live, except the French, who, as I found out when I joined them in their happy, fecund land, live to eat, drink and make love, which is perhaps why they had the freedom, energy and joy to overleap our pressing discontent and produce the world's first truly great art, in the Chauvet Cave, dating back 35,000 years, and have continued to do so, and—who knows?—might lead us all again when the age of non-art (non as in nonsense) is finally past.

T is for HOCK AUN TEH

Meeting Hock Aun Teh for the first time is bit like opening a door to a gale. He is usually splattered with paint, and it would never occur to him to hide what he does. But what hits you most directly is his energy, pent up in a lean, full-faced, frontal, black-haired frame, and his unequivocal stare. Since a kid, brought up in a Chinese community in Malaysia, he has practised martial arts, and soon developed his own technique, Tukido, which now has schools of followers. This served him in good stead once when he was surrounded by a bunch of thugs in a car park in Glasgow, who didn't like his 'chinky' face. He had the presence of mind to chuck his car keys to one of them, telling him to open the boot. 'There's a block of wood in there, hand it to me.' The fellow did, obediently. Hock Aun held it up, and said, 'If you mess with me, this is your head.' He smashed the block to smithereens with his other fist. They peeled away after that.

Fitness, for Hock Aun, is energy, and energy is what his art is all about, bottled explosions at the point of bursting. He never imitates appearance—that's too tame an activity—but works from memory, often at night, leaping immediately into the heart of the feeling, the emotional maelstrom of the experience. Some people seem to be born artists, like John Bellany and David Hockney. Others find out they are later, such as Beryl Cook, Niki de Saint Phalle and Francis Davison. Hock Aun Teh was among the first. He simply doesn't know what else to do with his life. 'Doubt,' as William Blake said, 'is self-contradiction.' I don't think Hock Aun has doubted in himself and what he's doing for one minute.

As a very young kid he was all play, growing up in a small village in the countryside in Malaysia. He escaped into the jungle whenever he could, climbing trees, swimming in rivers, escaping snakes and playing truant from schools before he was expelled, an impossible, unteachable child until he saw a Western painting of a bridge over a river and was literally stopped in his tracks. From that moment on he knew what he wanted to do with his life, and applied himself, relentlessly to the task. He had, first to learn traditional Chinese representational painting—birds on branches in watercolour. He fed the sparrows seeds soaked in alcohol—they flapped about on the floor drunk, so he could paint them more easily—these early studies are a delight.

But he also had the good fortune to be born into a culture where brushwork is essential to meaning and expression—before the era of the computer. He taught himself calligraphy and was particularly inspired by the 'Mad Grass' writers of the Tang dynasty, especially the work of Huai Su who developed a dazzlingly original, daring style in which the brushmarks stretched the meaning of the words until they almost disappeared in abstract flourishes that expressed feelings not literal meanings. Another Tang dynasty painter, Zhang Yan Yuan, wrote: the artist's job is to 'peel away the physical appearance to discover the spirit within'. This has been Hock Aun's ambition in all his work, but he only realised how to do it by marrying the freedom of expression in the West with the Chinese tradition. He consumed all the books he could on Western art, particularly Post-Impressionism and Abstract Expressionism. He then met, by chance, a Scottish soldier on a train who told him Glasgow Art School was the best in the West. So he came to study there and stayed, travelling to America as soon as he could to see the modern American painters work in the flesh, many of whom had been inspired by expressive graphic expression in the East. Hock Aun's art builds on this circular attraction.

He is at his strongest and most inventive when the original feeling is intense. I commissioned him once to go on an art expedition I funded with the Ysbrand Brouwers' Artists for Nature Organisation to produce paintings for an exhibition I wanted to do at the Burrell Collection to celebrate the Chinese Year of the Tiger in 1998. Hock Aun himself was born in the Year of the Tiger 1950 and learnt painting first from a Chinese master who specialised in tigers. The survival of tigers in the wild seemed to me to be a crucial turning point in the history of humanity. It takes a mother tiger two years to teach her cubs how to hunt, and only a tiger can do that. Tigers can't be reintroduced into the wild; they wait for food, not knowing what to do. If tigers only survive in zoos, what will be lost is tiger culture, which is irreplaceable. I wanted the exhibition to be about that.

Hock Aun went with all the other artists to Bandhavgarh Reserve in India, but unlike them he didn't draw anything; he just watched. He was amazed by the tiger's camouflage. Once on the back of an elephant, a tiger came close and reared up at him. He felt the hair rise on the back of his neck. He'd experienced that rarest of all human feelings today—to know oneself to be potential prey. The huge triptych he did when he came back is called *Tigers Do What Tigers Like*. It's an extraordinary painting, one of his most haunting. Entirely abstract, you don't see the tiger at all, but eerily sense its presence and movement through the high grasses so strongly that you can almost smell it. Patrick Davies, Hock Aun's enterprising dealer was at the opening of the exhibition and there saw the wire sculptures of Kendra Haste, another participant in the project. Though, like so many in the contemporary art world, he'd resolved to have nothing to do with 'nature artists'— a telling indication in itself of the blinkered view of art today— he fell in love with her deeply felt work, and they've enjoyed an extremely productive artist/dealer relationship ever since.

Hock Aun invited me on different occasions to China and Malaysia, to give talks at and write catalogues for the major

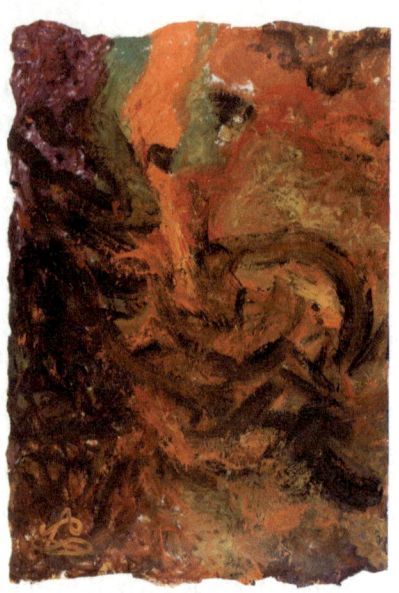

Hock Aun Teh, Triptych: Tigers Do What Tigers Like, 1998

exhibitions he has had in Beijing and Kuala Lumpur. At one banquet in Beijing, news was brought in that 'my' country had just voted Brexit. The whole table—mostly of Chinese businessmen—fell about laughing. I asked Hock Aun why they were laughing. They were laughing, he told me, for three reasons. First was the mere idea that a government could ask the people to vote no or yes on an issue as complex as whether Britain's economy would do better inside or outside Europe was laughably absurd. Secondly, they were laughing at the idea that the majority would necessarily be right about such a subject. And thirdly, they were laughing as they discussed what this might mean for their investments—should they buy Euros now, or dollars, or, even one suggested, with much hilarity, sterling?

At one banquet (there were always banquets—the Chinese don't trust you if you don't drink, Hock Aun told me, which was a pleasure for me, though not for him) after a ceremony celebrating the spirit of his grandfather in the little village in

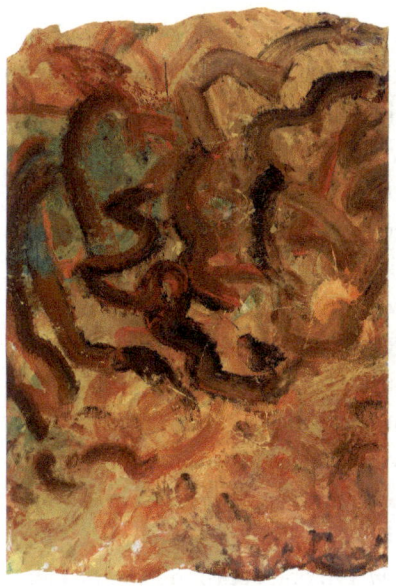
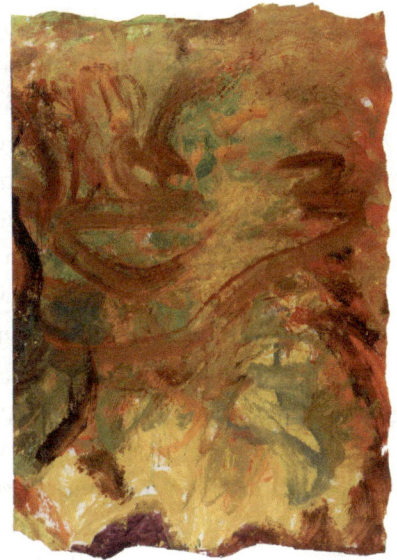

Southern China where his ancestors came from, I was sitting at a big round table (they are always round and big), dipping into the delicious local dishes spinning round before me, when a huge moth flew in and settled on the wall just above me. I am interested in moths and got up to look. It was a silk moth of the Atlas type, a great, arched, moon-patterned creature, much wider than my palm.

I felt it shouldn't be inside, in the glaring artificial light, and carefully nudged it to walk on to my palm and carried it outside, to everyone's surprise. I released it into the dark, warm air, but it flew round and immediately came back inside, settling on the wall where it was before. I took objection to this and carried it outside again, releasing it further down, at the very end of the balcony in front of the house. But it flapped lazily back through the warm, black night, came in again and settled on the wall once more almost exactly where it had been before. I gave up and sat down again.

Everyone was bewildered by what I'd just done. Hock Aun explained, 'Didn't I realise that the moth was the spirit of his grandfather?' I almost believed him and I was much more sympathetic, when some years later, Christine Measures, the wife of David, told me that shortly after he'd died, a butterfly had flown into their greenhouse and looked down at her from a leaf on the vine above her head in such an insistent way that she was sure it was David, telling her that he was all right and not to worry—a message from the afterlife. There are, quite possibly, more things in heaven and earth than are dreamt of in our Western philosophy, as Hamlet hinted, and Hock Aun at his best is about that.

I often took the opportunity when attending one of Hock Aun's exhibitions, to visit, by myself, some of the ancient sites of China, as part of my ongoing research into world art for my books, *The Art of Wonder* and, later, *Realisation*. On one occasion I went to see the Flower Mountain, at Hua Shan, in the southern Guangzhou Province, the largest area of rock painting in the world, though by no means the earliest, dating from the first century CE. My son, Daniel, was working as a teacher of English in Nanning, the capital of the province, and I thought he could help me get to see the site, which was buried deep in the countryside. He had learnt Chinese, so he told me, by playing badminton and getting drunk with friends. He asked around; no one had heard of the place, not even his professor—such was the interest in China's history after the Cultural Revolution. Nevertheless, Daniel thought he could get us there. It was only a four-hour bus ride away, a mere stone's throw in Chinese distances.

We arrived at a dot on the map—supposedly a village but in fact a town of over a million inhabitants. The bus stopped in the middle of a market place, packed with geese in bamboo baskets, their heads extended, snapping at anyone who got too close. It was a vast public space surrounded by tower blocks. Daniel asked around. A motorised rickshaw could take us to the place, about an hour away—a real village, it seemed, and it was. We were dropped on an earth track with a couple of lean-to farm buildings nearby. 'There's supposed to be a hotel here,' said Daniel, looking around. We needed somewhere to stay the night. 'Ah, there's a sign for a hotel,' he noticed, 'hanging between those trees.' We went up a lane in the woods and came to a wooden building utterly boarded up with a huge lock on the front door. My heart sank; it didn't look as though it had been used for centuries.

'No worries,' said Daniel, 'there's some smoke over there—there must be a house. I'll go and ask.' He came back a little later with a woman carrying a huge key. 'She's going to open the hotel for us.' And she did. We put our things in the room and went off to see if we could find the Flower Mountain. Daniel asked around. A boat went there, he was told. We could buy tickets for it in a booth; the two girls sitting inside sold us two to their great surprise and with much giggling. We eventually found the boat further on, moored against the steep mud bank of a wide river, a rickety old metal pleasure vessel with an outboard motor and about thirty seats, and a man asleep in the bow. Daniel woke him up. Yes, it was the right boat. He clicked our two tickets, and we sat down.

'How long do we have to wait?' I asked, after a pause. The boatman was almost asleep again. Daniel asked him. Until the boat fills up. We could be waiting all week; there was no one else around. Can I buy all the seats? The boatman almost fell out of the boat laughing at the suggestion. I had to go back to the booth to buy them. There was a job for everyone in Communism—not a totally bad idea, when you think about it. I remember once talking to a middle-aged man hanging about in Istanbul, one of the many who happened to know a little English. He asked me if I had a job. I replied, 'Yes.' I have never forgotten the look of despair on his face (see Percy Horton's *Unemployed Man*, p. 10) and his heartfelt sigh, 'Oh, how I would love to have a job.' This affected how I later reorganised museums. The extra tickets cost me just over a pound. I gave them to the boatman, and we set off.

It was an hour's journey up the river, through real rural China, with women washing linen on the banks and men fishing, balancing on long rafts of two or three bamboo poles lashed together. Eventually we arrived at the site, a vertiginous cliff overlooking the river where it bent abruptly south. The paintings were many metres up, under an overhang, so they couldn't have been painted from ropes suspended from above. They had to have been painted on immensely high bamboo-pole scaffolding. But the pictures looked as though they had just jumped onto the rock from mid-air or emerged from within the cliffs themselves—bright red splats of men, their arms and legs spread-eagled like frogs, some looking as though they were dancing, or rather jumping around big drums. Their appearance must have seemed magical, and probably frightening, to anyone venturing into this territory. I found out later that a frog dance was still performed by traditional people in the area, a celebration of the spirits of spring and rebirth.

We came back after I'd spent as long as I wanted looking and sketching. I prefer to draw than take photos because that sticks in the memory better, and you notice so much more. Arriving back there was the problem of food. There wasn't a restaurant anywhere, hardly even a house. Daniel wasn't at all concerned. 'We just look for a temple,' he said. He asked around. 'There's one over there, across those fields,' he was told. We wandered over—there was a small Buddhist temple. There was no one about. 'Just light an incense stick or two,' he said, 'there'll be someone here.' Sure enough, after a while, an old woman's face appeared from behind the altar. Daniel immediately asked her for some beer. 'They always have beer,' he told me. She brought two bottles. We sat down and sipped.

There was a movement to our left. Across the yard beside the temple, a younger woman came over from some buildings we hadn't at first noticed behind a stand of high bamboo. She asked us if we'd like some food. 'It would be impolite to refuse,' Daniel said, 'but I can't guarantee what it will be like.' It was just a few beans in a dish. We sat down beside an old man perched on a sawn-off tree stump, like an elf, his trouser legs rolled up, his arms hugging his bare knees, rocking himself gently with silent laughter. Suddenly a young man appeared, about Daniel's age, and shouted furiously at him, sending the old man packing. Daniel told me he was angry with him for baring his knees in public.

Daniel suddenly splayed the fingers of his right hand and challenged the young man to a guessing game—like our paper, scissors, stone except that players have to guess in advance the total number of fingers displayed. It's played very fast. They started calling, quick fire, and soon were laughing. Their voiced bets soon became calls for drinks. Then the young man shouted. I saw a woman through the bamboo stalks wring a chicken's neck and start plucking vigorously. A fire was lit. Before you could think, there were bowls of food before us. Others gathered. The wine flowed. Singing started, and the full moon rose above us in the still, clear night. And, somehow, we found our way back to the hotel.

Daniel told me that he and his friends and professor were surprised when the government chose to show their local 'treasure', the Hua Shan paintings, at the start of the Beijing Olympics' magnificent, balletic opening ceremony. The Chinese are only just beginning to rediscover their artistic past. But when I'd shown these images to Hock Aun, he was totally uninterested. They were stiff and simplistic, not at all like the much older cave paintings of France and Spain. Even early Chinese calligraphy is much more sophisticated, fluid and lively. Hock Aun Teh's remarkable art took off from that—a genuine, inspiring fusion of East and West.

T *is for* MRS THATCHER

Mrs Thatcher came to Glasgow in the last year of her term of office. She didn't want to be there, I'm sure, and this no doubt influenced her state of mind when she arrived. She was much hated in Scotland for using the country to test her community charge, commonly known as the 'poll tax'. And Glasgow was Scotland's Labour stronghold, not her favourite place on earth. But she had to come. The European Community had made Glasgow its cultural capital, in the early days of this idea of Melina Mercouri. European Cultural Capitals were then supposed to be capitals—and London was next in line. The problem was that Thatcher had just abolished the Greater London Council, so no one there could make a bid or run the event even if they'd got it. Glasgow, with typical cheek, stepped in, put a lot of money down, and the UK government and the European Commission had no option but to accept its offer, much, I would imagine, to Mrs T's chagrin. The Queen came to launch the Year (see Q for the Queen), but security wouldn't allow Mrs Thatcher to be in the city at the same time. The risks were too great, so she came separately a couple of weeks later.

It was decided that she'd hold a reception at the Burrell Collection, one of the museums I was responsible for. The arrangements were fascinating. She was such a security risk at the time that not only the museum itself but the whole of Pollok Park, in which it was situated, had to be closed on the day without any warning or any explanation given to the public. And no one was allowed to tell anyone she was coming. I was one of the very few who knew. Even the invitations to the event that were sent out couldn't mention her name, but just referred to a 'special guest'. This might, in part, explain the embarrassingly small attendance at her appearance, but then Conservatives had always been a bit thin on the ground in Scotland. Security was so tight that even I had to leave my car a mile away outside the park and was then taxied to the museum with a police escort.

Among the cluster of suits standing around the foyer waiting for the Prime Minister to arrive, by helicopter, was Mary Baird, then Lord Provost of Glasgow, pointedly wearing a brilliant red dress, which suited her, it has to be said. 'You will have to go and get her from the helicopter,' she told me at once. 'I'm not going out to meet that woman.' It was also, typically, raining. Malcolm Rifkind came up to me and assured me that the Prime Minister wouldn't be staying long and wouldn't want to look round my museum. 'She wanted to talk to people,' he said. This was a bit of a relief. I didn't mind going out to meet her, for my job would then be over and brief. I'd met her once before—well, meet is not quite the right word—and had not exactly warmed to her.

I'd been invited to a reception for the arts she'd held at 10 Downing Street while I was director of Manchester City Art Galleries. I rather proudly announced, 'No. 10 Downing Street' when I got into the taxi, but the driver was not impressed. I was dropped at the end of the street. I found myself strolling up with another guest. We were both late, nearly the last to arrive. I turned to see who it was. The profile was familiar, even to me. Obi-Wan Kenobi—Alec Guiness, no less. We had an amiable chat. No, he hadn't been there before either. I'd loved him in the *Lady Killers*—a repeat performance tonight? I suggested. It was like a film set, walking up that famous, empty street with that famous voice in my ears, under that old fashioned lamp-post, to that famous door. Unfortunately it was still open. I'd love to have knocked, and should have asked to, but missed my chance.

We were both surprised at the smallness of the entrance-way—No. 10 really was a domestic terrace house. We climbed the narrow stairway to the side, ranked with photos of previous PMs, and arrived at the landing on the top. The scale of the interior suddenly changed and broadened. We realised we'd stepped up into a palace. Tall pillars flanked the big double door facing us. This one was closed. A flunkey asked us our names. The modest entrance downstairs had been a front. How very British, I thought. My companion had noticed the light under the doors. It was blue. 'Curses,' he said, 'television cameras. I said I would only come if there weren't any.'

'You can't go back now,' I said, encouraging him to go ahead. I was eager to keep behind him, not in any hurry myself to be filmed or photographed enthusiastically shaking the hand of Mrs Thatcher by my ardent left-wing employers in Manchester. The doors were opened. He went in. The blue lights flared while I slipped past totally unnoticed, round the side.

Mrs Thatcher was wearing a tight-fitting dress in bright blue, covered from neck to hem in tiny, shimmering sequins that made her look like a strutting, armoured peacock. Not seeing anyone I knew at first, I looked at the pictures on the wall, a collection of modest, early twentieth-century examples of the British School. One showed a policeman arresting someone in the street. 'Oh, I've got to remove that,' the keeper of the Government Collection, who supplies such furnishings, told me. She came up when she'd seen me looking at them. 'Mrs Thatcher's totally uninterested in art,' she said, 'but she spotted that picture right away, and told me she didn't like what it showed in no uncertain terms. Nothing gets past her. It's got to go.'

A little later I was chatting to Peter Blake and Howard Hodgkin when suddenly we felt Mrs Thatcher's sparkling blue arms encompass us, in what we first thought was some sort of embrace. 'Now, come along,' she said, and waltzed together with us across the floor. It must have made an extraordinary sight, for Peter and

Howard were both, if plumper, about her height. I was the only one who stood a bit above this sparkling blue roly-poly gliding across the floor. We each thought she was about to show us something, but then she abandoned us without a word. We realised that we'd just been used to cross a gap in the assembly which she didn't want to be seen crossing alone. She had no idea that she had in her arms in that moment two of the finest painters in England! That was as close as I'd got to any communication with the Prime Minister. I didn't expect any more on her visit to my museum.

We heard the sound of the helicopter's whirr. It slowly landed on the lawn outside. It was still drizzling, and the red carpet we'd laid across the grass was wet. I went out and shepherded the Prime Minister inside, under a held-high umbrella. She was smaller than I remembered, barely more than Queen-height, and more discreetly dressed than last time, in a pale grey, checked jacket and matching skirt that hinted at tartan. The din of the still-turning blades was terrific, which was a relief, because I didn't have to speak. I hurried her inside and once through the doors, searched desperately, then spotted the Lord Provost, an only just visible sliver of red between some dark suits, which revealed where Susan Baird was deliberately hiding. I steered the Prime Minister over to her, coughed and the suits parted. I introduced the two and backed away. My job, I thought, was done.

Mrs Thatcher chatted to the few of the sparsely littered company, then perched on the bottom of some steps in the ample, tree-clad foyer of the Burrell, to give a speech. I totally failed to register what she was talking about because I was too riveted by the sight of the back of her jacket, which I could see clearly from where I was standing. It was heavily creased. I was reminded of the time when I'd seen Harold Wilson give a talk in Orpington, my childhood local town, and my first and last attendance at a political rally, during the run-up to the by-election that gave the Liberals a famous victory. I watched Wilson, as he mounted the platform, slip off his jacket as he was handed a freshly pressed one by a female assistant—a performance he always went through, I was later told, whenever he appeared in public. It seemed to me that Mrs Thatcher was, surprisingly, less concerned about appearances.

After her short speech, Malcolm Rifkind came up to me again. 'The Prime Minister,' he told me, 'would like to go round the museum.' She had evidently run out of things to say to anyone there. 'But,' he assured me solemnly, 'she doesn't want to be spoken to. She has much too much on her mind.' I thought Mrs Thatcher's back looked so hacked about she couldn't have been watching it. But all the papers reported that the knives were out. (As it turned out, in fact, she hadn't long to go.) A silent tour was a novelty, but try anything once I thought as an old friend used to say, apart from incest, of course, and country dancing.

I led the Prime Minister up the stairs to the painting collection, and took her into the first gallery without uttering a word—a sort of mime show by me indicating the way. She studied for a minute our magnificent painting by Cranach of a deer hunt. Suddenly she turned to me and barked, 'That wouldn't look good over the mantelpiece, would it?' I presumed the question was rhetorical, and kept my lips sealed. The idea of this great work of art over any mantelpiece was clearly absurd.

We walked further. She moved as if she were mechanical, not really fully human, neither her arms nor legs quite in sync, each making separate jerking movements attributable, I imagined, to the high wiring of her mental concentration. By chance I'd once met Stanley Booth, the man who gave her her first job after leaving university as a research chemist in his BX Plastics factory in Manningtree. Later in life he became chairman of the Alfred Munnings Trust, which is why we met. He said Margaret was remarkable for two things: for never being without her handbag and for being the only young woman he'd ever met who had absolutely nil sex appeal. The animated being beside me was an aged concentration of that absence, handbag still swinging.

She paused at a small painting of a mixed bunch of floppy pink flowers in a vase by the French painter, Henri Fantin-Latour. 'Oh, I like that!' she suddenly exclaimed. Her mind had flitted onto it for a second, then rapidly flitted elsewhere. There was anyway nothing I could add to this observation, so we moved on. We walked through the rest of the paintings in utter silence, past all the Boudins, Cézannes and the wonderful collection of Degas, and descended the stairs into the Chinese section. She stopped abruptly in front of a case of Chinese porcelain, a superb selection of Sung ware. She turned to me, and for the first time looked at me straight in the eye. 'I collect porcelain,' she announced. I was momentarily confused. Was this statement inviting a question? Was she actually wanting to engage in some sort of conversation? If not, why was she looking at me so intently? I took a risk and asked, 'Oh, why do you collect porcelain?'

The look in her eye changed. I realised in that moment that she hadn't actually up to that point been looking at me at all, but through me in a general, vague sort of way as at a crowd. Now I was a person and had to be replied to, if only out of politeness. Her gimlet glance told me how furious she was to have had her thoughts interrupted in this way. She waved both arms in the air, her handbag swinging dangerously, in a chopping motion to indicate the size of the case in front of her, and barked, 'Oh, for a case this size, you can get so much more colour for half the price of a picture!' I hope I didn't betray my surprise; a few Sung pots as rare as these could buy you almost any picture you desired. I only found out later that she's actually commissioned a group of Falkland War heroes, sculptured in ceramic for her mantlepiece— hence her interest in porcelain.

We went on, through the galleries of Rembrandts, wonderful ancient tapestries, oriental carpets, furnishings and silverware, without a murmur, even a turn of hair. Then, in the gallery of superb medieval stained glass, every piece lit beautifully from behind, she suddenly turned to me and said, 'These things are so expensive nowadays.' I looked confused. You can't buy medieval stained glass anywhere, at any price. I then learnt the one thing you don't do is look confused in the presence of Mrs Thatcher. She fixed me with a withering glare—an unforgettable experience in itself—and almost barked, 'What about that £30 million for those chrysanthemums?'

'Oh, I think you mean sunflowers, Prime Minister,' I replied, for indeed a Japanese businessman had just paid something like that sum for one of the versions of the painting. 'Yes, that's right. sunflowers. And who were they by?'

'I think they were by Van Gogh,' I replied, not wanting to appear too knowing.

'Yes, that's right,' her voice clipped out. 'Van Gogh. But they weren't even Van Gogh's best chrysanthemums, were they?'

Thinking about it in the silence of the rest of our walk back to the reception area, I realised that Mrs Thatcher had never really seen Van Gogh's *Sunflowers*, let alone, for a moment, responded to their profound symbolism and feeling. They were to her just flowers in vases, like the Fantin-Latour she'd admired, and you didn't get sunflowers in vases—at least not then, now they are everywhere (see illustration on p. 159). You got chrysanthemums in vases—at least in Britain, but not in France where they're only given to the dead on All Souls' Day—so Mrs Thatcher had actually seen Van Gogh's sunflowers as chrysanthemums in her mind, in the same way that she saw all art as something to go over a mantelpiece. And being Mrs Thatcher, having been told by someone that there was more than one version of this painting, she had to have an opinion about which was the best. And, being Mrs Thatcher, she had to be right.

Michael Forsyth, later an enterprising minister of state for Scotland, came up to me when Mrs Thatcher had left in the helicopter, and asked, 'Did you enjoy that? She knows so much about art.'

I replied, 'She knows nothing at all.' But since then, I have found out that her distracted state of mind might have been due not to her survival but to her preparation of the remarkable, potentially world-transforming speech she gave warning about the sacrifices we would all have to make to prevent global warming at the Second World Climate Change Conference held in Geneva after her visit. If this was the case, then I forgive her, almost, everything.

Except, of course, for the fundamental shift in British culture that, perhaps, really kick-started during her premiership—the transformation that I've seen over the years in people's personal ambitions: we see ourselves now, in the main, as consumers, not as citizens contributing creatively to our own and other people's lives. This has been the death of individual creativity, the demise of art.

T *is for* JEAN TINGUELY

A long, low, open-top, dark green vintage car moved round the corner. It could have been a Bugatti, but I wasn't sure. Tinguely was driving, but next to him was a strikingly beautiful, small, sleek young woman. When she got out, her clothes were tight fitting. She wore knee-length, dark brown leather boots. She was military in a diminutive way. I could image her with a whip. In comparison, Tinguely was wild, a ramshackle bear in worker's overalls, hirsute and grizzled, but boyish as well, almost bouncing, as if both Marxes, Karl and Harpo, had got mixed up in the same film.

We'd arranged to meet at a huge, old factory dug into the green, rolling hills, just north of Lausanne, which Tinguely had decided to convert into a museum for his work. This is where he now spent most of his time installing his vast collection in an elaborate complex of underground caverns. He'd recently had a triple-bypass heart operation (though you would never know it by the light energy in his step) and was thinking about what would happen to his art in the future. He couldn't just leave the problem of what to do with all these crazy machines to someone else—he had to find a solution himself. He was interested in the lasting quality of art—despite his *Homage to New York*, which had destroyed itself in 1960—the piece that had first got me interested in him. But he was also interested in living to the full in the present. Before he had the operation, he'd insisted on watching it being performed on someone else. Eventually the surgeons let him. He was fascinated by the mechanics of existence, and to him these were wonderful and inspiring.

We went up to a sort of jumble room, which served, I think, as an office. The young military lady had disappeared. There were papers everywhere. He flung a small suitcase he'd been carrying down on the littered desk and clicked open the catches. 'Look at this!' he said laughing (his English was fluent). He grubbed about in a jungle of wires and held up proudly two bundles of red sticks of dynamite. 'I've just brought them on the plane. I told them I was an electrician, and they just waved me through!' He laughed again. 'Very good, these overalls,' he said, adding, with a glance at me, 'very good for attracting women.'

He asked me what I wanted. 'No,' he said, 'Glasgow—Scotland—that's across the sea—that's America to me. I'm never

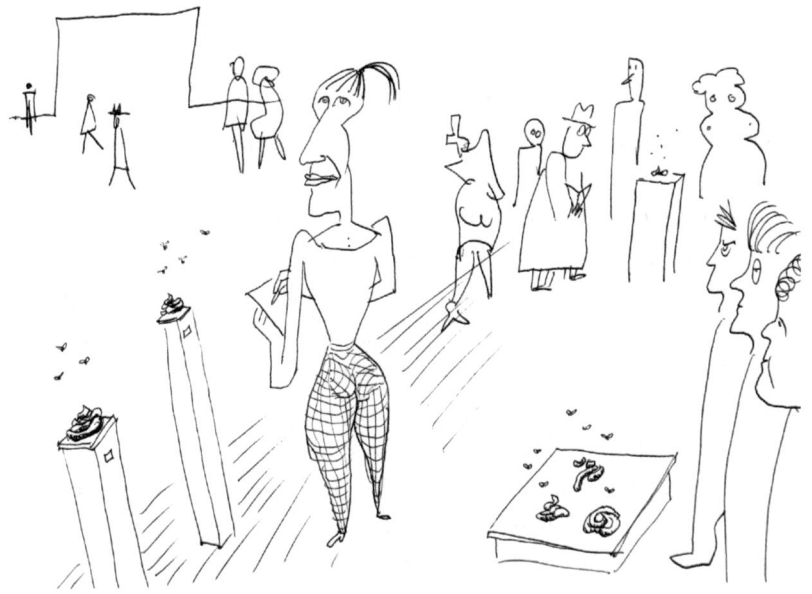

Peter Angermann, Portrait of a Curator, 1990

crossing the sea again.'

'But I want to do an exhibition of your work, your latest work.'

'No,' he said, abruptly again: 'I hate Shit Art Venues'. He pronounced the words slowly, with emphasis, which is why I have capitalised them. 'I'm never showing in a Shit Art Venue again.'

'But it's not a shit art venue,' I replied.

Luckily I'd brought with me a set of photos and a book about Kelvingrove, which I showed him. His face lit up when he saw this huge Victorian Gothic pile in a park and the voluminous spaces and galleries inside, and the fact that it was a general museum, with natural history and design, not just art. Everything changed. He became wired up with excitement. 'I'll show there!' he announced, thumping the table with his fist.

He gathered photos that were lying about, 'This and this, we'll include this,' he said. 'And we'll make new stuff.' He reached for a big black book and began leafing through the illustrated pages—pointing at machines. One had a photo of the famous curator Pontus Hultén, who had done so many exhibitions with him, standing talking to a woman. Tinguely laughed again and conjuring a felt-tip pen from a pocket—he always had pens about him, though he appeared to be carrying nothing—scrubbed the image of the women out, saying: 'that's not his wife. He's got a new one—ask him for a new pic.' He laughed: 'All I'll want is a big book, like this. The show will cost nothing—just send a van, no, a couple of vans. No insurance—they're not "art works"—they're just junk, scrap ... Come. I'll show you round.'

I laugh a lot, but I've rarely laughed so much. We walked into a huge dark chamber. At the end was a colossal Nana figure by his former wife, Niki de Saint Phalle, with multicoloured, efflorescing and spiralling breasts, belly and thighs. Oddly I don't remember a head, and if she had one, it was probably small and featureless, a knob without a face. She was all body and bulging and immense in her luxuriousness. I imagined that the gargantuan, chryselephantine figure of the Goddess Athena, and perhaps also brightly coloured (as many Ancient Greek sculptures were), might well have looked a bit like this at the end of the high, dark hall inside the Parthenon. The figure had an ancient, modern and eternal presence. Then Tinguely darted to one side, pressed a button and to my amazement and delight, the monster began to move towards me, swallowing up everything, including I thought soon me, in its gargantuan, multicoloured, piebald embrace. My laughter was, it's true, tinged with nervousness; I'd never seen, or witnessed, such a joyous manifestation of all-devouring womanhood.

He was putting on a show, a big retrospective, in the small town where he'd been born, Fribourg in Switzerland, and he invited me to the opening. 'Everyone's invited,' he said. And they were. I had never seen such a crowd, and such a feast, in the open air between the various venues, including the local art gallery, which had been hijacked for the occasion. There were huge barbeques cooking literally hundreds of sausages, with pigs roasting on spits, and for balloons he'd blown up the intestines of dozens of beasts of all sizes. He clearly wasn't keen on vegetarianism. Glasgow is going to love this, I thought. We'll have the opening in the park outside Kelvingrove. Everyone and anyone will be invited too.

The show itself, inside the various buildings, was even more exciting. In the apse in the church was one of his latest pieces. I realised I'd made the right choice in finding one of the great artists of our day. Here was the equivalent to Kelvingrove's Dalí, no, to Picasso's *Guernica*, in our times. Here was a waving, moving elephant-skull-headed monster. Its arms were charred timbers, and from its body crept insect-like creatures crawling out on wires, creeping everywhere. This is what we were doing to the planet, and more. It was called *Mengele Totentanz*, after Josef Mengele, the almost unbelievably cruel doctor in the Auschwitz concentration camp, who not only personally murdered thousands of people but also took the opportunity to conduct terrifying, often fatal medical experiments on his living victims, in his attempt to prove the Nazi theory of the supremacy of the non-existent Aryan race.

In Tinguely's hands, this Angel of Death had transformed into a monstrous humanity destroying nature itself. He told me how he'd seen a farm burn down after a lightning fireball had bounced along its roof. He'd dashed to see the wreckage in the morning, many of the timbers still burning, and collected pieces. He felt inspired. The whole of the Holocaust was there, and more. This was the right artist to make something wonderful for Kelvingrove (it was long before I'd thought of creating a new Gallery of Modern Art).

One day, a couple of months later, I got a phone call out of the blue. It was Tinguely. He said he'd be outside Kelvingrove at 9 a.m. the next Sunday morning. He'd been in a boat off the Scottish coast with his friend, Jackie Stewart, the famous racing driver (Tinguely loved car racing). When I arrived a bit early, he was already there, pacing up and down under the arcade at the top of the stairs, with a small case in his hand (containing sticks of dynamite I presumed). The night watchman let us in. Even I have rarely walked around a museum so fast. He wanted to see everything and grew more and more excited as we explored all the corridors, stairways, archways and galleries, taking everything in, including the Dalí, which made him grin. We had on an exhibition of the British painter Stanley Spencer, focusing on the paintings he'd done of the Glasgow shipyards during the war. Tinguely had never seen his work before and stopped longer than anywhere, looking closely at his brushwork and his drawing, absolutely fascinated.

I took him to my office, I can't quite remember why, and he asked, in the outer room, is that where your secretary sits? I nodded. He seized her diary, which was lying closed in front of her typewriter (those were the days!), opened it at the very last, vacant flyleaf page and sat down. He asked me her name—Hilary, I replied—and grabbing coloured pens and pencils from his case (there was no dynamite), he began to draw a painting for her, with her name emblazoned across the middle. 'It's very important,' he said, 'that your secretary is fully behind this project'—anticipating, goodness knows, what sort of difficulties. In a corner he suddenly stopped and mused, his usual exuberant flourishes paused, and he began to draw, with a sharpened pencil tip, sequences of closely contoured curving, breast-like lines and wrote under them,

Stanley Spencer. He'd been impressed. Hilary, when she opened her diary next morning was vaguely horrified, I could see, but much too polite to show it. Her eyebrows fluttered up a little, as if to say, 'Artists! What do you expect?' and resigned herself to what the future might bring.

We then went to see the McLellan Galleries where I'd put on a big exhibition, called *Out of Order*, of the work of three living artists, one of whom, Jim Whiting, knew Jean well. He was tremendously impressed by all their work and kept glancing at me, partly in surprise, that I admired such things. I felt—I might have been flattering myself, but I don't think so—that he was becoming more and more relaxed and warm with me, and confident that he wanted to work with me. We could be on a similar, imaginative, funny wavelength. The first galleries were full of Ron O'Donnell's huge colour photographs of his crazy installations. The Scotsman showed a hole punched through a brick wall to reveal the room inside, a knobbly-kneed manikin in a kilt, with a football for a head sitting watching TV in a tartan-wallpapered room littered with all the icons of Scottishness. One of the funniest was a comment on Scottish Independence, a photo from space of the British Isles, with Scotland being torn apart from England, blood dripping from the broadening gap. Jean laughed almost as much as I did.

David Kemp filled the next galleries. Jean turned to me and asked, 'Why are these all here?' He was including Ron's work in this observation. 'Why aren't they all sold?' Well, I explained, some of them are—and have been borrowed back from their owners—this is a public show, not a selling one—and David has more sculptures in public places in Britain that almost anyone. Among his masterpieces are *The Old Transformers*, an immense ironmaster and a coal miner, made from old boilers and scrap metal from the vast Consett Iron Works in County Durham, staring like lost

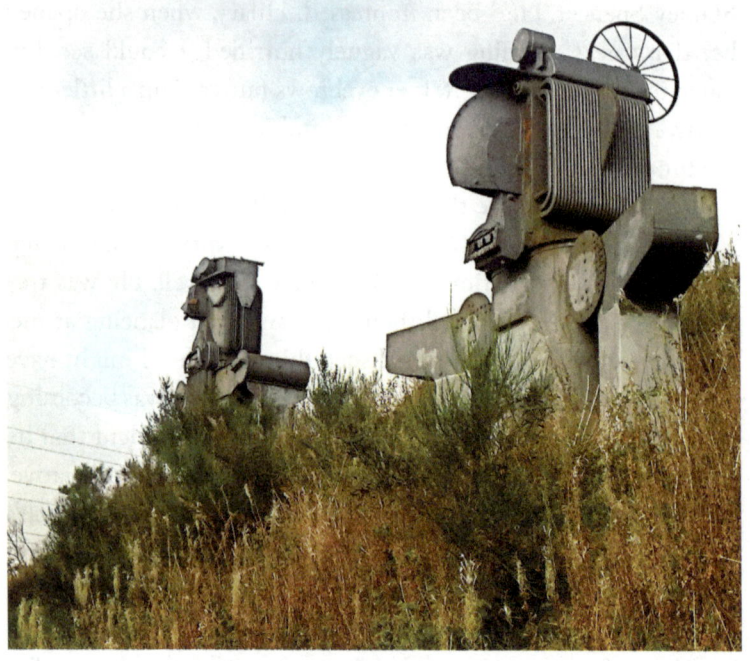

David Kemp, The Old Transformers, 1990

Easter Island gods over the flat, vacant 'redeveloped' green fields where these factories had so recently stood.

These figures were so much more redolent than Antony Gormley's much more famous and more strategically placed *Angel of the North*, with is soft-form body, cast on Gormley's own, and arms held straight out, like Messerschmitt wings, dubbed locally as the 'Gateshead flasher'. As another wit put it, 'I've seen a miner and a steel worker around here, but never a fucking angel.' But in a way, Jean was right, and I tried to explain why I thought he was— how artistic creativity in Britain was being overcast by the fake, dark cloud of conceptualism, the exterminating angel of Antony Gormley, the hollow man of British art, and others like him. 'Oh, shit art!' he laughed, and seemed all the more determined to do something with us.

The back galleries were full of the wire cages and animated manikins of Jim Whiting, an old friend of Jean's. He was one of the most brilliant contemporary artists I'd came across, but I never managed to buy any of his sculptures for any of the galleries I worked for, despite trying. I wanted, in particular, two drunken manikins of tramps, lying prone, twitching on the gallery floor. Jim wasn't totally against the idea, but somehow never got round to doing anything about it or getting them into a state where the piece could be sold. He just wasn't interested in that sort of immortality. Even Jean wasn't as cavalier about his lasting reputation, or anything lasting, as was and still is Jim. I've rarely come across an artist so totally absorbed in his creative life.

I once went to see the nightclub he'd created in Leipzig, in a disused factory in Baumwollspinnerei, an industrial area turned into a subsidised haven for artists after the Wall came down. The nightclub, called Bimbotown, only opened one night a month, but thousands flocked when the doors opened just before midnight. There were Jim Whiting sculptures everywhere: his suits flying in the air and his dancing trouser legs made famous in the pop video he made for Herbie Hancock's *Rockit*. The highchairs at the bar would, of a sudden, start to spiral up, leaving you, and your cocktail, perilously balanced in mid-air. One tempting sofa, if you were unwise enough to sit down on it with a friend, would suddenly yawn wide like a mouth and gobble you down, throwing you backwards onto a passing bed. There were travelling beds everywhere, which visitors in the know got on early, carrying them on a ghost tour through the maddest, most wonderful nightclub in the world. Art for the people, in the streets, with nothing, absolutely zilch, to do with contemporary fine art and all its pretensions and sickening wealth.

I'd shown Jim's work twice before—in Sheffield at the Mappin Art Gallery and in Manchester City Gallery—and now in Glasgow. There he'd been fascinated by different layers of existence; there were always figures high up near the ceiling, pink tailor-dummy legs sawing the air but held up by wings, flying heavenly sex bodies. Purgatory, with glimpses of heaven above and hell beneath—an instinctive meditation, I often wondered, on a religious upbringing? These higher flights of fancy had been reduced in Glasgow to a few circling, air-born wisps of cloth, strange eerie insect-like creatures, without substance. Jim seemed more interested now in earthbound activity and captivity: cages and tunnels. One stray creature was a handbag, on the end of a twisting wire that seemed to sense your presence as you walked past and suddenly sprang at you across the floor and started snapping at your ankles, as you jumped clear, like a demented dog. I'd recently met Mrs Thatcher and laughed so much; it was a perfect portrait of her—a neat, shiny handbag with a metal clip opening and shutting obsessively, rapaciously, the common denominator of human motivation, the devouring, respectable propriety of consumerism.

We took a taxi back to the airport. Then something odd happened. The taxi took a wrong turning at a building site and we suddenly found ourselves on an unmade track of road, surrounded by half-built, high-rise blocks, a high wire fence and building machines, and one of these, a huge mechanical digger, was driving straight towards us. The taxi driver panicked and started to reverse and spin round as quickly as he could while Jean was literally leaping up and down in the taxi beside me, shouting with delight. 'It's Jim! It's Jim!' We managed to drive out, the sweat pouring off the taxi driver's face. When we were clear and on the road again, he asked, 'How did that happen? I've never done that, gone there before!' I didn't tell him that he'd had a brush with the genius of fresh artistic feeling—that was all.

I never met Jean again. He died, quite soon after, of a massive heart failure. But then Jim said he'd never known anyone work so hard as Jean, endlessly, and, coming from him, that was quite an accolade. He didn't stop, until he was stopped. But we, and Glasgow, missed out. I went to the opening of the museum dedicated to him in Basle. I'd tried to persuade Niki de Saint Phalle to stick to his plans for his museum in the factory in Lausanne, but she said she didn't have the money. She could get the money if she moved it to Basle, which she did, from the Roche pharmaceutical company.

This also enabled her to shave off many of Jean's artistic friends, 'hangers on' which she told me she thought reduced his own standing. I wasn't at all happy about this either. I admired Jean's enthusiasm for other artist's work, and his eagerness to encourage them and embrace them, without in any way taking them over, an unusually generous trait in a man of genius. He was so right, I think, in maintaining that art today need not be seen as a battery of sheer cliff faces, with individual reputations standing alone and apart, but is more truly a continuum of creativity that infects others and can inspire them to produce work of similar merit and therefore value to those elevated by the market onto exclusive investment platforms above the common run. Many people inspired by Hockney, for example, have at times painted more powerful and profound pictures than he his—Peter Angermann is just one example. This whole business of the value of names and brands needs to be broken down and meaning given the upper hand, even if it's a masterpiece done by someone who did little else, which was not the case with Angermann.

I had to accept the reality of the money, but the new building Niki commissioned from Mario Botta was really disappointing; it was too cavernous, too exposed, shopping-centre architecture that lacked the mystery and discovery of the tunnelled, under-ground spaces Jean had originally selected. The same thing hap-pened to the Ruskin Gallery in Sheffield, when it was moved from the converted old drinking lodge, where it was intimate and perfect, to the anonymous arches of the Millennium Gallery. Again, to use the critic Bryan Robertson's memorable phrase, it was an 'architect's revenge on art'—they need to imagine muse-ums from the meaning of the exhibits out, not build the case first and then ram them in.

I also went to the opening by President Mitterrand (a great fan of Niki and Jean's work) of the *Cyclop* in the woods of Milly-la-Forêt, near Fontainebleau, south of Paris. Tinguely had started building this monster deep in the forest without any planning permission in the late 1960s and got Niki de Saint Phalle in-volved. He lifted a railway truck on rails twenty metres into the air and built beneath it a framework for a face, with inner passag-es, staircases and chambers inside which he hoped many artists he admired would show their work. He'd just begun to do this when he died. Niki was left having to continue the work. One of the artists Jean wanted to include was Jim Whiting. He went to see Niki and the *Cyclop*. She asked him what he was going to do. He took one look at her, turned and left. He was furious. She, of all people, should have known that artists don't know what they're going to do until they do it. That's the point of doing it.

Many have argued that Duchamp, whom Jean knew in New York, was a big influence on him, but that's not my reading, even though I'm looking back with hindsight. Of course, Duchamp's *Rotoreliefs* have a passing relationship to Jean's work, though noth-ing of the latter's zany meaning. Jean didn't really relate himself to Duchamp, whose work he found essentially intellectual and calculated, whereas he was instinctive, 'working from the bottom up', unlike Duchamp as he said. He always insisted that the big early influences on him, as far as using found objects was concerned, were Kurt Schwitters, Hans Arp and Picasso, but he, like everyone, was, of course, bowled over by the fact that Duchamp had submitted a urinal to an exhibition. That was sensational and made Duchamp as big a star on the scene as anyone. It never occurred to Jean or anyone at that time that Duchamp hadn't done it.

I sometimes wonder what Tinguely would have done, what he would have made, if he'd discovered the truth that Duchamp had stolen the urinal from Baroness Elsa von Freytag-Loringhoven, especially as her own portrait of Duchamp of 1919, which only survives in a photograph—a trembling, attenuated construction of feathers, wire and springs balancing crazily in a wine-glass— looks extraordinarily like a Tinguely in miniature—a remarkable premonition of the future by the greatest Dada artist ever. What would he have done? What's even more extraordinary, working as instinctively as he did, in way he'd already done what he might have done if he'd known the truth. He took Duchamp's fridge, which Duchamp and his wife Teeny were throwing out, and wired it up so that when anyone opened its door, the inside blazed with a volcanic red and New York fire sirens screeched inside. Of course it was on one level a response to what was happening to the world—refrigeration emissions were then seen to be one of the main causes of ozone layer depletion—but it could also be read, and I like this interpretation, as a warning to anyone to have nothing to do with Duchamp because he was a cold, calculating liar and not really creative at all.

Overleaf: Jean Tinguely, personal communication
with the author, 1990

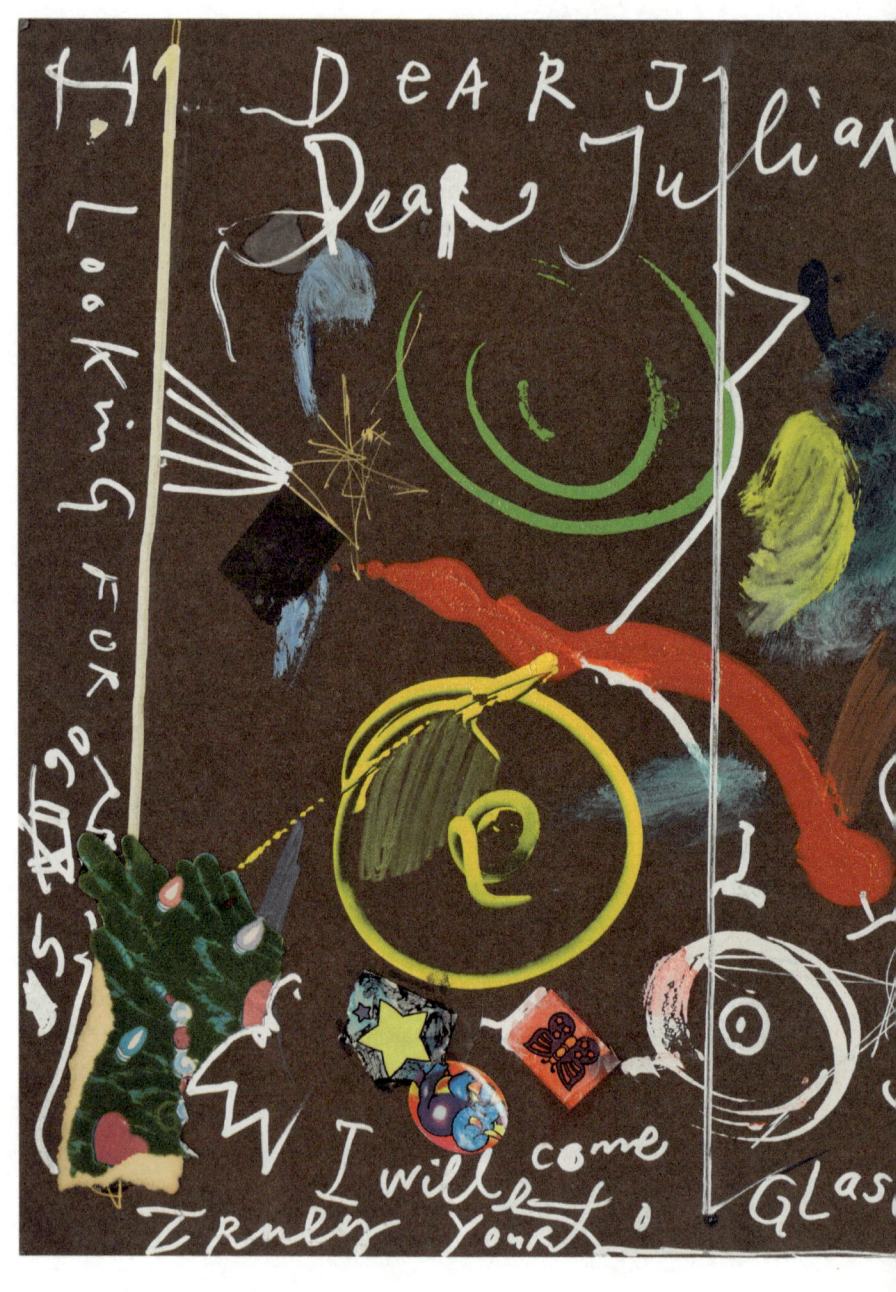

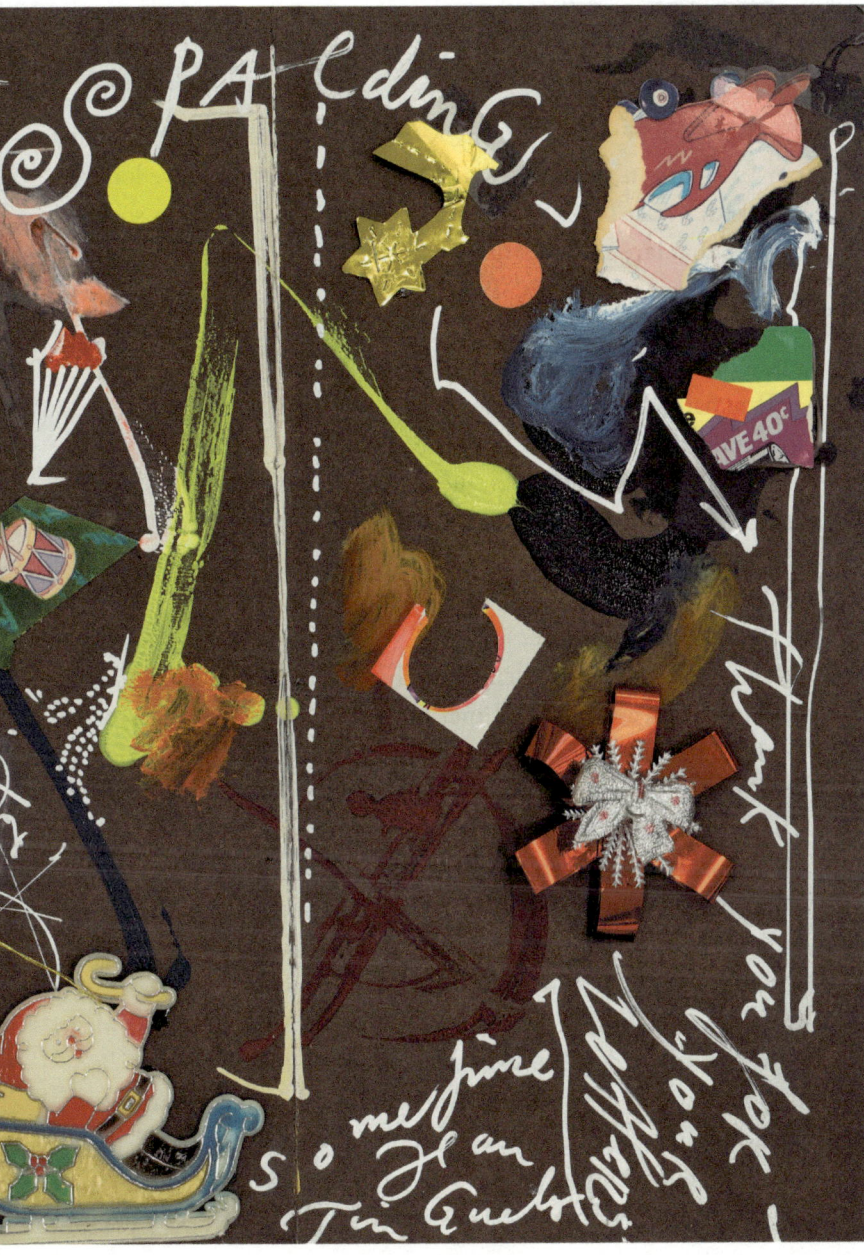

W is for PAUL WAPLINGTON

During Kate and William's wedding, Paul rang me, furious, from Portugal. 'Are you watching that wedding?' he asked. I wasn't and I was surprised he was as a life-long socialist. 'See that lace she's wearing?' ignoring my silence, 'It's Nottingham lace made in Calais! They bought all our Leavers machines when the Nottingham factories were closed down. That's the future Queen of England wearing French lace!!'

Paul had begun as a lace designer. There were not many options for work for a lad who'd left school at fifteen from Broxtowe, a very rough housing estate on the fringes of Nottingham. A teacher once asked him, 'Waplington, are you fond of fighting?'

'No sir.'

'Why not?'

'Because I always lose, sir.'

The class collapsed in laughter. His answer was surprising, because he is big, and when I met him, bushy-haired and bearded, leonine. His mother didn't want him to follow his father down the pit and managed to get him apprenticed to the lace trade. To his surprise, at first, he not only enjoyed it and found he was exceptionally good at it, but over time he got a bit fed up with 'designing knickers', as he put it, 'for tart's arses'. There had to be more to life. Pattern making irritated him; he wanted more, space and depth, form and the warmth of human feeling.

He wondered if he could become a painter but had no idea how. He hitched a lift to Cornwall one summer—where he'd heard artists lived—and earned pennies as a pavement portraitist. Two families, sharing a holiday, took to him. He drew all their portraits, but when he got to the youngest child, he said 'I know who your dad is—that nose!' It was the wrong dad. The two happy families disintegrated before his eyes. He chanced to meet the painter Herman Minner in a pub on a trip to Brussels, who told him, 'If you want to be a painter, throw away your watch, eat when you're hungry, sleep when you're tired, and fuck whenever you can—otherwise you're one of them.'

He kept on working, however, but went freelance, married, had kids and started to teach himself to draw and paint—local scenes around Nottingham, above all men at work in the lace factories and kids at play. One haunting one—a big triptych called *View over Sneinton Dale*—showing older youths idling their time away on a kid's climbing frame too small for them, the rolling terraced landscape swinging behind and beneath as they somersault and turn upside down (see overleaf). It was a time of increasing unemployment in the Thatcher years as mines and factories closed down. The painting asks, poignantly and powerfully, what are these kids going to do—without spelling any answers out. Paul just paints what he sees, sights that sum things up.

He was able, because of his art-barren background and his skill at craft, to steer a totally original path. He rejected the formalism of modernist abstraction, of Rothko and Pollock, Riley and Hoyland, where 'flatness' reigned supreme. He'd had enough of flatness designing lace. At the same time, being experienced in real working-class politics, he was deeply suspicious of any attempt to turn art into propaganda. He was invited once to speak at a conference organised by socialists about the future of art, at the ICA in London. Sitting on the platform, he was eventually asked by the chairman, 'Paul, you haven't said anything—what do you think?' One delegate had commented that they thought the TUC and the Labour Party might do something for art. All he could think to say was, 'I wouldn't expect too much to come out of those people.' He wasn't invited again.

What interested Paul was capturing real human feelings. In his

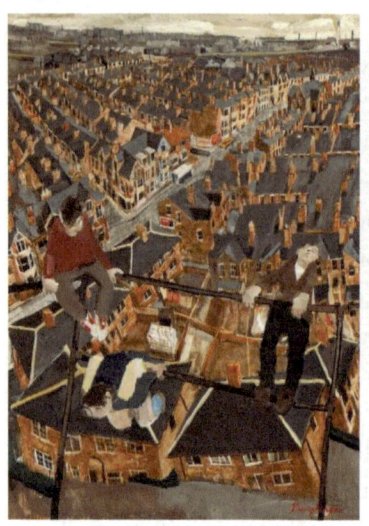
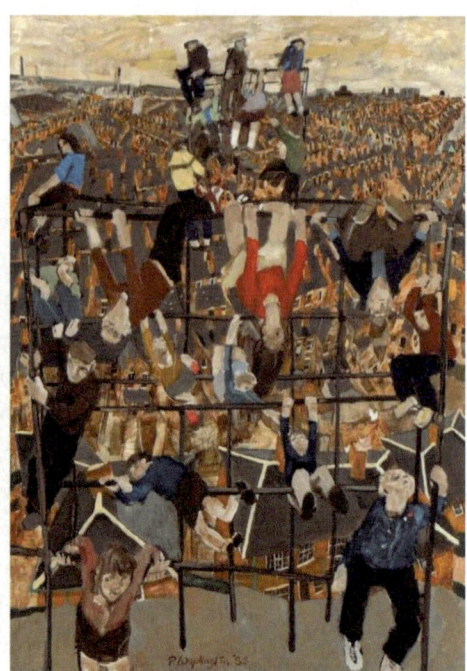

marvellous painting, *Retired Miner*, the old man sits by himself in the pub, wringing his large hands, now useless, on the table before him, his eyes withdrawn into his memories, with resignation but no self-pity though he knows he's dying of emphysema. Another portrait, *Viuva de Panque: Sra. Torres,* is of a widow, painted in Portugal. Her massive body, her waistcoat barely stretching over it, fills the frame, her large hands which have done so much work, her spreading knees and heavy feet that have carried her so far and now bear her weight so slowly are all painted as solidly as the stone bench on which she sits. Then you notice the woman's face, her sad, quivering, strong, knowing smile—how can one shaded line say so much? Her nose, flushed with age and wine and, higher up, her tiny eyes, one unseeing, sunken, sliding

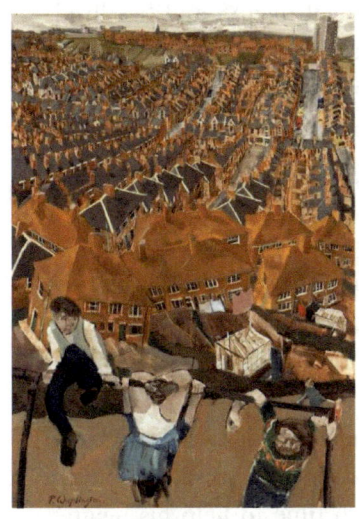

Paul Waplington, Triptych: View over Sneinton Dale, 1983

sideways like a faded sunset, the other as sharp, dark and searching as a needle. A whole life's experience is there, carved out of now-dried paint.

I was so impressed by his work that I commissioned him to do a series of paintings of the steelworks in Sheffield. There were, surprisingly, very few images of this major industry. It wasn't very successful. The sheer scale of operation, the vast, cavernous darkness, the towering machinery and brilliant blaze of the pouring metal belittled the workers and on the whole quite defeated even Paul. The best thing he produced, I think by far, was when I commissioned him to make a huge mural in different coloured bricks of a portrait of a steelworker, Ron Mason, for a blank sidewall in the city centre as part of my campaign to introduce art into public places. Despite the scale, it is immensely human, a real person. But then the puzzle of building a vivid three-dimensional image in slightly different toned and coloured bricks appealed to Paul and brought all his experience as a lace designer into play.

Paul moved to rural, northern Portugal in 1988 and has lived there ever since. He learnt Portuguese, married again and slowly but surely started to paint his adopted land—his paintings of long-horned, golden Barrosã cattle (he has one) and of ancient traditional farming in the Douro Valley (now beginning to disappear) are superb.

One day, on his doorstep, he found a toad with its mouth sewn up, a curse, put there by someone who didn't like him. But when his neighbour's father's corpse was moved to be reburied (a regular practice after seven years), it was found not have deteriorated (Paul thinks because he was so pickled in alcohol), and the man instantly became a local saint. A lean-to brick shed was built against the local church to accommodate the corpse, the pallor of which Paul touches up from time to time to help his neighbour who has meanwhile become rich from all the offerings and bought all the fields around Paul, making him wonder if this very neighbour hadn't put the toad on his doorstep in the first place.

Paul is one of the funniest people I have ever met; his maundering monologues about the state of the world are hilarious as they sink lower and lower and slower into eternal gloom, alleviated with quotes of poetry and the occasional snatches, now deeply ironic, of rousing socialist songs. 'I can live without God,' as he says. 'I can live without money—well, without much. But I can't live without hope. And since I don't believe in that any more, I don't like to think about it.' But his own personal stories are even better.

He told me how when in Nottingham, he'd kept chickens in a cage in the back garden. One neighbour complained that the crowing of the cock woke him up at dawn and he took him to court for disturbing the peace. Before the case was heard, Paul himself made a peace offering. He raised the perch so that the cock, when it flew up to the perch to stretch its neck up to crow in the morning, hit its head on the cage on top and baffled, looking round, failed to make a sound. But despite this solution, the neighbour insisted on continuing with the case.

Paul got another neighbour to stand in the witness box and say he liked hearing the cock in the morning because it reminded him of the countryside. The magistrate asked him to speak up. He cupped his fingers behind his ear and, looking confused, asked the magistrate to speak up himself because he was a little hard of hearing. The court collapsed in laughter, while some heard Paul over the din ask his neighbour, 'Why didn't you tell me you're as deaf as a post?' Nevertheless, Paul won the case, with the costs being charged to the police. He briefly became a national celebrity, as a champion of natural justice and an alternative way of living. His paintings do that for everyone.

I told him I was putting him in this book and that since it was alphabetical he was at the end, if not the conclusion, nor perhaps the climax, at least something of a victory sign. He laughed, 'Oh, that reminds me of the old Anthony Rowley song. It begins with A is for ... and ends with...' Then he burst into deep-throated song:

> W is for whore
> Who thinks fucking's a farce
> Heigh! Ho! Says Anthony Rowley
> And X, Y and Z
> You can shove up your arse
> With a roly poly up 'em and stuff 'em
> Heigh! Ho! For Anthony Rowley.

Which is as good a note to end on as any.

List of illustrations

p. 121: Francis Davison, *Collage, c.* 1980. Torn, cut and pasted self-coloured papers, 1000 x 1400 mm. Private collection. © Francis Davison's estate.

p. 129: Unknown photographer, *Baroness Elsa von Freytag-Loringhoven*, 1922. Photograph. Library of Congress, Washington, DC.

p. 130: Alfred Stieglitz, *The Urinal by Baroness Elsa von Freytag-Loringhoven* (*Fountain by Marcel Duchamp*), 1917. Photograph. Wikimedia Commons

p. 135: Glyn Thompson, *Reconstructing Stieglitz*, 23 February 2023. Photograph. © Glyn Thompson

pp. 148–49: Martin Handford, *The Battle of Chacabuco (1817)*, 1978. Pen, ink, pencil on paper, 345 x 472 mm. Arts Council Collection, Southbank Centre, London. © Martin Handford

p. 159: David Hockney, *Photography is Dead, Long Live Painting*, 1995. Digital inkjet print on paper, 836 x 106 mm. Glasgow Museums. © David Hockney

p. 164: Durham Miners Gala, 2008. The banners and bands coming down Old Elvet Bridge. Photograph. © Paul Simpson. Wikimedia

p. 177: Alexander Stoddart, *Biederlally*, 1992–93. Glass reinforced polymer, height 3467 x 686 x 482 mm. Glasgow Museums. © Alexander Stoddart

p. 183: Steven Campbell, *Painting in Defence of Migrants*, 1993. Oil on canvas, 271 x 256 cm. Glasgow Museums, © Steven Campbell

p. 184: Peter Howson, *The Patriots*, 1991. Oil on canvas, 206 x 274 cm. Glasgow Museums, © Peter Howson. All Rights Reserved, DACS 2023

pp. 186–87: Ken Currie, *The Bathers*, 1991–92. Oil on linen, 259 x 420 mm. Glasgow Museums, © Ken Currie, courtesy Flowers Gallery

pp. 188–89: John Bellany, *Journey to the End of the Night*, triptych, 1972. Oil on three panels of hardboard, left: 209 x 138 cm; centre 209 x 184 cm; right: 209 x 138 cm. Glasgow Museums, © John Bellany

p. 191: Front façade of the Gallery of Modern Art, Glasgow, showing the Niki de Saint Phalle panel and lettering by Lida Kindersley. Photograph © Helen Simonsson via Flickr

p. 205: L. S. Lowry, *Seascape*, 1950. Oil on canvas, 63 x 76 mm. Glasgow Museums, © L. S. Lowry's estate

p. 221: Julian Spalding, Gilmerton Cove, inner chamber, Edinburgh. Photograph. Collection of the author

p. 231: Charles Rennie Mackintosh and Margaret Macdonald, interior of the White Dining Room, Ingram Street Tea Rooms, partial reconstruction in 1995/6 with original features and gesso panels. Original 1900–12. © CSG CIC Glasgow Museums Collection

pp. 232–33: Charles Rennie Mackintosh and Margaret Macdonald, panels from the White Dining Room. Jean-Pierre Dalbéra, Wikimedia Commons

pp. 362–63: Jean Tinguely, postcard to Julian Spalding, 1990. Pen, ink, paint and collage on card, 500 x 350 mm. Collection of the author, © John Tinguely estate

pp. 366–67: Paul Waplington, *View over Sneinton Dale*, triptych. 1983. Oil on canvas, left: 175 x 126 cm; centre: 207 x 151 cm; right: 175 x 126 cm. Glasgow Museums, © Paul Waplington

Index

of people mentioned in this book

Numbers in *italic* denote illustrations

INDEX

INDEX

First published 2023 by
Pallas Athene (Publishers) Limited, 2 Birch Close, London N19 5XD
Reprinted 2024

www.pallasathene.co.uk

Design and layout by Alexander Fyjis-Walker.
Editing by Caroline Brooke Johnson
Cover image: detail of Beryl Cook's birthday card for
the author (ill. p. 93) © Estate of Beryl Cook

ISBN 978 1 84368 240 0

Printed in Great Britain by TJ Books Limited, Padstow, Cornwall

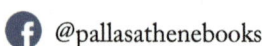 @pallasathenebooks   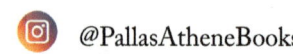 @PallasAtheneBooks

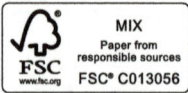